Other Books and Series by Jeff Bowen

Cherokee Granted Enrollment Cards & Dawes Packets 1900 - 1907
Volumes I, II & III

COMPLIMENT ALL CHEROKEE SERIES WITH THE GREATEST CHEROKEE HISTORY AND GENEALOGICAL BOOK PUBLISHED!

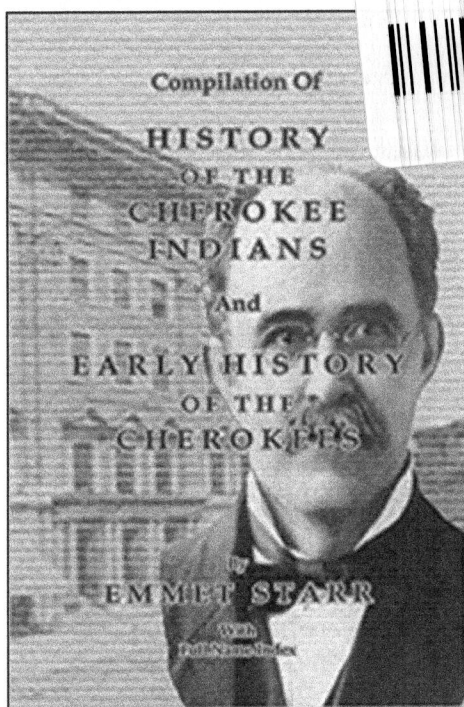

> Softback ISBN: 978-1-64968-119-5
> Hardback ISBN: 978-1-64968-127-0

Other Cherokee Publications You May Not Know About

- *Compilation of History of the Cherokee Indians and Early History of the Cherokees* by Emmet Starr *with Combined Full Name Index* (Hardbound & Softbound)

- *Eastern Cherokee by Blood, 1906-1910, Volumes I thru XIII*

- *Eastern Cherokee Census Cherokee, North Carolina 1930-1939 Census 1930-1931 with Births And Deaths 1924-1931 Taken By Agent L. W. Page Volume I*
- *Eastern Cherokee Census Cherokee, North Carolina 1930-1939 Census 1932-1933 with Births And Deaths 1930-1932 Taken By Agent R. L. Spalsbury Volume II*
- *Eastern Cherokee Census Cherokee, North Carolina 1930-1939 Census 1934-1937 with Births and Deaths 1925-1938 and Marriages 1936 & 1938 Taken by Agents R. L. Spalsbury And Harold W. Foght Volume III*

- *Texas Cherokees 1820-1839 A Document For Litigation 1921*

- *Starr Roll 1894 (Cherokee Payment Rolls) Districts: Canadian, Cooweescoowee, and Delaware Volume One*
- *Starr Roll 1894 (Cherokee Payment Rolls) Districts: Flint, Going Snake, and Illinois Volume Two*
- *Starr Roll 1894 (Cherokee Payment Rolls) Districts: Saline, Sequoyah, and Tahlequah; Including Orphan Roll Volume Three*

- *Cherokee Descendants East An Index to the Guion Miller Applications Volume I*
- *Cherokee Descendants West An Index to the Guion Miller Applications Volume II (A-M)*
- *Cherokee Descendants West An Index to the Guion Miller Applications Volume III (N-Z)*

Other Books and Series by Jeff Bowen

Compilation of History of the Cherokee Indians and Early History of the Cherokees by Emmet Starr with Combined Full Name Index (Hardbound & Softbound)

1901-1907 Native American Census Seneca, Eastern Shawnee, Miami, Modoc, Ottawa, Peoria, Quapaw, and Wyandotte Indians (Under Seneca School, Indian Territory)

1932 Census of The Standing Rock Sioux Reservation with Births and Deaths 1924-1932

Kiowa, Comanche, Apache, Fort Sill Apache, Wichita, Caddo and Delaware Indians Birth and Death Rolls 1924-1932

Census of The Blackfeet, Montana, 1897- 1901 Expanded Edition

Eastern Cherokee by Blood, 1906-1910, Volumes I thru *XIII*

Choctaw of Mississippi Indian Census 1929-1932 with Births and Deaths 1924-1931   Volume I
Choctaw of Mississippi Indian Census 1933, 1934 & 1937, Supplemental Rolls to 1934 & 1935 with Births and Deaths 1932-1938, and Marriages 1936-1938 Volume II

Eastern Cherokee Census Cherokee, North Carolina 1930-1939 Census 1930-1931 with Births And Deaths 1924-1931 Taken By Agent L. W. Page   Volume I
Eastern Cherokee Census Cherokee, North Carolina 1930-1939 Census 1932-1933 with Births And Deaths 1930-1932 Taken By Agent R. L. Spalsbury   Volume II
Eastern Cherokee Census Cherokee, North Carolina 1930-1939 Census 1934-1937 with Births and Deaths 1925-1938 and Marriages 1936 & 1938 Taken by Agents R. L. Spalsbury And Harold W. Foght Volume III

Seminole of Florida Indian Census, 1930-1940 with Birth and Death Records, 1930-1938

Texas Cherokees 1820-1839 A Document For Litigation 1921

Starr Roll 1894 (Cherokee Payment Rolls) Districts: Canadian, Cooweescoowee, and Delaware Volume One
Starr Roll 1894 (Cherokee Payment Rolls) Districts: Flint, Going Snake, and Illinois   Volume Two
Starr Roll 1894 (Cherokee Payment Rolls) Districts: Saline, Sequoyah, and Tahlequah; Including Orphan Roll   Volume Three

Cherokee Intruder Cases Dockets of Hearings 1901-1909 Volumes I & II

Indian Wills, 1911-1921 Records of the Bureau of Indian Affairs
Books One thru *Seven*
Native American Wills & Probate Records 1911-1921

Other Books and Series by Jeff Bowen

Turtle Mountain Reservation Chippewa Indians 1932 Census with Births & Deaths, 1924-1932

Chickasaw By Blood Enrollment Cards 1898-1914 Volume I thru V

Cherokee Descendants East An Index to the Guion Miller Applications Volume I
Cherokee Descendants West An Index to the Guion Miller Applications Volume II (A-M)
Cherokee Descendants West An Index to the Guion Miller Applications Volume III (N-Z)

Applications for Enrollment of Seminole Newborn Freedmen, Act of 1905

Eastern Cherokee Census, Cherokee, North Carolina, 1915-1922, Taken by Agent James E. Henderson   *Volume I (1915-1916)*
                                  Volume II (1917-1918)
                                  Volume III (1919-1920)
                                  Volume IV (1921-1922)

Eastern Cherokee Census, Cherokee, North Carolina, 1923-1929, Taken by Agent James E. Henderson   *Volume I (1923-1924)*
                                  Volume II (1925-1926)
                                  Volume III (1927-1929)

Complete Delaware Roll of 1898

Applications for Enrollment of Seminole Newborn Act of 1905 Volumes I & II

North Carolina Eastern Cherokee Indian Census 1898-1899, 1904, 1906, 1909-1912, 1914   Revised and Expanded Edition

1932 Hopi and Navajo Native American Census with Birth & Death Rolls (1925-1931) Volume 1 - Hopi
1932 Hopi and Navajo Native American Census with Birth & Death Rolls (1930-1932) Volume 2 - Navajo

Western Navajo Reservation Navajo, Hopi and Paiute 1933 Census with Birth & Death Rolls 1925-1933

Cherokee Citizenship Commission Dockets 1880-1884 and 1887-1889 Volumes I thru V

Applications for Enrollment of Chickasaw Newborn Act of 1905 Volumes I thru VII

Cherokee Intermarried White 1906 Volume I thru X

Applications for Enrollment of Creek Newborn Act of 1905 Volumes I thru XIV

Other Books and Series by Jeff Bowen

- *Cherokee Intruder Cases Dockets of Hearings 1901-1909 Volumes I & II*

- *Eastern Cherokee Census, Cherokee, North Carolina, 1915-1922, Taken by Agent James E. Henderson   Volume I (1915-1916)*
    - *Volume II (1917-1918)*
    - *Volume III (1919-1920)*
    - *Volume IV (1921-1922)*

- *Eastern Cherokee Census, Cherokee, North Carolina, 1923-1929, Taken by Agent James E. Henderson   Volume I (1923-1924)*
    - *Volume II (1925-1926)*
    - *Volume III (1927-1929)*

- *North Carolina Eastern Cherokee Indian Census 1898-1899, 1904, 1906, 1909-1912, 1914   Revised and Expanded Edition*

- *Cherokee Citizenship Commission Dockets 1880-1884 and 1887-1889   Volumes I thru V*

- *Cherokee Intermarried White 1906 Volume I thru X*

- *Cherokee Granted Enrollment Cards & Dawes Packets 1900 - 1907   Volumes I, II & III*

Visit our website at *www.nativestudy.com* to learn more about these other books and series by Jeff Bowen

CENSUS OF THE OSAGE INDIANS OF OSAGE AGENCY, OKLAHOMA, 1906 - 1929 1906 - 1911 VOLUME I

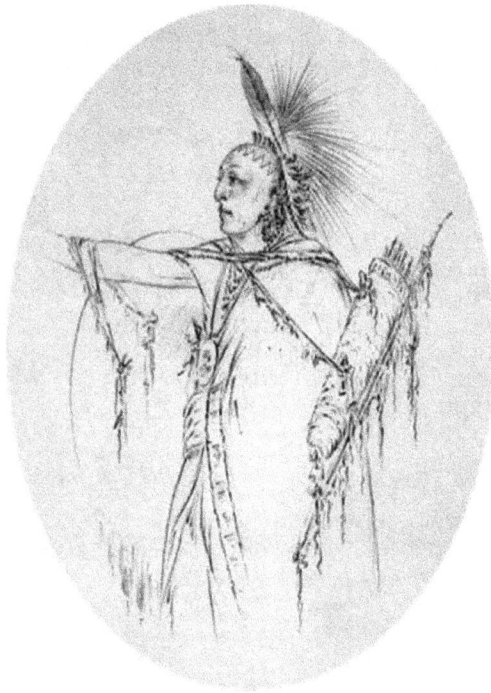

TRANSCRIBED BY
JEFF BOWEN

NATIVE STUDY
Gallipolis, Ohio
USA

Native Study LLC
Gallipolis, OH
www.nativestudy.com

Library of Congress Control Number: 2025903766

ISBN: 978-1-64968-176-8

Bookcover: Tal-lee, Pencil   portrait by George
Catlin, Newberry Library.
Drawing No. 123. Portrait of the most distinguished warrior
of the Osage tribe. He is carrying his shield, bow and quiver
set. He is wearing a peace medal, some strands of beads, and
multiple earrings. He has a shaved head and is wearing a
large headdress with animal hair and a feather, 1852 [possibly
drawn 1834-1852]
NL004826_o2.jpg

Made in the United States of America.

This series is dedicated to the
Osage of Oklahoma and those throughout the country,
past, present and future.

Table of Contents

[The year 1908 is missing from the archival record
not able to be retrieved by the transcriber.]

Other Books and Series by Jeff Bowen

Applications for Enrollment of Choctaw Newborn Act of 1905 Volumes I thru XX

Choctaw By Blood Enrollment Cards 1898-1914 Volumes I thru XX

Oglala Sioux Indians Pine Ridge Reservation 1932 Census Book I
Oglala Sioux Indians Pine Ridge Reservation Birth and Death Rolls 1924-1932
Book II

Census of the Sioux and Cheyenne Indians of Pine Ridge Agency
1896 - 1897 Book I
Census of the Sioux and Cheyenne Indians of Pine Ridge Agency
1898 - 1899 Book II

Northern Cheyenne Tongue River, Montana 1904 - 1932 Census
1904-1916 Volume I
Northern Cheyenne Tongue River, Montana 1904 - 1932 Census
1917-1926 Volume II
Northern Cheyenne Tongue River, Montana 1904 - 1932 Census
1927-1932 Volume III

Sac & Fox - Shawnee Estates 1885-1910 (Under Sac & Fox Agency)
Volumes I-VIII
Sac & Fox - Shawnee Estates 1920-1924 (Under The Sac & Fox Agency,
Oklahoma) & Wills 1889-1924 Volume IX
Sac & Fox - Shawnee Deaths, Cemetery, Births, & Marriage Cards (Under The Sac
& Fox Agency, Oklahoma) 1853-1933 Volume X
Sac & Fox - Shawnee Marriages, Divorces, Estates Log Books Volumes 1 & 2, Log
Book Births & Deaths (Under Sac & Fox Agency, Oklahoma)1846-1924 Volume XI
Sac & Fox - Shawnee Guardianships Part 1 (Under Sac & Fox Agency, Oklahoma)
1892-1909 Volume XII
Sac & Fox - Shawnee Guardianships, Part 2 (Under The Sac & Fox Agency,
Oklahoma) 1902-1910 Volume XIII
Sac & Fox - Shawnee Guardianships, Part 3 (Under The Sac & Fox Agency,
Oklahoma) 1906-1914 Volume XIV

Census of the Pima, Tohono O'odham (Papago), and Maricopa Indians of the Gila
River, Ak Chin & Gila Bend Reservations 1932 with Birth and Death Rolls 1924-
1932

Identified Mississippi Choctaw Enrollment Cards 1902-1909 Volumes I, II, III
Identified Mississippi Choctaw Enrollment Cards' Dawes Packets 1902-1909
Volumes IV, V, VI & VII

Census of the Northern Navajo, Navajo Reservation, New Mexico, 1930 Volume I
Census of the Northern Navajo, Navajo Reservation, New Mexico, 1931 Volume II

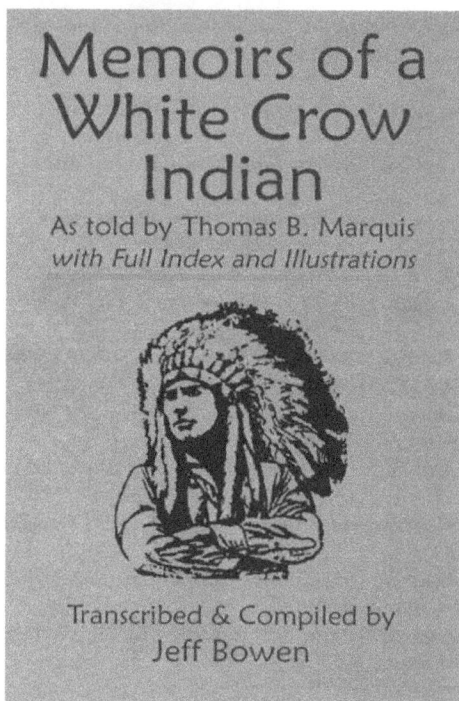

George Catlin
An Artist's Rendering
July 26, 1796 – December 23, 1872

The advocacy of youth reading books is important. Case in point; the image on the cover of this series was drawn by the famous artist and ethnologist George Catlin. By reading, questions about the image's appearance would never have been found if not for having an interest in Mr. Catlin and his participation with the Osage and other tribes. For instance while searching out Catlin's presence among the Osage this example was found on page 72, paragraph 3, of Marjorie Roehm's book. During one of his first times out west while at Fort Gibson he mentions through either family legend or his many notes that while with then well-known Col. Henry Dodge in the southwest, he, Catlin during 1834 bought a horse he named Charlie, "a wild horse that had been beautifully trained by the Osages."

Reading informed; it answered questions today for his reasoning then 195 years earlier, (he started out west in the 1830's and continued well into the future). From Marjorie Catlin Roehm's book, the granddaughter of George's youngest brother Francis, *The Letters of George Catlin and his family* (©1966), beginning on page 47, paragraph 6:

"Catlin painted rapidly all the time he was in Indian country. He had to. He could not take the time to make "finished" paintings; he would need hundreds for his museum-to-be. It was the main characteristics he was after: the face, a true likeness of his subject and how it might differ from that of another tribe; the clothes painted faithfully to preserve tribal individuality, either on the spot, or, with his copious notes giving minute detail, finished when he arrived home. Hands he practically ignored, giving them but crude strokes of his brush. There had been much criticism on this point, and also on the proportions of some of his figures in group pictures. He just did not take the time to consider such matters before he splashed the paint on the canvas. When not painting he was filling one notebook after another with remarks on each tribe, notes that later would be carefully written in detail."

You can see Catlin getting off of the stagecoach and reporting to the head of Indian Affairs realizing he alone was the key to his passage further west and safety. General William Clark would soon give Catlin the invitation to attend council meetings with tribal leaders entering tribal lands where these Native heads of state would be dressed in their best attire for these talks and just the colors of their robes alone appearing statuesque and primed for canvas. Catlin must have been in his element. From earlier days while still east hungering for a path forward with his art he would see, from page 30, Paragraph 2:

"... my mind was continually reaching for some branch or enterprise of the arts, on which to devote a whole life-time of enthusiasm; when a delegation of some ten or fifteen noble and dignified-looking Indians, from the wilds of the 'Far West,' suddenly arrived in the city, arrayed in all of their classic beauty—with shield and helmet—with tunic and manteaux—tinted and tasseled off, exactly for the painter's palette!"

You will find many drawings by this blessed example of history's gift to us with hands and other features but the image on this series and its detail was explained by reading a book. Catlin's life alone is fascinating and his subjects as, he thought, more so....

Also from; **George Catlin, Letters and Notes on the Manners, Customs, and Conditions of the North American Indians... (2 vols.; London: published by the author, 1841), I, 2. [Footnoted on page 30 of Marjorie Catlin Roehm's book.]** Reading this text from the past makes one want to read more of what this man went through to give us his vision of a people.

GEORGE CATLIN'S "INDIAN CREED"

"Catlin found tribes living near the frontiers and settlements, and thus in contact with the white men, degenerate in both morals and constitution. Not so with the strong, healthy and clear-eyed Indians west of the Missouri. These were the people for whom he was fighting, and would continue to do so all his life. Though some writers speak of his purely altruistic conception of the red men, they often forget his over-all goal: to picture them for future generations and to have fairer laws enacted for these children of the forests and prairies who still roamed in comparative freedom. Perhaps he omitted that which was detrimental to the Indian character. He saw more good in them than bad. Here is his Indian Creed, written in 1868 in answer to the critics who spoke of him as 'Indian loving Catlin':

I love a people who have always made me welcome to the best they had.

I love a people who are honest without laws, who have no jails and no poorhouses.

I love a people who keep the commandments without ever having read them or heard them preached from the pulpit.

I love a people who never swear, who never take the name of God in vain.

I love a people who love their neighbors as they love themselves.

I love a people who worship God without a Bible, for I believe that God loves them also.

I love a people who have never raised a hand against me, or stolen my property, where there was no law to punish for either.

I love a people whose religion is all the same, and who are free from religious animosities.

I love a people who have never fought a battle with white men, except on their own ground.

I love and don't fear mankind where God has made and left them, for there they are children.

I love a people who live and keep what is their own without locks and keys.

I love all people who do the best they can. And oh, how I love a people who don't live for the love of money!"

The above taken from *The Letters of George Catlin and his family Chronicle of the American West* by Marjorie Catlin Roehm, pgs. 120-121.

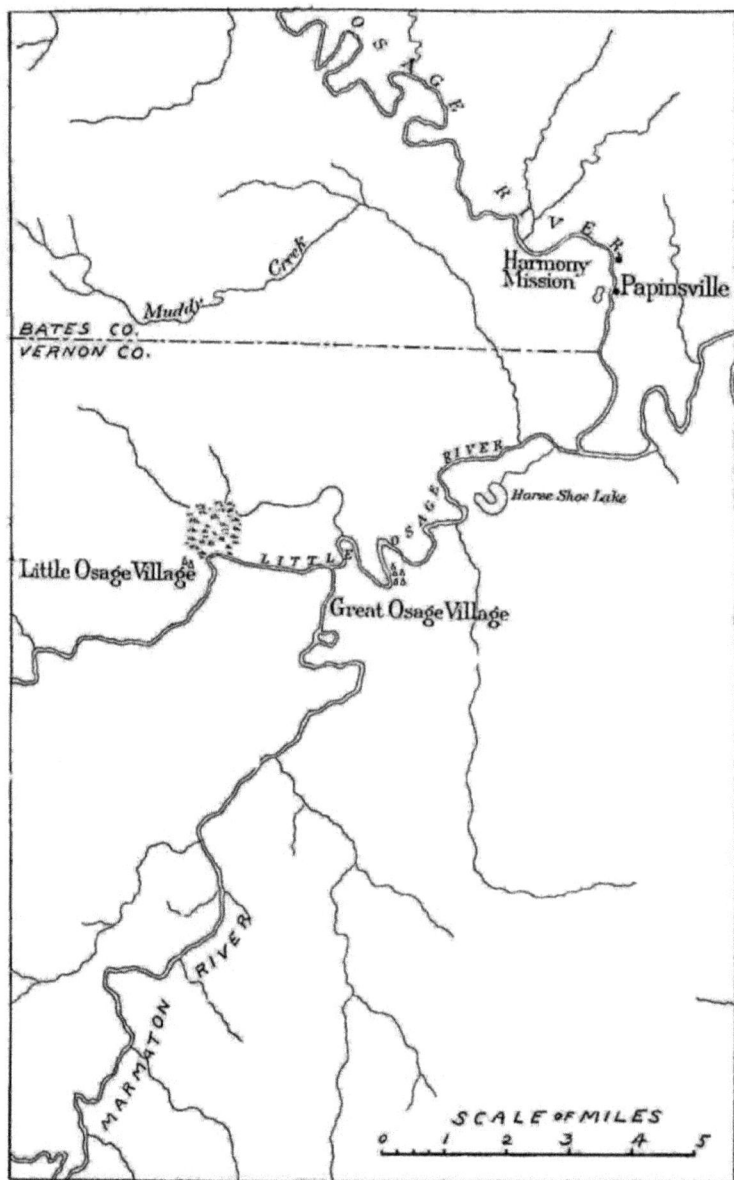

MAP OF PARTS OF VERNON AND BATES COUNTIES

Homes of the Great and Little Osages on the Little Osage River at the time of the visit of Capt. Zebulon M. Pike in 1806.

Captain Black Dog
Also known as Young Black Dog, of Co. B, 1st Osage
Battalion, wearing bear claw necklace.

Photographer: William Henry Jackson (1843-1942)
1876
Publisher: Department of the Interior, U.S. Geological &
Geographical Survey of the Territories, F.V. Hayden, U.S.
Geologist in charge
Library of Congress Control Number: 2022631308

Wah-chee-te

Drawing No. 126. Portrait of a seated Osage woman and child. She is wearing a wrapped, embroidered robe, strands of beads, earrings and her hair is worn loose.

Creator: George Catlin (1796-1872)
Date: 1852/1860 [possibly 1834-1860]
Newberry Library (NL004829_o2.jpg)

THE

Constitution and Laws

OF THE

OSAGE NATION,

PASSED AT

PAWHUSKA, OSAGE NATION,

In the Years 1881 and 1882.

WASHINGTON, D. C.:
R. O. POLKINHORN, PRINTER,
1883.

CONSTITUTION
OF
THE OSAGE NATION.

The Constitution of the Osage Nation, prepared by the authorized committee and adopted by the National Council.

The Great and Little Osages having united and become one body politic, under the style and title of the Osage Nation; therefore,

We, the people of the Osage Nation, in National Council assembled, in order to establish justice, insure tranquility, promote the common welfare, and to secure to ourselves and our posterity the blessing of freedom—acknowledging with humility and gratitude the goodness of the Sovereign Ruler of the universe in permitting us so to do, and imploring his aid and guidance in its accomplishment—do ordain and establish this Constitution for the government of the Osage Nation.

ARTICLE I.

SECTION 1. The boundary of the Osage Nation shall be that described in the treaty of 1876 between the United States and the Great and Little Osages, except that portion purchased by the Kaws.

SEC. 2. The lands of the Osage Nation shall remain common property, until the National Council shall request an allotment of the same, but the improvements made thereon and in possession of the citizens of this Nation are the exclusive and indefeasible property of the citizens respectively who made or may rightfully be in possession of them. *Provided*, That the citizen of this Nation possessing exclusive and indeasible right to their improvements, as expressed in this article, shall possess no right or power to dispose of their improvements in any manner whatever, to the United States, individual States, or to individual citizens thereof; and that, whenever any citizen shall remove with his effects out of the limits of this Nation, and become a citizen of any other government, all his rights and privileges as a citizen of this Nation shall cease; *Provided, nevertheless*, That the National Council shall have power to re-admit by law, to all the rights of citizenship any such persons who may at any time desire to return to the Nation, on memorializing the National Council for such re-admission.

Moreover, the National Council shall have power to adopt such laws and regulations as it may deem expedient and proper to prevent citizens from monopolizing improvements with the view of speculation.

ARTICLE II.

SECTION 1. The power of this government shall be divided into three distinct departments, the Legislative, the Executive, and the Judicial.

SEC. 2. No person or persons belonging to one of these departments shall exercise any of the powers properly belonging to either of the others, except in the cases hereinafter expressly directed or permitted.

ARTICLE III.

SECTION 1. The legislative power shall be vested in a National Council, and the style of their acts shall be :—Be it enacted by the National Council.

SEC. 2. The National Council shall make provision, by law, for laying off the Osage Nation into five districts, and, if subsequently it should be deemed expedient, one or two may be added thereto.

SEC. 3. The National Council shall consist of three members from each district, to be chosen by the qualified electors in their respective district, for two years, the elections to be held in the respective districts every two years, at such times and places as may be directed by law,

The National Council shall, after the present year, be held annually, to be convened on the first Monday in November, at such place as may be designated by the National Council, or, in case of emergency, by the Principal Chief.

SEC. 4. Before the districts shall be laid off, any election which may take place, shall be by general vote of the electors throughout the Nation, for all officers to be elected.

The first election for all officers of the government.— Chiefs, Executive Council, members of the National Council, Judges, and Sheriffs—shall be held at Pawhuska, before the rising of this council; and the term of service of all officers elected previous to the first Monday in November, 1882, shall be extended to embrace, in addition to the regular constitutional term, the time intervening from their election to the first Monday in November, 1882.

SEC. 5. No person shall be eligible to a seat in the National Council, but an Osage male citizen, who shall have attained to the age of twenty-five years.

SEC. 6. The members of the National Council shall in all cases, except those of felony or breach of the peace, be privileged from arrest during their attendance at the National Council, in going to, and returning.

SEC. 7. In all elections by the people the electors shall vote *viva voce*. All male citizens, who shall have attained to the age of eighteen years, shall be equally entitled to vote at all public elections.

SEC. 8. The National Council shall judge of the qualifi-

cations and returns of its own members, determine the rules
of its proceedings, punish a member for disorderly behavior,
and with the concurrence of two-third, expel a member;
but not a second time for the same offence.

Sec. 9. The National Council, when assembled, shall
chose its own officers; a majority shall constitute a quorum
to do business, but a smaller number may adjourn from
day to day and compel the attendance of absent members,
in such manner, and under such penalty as the council may
prescribe.

Sec. 10. The members of the National Council shall each
receive a compensation for their services, which shall be
one hundred dollars per annum : *Provided,* That the same
may be increased or diminished by law ; but no alteration
shall take effect during the period of services of the members of the National Council by whom such alteration may
have been made.

Sec. 11. The National Council shall regulate by law, by
whom, and in what manner, writs of elections shall be issued to fill the vacancies which may happen in the Council thereof.

Sec. 12. Each member of the National Council, before
he takes his seat, shall take the following oath or affirmation :

"I, A. B., do solemnly swear (or affirm, as the case may be) that I
have not obtained my election by bribery, treat, or any undue and unlawful means, used by myself, or others, by my desire or approba-
tion for that purpose; that I consider myself-constitutionally qualified
as a member of—————, and that on all questions and measures
which may come before me, I will so give my vote, and so conduct
myself, as, in my judgment, shall appear most conducive to the interest and prosperity of this Nation, and that I will bear true faith and
allegiance to the same, and to the utmost of my ability and power, ob-
serve, conform to, support, and defend the constitution thereof."

Sec. 13. No person who may be convicted of felony shall

be eligible to any office or appointment of honor, profit or trust, within this Nation.

SEC. 14. The National Council shall have power to make all laws and regulations which they shall deem necessary and proper for the good of the Nation, which shall not be contrary to this constitution.

SEC. 15. It shall be the duty of the National Council to pass such laws as may be necessary and proper to decide differences by arbitration, to be appointed by the parties who may choose that summary mode of adjustment.

SEC. 16. No power of suspending the laws of this Nation shall be exercised, unless-by the National Council or its authority.

SEC. 17. No retrospective law, nor any law impairing the obligations of contracts, shall be passed.

SEC. 18. The National Council shall have power to make laws for laying and collecting taxes for the purpose of raising a revenue.

SEC. 19. All acknowledged treaties shall be the supreme law of the land, and the National Council shall have the sole power of deciding on the constructions of all treaty stipulations.

SEC. 20. The Council shall have the sole power of impeaching. All impeachments shall be tried by the National Council, when setting for that purpose; the members shall be upon oath or affirmation; and no person shall be convicted without the concurrence of two-thirds of the members present.

SEC. 21. The Principal Chief, Assistant Principal Chief, and all civil officers shall be liable to impeachment for misdemeanor in office; but judgment in such cases shall not extend further than removal from office, and disqualification to hold any office of honor, trust, or profit under the government of this Nation. The party, whether convicted or acquitted, shall, nevertheless, be liable to indictment, trial, judgment, and punishment according to law.

ARTICLE IV.

SECTION 1. The supreme executive power of this Nation shall be vested in a Principal Chief, who shall be styled "The Principal Chief of the Osage Nation." The Principal Chief shall hold his office for the term of two years, and shall be elected by the qualified electors on the same day, and at the place where they shall respectively vote for members to the National Council. The returns of the elections for Principal Chief shall be sealed up and directed to the President of the National Council, who shall open and publish them in the presence of the Council assembled. The person having the highest number of votes shall be Principal Chief, but if two or more shall be equal and highest in votes, one of them shall be chosen by vote of the National Council; the manner of determining contested elections shall be directed by law.

SEC. 2. No person, except a natural born citizen, shall be eligible to the office of Principal Chief; neither shall any person be eligible to that office who shall not have attained to the age of thirty-five years.

SEC. 3. There shall also be chosen, at the same time, by the qualified electors, in the same manner, for two years, an Assistant Principal Chief, who shall have attained to the age of thirty-five years.

SEC. 4. In case of the removal of the Principal Chief from office, or of his death, or resignation, or inability to discharge the powers and duties of the said office, the same shall devolve on the Assistant Principal Chief.

SEC. 5. The National Council may, by law, provide for the case of removal, death, resignation, or disability of both the Principal and Assistant Principal Chief, declaring what officer shall then act as Principal Chief until the disability be removed or a Principal Chief shall be elected.

SEC. 6. The Principal Chief and Assistant Principal Chief shall, at stated times, receive for their services a compensation which shall neither be increased nor diminished during the period for which they shall have been elected, and they shall not receive within that period any other emolument from the Osage Nation or any other government."

SEC. 7. Before the Principal Chief enters on the execution of his office, he shall take the following oath or affirmation: "I do solemnly swear or affirm that I will faithfully execute the duties of Principal Chief of the Osage Nation, and will, to the best of my ability, preserve, protect, and defend the Constitution of the Osage Nation.

SEC. 8. He may, on extraordinary occasions, convene the National Council at the seat of government.

SEC. 9. He shall, from time to time, give to the Council information of the state of the government, and recommend to their consideration such measures as he may deem expedient.

SEC. 10. He shall take care that the laws be faithfully executed.

SEC. 11. It shall be his duty to visit the different districts at least once in two years, to inform himself of the general condition of the country.

SEC. 12. The Assistant Principal Chief shall, by virtue of his office, aid and advise the Principal Chief in the administration of the government at all times during his continuance in office.

SEC. 13. Vacancies that may occur in offices, the appointment of which is vested in the National Council shall be filled by the Principal Chief during the recess of the National Council, by granting commissions, which shall expire at the end of the next session thereof.

Sec. 14. Every bill, which shall pass the National Council, shall, before it becomes a law, be presented to the Principal Chief; if he approves, he shall sign it, but if not, he shall return it with his objections to the Council, who shall enter the objections at large on their journals, and proceed to reconsider it.

If, after such reconsideration, two-thirds of the Council shall agree to pass the bill, it become a law, if any bill shall not be returned by the Principal Chief within five days (Sunday excepted) after the same has been presented to him, it shall become law, in like manner as if he had signed it. Unless the National Council, by their adjournment, prevent its return, in which case it shall be a law, unless sent back within three days after their next meeting.

Sec. 15. Members of the National Council and all officers, executive and judicial, shall be bound by oath, to support the Constitution of their Nation; and to perform the duties of their respective offices with fidelity.

Sec. 16. The Principal Chief shall, during the session of the National Council, attend at the seat of government.

Sec. 17. The Principal Chief shall recommend three persons, to be appointed by the National Council, whom the Principal Chief shall have full power at his discretion to assemble; he, together with the Assistant Principal Chief and the Counsellors, or a majority of them, may, from time to time, hold and keep a Council for ordering and directing the affairs of the Nation according to law.

Sec. 18. The members of the Executive Council shall be chosen for the term of two years.

Sec. 19. The Treasurer of the Osage Nation shall be chosen by the National Council for the term of two years.

Sec. 20. The Treasurer shall, before entering on the duties of his office, give bond to the Nation with Sureties to the satisfaction of the National Council, for the faithful discharge of his trust.

SEC. 21. No money shall be drawn from the treasury, but by warrant from the Principal Chief, and in consequence of appropriations made by law.

SEC. 22. It shall be the duty of the Treasurer to receive all public moneys, and to make a regular statement and account of the receipts and expenditures of all public moneys at the annual session of the National Council.

SEC. 23. The "Fiscal Year" of the Osage Nation shall begin on the 1st day of October, and close on the 30th day of September of each year; and all books and accounts of the Treasurer, shall be kept, and duties of his office performed with regard to the beginning and ending of the fiscal year, The National Treasurer shall receive for his services ten (10) per cent. of all moneys that may pass through his hands as provided by law.

ARTICLE V.

SECTION 1. The judicial powers shall be vested in a supreme court, and such circuits and inferior courts as the National Council may from time to time ordain and establish.

SEC. 2. The judges of the supreme and circuits courts shall hold their commission for the term of two years, but any of them may be removed from office on the address of two-thirds of the National Council to the Principal Chief, for that purpose.

SEC. 3. The judges of the supreme court and circuits courts, shall at stated times receive a compensation which shall not be deminished during their continuance in office, but they shall receive no fees or perquisites of office, nor hold any other office of profit or trust under the government of this Nation or any other power.

SEC. 4. No person shall be appointed a judge of any of the courts, until he shall have attained the age of thirty years.

SEC. 5. The judges of the Supreme and Circuits courts shall be elected by the National Council.

SEC. 6. The judges of the Supreme courts and of the Circuits courts shall have complete criminal jurisdiction in such cases and in such manner as may be pointed out by law.

SEC. 7. No judge shall sit on trial of any cause when the parties are connected (with him) by affinity or consanguinity except by consent of the parties. In case all the judges of the supreme court shall be interested in the issue of any court or related to all or either of the parties, the National Council may provide by law for the selection of a suitable number of persons of good character and knowledge for the determination thereof, and who shall be specially commissioned for the adjudication of such case by the Principal Chief.

SEC. 8. All writs and other process shall run "in the name of the Osage Nation " and bear test and be signed by the respective clerks.

SEC. 9. Indictments shall conclude against the peace and dignity of the Osage Nation.

SEC. 10. The supreme court shall, after the present year, hold its session three times a year, at the seat of government, to be convened on the first Monday in October, February, and August, of each year.

SEC. 11. In all criminal prosecutions the accused shall have the right of being heard; of demanding the nature of the accusation; of meeting the witnesses face to face; of having compulsory process for obtaining witnesses in his or their favor, and in prosecutions by indictment or information a speedy public trial; nor shall the accused be compelled to give evidence against himself.

SEC. 12. All persons shall be bailable by sufficient securities, unless for capital offences when the proof is evident or presumption great.

ARTICLE VI.

SECTION 1. No person who denies the being of a God or a future state of reward and punishment, shall hold any office in the civil department in this Nation.

SEC. 2. When the National Council shall determine the expediency of appointing delegates, or other public agents for the purpose of transacting business with the Government of the United States, the Principal Chief shall recommend, and by the advice and consent of the National Council appoint and commission such delegates or public agents accordingly on all matters of interest touching the rights of the citizens of this Nation which may require the attention of the United States Government.

SEC. 3. All commissions shall be in the name and by the authority of the Osage Nation, and signed by the Principal Chief. The Principal Chief shall make use of his private seal until a national one shall be provided.

SEC. 4. A sheriff shall be elected in each district by the qualified electors thereof, who shall hold his office two years unless sooner removed. Should a vacancy occur subsequent to election, it shall be filled by the Principal Chief as in other cases, and the person so appointed shall continue in office until the next regular election.

SEC. 5. The appointment of all officers not otherwise directed by this constitution shall be for voted in the National Council.

SEC. 6. The National Council may propose such amendments to this Constitution as two-thirds of the Council may

deem expedient, and the Principal Chief shall issue a pro-
clamation directing all officers of the several districts to
promulgate the same as extensively as possible within their
respective districts at least six months previous to the next
general election, and if, at the first session of council after
such general election, two-thirds of the council shall by ayes
and noes ratify such proposed amendments, they shall be
valid to all extent and purposes as part of this Constitution,
Provided, that such proposed amendments shall be read on
three several days in Council, as well as when the same are
proposed as when they are ratified.

Done in convention at Pawhuska, Osage Nation, this
thirty-first day of December, A. D. 1881.

JAMES BIGHEART,
President of the National Convention

Ne-kah-ke-pon-ah.
Wah-ti-an-kah.
Saucy Chief.
Tah-wah-che-he.
William Penn.
Clamore.
Two-giver.
Tall-chief.
Sa-pah-ke-ah.
Black Dog.
Thomas Big-chief.
Ne-kah-wah-she-ton-kah.
Joseph Pawnee-no-pah-she
White Hair.
Cyprian Tayrian.

PAUL AKIN, *Interpreter.*
E. M. MATTHEWS,
Secretary.

LAWS

THE OSAGE NATION.

CHAPTER 2.

ARTICLE I.

An Act for the punishment of criminal offences.

SECTION 1. That in all cases of wilful murder, the offender, upon trial and conviction by the authorized court of this Nation, shall suffer death, and when sentence of death shall have been passed, the court shall grant a respite of five days before such criminal shall be executed.

SEC. 2. That any person who shall, with malice aforethought, assault another with intent to kill, shall, upon conviction thereof, be fined in a sum, for the benefit of the party injured, not less than fifty nor more than one hundred dollars, at the discretion of the court, and receive fifty lashes on the bare back. But if any person shall kill in self-defence or by accident, without any previous intent to do the same, he shall not be held accountable for such act, and be exempt from any fine or punishment whatever.

SEC. 3. That upon trial and conviction of any person charged with the offence of having committed a rape on any female, he shall be punished with fifty lashes on the bare back.

ARTICLE 2.

An Act for the punishment of thefts and other crime.

SEC. 4. That any person who shall be convicted of stealing a horse, mule, jack or jinney, shall be punished by not less than twenty-nine nor more than fifty lashes on the bare back, and be compelled to make payment to the amount of damages or injuries sustained, if such stolen property be not restored, for the benefit of the person so injured ; and for all other property which may be stolen, upon conviction of the party so offending, the punishment shall be in proportion to the magnitude of the offence, at the discretion of the court, and judgment against the offender for damages to the party injured.

SEC. 5. That if any person shall wilfully and maliciously burn the house or other property of another, or otherwise kill or destroy the property of any person for the purpose of injuring or gratifying a spirit of revenge, such offender, upon conviction, shall be punished in like manner as provided in the section above, and be compelled to make ample remuneration by such compensation as the Court may determine.

SEC. 6. That any person who shall employ another, or aid or abet in the perpetration of any criminal offence, upon conviction thereof, such person or persons shall suffer such punishment as may be inflicted upon the principal offender ; and be likewise subject to the same judgment for damages.

ARTICLE III.

AN ACT *in relation to contracts.*

SEC. 7. That all lawful contracts shall be binding, and any person upon failure to comply with the terms of such contracts shall be liable to a suit at law, in the Court having jurisdiction in the matter, to be instituted by the creditor, and if upon trial, the law and testimony shall justify judgment shall be rendered in favor of such creditor for the amount which may be due by the defendant.

SEC. 8. That in all cases where a debt may be contracted, and it is agreed that property or trade shall be taken in payment of such debt, judgment shall be rendered accordingly ; and the officer shall proceed to levy on the property of such debtor, and to summons two disinterested citizens, who shall be sworn by him, to aid in the valuation of such property, fairly and impartially, and when such property is so valued by the sheriff and such other persons, the creditor shall receive the same at such valuation as may be fixed by them.

SEC. 9. The following description of property shall be exempt from sale to satisfy any debt or judgment, and shall be reserved for the benefit of the owner thereof; viz : one horse or in lieu thereof, one yoke of oxen, one cow and calf, one sow and pigs, farming utensils, household and kitchen furniture, and fifty bushels of corn, and fire-arms, one saddle and bridle, and it shall not be lawful for an officer to levy on any of the above-mentioned property.

SEC. 10. When judgment is rendered, and the officer in whose hands an execution may be placed shall fail to find any property or effects in possession of the debtor to satisfy the same, and has cause to believe that some other person has in hands property or effects belonging to such debtor, the officer shall proceed to make inquiry of such person; and if such property or effects shall be pointed out, he shall proceed to make levy ; but if such person shall refuse to give such information as may be satisfactory, the officer shall summon him before the clerk of the court, who shall require of him an oath to answer to the charges of holding in his possession the property or effects of such debtor.

SEC. 11. It shall not be lawful for any officer to levy on

the house, farm, or any other improvements, of any person or persons.

ARTICLE IV.

AN ACT *respecting persons who may be summoned by an officer.*

SEC. 12. Any person or persons who may be summoned to appear before the court to give in testimony, and shall refuse or fail to attend, unless on account of sickness or other lawful excuse—such person shall be fined in a sum not less than twenty, nor more than fifty dollars, at the discretion of the court; and any person who may be summoned by an officer to aid in the arrest of any criminal, and shall refuse, unless it shall be on account of sickness, or other lawful excuse, shall be fined twenty-five dollars.

SEC. 13. Any citizen who may be summoned to assist in arresting criminals shall be entitled to one dollar per day for his services out of the national treasury; and all persons summoned to give in testimony in court shall be entitled each to one dollar per day during their attendance at court, including going and returning home—against whom judgment may be rendered.

ARTICLE V.

AN ACT *relating to estates and administrators.*

SEC. 14. All written or verbal wills of deceased persons, when proved to the satisfaction of one of the judges of the court, shall be valid, and if by such will, any person or persons are designated to manage the business of any estate so left, such person shall receive from one of the judges of the court a written appointment for that purpose, and be required to enter into bond with sufficient security, for the faithful management of such business, in accordance with the provisions of said will, and for the careful preservation of all property and effects so left, all such wills shall be registered by the clerk of the court. All persons so appointed shall furnish, on oath, a schedule and discription of all property and effects belonging to such estate, and which shall likewise be registered by the said clerk.

SEC. 15. Executors of wills and administrators on estate of deceased persons shall report annually to the judges of the court at the August term of the Supreme Court, the condition of, and all that may have been done by them in reference to the business, property, and effects of such estate, as such persons may have in charge.

SEC. 16. Executors of wills and administrators shall be entitled to a compensation of eight per cent. upon the amount of property and effects belonging to an estate, for their services, which shall be appraised by two or more persons to be appointed by the Chief Justice under oath.

SEC. 17. When a person dies without having made a will, one of the judges shall grant letters of administration to some competent and responsible person, to be selected from among the relatives of the deceased, if the safety of such property as may be left seems to warrant, and who shall be required to enter into bond, as provided above. And the property and effects shall belong equally to the children; the widow, also, of such deceased person shall be entitled to an equal share with the children, to be apportioned to her whenever she requires it, and the settlement of the business will safely permit, and the residue to the children as they become of age, to wit, males at eighteen years, and females at fifteen years, and in case such widow shall again marry and hold her property separately from her husband, and shall die without issue from her second marriage, such property shall be divided among the aforesaid children, and in all cases where the wife dies holding property as above, and has children, and the husband survives, such property shall likewise be equally apportioned among the children and the

husband; and if such husband should again marry and die
without issue from such second marriage, his property shall
be divided equally among his children. Any administra-
tor, who may have charge of an estate, shall settle all just
debts due out of its effects, and collect all outstanding claims
in its favor. He shall cause public notice to be given, by
written advertisements, for all persons having demands
against such estate to bring them forward for settlement
within twelve months, otherwise they shall be void and not
recoverable by law.

ARTICLE VI.

An Act relating to Public Domain.

SEC. 18. No person or persons shall be permitted to settle on
or erect any improvements within one-fourth of a mile of the
house, field or other improvements of another citizen, without their consent, under the penalty of forfeiting such improvements and labor for the benefit of the original settler;
provided it may be lawful, however, where there may be a
stream of running water for another citizen to improve one
hundred yards from such field so situated.

SEC. 19. All improvements which may be left by any
person or persons removing to another place, and the improvements so left remaining unoccupied for the term of
two years, such improvements shall be considered abandon-
ed, and other person or persons whosoever may take and go
in possession of such improvements in the same manner as
if there were no improvements.

ARTICLE VII.

An Act to legalize intermarriage with white men.

SEC. 20. Whereas the peace and prosperity of the Osage
people require that, in the enforcement of the laws, jurisdiction of the civil laws should be exercised over all persons whatever, who may, from time to time, be privileged

to reside within the limits of the Osage Nation; therefore, any white man or citizen of the United States, who may hereafter come into the country to marry an Osage woman, shall first be required to make known his intentions to the National Council by applying for a license, and such license may, under the authority of the National Council, be issued by the clerk thereof; any person so obtaining a license shall pay to the clerk the sum of twenty dollars for such license, and take an oath to support the Constitution and abide by the laws of the Osage Nation; which oath may be administered by the President of the National Council, or the Clerk of the body, authorized for that purpose, and it shall be the duty of the Clerk to record the same in the Journals of the National Council. But if any such white man, or citizen of the United States, shall refuse to ubscribe to the oath, he shall not be entitled to the rights of citizenship, and shall forthwith be removed without the limits of the Osage Nation as an intruder.

ARTICLE VIII.

An Act respecting stray property.

SEC. 21. It shall be the duty of each of the sheriffs of the several districts to receive and advertise for public sale to the highest bidder all stray property that may be found or reported to them in their respective districts—such as horses, mules, asses, cows, hogs, sheep, and goats—giving a description of color, brands, ear and flesh marks, age and sex, and such property shall be sold for prompt payment in cash, national warrants, or certificates, at the regular term of court, and on the first day thereof, and not before the hour of ten in the morning.

SEC. 22. All stray property, before being sold, shall be advertised at least sixty days by written advertisements, and posted at the court-house, and in like manner in the register-book, which shall be kept by the clerk of the court;

and any person having property advertised under the provision of this act shall have the right of reclaiming such property by providing the same, on or before the day of sale, before one of the judges of the court ; and the judge, if satisfied of the proof, after recording the same, and making his decision thereon, shall issue an order directing the sheriff posting the property to deliver it to the owner.

SEC. 23. If any person having property advertised under this act shall fail to prove the same, before the sale of the same, he shall forfeit his right to such property, except as hereinafter provided ; but any person who shall prove such property in the manner thereinbefore provided for, within nine months after the sale of the same, shall be entitled to receive from the Treasurer, on the certificate of the judge before whom the proof is made, the proceeds in kind of the sale of the same, deducting therefrom the sheriff's fees.

SEC. 24. Any person who may take up stray property shall, within ten days thereafter, be required to have the same posted ; and any person failing to comply with this provision shall be liable to a fine of not less than ten nor more than twenty-five dollars.

SEC. 25. Any person who shall dispose of or wilfully take any stray property not his own, or shall wilfully kill or maim any such property, either before or after such property is posted, shall be deemed guilty of the same offence as if the act was committed upon the property of a citizen, and shall, upon conviction, be punished accordingly.

SEC. 26. It shall be the duty of the several sheriffs to have, if possible, all property that may be posted by them at the Court-house on the day of sale, and to place the purchaser there in possession of the same when sold, or within a reasonable time, if required to do so; the sheriff may retain ten per cent. in kind of all proceeds of sales of stray property, and be required to turn over the residue to the treasurer. The clerk of the court shall be present at all sales of stray property, and shall make and keep on record in his office a register of all sales by the sheriff, to whom made, amount in kind paid, date of sale and kind of property sold, and make therefrom a quarterly report to treasurer as he may direct.

ARTICLE IX.

AN ACT *relating to the duties of the High Sheriff.*

SEC. 27. The office of High Sheriff is hereby created. He shall be elected by the National Council for the term of two years.

SEC. 28. It shall be the duty of the High Sheriff to keep the Capitol, the furniture, and other property therein and thereto belonging in a State, of the keys and fastening of the door of the Capitol during the session of the National Council and the sitting of the Court.

SEC. 29. The Sheriff shall at all times keep the room of the Capitol clean and properly ventilated, and during the session of the National Council and Court well-warmed and supplied with pure water. It shall be his especial duty to cause to be prosecuted every person who shall be accused of violating the laws.

SEC. 30. The High Sheriff shall be a conservator of the peace with such general powers as are exercised by Sheriffs, besides such special or extraordinary powers as may be conferred upon him by law. He shall wait upon, open and adjourn the session of the Court and execute its mandates. He shall also wait upon and execute all orders of the National Council we shall have full authority during the session of the Council, and at all other times to suppress within the vicinity of the Capital all riotous broils, obscene, or other improper conduct, and to enforce obedience to the law and may, whenever necessary, summons any extra adequate force to his assistance; he may summarily arrest, imprison, and hold until duly sober, any person acting improperly, while under the influence of intoxicating drinks, and arrest, and imprison, all persons who may be guilty of a breach of the peace at or about the same of government.

SEC. 31. The High Sheriff shall have general supervision of the lower sheriffs, and see that they properly execute the laws in their respective districts, and he shall see that all taxes are collected as provided by law.

ARTICLE X.

Duties of the Prosecuting Attorney.

SEC. 32. The Prosecuting Attorney shall be elected at the same time and in the manner that executive councilors are elected, and his term of office shall be that of the National Council electing him, and such prosecuting attorney before he enters upon the duties of his office shall be commissioned by the principal chief, his compensation shall be two hundred dollars per annum.

SEC. 33. That it shall be the duty of the prosecuting attorney to prosecute in behalf of the Nation all persons charged with criminal offences that may be brought before the court of the Nation, and be required to take the following oath or affirmation : " You do solemnly swear that you as prosecuting attorney for and on behalf of the Nation, will, to the best of your skill and ability prosecute all persons charged with criminal offences that may be brought before the court, and that you will not take or receive any remuneration of any person charged with any criminal offence, but will be faithful to the Osage Nation in all prosecutions to the best of your ability, so help you God."

SEC. 34. There shall be a National Secretary, who shall be elected by the council for the term of two years, he shall be clerk of the council and court and shall keep a record of all the proceedings of both the council and court; and perform such other duties that may be provided by law.

ARTICLE XI.

Attorney.

SEC. 35. Before any citizen shall be allowed to appear before the court of this Nation for the purpose of practicing at law he shall obtain a license from the clerk thereof, and pay in advance annually the sum of five dollars to practice before the court, and be required to take an oath that he will to the best of his knowledge and ability support and defend all cases that may be entrusted to his care.

SEC. 36. Any person engaged in the practice of law agreeable to the provisions of this act, who shall be convicted before the court of bribing or otherwise influencing any person to keep them from appearing at court, or proving unfaithful to their duties and oaths, shall be subject to a fine of twenty-five dollars, and the revocation of their license. All fines collected under the provision of this act shall be paid into the treasury.

ARTICLE XII.

Lawful Fences.

SEC. 37. A fence nine rails high, with cracks not exceeding four inches wide, for four rails up said fence, and a fence seven good rails high well staked and ridered, shall also be considered a lawful fence, and a board or wire fence four feet high with post eight feet apart, shall also be a lawful fence; and any stock whatever, that may breake into the field of any person or persons having a lawful fence, the owner of such property shall be responsible for the damages done.

ARTICLE XIII.

AN ACT *prohibiting the sale of timber and stone.*

SEC. 38. No person or persons shall be allowed to sell to citizens of the United States any timber, rails, boards, or stones, under the penalty of being liable to a fine in a sum of not less than twenty-five nor exceeding fifty dollars for every such offence, or in default of payment shall be imprisoned for any term not exceeding thirty days at the discretion of the court.

ARTICLE XIV.

Permits to employ or rent to U. S. citizen.

SEC. 39. Any citizen of this Nation who may desire to employ or rent to a citizen of the United States shall be required to obtain a permit for that purpose from the Osage Council, and be approved by the Indian agent and the Indian Office at Washington.

SEC. 40. For all such permits granted the national secretary shall require of the person obtaining it one dollar for every month or fraction of a month for which it is granted. He shall report to the treasurer at the end of each quarter and turn over to him all the receipts that may come into his hands for the quarter then ending.

SEC. 41. After the expiration of the time of the permits, such person shall be deemed an intruder, and it is made the duty of prosecuting attorney to report the same to the Indian agent.

SEC. 42. Any citizen of this Nation who shall hire or employ any citizen of the United States in any other manner than as provided in the first section of this article shall be deemed guilty of a misdemeanor, and, upon conviction, be fined in any sum not less than twenty-five nor exceeding fifty dollars, at the discretion of the court; and in default of payment be imprisoned, not less than fifteen nor exceeding thirty days. No permits shall be granted longer than one year. Persons holding such permits shall be allowed two span of horses or oxen, two cows and calves, and ten hogs, all stock over this number as above specified shall be taxed.

ARTICLE XV.

Drover's Taxes.

SEC. 43. Every person not a citizen of this Nation, driving stock into this Nation for the purpose of grazing or feeding the same shall be liable to a tax at the rate of five cents a head per month.

SEC. 44. It shall not be lawful for any citizen of this Nation to hold within the limits of the Osage Nation, for the purpose of grazing or feeding, any stock belonging to a citizen of the United States, until first procuring a permit from the National Council for that purpose, and paying a tax as provided by law. Any citizen of this Nation violating the provisions of this act shall be liable to a fine of one hundred dollars, and in default of payment be imprisoned not less than thirty nor more than fifty days.

In all cases where a sheriff or other person acting under lawful authority, has reason to believe that efforts are being made to evade the provisions of this Act by collision of some citizen of this Nation, with the owner of stock, such citizen claiming to be the owner, such sheriff or other person shall require the claimant to exhibit his bill of purchase of the stock in question; if deemed necessary to arrive at the facts, he may put such claimant or any other person supposed to be cognizant of the facts in the premises, upon oath, and question him or them as to the bona fide ownership of such stock, and in all such cases, if it appears that there has been fraud attempted for the purpose of evading the revenue laws of this nation, then and in that case there shall be levied double the amount of tax which would otherwise have been made. All money collected under the provisions of this Act shall be paid into the Treasury.

ARTICLE XVI.

Fixing Compensation of Officers.

SEC. 45. From and after the first Monday of November, 1882, the salary and pay of the following officers and persons in the employ of the Osage Nation shall be as follows. to wit:

Principal Chief. ....Per annum. .		$300 00
Assistant Principal Chief.......... " "		200 00
Supreme Judges, each............ " "		100 00
Members of National Council, each. " "		100 00
National Clerk.................. " "		200 00
High Sheriff..................... " "		100 00
Sheriffs, each................... " "		80 00

Executive Councilors shall each receive a compensation for their services which shall be two dollars per day while in actual service.

CHAPTER III.

ARTICLE I.

AN ACT *relating to the judiciary.*

SECTION 1. That the seat of the Osage Government is hereby established at Pawhuska.

SEC. 2. The court established under the Government of this Nation, shall have jurisdiction of all suits rising under the Constitution and laws of the Osage Nation.

SEC. 3. There shall be established a Supreme Court which shall consist of one Chief Justice, and two associate judges. who shall decide all civil cases.

SEC. 4. It shall be the duty of the three judges to choose two persons of good character and knowledge, who shall in

conjunction with them, constitute a court for the purpose
of hearing and deciding, all criminal cases. The compensation of persons chosen shall be one dollar and fifty cents
per day while in actual service.

Sec. 5. No citizen of the Osage Nation who may be em-
ployed by the United States Government, as police, shall be
chosen to sit as judge in the court of the Osage Nation.

Sec. 6. The commencement of all suits shall be by summons obtained from the clerk of the court, and which summons shall state the nature of the case upon which proceedings are founded, and be served by some lawful officer at
least twenty days before the holding of said court, and such
summons shall be returnable to the clerk with a certificate
of service, and the court shall give judgment as the right of
the cause, and the matter in law shall appear under them
without regarding any imperfection, defect or want of form
in such summons in process.

ARTICLE II.
Duties of Sheriffs.

Sec. 7. There shall be one Sheriff in each District, who shall
enter into bonds with security to the amount of three hundred
dollars for the faithful execution of duties of his office, and
take the following oath. "I. A. B.," having been elected to the
office of Sheriff of —— District, do solemnly swear that I
will, well and truly execute the duties of said office ; according to the best of my ability, without fraud or par-
tiality. It shall be the duty of the Sheriffs to attend the
court to serve all summons or other process, which may be
placed in their hands, and to take all necessary and proper
measures in the execution of the judgements of the court,
and also to arrest and cause to be tried all persons who may
be charged with criminal offences, and in case of resistance
or strong apprehensions of resistance, the Sheriff shall summons such number of citizens as may be necessary to arrest

any person or persons against whom criminal charges may
be alleged, and to confine the same in jail until convicted
or acquitted ; should any person charged with criminal vio-
lation of law resist any lawful officer, or person authorized
to cause arrest, while in the discharge of his or their duty,
and such persons should be killed on account of unlawful
resistance, such officer or other person shall not be held
guilty of murder.

ARTICLE III.

Relating to District.

The following divisions of the Osage Nation into five districts shall continue until altered by law, to wit :

PAWNEENOPAHSHE DISTRICT.

SEC. 8. Commencing at the Pawnee crossing on the Arkansas River, thence along the old Pawnee road, to the Elm
Spring, thence along the Salt Creek road to the top of the
dividing ridge between Hominy and Clear Creeks, thence
in a direct line to where the Kaw road crosses the flint
hills, thence along said flint hills to the State line, thence
west along said line to the Kaw boundary, thence along
said boundary to the Arkansas River, thence along said
river to the place of beginning.

BLACK DOG DISTRICT

SEC. 9. Commencing at the Elm Spring, thence south in a
direct line to Prominent mound, thence in a direct line to
where the Cherokee line crosses Delaware creek, thence south
along said line to the Arkansas river, thence up said river
to the Pawnee crossing, thence bounded by the first district.

CLAMMORE DISTRICT.

SEC. 10. Commencing at the top of the dividing ridge, between Hominy and Clear creeks, thence east along said division to where the Cherokee line crosses Bird creek, thence

south along said line to Delaware creek, to be bounded on the south by the Second, and on the west by the First districts.

PAWHUSKA DISTRICT.

SEC. 11. Commencing where the Cherokee line crosses Bird creek, thence north along said line to Sand creek, thence west in a direct line to Gus Strikeaxe's place, between Mission and Rock creeks, thence in a direct line to where the Elgin road crosses Rock creek, thence in a direct line to the flint hills at the head of Bird creek, to be bounded on the west by the First, and on the south by the Third districts.

STRIKEAX DISTRICT.

SEC. 12. Commencing where the Cherokee line crosses Sand creek, thence along said line north to the State line, thence along said line to the Flint hills, thence along said hills to the head of Bird creek, to be bounded on the south by the Fourth district.

Resolved by the National Council:

SEC. 13. That we accept the sum of one hundred (100) dollars per year from the Indian agent in charge, in full for all salaries due us for services as members of the Osage Council, and that we ask the judges of the Osage Nation to acccept one hundred (100) dollars per annum in full for their services as judges of the Osage Nation, to be paid as aforesaid, also, that all other officers whose salaries are prescribed at a stated amount per annum, be asked to receive thereby as above; all of the above salaries to be paid from our tribal funds in the hands of the United States Government.

Provided, That all the aforesaid officers shall receipt for the same in full for all moneys due them as officers of this nation, for the time for which they are paid.

Approved March 4th, 1882.

(SIGNED,) JOSEPH PAW-NE-NO-PAN-SHE,
Principal Chief.

E. M. MATHEWS, *Secretary.*

Ratified Indian Treaty 338: Osage (Great and Little) – Canville Trading Post, Osage Nation, Kansas, September 29, 1865

Andrew Johnson,

President of the United States of America,

To all and singular to whom these presents shall come,
greeting:

Whereas a Treaty was made and concluded at
Canville Trading Post, Osage Nation, in the State of
Kansas, on the twenty-ninth day of September, in
the year of our Lord one thousand eight hundred and sixty-five, by and between D. N.
Cooley and Elijah Sells, Commissioners, on the
part of the United States, and White Hair,
Little Bear, (Me-tso-shin-ca,) and other Chiefs
of the Tribe of Great and Little Osage Indians,
on the part of said tribe of Indians and duly
authorized thereto by them, which Treaty is in the
words and figures following, to wit:

08

Articles

Of Treaty and Convention, made and Concluded, at Canville Trading Post, Osage Nation. within the boundary of the State of Kansas. on the twenty-ninth day of September Eighteen hundred and sixtyfive by And between D. N. Cooley Commissioner of Indian Affairs And Elijah Sell Superintendent of Indian Affairs for the Southern Superintendency. Commissioners on the part of the United States, and the Chiefs of the Tribe of Great and Little Osage Indians, the said Chiefs being duly authorized to negotiate and Treat, by said Tribes.

1

Article 1.

The tribe of the Great and Little Osage Indians having now more lands than are necessary for their occupation, and all payments
from the Government to them, under former treaties,
having ceased, leaving them greatly impoverished,
and being desirous of improving their condition
by disposing of their surplus lands, do hereby
grant and sell to the United States the lands contained within the following boundaries— that is
to say— Beginning at the south-east corner of
their present Reservation and running thence
north with the eastern boundary thereof fifty
miles to the north-east corner, thence west
with the northern line thirty miles, thence south
fifty miles to the southern boundary of said Reservation, and thence east with said southern
boundary to the place of beginning: Provided,
That the western boundary of said land herein
ceded, shall not extend further westward than
upon a line commencing at a point on the
southern boundary of said Osage county one
mile east of the place where the Verdigris river
crosses the southern boundary of the State of Kansas:
And, in consideration of the grant and sale to
them of the above described lands, the United States
agree to pay the sum of three hundred thousand
dollars; which sum shall be placed, to the

28 credit of said tribe of Indians, in the Treasury
29 of the United States; and interest thereon, at the
30 rate of five per centum per annum, shall be paid
31 to said tribe semi-annually, in money, clothing,
32 provisions, or such articles of utility, as the Secretary
33 of the Interior may, from time to time, direct. —
34 Said lands shall be surveyed, and sold under
35 the direction of the Secretary of the Interior, on the
36 most advantageous terms, for cash, as public
37 lands are surveyed and sold under existing
38 laws; but no pre-emption claim or homestead
39 settlement shall be recognized; and after reimbursing the United States the cost of said survey
and sale, and the said sum of three hundred
thousand dollars placed to the credit of said
Indians, the remaining proceeds of sales shall be
placed in the Treasury of the United States, to the
credit of the "Civilization Fund," to be used, under
the direction of the Secretary of the Interior, for
the education and civilization of Indian tribes
residing within the limits of the United States.

Article 2.

1   The said tribe of Indians also hereby cede to
2 the United States a tract of land twenty miles in
3 width from north to south, off the north side of
4 the remainder of their present Reservation, and
5 extending its entire length from east to west;
6 which land is to be held in trust for said

7 Indians, and to be surveyed, and sold for
8 their benefit, by the Secretary of the Interior, under
9 such rules and regulations as he may, from time
10 to time, prescribe, under the direction of the Com-
11 missioner of the General Land Office, as other lands
12 are surveyed and sold; the proceeds of such
sales, as they accrue, after deducting all expenses incident to the proper execution of the
trust, shall be placed in the Treasury of the United
States to the credit of said tribe of Indians; and
the interest thereon, at the rate of five per centum
per annum, shall be expended annually, for
building houses, purchasing agricultural implements
and stock animals, and for the employment of a
physician and mechanics, and for providing such
other necessary aid as will enable said Indians to
commence agricultural pursuits under favorable
circumstances: Provided, That twenty-five per
centum of the net proceeds arising from the sale of
said Trust Lands, until said percentage shall
amount to the sum of eighty thousand dollars,
shall be placed to the credit of the School Fund of
said Indians; and the interest thereon, at the rate
of five per centum per annum, shall be expended
semi-annually, for the boarding, clothing, and education of the children of said tribe.
Article 3.
    The Osage Indians, being sensible of the great

benefits they have received from the Catholic Mission
situate in that portion of their Reservation herein
granted and sold to the United States, do hereby
stipulate that one section of said land, to be selected
by the Commissioner of Indian Affairs, so as to include the
improvements of said Mission, shall be granted in
fee simple to John Schoonmaker, in trust, for
the use and benefit of the Society sustaining
said Mission, with the privilege to said Schoonmaker, on the payment of one dollar and
twenty-five cents per acre, of selecting and purchasing two sections of land adjoining the
section above granted, the said selection
to be held in trust for said Society, and to
be selected in legal subdivisions of surveys,
and subject to the approval of the Secretary
of the Interior.

Article 4.

1   All loyal persons, being heads of families and
2   citizens of the United States, or members of any
3   tribe at peace with the United States, having
4   made settlements and improvements as pro-
5   vided by the pre-emption laws of the United States,
6   and now residing on the lands provided to
7   be sold by the United States, in trust for said
8   tribe, as well as the said lands herein granted
9   and sold to the United States, shall have the
10 privilege, at any time within one year after

the ratification of this treaty, of buying a quarter section each, at one dollar and twenty-five cents per acre; such quarter section to be selected according to the legal subdivision of surveys, and to include, as far as practicable, the improvements of the settler.

Article 5.

The Osages being desirous of paying their just debts to James N. Coffey and A. B. Canville for advances in provisions, clothing, and other necessaries of life, hereby agree that the Superintendent of Indian Affairs for the Southern Superintendency and the Agent of the tribe shall examine all claims against said tribe, and submit the same to the tribe for approval or disapproval, and report the same to the Secretary of the Interior, with the proofs in each case, for his concurrence or rejection; and the Secretary may issue to the claimants Scrip for the claims thus allowed, which shall be receivable, as cash, in payment for any of the lands sold in trust for said tribe: Provided, the aggregate amount thus allowed by the Secretary of the Interior shall not exceed five thousand dollars.

Article 6.

In consideration of the long and faithful

Article 6.

In consideration of the long and faithful
services rendered by Charles Mograin, one
of the principal Chiefs of the Great Osages, to the
people, and in consideration of improvements
made and owned by him on the land by
this treaty sold to the United States, and in lieu
of the provision made in Article fourteen
for the half-breed Indians, the heirs of the said Charles
Mograin dec'd may select one section of land, including his improvements, from the north half
of said land, subject to the approval of the
Secretary of the Interior, and upon his approval of such selection, it shall be patented to the heirs of
the said Mograin dec'd in fee simple; ~~and it is further agreed that the said Charles Mograin
shall, for the reasons stated, receive out of the
first payment to said tribe the sum of
five hundred dollars.~~

Article 7.

It is agreed between the parties hereto,
that the sum of five hundred dollars shall
be set apart, each year, from the moneys of
said tribe, and paid by the Agent to the Chiefs,
~~and Headmen of the tribe, for their services.~~

Article 8.

The Osage Indians being anxious that a
School should be established in their new
home, at their request it is agreed and provided that John Schoenmaker may select

one section of land within their diminished
Reservation, and, upon the approval of such
selection by the Secretary of the Interior, such
section of land shall be set apart to the
said Schoenmaker and his successors, upon
condition that the same shall be used, improved, and occupied, for the support and
education of the children of said Indians
during the occupancy of said Reservation
by said tribe: Provided, that said lands
shall not be patented, and upon the discontinuance of said School shall revert
to said tribe and to the United States as
other Indian lands.

Article 9.

It is further agreed that in consideration
of the services of Darius Rogers to the Osage
Indians, a patent shall be issued to him for
one hundred and sixty acres of land, to
include his mill and improvements, on paying one dollar and twenty-five cents per
acre; and said Rogers shall also have the
privilege of purchasing, at the rate of one dollar and twenty-five cents, one quarter section
of land adjoining the tract above mentioned,
which shall be patented to him in like
manner; said lands to be selected subject
to the approval of the Secretary of the Interior.

Article 10.

The Osages acknowledge their dependence on the Government of the United States, and invoke its protection and care; they desire peace, and promise to abstain from war, and commit no depredations on either citizens or Indians; and they further agree to use their best efforts to suppress the introduction and use of ardent spirits in their country.

Article 11.

It is agreed that all roads and highways, laid out by the State or General Government, shall have right of way through the lands herein reserved, on the same terms as are provided by law when made through lands of citizens of the United States; and Railroad Companies, when the lines of their roads necessarily pass through the lands of said Indians, shall have right of way, upon the payment of fair compensation therefor.

Article 12.

Within six months after the ratification of this treaty the Osage Indians shall remove from the lands sold and ceded in trust, and settle upon their diminished Reservation.

Article 13.

The Osage Indians having no annuities from which it is possible for them to pay any of the expenses of carrying this treaty into effect, it is agreed that the United States shall appropriate twenty thousand dollars, or so much thereof as may be necessary, for the purpose of defraying the expense of survey and sale of the lands hereby ceded in trust; which amount so expended shall be re-imbursed to the Treasury of the United States from the proceeds of the first sales of said lands.

Article 14.

The half-breeds of the Osage tribe of In-dians, not to exceed twenty-five in number, who have improvements on the north half of the lands sold to the United States, shall have a patent issued to them, in fee simple, for eighty acres each, to include as far as practicable their improvements:—Said half-breeds to be designated by the Chiefs and Headmen of the tribe; and the heirs of Joseph Swiss, a half-breed and a former Interpreter of said tribe, shall, in lieu of the above provision, receive a title, in fee simple, to a half section of land, including his house and improve-ments, if practicable, and also to a half

section of the Trust Land— all of said lands
to be selected by the parties, subject to the
approval of the Secretary of the Interior.

Article 15.

It is also agreed by the United States
that said Osage Indians may unite with
any tribe of Indians at peace with the
United States, residing in said Indian Territory, and thence afterwards receive an
equitable proportion, according to their numbers, of all moneys, annuities, or property, payable by the United States to said Indian tribe with
which the agreement may be made; and
in turn granting to said Indians, in proportion to their numbers, an equitable proportion of all moneys, annuities, and property,
payable by the United States to said Osages.

Article 16.

It is also agreed by said contracting parties that if said Indians should agree to
remove from the State of Kansas, and settle
on lands to be provided for them, by the
United States, in the Indian Territory, on such
terms as may be agreed on between the
United States and the Indian tribes now
residing in said Territory, or any of them,
then the diminished reservation shall be
disposed of by the United States in the

same manner and for the same purposes
as hereinbefore provided in relation to said
Trust Lands— except that fifty per cent. of the
proceeds of the sale of said diminished
reserve may be used by the United States in
the purchase of lands for a suitable home
for said Indians, in said Indian Territory.

Article 17.

Should the Senate reject or amend any
of the above Articles, such rejection or amendment shall not affect the other provisions of
this treaty, but the same shall go into effect
when ratified by the Senate and approved
by the President.

Note   The interlineations and erasures on the seventh and
tenth pages were made before signing

D. M. Cooley,
Com'r of Indian Affairs,

Elijah Sells
Supt Ind aff South. Supt'cy
and Commissioner

Me tso shin ca (Little Bear)	White Hair his x mark
Chf Little Osage his x mark	Principal Chief Osage Nation
No pa wah la his x mark	Ta wah the he his x mark
2d Chief to Little Bear	Chf Big Hill Band
Ta cha hum kah, his x mark	Beaver his x mark
Little Chief L.B. Band	Second chief White Hair Band

Glermont   his x mark
Chief Clermont Band | Wa She pe She his x mark
Opo ton koh   his x mark | Little chief W H Band

Witnesses

Ma sho hun ca   his x mark
Councellor Little Bear Band
Wa sha pa wa ta ne ca   his x mark
Wa du ha ka   his x mark
Shin ka Wa ta ne kah   his x mark
She weh teh   his x mark
Gra Ma   his x mark
Hur la wah sho Sha   his x mark
Wa ta ton ca Wa ki   his x mark
hun pa wah ca   his x mark
Ha Ska mon ne   his x mark

Attest
   G. C. Snow U. S. Neosho Ina agent
   Milton W. Reynolds, acting clerk
   Theodore C. Wilson Phonographic Reporter.

   Alexander Beyett
        Interpreter Osage Nation

lxii

Witnesses   Little Raven Band

Ka wah ho tza   his x mark

O ke pa hola   his x mark

Me hy tha   his x mark

~~Little~~ White Hair Band

of Witness

Han ka wa tha   his x mark

      Councellor of White Hair

Wa tha wa   his x mark

Ka he ka tza jeh   his x mark

Ka he ka wa shin pe the   his x mark

Taw pe ka la   his x mark

Wa tza shin ka   his x mark

Wa no pa the   his x mark

shin be ka thi   his x mark

Ne koole bl.   his x mark

O ke pa ca loh   his x mark

Ke nu in ca   his x mark

Pa tu mo na   his x mark

We the undersigned Chiefs and head men of the Clermont and Black Dog Band of the Great Osage Nation in Council at Fort Smith Ark. have had the foregoing treaty read and explained in full by our interpreter L. P. Chouteau and fully approve the provisions of said treaty, made by our brothers the Osages, and by thus signing make it our act and deed

of Clermont Band

Clermont Chf,		his X mark
Talley 2d Chf C. Band		his X mark
Wah ti ingah (Dry Father) Counsellor		his X mark
Kah ha che la ton. Brave		his X mark
Do tah cah she "		his X mark
Black Dog Chf Black Dog Band		his X mark
William Penn 2d Chf " " "		his X mark
Broke arm Counsellor		his X mark
Ne kah ke Pon nah Brave		his X mark
Ne kah gah he "		his X mark

23

Witnesses

Wah skon mon ney	his X mark
Wah kon che la	his X mark
Wah sha she wah ti in jah	his X mark
Pah cha hun jah	his X mark
Long Bow.	his X mark
Wah she wah ba.	his X mark
War Eagle	his X mark
Pon hon gle jah hue	his X mark
San down	his X mark
Ton won jehe	his X mark
Wah cha o nan she	his X mark

I certify that the foregoing treaty was fully explained by me, and that the above signatures, the first as Chiefs and the head men, and the others as witnesses signed the same as their free act and deed

L. P. Chouteau
Interpreter.

And whereas the said Treaty having been sub=
mitted to the Senate of the United States for its
constitutional action thereon, the Senate did,
on the twenty-sixth day of June, one thousand
eight hundred and sixty-six, advise and
consent to the ratification of the same by a reso=
lution with amendments in the words and figures
following, to wit:

In Executive Session
Senate of the United States,
June 26. 1866

Resolved, (two thirds of the Senators present concurring) That the Senate advise and consent to the ratification of the Articles of Treaty and Convention made and concluded at Canville Trading Post, Osage nation, within the boundary of the State of Kansas, on the twenty-ninth day of September, eighteen hundred and sixty-five, by and between the Commissioners on the part of the United States, and the Chief of the tribes of Great and Little Osage Indians, the said chief being duly authorized to negotiate and treat by said tribes, with the following.

Amendments

1st   Article 1. line 58, after the word "laws," insert the following:— including any act granting lands to the State of Kansas, in aid of the construction of a railroad through said lands,

2nd   Article 2 Strike out all after the word "benefit" in line 8 to and including the word "sold" in line 12, and insert in lieu thereof the following:— under the direction of the Commissioner of the General Land Office at a price not less than one dollar and twenty-five cents per acre as other lands are

are surveyed and sold, under such rules and regulations as the Secretary of the Interior shall from time to time prescribe.

3° Article 4. line 8 After the word "as" where it occurs the second time, insert : upon

4th Article 9 line 9 after the word "cents" insert :- per acre

5th Article 11 line 3 After the words "through the" insert :- remaining

6th Same Article line 4. Strike out "herein reserved" and insert in lieu thereof :- of said Indians.

Attest :

_____ Secretary

lxviii

And whereas the foregoing amendments having been fully interpreted and explained to White Hair, Little Beaver, Clarmont, Ta-wah-she-he, Met-so-shinca, (Little Bear,) No-paw-ahla, and Black Dog, chiefs of the and tribe of Great and Little Osage Indians, they did, on the twenty-first day of September, one thousand eight hundred and sixty-six, give their free and voluntary assent to the same, in the words and figures following, to wit:

Whereas, A certain treaty was made by and between Commissioners on the part of the United States, and the chiefs representing the Great and Little Osage Indians, on the 29th of September, 1865, to the ratification of which treaty the Senate of the United States has advised and consented, with the following amendments, viz;

Amendments

1st. Art. 1. Line 38; After the word "laws" insert the following;
"including any act granting lands to the
"State of Kansas, in aid of the construction of
"a railroad through said lands"

2d. Art. 2. Strike out all after the word "benefit" in line 8 to
and including the word "sold" in line 12, and
insert in lieu thereof the following;— "under the
"direction of the Commissioner of the General Land
"Office, at a price not less than one dollar and
"twenty five cents per acre, as other lands are
"surveyed and sold, under such rules and regu—
"lations as the Secretary of the Interior shall from
"time to time prescribe"

3d. Art. 4. Line 8. After the word "as", where it occurs the second time, insert "upon".

4th. Art. 9 – line 9. After the word "cents", insert "per acre"

5th. Art. 11 – line 3. After the words "through the", insert "remaining"

6th. Art. 11 – line 4. Strike out "herein reserved", and insert in lieu
   thereof, "of said Indians", —

Now, therefore, we, the undersigned, chiefs and headmen
of the said Great and Little Osage Indians, having
heard the above amendments read, and fully
explained to us, on this Twenty first day of
September one thousand eight hundred and sixty six,
do hereby accept and consent to the aforesaid
amendments.

White Hair   his X mark. Principal Chief Osage Nation
Little Beaver   his X mark. 2d Chief White Hairs Band
Clarmont   his X mark. Chief Clarmont's Band
Joe wah she she   his X mark. Chief Big Hill Band
Met so she new (Little Bear)   his X mark. Chief Little Osages
Nei pau ahla   his X mark. 2d Chief Little Osages
Black Dog   his X mark. Chief Black Dogs Band

Attest

    G. C. Snow U.S. Neosho Ind. agent
    Joseph Pawnee no pashe E. Indian
    Alexander Beyett Interpreter
    Moses Neal
    E. C. Amos
    George W. Douglass
    Jno. Tibbetts
    John Brinkley

lxxi

Now, therefore, be it known that I, Andrew Johnson, President of the United States of America, do in pursuance of the advice and consent of the Senate, as expressed in its resolution of the twenty-sixth of June, one thousand eight hundred and sixty-six, accept, ratify, and confirm the said Treaty with the amendments as aforesaid.

In testimony whereof I have hereto signed my name, and caused the seal of the United States to be affixed.

Done at the city of Washington this twenty-first day of January, in the year of our Lord one thousand eight hundred and sixty-seven, and of the Independence of the United States of America the ninety-first.

Andrew Johnson

By the President:

William H. Seward,
Secretary of State.

Ratified Indian Treaty 338: Osage (Great and Little) – Canville Trading Post, Osage Nation, Kansas, September 29, 1865

Department of State,

Washington June 28, 1866

Hon James Harlan

Secretary of the Interior.

Sir

I have the honor to transmit to you herewith the Treaty with the Western Bands of Soshone Indians, concluded on the 1st of October, 1863, to the ratification of which the Senate has by resolution without date advised and consented with an amendment; in order that said amendment may be submitted to the Indians concerned, for their acceptance. I have the honor also to transmit to you herewith the Treaty, concluded on the 29th of September, 1865, with the Great and Little Osage Indians, to the ratification of which the Senate has by resolution of the 26th instant advised and consented with certain amendments. The last article of this treaty provides that "should the Senate reject or amend any of the above articles, such rejection or amendment shall not affect the other provisions of this treaty, but the same shall go into effect when ratified by the Senate and approved by the President". It will be perceived, however, that if, under these circumstances, the treaty were promulgated at this time, it would be in a very incomplete and indeterminate state until the consent of the

#338.

Indians concerned should have been given to the Senate's
amendments. It is therefore respectfully suggested it might
be well prior to the promulgation of the treaty to submit it
to the Great and Little Osage Indians, with a view of obtaining such consent, which would remove all complexity from the
matter.

                I am Sir

                    Your obedient servant

                      William H. Seward.

RECEIVED,

Dept. of State,

JUL 2 1866

> DEPARTMENT of the INTERIOR,
> WASHINGTON D. C. June 30, 1866

Sir

      I have the honor to acknowledge the receipt of your letter of the 28th inst; transmitting the Treaty concluded on the 29th of Sept. 1865, with the Great and Little Osage Indians to the ratification of which the Senate by resolution of the 26th inst; advised and consented, with certain amendments; which amendments will be submitted to the Indians interested for their acceptance.

> I am Sir
> Very respectfully
> Your ob't Serv't
> Jas Harlan
> Secretary

Hon Wm H. Seward

  Sect'y of State.

#336.

Department of State,

Washington January 23, 1867.

Hon. O. H. Browning,

Secretary of the Interior.

Sir:

I have the honor to request that you will be
pleased to designate the newspaper in which the Treaty of
the 29th of September, 1865, between the United States and
the Great and Little Osage Indians, shall be published.

I am, your obedient servant,

William H. Seward

#338.

RECEIVED

FEB 4 1867

DEPARTMENT of the INTERIOR,

WASHINGTON D. C. Jany 31st 1867.

Sir:

Agreeably to the recommendation of the Commissioner
of Indian Affairs, I have to request, in reply to your
letter of the 23rd inst., that the treaty with the Great
and Little Osage Indians be published in the Topeka
'"Record", Kansas.

Very respectfully,

Your obedient servant,

O H Browning

Secretary.

Hon. W^m_H H. Seward,

Secretary of State.

#338.

Domestic Letters - Volume 75, page 243.

Department of State
Washington February 12, 1867.

Hon. O H Browning
    Secretary of the Interior.

Sir:

    I have the honor to transmit, herewith, 250 print-
ed copies of the Treaty with the Great and Little Osage
Indians, concluded September 29, 1865; one copy of the same
having been transmitted to the Editor of the "Record", at
Topeka, Kansas, for promulgation, agreeably to your request
of the 31st ultimo.

                    I am, your obedient servant,
                        William H. Seward

#338.

RECEIVED

MAY 25 1867

> Department of the Interior
>
> General Land Office
>
> May 23^{d} 1867.

Hon: William H. Seward
  Secretary of State

              Sir,

              I have the honor to acknow-
ledge the receipt of a communication from your Department
dated the 20$^{"}$ instant, covering a copy of dispatch N° 191
of the 16$^{"}$ May from the U. S. Consul at Toronto, Canada
West, inclosing a copy of a letter to him of even date from
Mr Donald McDonald relative to a tract of land which his
friend desires to purchase in the southern part of Kansas.

              As your Department desires the information in regard
to the matter furnished by this Office for the purpose of
transmitting the same to the U. S Consul at Toronto, I have
to state for the information of the party concerned as follows: -

              The land referred to by Mr McDonald appears to fall
within the Osage Lands ceded in trust to the United States
per 2^{d} Article of the Treaty concluded September 29. 1865,

                                                        #338.

copy of which is herewith inclosed together with Map of
Kansas & Nebraska whereon the Osage lands sold to the U.
States, ceded in trust and those reserved by Osage Indians
are represented. The treaty stipulations, it will be perceived, require the ceded lands in trust to be sold as
other public lands are sold under such rules and regulations
as the Secretary of the Interior shall from time to time pre-
scribe- The returns of the surveys not having as yet been
fully made to this Office by government surveyors, no procla-
mation for the sale of the lands has been made nor the rules
and regulations have been prescribed by the Secretary of the
Interior and therefore the section of those lands, desired
by Mr M^CDonald's friend for stock farming and residence, cannot
be purchases at the seat of the government, but will have to
be applied for to the local Land Office at Humboldt, Kansas,
where the Register & Receiver of the Osage District reside -

I have the honor to be

Very respectfully

Your Ob't Serv't

Jo^s S. Wilson

Commissioner

Miscellaneous Letters - May, Part II, 1867. (Enclosure to
letter of May 23, 1867, from General Land Office, Department
of Interior.)

Extracts

Treaty

between

The United States of America

and the

Great and Little Osage Indians

concluded,

September 29th 1865.

x   x   x   x   x   x

"Article 2.   The said tribe of Indians also hereby
cede to the United States a tract of land twenty miles in
width from north to south, off the north side of the remainder of their present reservation and extending its entire
length from east to west; which land is to be held in trust
for said Indians and to be surveyed and sold for their benefit under the direction of the Commissioner of the General
Land Office at a price not less than one dollar and twenty
five cents per acre, as other lands are surveyed and sold,
under such rules and regulations as the Secretary of the
Interior shall from time to time prescribe. The proceeds of
such sales, as they accrue after deducting all expenses incident to the proper execution of the trust shall be placed in

#338.

the Treasury of the United States to the credit of said
tribe of Indians; and the interest thereon at the rate of
five per centum per annum shall be expended annually for
building houses, purchasing agricultural implements and
stock animals, and for the employment of a physician and
mechanics, and for providing such other necessary aid as
will enable said Indians to commence agricultural pursuits
under favorable circumstances: Provided, That twenty-five
per centum of the net proceeds arising from the sale of
said trust lands, until said percentage shall amount to the
sum of eighty thousand dollars, shall be placed to the credit
of the school fund of said Indians; and the interest thereon
at the rate of five percentum per annum, shall be expended
semi annually for the boarding clothing and education of the
children of said tribe."

Ratified Indian Treaty 338:
Osage (Great and Little) –
Canville Trading Post,
Osage Nation, Kansas,
September 29, 1865

TREATY

THE UNITED STATES OF AMERICA

GREAT AND LITTLE OSAGE INDIANS.

CONCLUDED, SEPTEMBER 29, 1865.
RATIFICATION ADVISED, WITH AMENDMENTS, JUNE 26, 1866.
AMENDMENTS ACCEPTED SEPTEMBER 21, 1866.
PROCLAIMED JANUARY 21, 1867.

#338

ANDREW JOHNSON,

PRESIDENT OF THE UNITED STATES OF AMERICA,

TO ALL AND SINGULAR TO WHOM THESE PRESENTS SHALL COME, GREETING:

Whereas a Treaty was made and concluded at Canville Trading Post, Osage Nation, in the State of Kansas, on the twenty-ninth day of September, in the year of our Lord one thousand eight hundred and sixty-five, by and between D. N. Cooley and Elijah Sells, Commissioners, on the part of the United States, and White Hair, Little Bear, (Me-tso-shin-ca,) and other Chiefs of the Tribe of Great and Little Osage Indians, on the part of said tribe of Indians, and duly authorized thereto by them, which Treaty is in the words and figures following, to wit:

Articles of Treaty and Convention, made and concluded at Canville Trading Post, Osage nation, within the boundary of the State of Kansas, on the twenty-ninth day of September, eighteen hundred and sixty-five, by and between D. N. Cooley, Commissioner of Indian Affairs, and Elijah Sells, superintendent of Indian affairs for the southern superintendency, commissioners on the part of the United States, and the chiefs of the tribe of Great and Little Osage Indians, the said chiefs being duly authorized to negotiate and treat by said tribes.

ARTICLE 1.

The tribe of the Great and Little Osage Indians having now more lands than are necessary for their occupation, and all payments from the government to them under former treaties having ceased, leaving them greatly impoverished, and being desirous of improving their condition by disposing of their surplus lands, do hereby grant and sell to the United States the lands contained within the following boundaries, that is to say: beginning at the southeast corner of their present reservation, and running thence north with the eastern boundary thereof fifty miles to the northeast corner; thence west with the northern line thirty miles; thence south fifty miles, to the southern boundary of said reservation; and thence east with said southern boundary to the place of beginning: *Provided*, That the western boundary of said lands herein ceded shall not extend further westward than upon a line commencing at a point on the southern boundary of said Osage country one mile east of the place where the Verdigris river crosses the southern boundary of the State of Kansas. And, in consideration of the grant and sale to them of the above-described lands, the United States agree to pay the sum of three hundred thousand dollars, which sum shall be placed to the credit of said tribe of Indians in the treasury of the United States, and interest thereon at the rate of five per centum per annum shall be paid to said tribe semi-annually, in money, clothing, provisions, or such articles of utility as the Secretary of the Interior may

from time to time direct. Said lands shall be surveyed and sold, under the direction of the Secretary of the Interior, on the most advantageous terms, for cash.
as public lands are surveyed and sold under existing laws, but no pre-emption
claim or homestead settlement shall be recognised: and after reimbursing the
United States the cost of said survey and sale, and the said sum of three hundred thousand dollars placed to the credit of said Indians, the remaining proceeds
of sales shall be placed in the treasury of the United States to the credit of the
"civilization fund," to be used, under the direction of the Secretary of the Interior, for the education and civilization of Indian tribes residing within the limits
of the United States.

ARTICLE 2.

The said tribe of Indians also hereby cede to the United States a tract of
land twenty miles in width from north to south, off the north side of the remainder
of their present reservation, and extending its entire length from east to west;
which land is to be held in trust for said Indians, and to be surveyed and sold for
their benefit by the Secretary of the Interior, under such rules and regulations as
he may, from time to time, prescribe, under the direction of the Commissioner of
the General Land Office, as other lands are surveyed and sold. The proceeds of
such sales, as they accrue, after deducting all expenses incident to the proper
execution of the trust, shall be placed in the treasury of the United States to the
credit of said tribe of Indians; and the interest thereon, at the rate of five per
centum per annum, shall be expended annually for building houses, purchasing
agricultural implements and stock animals, and for the employment of a physician
and mechanics, and for providing such other necessary aid as will enable said
Indians to commence agricultural pursuits under favorable circumstances: *Provided*, That twenty-five per centum of the net proceeds arising from the sale of
said trust lands, until said percentage shall amount to the sum of eighty thousand
dollars, shall be placed to the credit of the school fund of said Indians; and the
interest thereon, at the rate of five per centum per annum, shall be expended
semi-annually for the boarding, clothing, and education of the children of said
tribe.

ARTICLE 3.

The Osage Indians, being sensible of the great benefits they have received
from the Catholic mission. situate in that portion of their reservation herein
granted and sold to the United States, do hereby stipulate that one section of said
land, to be selected by the Commissioner of Indian Affairs so as to include the
improvements of said mission, shall be granted in fee-simple to John Schoenmaker,
in trust, for the use and benefit of the society sustaining said mission, with the
privilege to said Schoenmaker, on the payment of one dollar and twenty-five
cents per acre, of selecting and purchasing two sections of land adjoining the
section above granted; the said selection to be held in trust for said society, and
to be selected in legal subdivisions of surveys, and subject to the approval of the
Secretary of the Interior.

ARTICLE 4.

All loyal persons, being heads of families and citizens of the United States,
or members of any tribe at peace with the United States, having made settlements and improvements as provided by the pre-emption laws of the United
States, and now residing on the lands provided to be sold by the United States,
in trust for said tribe, as well as the said lands herein granted and sold to the
United States, shall have the privilege, at any time within one year after the
ratification of this treaty, of buying a quarter section each, at one dollar and

twenty-five cents per acre; such quarter section to be selected according to the legal subdivison of surveys, and to include, as far as practicable, the improvements of the settler.

ARTICLE 5.

The Osages being desirous of paying their just debts to James N. Coffey and A. B. Canville, for advances in provisions, clothing, and other necessaries of life, hereby agree that the superintendent of Indian affairs for the southern superintendency and the agent of the tribe shall examine all claims against said tribe, and submit the same to the tribe for approval or disapproval, and report the same to the Secretary of the Interior, with the proofs in each case, for his concurrence or rejection: and the Secretary may issue to the claimants scrip for the claims thus allowed, which shall be receivable as cash, in payment for any of the lands sold in trust for said tribe: *Provided,* The aggregate amount thus allowed by the Secretary of the Interior shall not exceed five thousand dollars.

ARTICLE 6.

In consideration of the long and faithful services rendered by Charles Mograin, one of the principal chiefs of the Great Osages, to the people, and in consideration of improvements made and owned by him on the land by this treaty sold to the United States, and in lieu of the provisions made in article fourteen for the half-breed Indians, the heirs of the said Charles Mograin, dec[ease]d, may select one section of land, including his improvements, from the north half of said land, subject to the approval of the Secretary of the Interior, and upon his approval of such selection, it shall be patented to the heirs of the said Mograin, dec[ease]d, in fee-simple.

ARTICLE 7.

It is agreed between the parties hereto that the sum of five hundred dollars shall be set apart each year from the moneys of said tribe and paid by the agent to the chiefs.

ARTICLE 8.

The Osage Indians being anxious that a school should be established in their new home, at their request it is agreed and provided that John Schoenmaker may select one section of land within their diminished reservation, and, upon the approval of such selection by the Secretary of the Interior, such section of land shall be set apart to the said Schoenmaker and his successors, upon condition that the same shall be used, improved, and occupied for the support and education of the children of said Indians during the occupancy of said reservation by said tribe: *Provided,* That said lands shall not be patented, and upon the discontinuance of said school shall revert to said tribe and to the United States as other Indian lands.

ARTICLE 9.

It is further agreed that, in consideration of the services of Darius Rogers to the Osage Indians, a patent shall be issued to him for one hundred and sixty acres of land, to include his mill and improvements, on paying one dollar and twenty-five cents per acre; and said Rogers shall also have the privilege of purchasing, at the rate of one dollar and twenty-five cents, one quarter section of land adjoining the tract above mentioned, which shall be patented to him in like manner; said lands to be selected subject to the approval of the Secretary of the Interior.

ARTICLE 10.

The Osages acknowledge their dependence on the government of the United States, and invoke its protection and care; they desire peace, and promise to abstain from war, and commit no depredations on either citizens or Indians; and they further agree to use their best efforts to suppress the introduction and use of ardent spirits in their country.

ARTICLE 11.

It is agreed that all roads and highways laid out by the State or general government shall have right of way through the lands herein reserved, on the same terms as are provided by law when made through lands of citizens of the United States: and railroad companies, when the lines of their roads necessarily pass through the lands of said Indians, shall have right of way upon the payment of fair compensation therefor.

ARTICLE 12.

Within six months after the ratification of this treaty the Osage Indians shall remove from the lands sold and ceded in trust, and settle upon their diminished reservation.

ARTICLE 13.

The Osage Indians having no annuities from which it is possible for them to pay any of the expenses of carrying this treaty into effect, it is agreed that the United States shall appropriate twenty thousand dollars, or so much thereof as may be necessary, for the purpose of defraying the expense of survey and sale of the lands hereby ceded in trust, which amount so expended shall be reimbursed to the treasury of the United States from the proceeds of the first sales of said lands.

ARTICLE 14.

The half-breeds of the Osage tribe of Indians, not to exceed twenty-five in number, who have improvements on the north half of the lands sold to the United States, shall have a patent issued to them, in fee-simple, for eighty acres each, to include, as far as practicable, their improvements, said half-breeds to be designated by the chiefs and headmen of the tribe; and the heirs of Joseph Swiss, a half-breed, and a former interpreter of said tribe, shall, in lieu of the above provision, receive a title, in fee-simple, to a half-section of land, including his house and improvements, if practicable, and also to a half section of the trust land; all of said lands to be selected by the parties, subject to the approval of the Secretary of the Interior.

ARTICLE 15.

It is also agreed by the United States that said Osage Indians may unite with any tribe of Indians at peace with the United States, residing in said Indian territory, and thence afterwards receive an equitable proportion, according to their numbers, of all moneys, annuities, or property, payable by the United States to said Indian tribe with which the agreement may be made; and in turn granting to said Indians. in proportion to their numbers, an equitable proportion of all moneys, annuities, and property, payable by the United States to said Osages.

7

Article 16.

It is also agreed by said contracting parties, that if said Indians should agree to remove from the State of Kansas, and settle on lands to be provided for them by the United States in the Indian territory, on such terms as may be agreed on between the United States and the Indian tribes now residing in said territory or any of them, then the diminished reservation shall be disposed of by the United States in the same manner and for the same purposes as hereinbefore provided in relation to said trust lands, except that fifty per cent. of the proceeds of the sale of said diminished reserve may be used by the United States in the purchase of lands for a suitable home for said Indians in said Indian Territory.

Article 17.

Should the Senate reject or amend any of the above articles, such rejection or amendment shall not affect the other provisions of this treaty, but the same shall go into effect when ratified by the Senate and approved by the President.

Note.—The interlineations and erasures on the seventh and tenth pages were made before signing.

D. N. COOLEY,
Com'r. of Indian Affairs.
ELIJAH SELLS,
Sup't Ind. Aff. South'n Sup'cy, and Commissioner.
ME-TSO-SHIN-CA, (Little Bear.)   his x mark.
Chief Little Osages.
NO-PA-WAH-LA,   his x mark.
2d Chief to Little Bear.
PA-THA-HUN-KAH,   his x mark.
Little Chief L. B. Band.
WHITE HAIR,   his x mark.
Principal Chief Osage Nation.
TA-WAH-SHE-HE,   his x mark.
Chief Big Hill Band.
BEAVER,   his x mark.
Second Chief White Hair's Band.
CLERMONT,   his x mark.
Chief Clermont Band.
O-PO-TON-KOH,   his x mark.
WA-SHE-PE-SHE,   his x mark.
Little Chief W. H. Band.

Witnesses:
MA-SHO-HUN-CA,   his x mark.
Counsellor Little Bear Band.
WA-SHA-PA-WA-TA-NE-CA,   his x mark.
WA-DU-HA-KA,   his x mark.
SHIN-KA-WA-TA-NE-KAH,   his x mark.
SHE-WEH-TEH,   his x mark.
GRA-MA,   his x mark.
HU-LA-WAH-SHO-SHA,   his x mark.
NA-TA-TON-CA-WA-KI,   his x mark.
NUM-PA-WAH-CU,   his x mark.
HA-SKA-MON-NE,   his x mark.

8

Attest:
G. C. SNOW, *U. S. Neosho Ind. Agent.*
MILTON W. REYNOLDS, *Acting Clerk.*
THEODORE C. WILSON, *Phonographic Reporter.*
ALEXANDER BEYETT, *Interpreter Osage Nation.*

Witnesses, Little Bear's band:
KA-WAH-HO-TZA,	his x mark.
O-KE-PA-HOLA,	his x mark.
ME-HE-THA,	his x mark.

White Hair's band of witnesses:
SHIN-KA-WA-SHA, councillor of White Hair's,	his x mark.
WA-SHA-WA,	his x mark.
KA-HE-KA-STZA-JEH,	his x mark.
KA-HE-KA-WA-SHIN-PE-SHE,	his x mark.
SAW-PE-KA-LA,	his x mark.
WA-TZA-SHIM-KA,	his x mark.
WA-NO-PA-SHE,	his x mark.
SHIN-BE-KA-SHI,	his x mark.
NE-KOO-LE-BLO,	his x mark.
O-KE-PA-KA-LOH,	his x mark.
KE-NU-IN-CA,	his x mark.
PA-SU-MO-NA,	his x mark.

We, the undersigned, chiefs and headmen of the Clermont and Black Dog Bands of the Great Osage Nation, in council at Fort Smith, Ark., have had the foregoing treaty read and explained in full by our interpreter, L. P. Chouteau, and fully approve the provisions of said treaty made by our brothers the Osages, and by this signing make it our act and deed.

CLERMONT, chf. of Clermont Band,	his x mark.
PALLEY, 2d chf. of Clermont Band,	his x mark.
HAH-TI-IN-GAH, (Dry Feather,) counsellor,	his x mark.
KAH-HA-CHE-LA-TÓN, brave,	his x mark.
DO-TAH-CAH-SHE, brave,	his x mark.
BLACK DOG, chf. Black Dog Band,	his x mark.
WILLIAM PENN, 2d chf. Black Dog Band,	his x mark.
BROKE ARM, counsellor,	his x mark.
NE-KAH-KE-PON-NAH, brave,	his x mark.
NE-KAH-GAH-HEE, brave,	his x mark.

Witnesses—
WAH-SKON-MON-NEY,	his x mark.
WAH-KON-CHE-LA,	his x mark.
WAH-SHA-SHA-WAH-TI-IN-GAH,	his x mark.
PAH-CHA-HUN-GAH,	his x mark.
LONG BOW,	his x mark.
WAH-SHE-WAH-LA,	his x mark.
WAR EAGLE,	his x mark.
PON-HON-GLE-GAH-TON,	his x mark.
SUN DOWN,	his x mark.
TON-WON-GE-HI,	his x mark.
WAH-CHA-O-NAU-SHE,	his x mark.

8

9

I certify that the foregoing treaty was fully explained by me, and that the above signatures, the first as chiefs and headmen and the others as witness[es,] signed the same as their free act and deed.

L. P. CHOUTEAU, *Interpreter.*

And whereas the said Treaty having been submitted to the Senate of the United States for its constitutional action thereon, the Senate did, on the twenty-sixth day of June, one thousand eight hundred and sixty-six, advise and consent to the ratification of the same by a resolution with amendments in the words and figures following, to wit:

In Executive Session, Senate of the United States,
June 26, 1866.

Resolved, (two-thirds of the Senators present concurring,) That the Senate advise and consent to the ratification of the Articles of Treaty and Convention made and concluded at Canville Trading Post, Osage Nation, within the boundary of the State of Kansas, on the twenty-ninth day of September, eighteen hundred and sixty-five, by and between the Commissioners on the part of the United States, and the Chief of the tribes of Great and Little Osage Indians, the said Chief being duly authorized to negotiate and treat by said tribes, with the following

AMENDMENTS :

1st. Article 1, line 38, after the word "laws" insert the following: *including any act granting lands to the State of Kansas in aid of the construction of a railroad through said lands.*
2nd. Article 2, strike out all after the word "benefit," in line 8, to and including the word "sold," in line 12, and insert in lieu thereof the following: *under the direction of the Commissioner of the General Land Office at a price not less than one dollar and twenty-five cents per acre as other lands are surveyed and sold, under such rules and regulations as the Secretary of the Interior shall from time to time prescribe.*
3d. Article 4, line 8, after the word "as," where it occurs the second time, insert: *upon.*
4th. Article 9, line 9, after the word "cents" insert: *per acre.*
5th. Article 11, line 3, after the words "through the" insert: *remaining.*
6th. Same article, line 4, strike out "herein reserved," and insert in lieu thereof: *of said Indians.*
Attest:

J. W. FORNEY,
Secretary.

And whereas the foregoing amendments having been fully interpreted and explained to White Hair, Little Beaver, Clarmont, Ta-wah-she-he, Met-so-shinca, (Little Bear,) No-paw-ahla, and Black Dog, chiefs of the said tribe of Great and Little Osage Indians, they did, on the twenty-first day of September, one thousand eight hundred and sixty-six, give their free and voluntary assent to the same, in the words and figures following, to wit:

Whereas a certain Treaty was made by and between Commissioners on the part of the United States and the Chiefs representing the Great and Little Osage

Indians, on the 29th of September, 1865, to the ratification of which Treaty the Senate of the United States has advised and consented, with the following amendments, viz:

AMENDMENTS.

1st. Art. 1, line 38, after the word "laws" insert the following: "including any act granting lands to the State of Kansas, in aid of the construction of a railroad through said lands."

2d. Art. 2, strike out all after the word "benefit," in line 8, to and including the word "sold," in line 12, and insert in lieu thereof the following: "under the direction of the Commissioner of the General Land Office, at a price not less than one dollar and twenty-five cents per acre, as other lands are surveyed and sold, under such rules and regulations as the Secretary of the Interior shall from time to time prescribe."

3d. Art. 4, line 8, after the word "as," where it occurs the second time, insert "upon."

4th. Art. 9, line 9, after the word "cents," insert "per acre."

5th. Art. 11, line 3, after the words "through the," insert "remaining."

6th. Art. 11, line 4, strike out "herein reserved," and insert in lieu thereof "of said Indians."

Now, therefore, we, the undersigned, Chiefs and Headmen of the said Great and Little Osage Indians, having heard the above amendments read, and fully explained to us, on this twenty-first day of September, one thousand eight hundred and sixty-six, do hereby accept and consent to the aforesaid amendments.

WHITE HAIR,   his x mark.
Principal Chief Osage Nation.
LITTLE BEAVER,   his x mark.
2d Chief White Hair's Band.
CLARMONT,   his x mark.
Chief Clarmont's Band.
TA-WAH-SHE-HE,   his x mark.
Chief Big Hill Band.
MET-SO-SHINCA, (Little Bear,) his x mark.
Chief Little Osages.
NO-PAW-AHLA,   his x mark.
2d Chief Little Osages.
BLACK DOG,   his x mark.
Chief Black Dog's Band.

Attest:
G. C. SNOW, U. S. *Neosho Ind. Agent.*
JOSEPH PAW-NE-NO-PASH, *E. Indian.*
ALEXANDER BEYETT, *Interpreter.*
MOSES NEAL.
E. C. AMSDEN.
GEORGE W. DOUGLASS.
FRED. TIBBETTS.
JOHN BRINKLEY.

Now, therefore, be it known, that I, ANDREW JOHNSON, President of the United States of America, do, in pursuance of the advice and consent of the

Senate, as expressed in its resolution of the twenty-sixth of June, one thousand eight hundred and sixty-six, accept, ratify, and confirm the said Treaty with the amendments as aforesaid.

In testimony whereof I have hereto signed my name, and caused the seal of the United States to be affixed.

Done at the city of Washington, this twenty-first day of January, in the year

[L. S.]   of our Lord one thousand eight hundred and sixty-seven, and of the Independence of the United States of America the ninety-first.

ANDREW JOHNSON.

By the President:
WILLIAM H. SEWARD,
Secretary of State.

INTRODUCTION

It is intriguing to think about what the Osage from circa 1918 to approximately the mid to late 1930's dealt with through the greed, corruption and what we now call domestic terrorism. It's well documented what took place in Oklahoma from David Grann's important research and book (2018); *Killers of the Flower Moon* and recent movie (2023).

But let's not ignore their story from their early history and their beliefs of creation, their roots so to speak, their foundation. Not when they were masters of their own fate, before intrusion. Not when they were masters of the prairie only to become victims of land grabbers wanting what was theirs. It wasn't just the land but their headrights, the resources they didn't even ask for. When the currents below their feet brought untold millions they were under attack. The riches not only brought the pleasures of money but also excessive heartache.

Now they had to deal with fear and hate and deception. The good life brought death. They dealt with the injustices from another race and a government close behind them to make sure they became, Wards under fake Guardians who sought only to line their pockets no matter the price to the Osage.

The Osage people paid a steep price that haunts them to this day. Within this census every time during the transcription phase there appears periodically a picture of a character holding a pitch folk and wearing horns revealing the terms, Incompetent, D&D, Crazy, Blind, whatever, it makes you wonder and think really? They were placed in deadly circumstances every single day of their lives either by slow poisoning, gunshot, explosive destruction and who knows what else. But they had beliefs and history long before the demise by inhumane monsters. Read on and understand who the Osage were before they met civilization so to speak.

Back to the Osage Creation and Their Cultural Beliefs and History

Two different documents have been found describing the origins of their creation and early history and movement; first a look at the Osage's history and travel. There are within these text two separate tribal creations. These descriptions though somewhat different in nature would take much more concentration on the subject and several more sources which are difficult to find. Possibly, if able, an age old oral tradition could help from a storyteller carrying their legends and folklore. Story's from their ancestors. Hopefully from solid sources and through family traditions. But even then after so much time you'd still end up having to develop an educated guess.

But here are two from 1906 and 1914-1915. Even back then they were tales from the past; just putting it in print then and considering their accuracy had to be challenging. There's no telling who told these stories or even recorded their histories prior to the ones recording their history then, prior to 120 years ago? So even then it was nothing new. Thinking about it we should be thankful to those from our past willing to repeat their heritage rather than allowing their lives to fall into oblivion. For us to be able to have the privilege of taking a glimpse into what took place in the lives of these ancient people is an honor.

From the "THIRTY-SIXTH ANNUAL REPORT OF THE BUREAU OF AMERICAN ETHNOLOGY TO THE SECRETARY OF THE SMITHSONIAN INSTITUTION 1914-1915" beginning on page 35 by Francis La Flesche (pls. 1-23 figs. 1-15)

ACCOMPANYING PAPER - THE OSAGE TRIBE
RITE OF THE CHIEFS; SAYINGS OF THE ANCIENT MEN

By FRANCIS LA FLESCHE

The beginning text on page 43, paragraph 1. La Flesche's brief history Under INTRIDUCTION Ancient Home of the Osage states; "According to the Osage people made by the early travelers it appears that during the seventeenth century these Indians were living on the banks of the Little Osage near its confluence with the main Osage River. Marquette (1673) was the first traveler to mention the Osage. He did not visit the people in their villages, but, guided by information obtained from members of other tribes, he located the Osage upon his map as living at the head of the river bearing their name. How long prior to that time the Osages had made that particular locality their home, held it and the surrounding country by their valor while they lived upon its natural products, is not known, but it is certain that for more than a century since this first mention of them they had made this place their fixed abode. From this locality they went forth upon their hunting excursions and to this spot they returned. From here their war parties, both great and small, started when they went against their enemies, and when the fighting was over the war parties came back to this place. It was here that all their various ancient tribal ceremonies were held, and the hills that surrounded their villages were hallowed to the people by the graves of their ancestors, who were always remembered in the daily orisons of the tribe."

Also on page 44, paragraph 2-3. Titled: Visit of Captain Pike,

"In 1806 Capt. Zebulon M. Pike visited the Osages in their villages on the Little Osage River, where he stayed about a fortnight and became personally acquainted with the people and their condition. The year of this visit (1806) is epochal in the history of the Osage. It marks the beginning of a gradual process by which this people relinquished from time to time to the United State their territorial possessions. By the treaties of **1808** and **1818** they ceded large portions of their land. The Treaty of **1825** followed, by which they were obliged to give up their ancient home along the Little Osage River and take a reservation in Kansas. The treaties of **1834** and **1865** followed, and then, by an act of Congress passed in **1870**, they gave up their homes in Kansas to remove to what was then the Indian Territory."

On page 44, paragragh 6; Titled: Present Home and Condition of the Osage, "The present home of the Osage tribe is in Osage County, Oklahoma, to which the people moved from their old reservation in Kansas in **1872**; and took possession of the land." The commissioner of Indian affairs, in his report for the year 1872, speaking of the Osage and their new home, says:

Their reservation is bounded on the north by the south line of Kansas, east by the ninety-sixth degree of west longitude, and south and west by the Arkansas River, and contains approximately 1,760,000 acres. * * * By the act of **July 15, 1870**, provision was made for sale of all the lands belonging to the Osages within the limits of Kansas and for their removal across the line into the Indian Territory. * * * They still follow the chase, the buffalo being their main dependence for food. * * * They have since their removal begun farming to some extent, having already about 2,000 acres under cultivation. Their agent reports the reservation 'poorly adapted for civilizing purposes,' there being only one small valley of fertile soil, barely affording enough good farming land for 4,000 Indians. Having just located, they have at present but one school in operation, with an attendance of 38 scholars."

The government from the early days as it states, starting from the treaty in 1808 knew exactly what they were doing and what they wanted. From the book; *White Savage The Case of John Dunn Hunter* by Richard Drinnon, 1972; on page 63, paragraph 1.

"Both commissioners came to the council highly accomplished in the art of relieving Indians of their land. Clark arrived late, in fact, because he had stayed in St. Louis to wind up the details of a treaty by which the Osages ceded the great bulk of their remaining land to the United States." On page 84, paragraph 2. Clark makes a statement that reveals he knew what he was doing and was totally wrong,

"There is no evidence Chouteau ever regretted his role in negotiating this treaty [1825], but Clark later informed General Ethan Allen Hitchcock that this had been 'the hardest treaty on the Indians he [Clark] ever made and that if he was to be damned hereafter it would be for making that treaty.'

It's important to note the Auguste Pierre Chouteau was of French decent and a trader raised among the Osage while purposing the family's fur business during this early time worked with Clark of exploration fame; Lewis and Clark 1804. Though in many ways Clark was sympathetic to the Native peoples he still followed his destructive role in the decimation of the Native peoples land holdings and life forever.

Picking up again from La Flesche's short study "THE OSAGE TRIBE RITE OF THE CHIEFS" for the Osage gives the reasoning behind the great and sad circumstances the Osage innocently would face and show how degenerated a human or humans can become. On page 45, beginning at paragraph 1;

"Since that time it has been discovered that the land reported to be 'poorly adapted for civilizing purposes' is rich in minerals, particularly in oil, which has of late years been developed. The royalties received by the Osages on their oil leases have greatly increased their wealth, so that they are now reputed to be the richest people in this country as a community. They live in well-built houses, furnished with the best of furniture the stores can supply, and many of them have automobiles, which they have learned to drive themselves.

Up to the present time the Osages have lived upon their new reservation in three village communities, thus perpetuating the story of a division of the tribe that was forced by accident. The story handed down concerning this division is as follows: The Osage people had built their village upon the banks of a large river (perhaps the Mississippi), where they dwelt for a long period of time. It happened that the river overflowed its banks, forcing the people to flee in a panic toward a high hill for safety, taking with them only the things necessary for their living. A large group continued its flight until it reached the summit of the hill, where the people established their temporary camp. From that time this group was spoken of as Pa-ciu'-gthi^n, Dwellers-Upon-the-Hilltop. Another group halted at a forest where the people pitched their camp. These were spoken of as the Co^n-dscu'-ghti^n, Dwellers-in-the-Upland-Forest. A third group was caught in a thicket of thorny trees and bushes, where the people set up their temporary dwellings and became known by the name Wa-xa'-ga-u-gthi^n, Dwellers-in-the-Thorny-Thicket. A fourth group stopped near the foot of the hill, where they camped and were known by the name Iu-dse'-ta, The-Dwellers-Below. In later times the people of this group united with the Dwellers-in-the-Thorny-Thicket and now their identity as a distinct group is practically lost To-day the Dwellers-Upon-the-Hilltop have their village at Grayhorse; the Dwellers-in-the-Upland-Forest at Hominy; and the Dwellers-in-the-Thorny-Thicket at Pawhuska. This accidental division of the tribe into separate village groups, made permanent by tacit agreement, in no way disturbed the tribal and gentile organizations, and the tribal rites were continued by all three groups, although at times the villages were located long distances apart. It is said that in each of the villages all the gentes were represented, so that there was never any difficulty in making up the number of gentes required in a ceremony. In recent times, however, as the people were reduced in numbers from various causes, the three groups became dependent upon each other for a full gentile representation in a ceremony.

In Philip Dickerson's *History of the Osage Nation* (1906), page 3, para 1-2; he goes into another variation of the Osage past; briefly speaking about their movement west while inserting the opinions and knowledge of the subject from the famous Ethnologist Mooney of Cherokee history fame.

"From tribal traditions, according to Dorsey, the ancestors of the Omaha, Ponca, Kwapa, Kansa, and Osage were at first one family dwelling on the Ohio and Wabash rivers, but gradually wandered westward. They first separated at the mouth of the Ohio River. Those going down the Mississippi became the Kwapa, or down-stream people, those ascending the Mississippi, the Omaha or Nomaha, up-stream people. This separation occurring before De Sota's discovery of the Mississippi must have been in the 15th century. The Omahas, including the Osage, Ponka and Kansa group, ascended as far as the Missouri river where after a time the Omahas ascended the Missouri, leaving behind successively the Osage and Kansa families in the present territory of Missouri and Kansas, where the Omahas settled between the Platte and Niobrara, south of the Missouri, and the Ponkas continued into the Black Hills country where Lewis and Clark found them late in the 18th century reduced by smallpox from 3,500 to 300.

The Osage and Kansa ancestors seemed to have separated from the main Omaha group at the mouth of what was known as 'White Creek,' Grand Tuc (Grandes Eaux, according to Mooney) or Great Osage, which name it afterwards bore instead of referring to the Mississippi, as some claim. In 1673 Marquette refers to them as the 'Ouchage' and 'Autrechaha.' In 1791 Penicaut designates them 'Huzzau,' 'Ous,' and 'Wawha.'

Covering the two themes of Osage creation first from La Flesche's
Under the description, on page 59-62, paragraph 4.

Allegorical Story of the Organization

"In the beginning the peoples of the Wa-zha'-zhe, the Ho^n-ga, and the Tsi'-zhu came from the sky to the earth. After these three groups of people had descended they started forth to wonder over the earth, observing, as they marched, the sequence in which they had reached the earth; first the Wa-zha'-zhe, then the Ho^n-ga, and last the Tsi'-zhu. One day, after they had wandered for a great length of time, the Wa-zha'-zhe suddenly halted, and the leader looked back over his shoulder to his followers, who had also halted, and in an undertone said: 'We have come to the village of a strange people.' The leader of the Ho^n-ga looked back over his shoulder and said in the same manner passed the word to the Tsi'-zhu.

Overhearing the words cautiously spoken by the Wa-zha'-zhe leader and his followers, the people of the village sent a messenger to inquire who these strangers were and what was their mission. On the invitation of the messenger the Wa-zha"-zhe alone entered the village, for the Ho^n-ga and the Tsi-zhu declined to follow because they had noticed with revulsion that the bones of animals and of men lay scattered and bleaching around the village. It was the village of death to which they had come, when they had been seeking for life.

The Wa-zha'-zhe leader was conducted to the house of the leader of the strange people and there the two men exchanged words in friendly terms. The Wa-zha'-zhe presented a ceremonial pipe to the leader of this strange village, who in turn gave a pipe to the Wa-zha'-zhe, and then the two leaders conversed freely about the life and customs of their peoples. In the course of their conversation the Wa-zha'-zhe said the he belonged to a people who called themselves Ho^n-ga, whereupon the stranger said: 'I also am a Ho^n-ga.' He then told the Wa-zha'-zhe the manner in which his people destroyed life wherever it appeared on the earth, using for their weapons the four winds, and that whichever way the people turned the winds, the animals and men stricken by them fell and died. It was at this point that the Wa-zha'-zhe leader made known to his host that the Ho^n-ga and the Tsi'-zhu desired to dwell with him and his people, but did not like their habit of destroying life. The Wa-zha'-zhe leader then suggested that his host and his people move to a new country, where the land was pure and free from the signs of death. The Ho^n-ga U-ta-no^n-dsi (the isolated Ho^n-ga), as the Wa-zha'-zhe leader called these strange people, willingly accepted the invitation and moved with the Wa-zha'-zhe to a 'new country,' where they joined the Ho^n-ga and the Tsi-zhu.

All the four groups, the Wa-zha'-zhe, the Ho^n-ga, the Tsi-zhu, and the Ho^n-ga U-ta-no^n-dsi, thereupon moved to a new country, where the land was undefiled by decaying carcasses and where there were no visible signs of death. There they united themselves in friendship, and each pledging to the other its strength and support in resisting the dangers that might beset them in the course of their united tribal life.

It was at this time that the following dramatic incident took place between the Wa-zha'-zhe and the Ho^m-ga. The Wa-zha'-zhe offered to the Ho^m-ga a symbolic pipe, but before accepting it the Ho^m-ga asked, 'Who are you?' The Wa-zha'-zhe replied:

I am a person who has verily made of a pipe his body,
When you also make of the pipe your body,
You shall be free from all causes of death, O, Ho^m-ga.

The Ho^m-ga took the pipe and said in response:
I am a person who has made of the red boulder his body,
When you also make of it your body,
The maleviolent gods in their destructive course,
Shall pass by and leave you unharmed, O, Wa-zha'-zhe.

The expression of the Wa-zha'-zhe, 'I am a person who has made of a pipe his body,' is figurative and means that the pipe is the life symbol of his people, the medium through which they approach Wa-ko^m-da with their supplications. The words used by the Ho^m-ga in his response, 'I am a person who has made of the red boulder his body,' are also figurative and meaned that the red boulder is the life symbol of the Ho^m-ga people. The red boulder has a dual symbolism; it is the symbol of endurance and is also a symbol of the sun, the emblem of never-ending life.

It was thus that the two groups, the Wa-zha'-zhe and the Ho^m-ga, pledged support to one another in times of danger so long as tribal life should last. The words of the Wa-zha'-zhe and those of the Ho^m-ga were put in the wi'-gi-e form and are embodied in the rite called Ni'-ki-e, The Words of the Ancient Men, where the wi'-gi-es will be found in full. These two wi'-gi-es are also used in a certain part of the Wa-sha'-be A-thi^n, a war ceremony that will appear in a later volume, where it is intimated that the Wa-zha'-zhe also presented a ceremonial pipe to the Tsi'-zhu. The narrator of the foregoing paraphrase offered no information concerning the part of the Tsi'-zhu in this council of alliance, as he was not a member of that division.

At the time of this council the people of the three groups gave to the Ho^m-ga U-ta-no^n-dsi a house which they called Tsi' Wa-ko^n-da-gi, House of Mysteries. Both the house and its fireplace they consecrated to ceremonial uses and made them to represent the life-giving earth. To this House of Mysteries were to be brought all the infants of the four groups to be ceremonially fed upon the sacred foods of life that they might arrive safely at the age of maturity, and the children were here to be given their gentile names in order to take their established places in the tribal organization.

The council at this time also established another house, Tsi' Wa-ko^n-da-gi, House of Mysteries, which they called Ho^m-ga Tsi, and placed it in the keeping of the Wa-ca'-be gens of the Ho^m-ga group. In this house were to be performed the ceremonies that pertain to war. Within its fireplace, which was called Ho'-e-ga, Snare, were placed four stones, arranged at the cardinal points, one for each of the four winds. Upon these four stones was placed the Tse'-xe Ni-ka-po, a caldron for the boiling of certain plants that represented certain persons belonging to enemy tribes.

When the Tsi' Wa-ko^n-da-gi of the Wa-ca'-be gens and its fireplace had been consecrated, each of the gentes of the four groups placed within the house its life symbol. This statement is not meant to be understood in a literal sense, as some of the gentile life symbols are of the great objects in nature, such as the sun, moon, stars, earth, while there are others that are intangible, as the day, the night, and the sky. Therefore the act of placing the sacred life symbols in the House of Mysteries was represented by the reciting of the wi'-gi-es that relate to these various sacred life symbols.

These four warrior groups conducted both the war and hunting movements of the people, and no one group could act independently of the others. A war party thus ceremonially organized by all of these four groups was called Do-do^n-hi^n-to^n-ga, War Party in Great Numbers.

After living for a long period of time under this form of government the people were again seized with a desire to 'move to a new country' (a term expressive of a slow movement that preceded a change in the government of the tribe). It was while the tribe was in the 'new country' that the people made the Wa-xo'-be Zhi^n-ga, the Little Wa-xo'-be, one for each of the seven fireplaces of the Tsi'-zhu great division; one for each of the seven fireplaces of the Ho^n-ga subdivision; and one for each of the seven fireplaces of the Wa-zha'-zhe subdivision of the great Ho^n-ga division.

These wa-xo'-be were made of hawk skins and symbolized the courage of the warriors of each fireplace. The choice of the hawk to symbolize the courage and combative nature of the warrior proved satisfactory to all the people, for the courage of the hawk was considered as equal to that of the eagle, while the swift and decisive manner in which the smaller bird always attacks its prey ever excited the admiration of the warrior.

From the story relating to the adoption of the hawk as the warrior symbol, given in wi'-gi-e form by a member of the I^n-gtho^n-ga gens and by a member of the Tho'-xe gens in a paraphrase of the wi'-gi-e, it would appear that the ceremonies of the formal adoption and the acts of preparing the hawk skin for preservation were accompanied by dramatic action.

In the version of the I^n-gtho^n-ga, a gens belonging to the Ho^n-ga Great Division, the principal characters of the drama are left vague as to identity. But in the version of the Tho'-xe, a gens belonging to the Tsi'-zhu Great Division that symbolizes the sky, it becomes clear that the warrior whom the hawk typifies is a child born of the god of day and the goddess of night. In this version the principal characters are four brothers (stars), their sister (the moon), and the sun.

The supernatural birth of the wa-xo'-be, the symbolic hawk, is referred to in the words of three songs belonging to the ritual of the Wa-xo'-be degree of the Tho'-xe gens. The three songs bear in common the title "Little Songs of the Sun." (These songs, with their music, will appear in a later volume.)

Song 1

1

I go to the call of those who are assembled,
    To the call of those who are gathered around the hawk.

2

    I go to the call of those who are assembled,
    To the call of those who are gathered around the black bird.

3

    I go to the call of those who are assembled,
      To the call of those who are gathered around the One of the Night.

4

I go to the call of those who are assembled,
      To the call of those who are gathered around the One of the Day.

Song 2

1

      He is born! He is born!
      Behold, the hawk, he is born,
      They have said. They have said,
      He is born!

2

      He is born! He is born!
      Behold, the black bird, he is born,
      They have said. They have said,
      He is born!

3

      He is born! He is born!
      Behold, he is born of the One of the Night,
      They have said. They have said,
      He is born!

4

      He is born! He is born!
      Behold, he is born of the One of the Day,
      They have said. They have said,
      He is born!

Song 3

1

      Lo, it has come to pass,
      Behold, the hawk that lies outstretched,
      Is now born they proclaim. Is now born they proclaim.
      Welcome! be it said. Lo, it has come to pass.

2

      Lo, it has come to pass,
      Behold, it is of the One who is of the Day,
      He is born they proclaim. He is born they proclaim.
      Welcome! be it said. Lo, it has come to pass.

3

> Lo, it has come to pass,
> Behold, the black bird that lies outstretched,
> Is now born they proclaim. Is now born they proclaim.
> Welcome! be it said. Lo, it has come to pass.

4

> Lo, it has come to pass,
> Behold, it is of the One who is of the Night,
> He is born they proclaim. He is born they proclaim.
> Welcome! be it said. Lo, it has come to pass.

The No^m-ho^n-zhi^n-ga sat within their long house as they worked on the wa-xo'-bes. Their heads were still bent over the last one when they were startled by the angry bellowing of an animal. All eyes turned upon the Sho'-ka, who hastened to the door and quickly threw aside the flap. There stood an angry buffalo with his head lowered and his tail trembling in the air, pawing the earth and throwing clouds of dust toward the sky. Stricken with fear, the Sho'-ka asked with unsteady voice, 'Who are you?' The bull answered, 'I am Tho'-xe, lift ye your heads!' At that moment there came a crash of thunder that seemed to issue from the end of the ridgepole of the house. In an excited manner the No^m-ho^n-zhi^n-ga gathered up all the wa-xo'-bes and threw them toward the bull, who at once lowered his tail, ceased pawing the earth, and became friendly.

These two angry visitors, the bull and the thunder, were representatives of the Tho'-xe and the Ni'-ka Wa-ko^n-da-gi gentes. It was in this dramatic manner that these two gentes were jointly given the office of caring for the wa-xo'-bes. At an initiation of a member of one of the various gentes into the mysteries of the war rite, the hereditary caretaker of the wa-xo'-be, who belongs to the Ni'-ka Wa-ko^n-da-gi gens, is given the bird to redecorate, an act equivalent to its reconsecration for the benefit of the initiate. If the hereditary caretaker happens to be absent from the initiation, this duty is performed by the second official caretaker, who belongs to the Tho'-xe gens. It is said that all the wa-xo'-bes belong to these two gentes because the No^m-ho^n-zhi^n-ga had given them to the two gentes through fear; also that the Tho'-xe and the Ni'-ka Wa-ko^n-da-gi had originally brought the birds from the sky and given them to the people.

The Tho'-xe and the Ni'-ka Wa-ko^n-da-gi were also spoken of as the Tsi Ha-shi, Those Last to Come—that is, those of the gentes who were last to take part in the formulating of the war rite."

From Dickerson's History of the Osage Nation (1906) Page 11-13, Paragraph 2.

<u>BELIEF IN CREATION—IN THE GREAT GOD AND A MESSIAH.</u>

"In the mythological legends as to the creation of certain lands the beaver, otter, and muskrat hold the role of formation. The Iroquois narrated that their primitive female ancestor was kicked from the sky by her enrager spouse when there was yet no land for her habitation, but that it 'suddenly bubbled up under her feet, and waxed bigger till a whole country was in her possession.' Others claim that the beaver, otter and muskrat, seeing her fall rushed to the bottom of the deep to bring up mud sufficient to construct an island for her residence.

Among the Osages, Takahlis and Algonkin of the northwest tribes the muskrat was their simple, cosmogonic machinery of land formation. These latter tribes were philosophic enough to see no real creation in such an account, but only formation by the action of these amphibious animals. The earth was there but hidden by boundless waters, and heaved up for dry land by the muskrat, as a formation only, logically distinguishing between the terms formation and creation, not assuming to know anything of creation, and considered any questions concerning it nonsense. Their amphibians were not considered creative constructors, but merely reconstructors, a very judicious and important corollary. It supposed a previous existence of matter on earth anterior to ours, but one without light or human inhabitants. A lake they said, burst it bounds, and submerbed all lands (note some similarity to the Bible deluge) and became the primeval ocean. We find among all primitive peoples some marvelous parallels of belief in the mythic epochs of nature, the catastrophes, calamities and deluges of fire and water, which have held and swayed all human fancy in every land in every age. But all fancies have been lost in the dilemma of an explanation of a creation of matter from nothing on the one hand, and the 'eternity of matter' on the other. **'Ex nihilo nihil'** (est) is an apothem indorsed alike by the profoundest metaphysicians and the most uncultured of primeval man. Francis S. Drake, in his "Indian History for Young People" gives the following fabulous legend as the Osage metaphysician's natural philisophy for the origin of his 'people.' Many Osages believe that the first mand of their nation came out of a sheel: that while he was walking on earth he met the Great Spirit, who gave him a bow and arrow and told him to go a hunting. After he had killed a deer the Great Spirit gave him fire and told him to cook and eat his meat and told him also to take the skin and cover himself with it, and with the skins of other animals that he should kill. One day the Osage while hunting saw a beaver sitting on a beaver hut. Mr. beaver asked him what he was looking for. The Osage answered: 'I am thirsty and came for a drink.' The beaver then asked him who he was and when he came. The Osage replied that he had no place of residence. 'Well, then,' said the beaver, 'as you appear to be a reasonable man I wish you to come and live with me. I have many daughters and if any of them should be agreeabel to you, you may marry.' The Osage, as the legend goes, accepted his offer and married one of his daughters, by whom he had many children. The Osage ancestors gave this as their reason for not killing the beaver, as their offspring were believed to be Osage 'People.' Such were their former traditions not present."

OSAGE TREE OF LIFE AND HEAVEN MYTHOLOGY.

"Rev. J. Owen Dorsey, refers to a chart that was accompanied by chanting a tradition by the members of a secret society of Osages drawn by an Osage, Hada—cutse, Red Corn, early adopted by a white man named Matthews. Hence Rer Corn was named Wm. P. Matthews, or 'Bill Nix,' becoming one of the tribal lawyers. He belongs to the Sadekice gens. Other versions were given by Pahuska (present Pawhuska. While Hair, chief of the Bald Eagle sub-gens of the Tsicu gens, and from Saucy Chief, from the Wa-ca-ce gens, and from Good Voice of the Miki gens. The chart represents the tree of life, by a flowing river, both described in conferring the order. When a woman is initiated she was required by the head of her gens to take four sips of water (symbolizing the river). Then rubs cedar on the palms of his hands with which he rubs her from head to foot. If she belongs to the left side of the tribal circle he first strokes the left side of her head, making three passes, pronounciing the sacred name of the Great Spirit three times, repeating the process on her forehead, right side and back part of her head making twelve strokes in all (a perfect number).

Beneath the river were the following objects: The Watsetuka male slaying animal, or morning, (red), star, (2) six stars ('Elm Rod'), (3) the evening star (4), the little star. Beneath these are the moon, seven stars and sun. Under the seven stars the peace pipe and war hatchet which is close to the sun. The moon and seven stars are on the same side of the chart. Four parallel lines across the chart represent the four degrees through which the ancestors of the Tsicu people passed from the upper heavens to the earth. The lowest heavens rest on a red oak tree (Pusuku). The Sadekice tradition begins below the lowest heavens on the left side under the peace pipe The stanza of the chant point to the different periods of evolution, first when the children of the first period ('former end') of the race were without human bodies and human souls. Then birds over the arch denote the evolution of human souls in bird bodies. Then the progress from the fourth to the first heavens, followed by descent to the earth. The ascent to four and ddescent to three make up the sacred number seven. When they alighted, as the legend runs, it was on a beautiful day, when the earth was clothed in luxuritant vegetation. From this time the path of the Osages diverged, the war gens marching to the right, the peace gens to the left, including the Tsicu, who originated the chart. Then conflict and the question of rights begun. The Tsicu, peace gens, met the messenger and they sent him off to the different stars for aid. According to the chart he approached in order the morning star (Watse-tuka), sun (Hapata Wakanta—the God of day, the sun), moon (Wakantaka—the God of night), seven stars (Mikake-pecuda), (Ta-adxi Three deer?), Big Star (Mi-kake-tanka), and Little Star (Mikake-cinka). Then Black Bear went to the Wacinka-cutse, a female red bird sitting on her nest. This grandmother granted his request giving them human bodies, made from her own body. The Hankaucantsi, the most warlike people; made a treaty of peace with the Waccace and Tsico gems and from the union of the three resulted in the last Osage nation but not including the allied races. A somewhat different version is given by the other gens, but all showing more or less the Darwinian theory of man's evolution, or ascent—almost as plausible in reason, when we link to this the first man's marriage with the beaver's daughter.

Please forgive this author for the reproduction of the Osage's though limited in mention early history and creation story. The Osage history as well as the versions found of their early beliefs (creation), were thought to be vital to apply during this study because so much has been written about the Osages history during their serious dilemmas during the early to mid 1900's; so earlier materials were sought out through archival sources. Realizing through personal search there are few manuscripts readily available for perusing about these subjects. The Ethological reports from the early 1900's as well as Dickerson's history of the Osage (1906) were perfect for sharing especially since these references came through older tribal sources and from likely now (2025) reaching back approximatly 175 years today.

It also was noticed that you'd have to find dozens of small Osage mention through brief early articles and books then put them together to find any form of medium that would fit their story. Sources through journals from individuals such as Col. Henry Dodge during the early settlement of the west from the early to mid 1800's, or Dickerson the Osage Historian, George Catlin, artist and ethonoligist, James Mooney, ethonologist to name a few. These materials aren't overly abundant unless you plan on digging them up if you know how to and then reading overwhelmingly numerous pages. But hopefully the pages within this text will cover a little bit of what a friend considered information about a people that were some what enigmatic of which at the time they were likely better off.

It has been read that they were courageous warriors and very intelligent as well as capable. It is the hope that these censuses will provide a huge amount of family information for thousands who will turn their pages.

Also along with this series NativeStudy will be releasing with this series Philip Dickerson's, *History of the Osage Nation*. Though not as large but loaded with Osage history, family names and images, it is comparable to Emmet Starr's *History of the Cherokee*. He (Dickerson) made a real effort at putting these materials together showing himself as someone than admired the Osage for who they were and would be. So many times you order an early reproduction of some old manuscripts and receive them realizing they are just xerox copies of old books that can hardly be read because of the smaller images or poor images in general. The *History of the Osage Nation* from NativeStudy has been fully transcribed and in a font size that can be read comfortably as well as fully indexed and proofed. Though in many situations the spelling from the original of 1906 wasn't changed or noted during transcription not wanting to change what was witten in those early days.

Included within this present introduction you will find;

The full transcription of this series as titled covers from 1906-1929 National Archive Film Rolls, M-595; Rolls 316-323. ***Note: the header for 1907 has a mix up, it states, (1908.(?) 1907?); Example; Entry #1 in 1906 Tom Big Chief [Same Indian name] is age 47. Example; Entry #1 in 1907 Tom Big Chief is age 48. Example; Entry #1 in 1909 Tom Big Chief is age 50. So in 1908 he would be 49 years old. An attempt was made numerous times to contact the National Archives in Washington to see if the descrepency was where the film was just left out with their copy or there was a historical error for the year 1908 or was just lost. This question was never resolved likely due to the inadequacy of (shortage of) personnel available? After being passed on to a few different people it seemed a decent answer wouldn't be given. So the assumption unless later found 1908's record will not be shown.

Jeff Bowen
Gallipolis, Ohio
NativeStudy.com

Census of the Osage Indians

of

Osage Indian Agency, Oklahoma,

As of June 30, 1906

Ret Millard, U. S. Indian Agent

Census of the__**Osage**__Indians of__**Osage**__Agency__**Oklahoma**__taken
By____**Ret Millard**____, U. S. Indian Agent____**June 30, 1906**

Key: NUMBER; NAME; SEX; RELATION; AGE
* An Askerisk will be next to a number if repeated or out of sequence and inserted among a different family.

BIG CHIEF BAND.

1; Pah-hu-scah; M; Head; 47
2: Me-to-op-pe; F; Wife; 33
3: He-ah-to-me; F; Daut.; 15
4; Heh-kuh-mon-kah; F; Daut.; 7
5; Gra-to-me; F; Daut; 3

6; Nah-me-tsa-he; F; Head; 69

7; Moh-she-tah-moie; M; Head; 62
8; Mo-se-che-he; F; Wife; 62

9; Richard Rusk; M; Head; 24
10; May Rusk; F. Daut; 3

11; Wy-u-tsa-kah-she; M; Head; 72
12; Me-tsa-he; F; Wife; 54
13; Num-pah-wah-kon-tah; M; Son; 17
24; Moie-wah-kon-tah; M; Son; 13

15; Hun-kah-me; F; Head; 49
16; To-sho-ho; M; Son; 10
17; E-nah-min-tsa; Son; 2

18; Me-lo-tah-moie; M; Head; 43
19; Hum-pah-to-kah; F; Wife; 51
20; He-ah-to-me; F; Daut.; 5
21; Gra-tah-wah-kah; M; Son; 2

22; Howard Russell; M; Head; 18

23; Otis Russell; M; Head; 19

24; Pearly Murray; F; Head; 27
25; Wah-she-ke-pah; M; Son; 10
26; He-ah-shin-kah; M; Son; 6
27; Min-kah-she; F; Daut; 2/12

28; Herman McCarthy; M; Head; 27

29; Son-sah-kah-hah; M; Head; 58
30; Hlu-ah-to-me; F; Wife; 59

31; Wah-shah-she-me-tsa-me; F; Head; 73

3

Key: NUMBER; NAME; SEX; RELATION; AGE
* An Askerisk will be next to a number if repeated or out of sequence and inserted among a different family.

32; Wah-sho-shah; M; Head; 44
33; Me-se-che-he; F; Wife; 37

34; Mon-kah-sop-py; M; Head; 57
35; He-ah-to-me; F; Wife; 36
36; Wah-tsa-a-tah; M; S. Son; 12
37; E-ne-op-pe; F; S. Daut; 10
38; Hun-kah-me; F; Daut; 1

39; Wah-hre-she; M; Head; 43
40; Hlu-ah-me; F; Wife; 36
41; Mo-se-che-he; F; Daut; 10
42; Mon-kah-hah; M; Son; 5
43; Nah-me-tsa-he; F; Daut; 1

44; Luther Harvey; M; Head; 36
45; Ke-ah-som-pah; F; Wife; 33
46; He-ah-to-me; F; Daut; 11
47; Hlu-ah-wah-kon-tah; M; Son; 8
48; Num-pah-q-ah; M; Son; 7
49; Wah-tsa-su-sah; M; Son; 3
50; Mah-lah-to; F; Daut; 2

51; Me-ke-wah-ti-an-kah; M; Head; 49
52; Wah-hrah-lum-pah; F; Wife; 35
53; Kah-he-ah-gra; M; Son; 9
54; Me-to-op-pe; F; Daut; 9/12

55; Roy James; M; Head; 20

56; Me-tsa-he; F; Head; 53

57; Richard White; M; Head; 30
58; Edith White; F; Wife; 24
59; He-ah-to-me; F; Daut; 10
60; Joseph; M; Son; 2
61; Abraham; M; Son; 5/12

62; Sho-e-ne-lah (Blind); M; Head; 34

63; Wah-shin-kah-sop-py; M; Head; 59
64; E-ne-op-py; F; Daut; 15
65; E-gro-tah; M; Son; 13

66; Joseph Bacon; M; Head; 21
67; Esther; F; Wife; 19

Key: NUMBER; NAME; SEX; RELATION; AGE
* An Askerisk will be next to a number if repeated or out of sequence and inserted among a different family.

68; E-gron-kah-shin-kah; M; Head; 46
69; Hum-pah-to-kah; F; Wife; 34
70; We-heh; F; Daut.; 12
71; Sin-tsa-hu; M; Son; 17
72; Wah-sop-py-wah-kah; F; Daut; 5

JOE'S Band

73; Shun-kah-mo-lah; M; Head; 60
74; Wah-tsa-me; F; Wife; 52
75; Wah-shin-kah-hu; M; Son; 16

76; Daniel West; M; Head; 32
77; Hlu-ah-to-me; F; Wife; 35
78; Kah-shin-kah; M; Son; 5

79; Wah-hah-sah-e; F; Head; 69

80; Wah-ses-tah-shin-kah; M; Head; 48
81; Hlu-ah-to-me; F; Wife; 31
82; Moh-shon-tsa-e-tah; F; Daut; 11
83; Wah-hrah-lum-pah; F; Ward; 15

84; Pun-kah-shin-kah; M; Head; 41
85; He-ah-to-me; F; Wife; 30
86; Kah-scah; M; Son; 6

87; Kah-wah-c (Yellow Horse); M; Head; 49
88; Ke-ah-som-pah; F; Wife; 39
89; Pah-kah-me-tsa-he; F; Daut; 11
90; Ah-kah-hu; M; Son; 9
91; Hun-kah-me-tsa-he; F; Daut.; 7
92; Kah-ah-sum-pah; F; Daut; 1

93; Joseph Bates; M; Head; 19

94; Wah-hruh-lum-pah; F; Head; 64

95; Hun-tsa-me; F; Head; 62

96; Wah-tsa-moie; M; Head; 27
97; Hun-kah-me-tsa-he; F; Wife; 23
98; Michel; M; Son; 1

99; Pun-q-tah; F; Head; 55

5

Key: NUMBER; NAME; SEX; RELATION; AGE
* An Askerisk will be next to a number if repeated or out of sequence and inserted among a different family.

100; Andrew Berry; M; Head; 19
101; Grace Berry; F; Head; 21
102; Esther Berry; F; Head; 21

103; Nun-tsa-wah-hu; M; Head; 54
104; Num-pah-se; M; Son; 15
105; John; M; Son; 4

106; Frank Cannon; M; Head; 21

107; Alex Cannon; M; Head; 23

108; O-pah-su-ah; M; Head; 37
109; Wah-to-sah; F; Wife; 37
110; Pah-pah-ah-hah; M; Son; 12

111; Tsa-po-in-kah; M; Head; 57
112; Hlu-ah-me-tsa-he; F; Wife; 53

113; Lawrence Gray; M; Head; 20

114; Hazel Gray; F; Head; 22
115; Lawrence Gray; M; Son; 4

116; Amos Osage; M; Head; 34
117; Ne-kah-ah-se; F; Wife; 25
118; He-ah-to-me; F; Daut; 7

MOH-E-KAH-MOIE BAND.

119; Moh-e-kah-moie; M; Head; 72
120; Tsa-me-hun-kah; F; Daut; 16
121; Hlu-ah-to-me; F; Wife; 52
122; Me-hah-sah-e; F; Daut; 16
123; Me-ah-hre; F; Daut; 12

124; Adair Hickey; M; Head; 30

125; William Fletcher; M; Head; 35
126; Sin-tah-wah-kon-tah; M; Son; 9
127; E-to-moie; F; Daut; 6

128; Gro-tun-kah; M; Orphan; 16

129; To-wan-gah-she; M; Head; 47
130; He-ah-to-me; F; Wife; 43

6

Key: NUMBER; NAME; SEX; RELATION; AGE
* An Askerisk will be next to a number if repeated or out of sequence and inserted among a different family.

131;   Gra-tah-su-ah; M; Son; 13

132;   Eugene Butler; M; Head; 15

133;   Me-gra-to-me; F; Head; 40

134;   U-ses-tah-wah-hah; M; Head; 74
135;   Gilbert Cox; M; Head; 35

136;   Roscoe Conklin; M; Head; 43

137;   Me-ti-an-kah; M; Head; 43
138;   Mo-se-che-he; F; Wife; 37
139;   Wah-pah-ah-hah; M; Son; 9
140;   Hun-kah-hop-py; M; Son; 5
141;   Wah-ne-en-kah; M; Son; 5/12
142;   Bernadette Elkins; F; Head; 18
143;   Luther Elkins; M; Head; 20

144;   Ne-kah-she-he (Blind); F; Wife; 32
145;   Ne-wal-la; M; Son; 10

146;   Charles West; M; Head; 23
147;   Don Dickinson; M; Head; 28

148;   Herbert Spencer; M; Head; 30
149;   Jennie Spencer; F; Wife; 22

150;   Me-sah-e; F; Head; 24
151;   Gra-to-me-tsa-he; F; Daut; 5
152;   Gra-to-ah; F; Daut; 2

153;   Gra-tah-su-ah; F; Orphan; 15
154;   Mable Cole; F; Head; 18
155;   Fidelis Cheshowaahkepah; M; Head; 24
156;   To-wan-gah-he; M; Head; 47
157;   Son-se-grah; F; Wife; 33
158;   He-ah-to-me; F; Daut; 15

159;   Edward Cox; M; Head; 30
160;   A-non-to-op-pe; F; Wife; 19
161;   Wah-tsa-ah-tah; M; Son; 2

162;   Clinton Bigheart; M; Head; 35
163;   Moh-shon-tsa-e-tah; F; Wife; 25
164;   Hum-pah-to-kah; F; S.Daut; 10

Key: NUMBER; NAME; SEX; RELATION; AGE
* An Askerisk will be next to a number if repeated or out of sequence and inserted among a different family.

165; Wah-kon-tah-he-um-pah; F; Head; 57
166; Ne-wal-la; M; Son; 7

167; Stevens Neal; M; Head; 27
168; Rose; F; Wife; 19

169; Wilson Kirk; M; Head; 49
170; Dora Kirk; F; Daut; 5
171; Rosie Kirk; F; Daut; 10/12

172; A-non-to-op-pe; F; Head; 79
173; Pah-she-he; F; Orphan; 16

NE-KAH-WAH-SHE-TUN-KAH

174; Ne-kah-wah-she-tun-kah; M; Head; 66
175; Wah-hrah-lum-pah; F; Wife; 54

176; Nicholas Webster; M; Head; 31

177; E-to-moie; M; Head; 37
178; Wah-to-sah-e; F; Wife; 37
179; Gra-tah-ah-kah; M; Son; 6
180; Tom-pah-pe; F; Daut; 3
181; E-kah-pah-she; F; Daut; 6/12

182; Che-sho-wah-ke-pah; M; Head; 36
183; Wah-hrah-lum-pah; F; Wife; 39
184; Hum-pah-to-kah; F; Daut; 9
185; Ke-ah-som-pah; F; Daut; 6
186; Mary; F; Daut; 3

187; Mille Kirk; F; Head; 22
188; Hun-wah-ko; F; Head; 70

189; Pun-kah-wah-ti-an-kah; M; Head; 44
190; Wah-tsa-a-tah; M; Son; 10
191; Wah-hrah-lum-pah; F; Wife; 31
192; Wah-te-sah; F; S.Daut; 4
192; Wah-se-tah; M; Son; 1/12
193; Pah-nee-wah-with-tah; M; Head; 64
194; Grah-to-me-tsa-he; F; Wife; 45

195; Ne-kah-lum-pah; M; Head; 50
196; Hlu-ah-to-me; F; Wife; 48
197; Hah-moie; M; Son; 15

8

Key: NUMBER; NAME; SEX; RELATION; AGE
* An Askerisk will be next to a number if repeated or out of sequence and inserted among a different family.

198; Gurney Miller; M; Head; 39
199; Grace; F; Daut; 5
200; Howard; M; Son; 3

201; Ne-ah-tse-pe; F; Head; 64
202; Annie Turpie; F; Head; 19

203; Bro-ki-he-kah; M; Head; 50
204; E-ne-op-pe; F; Daut; 12

205; Herbert Brokey; M; Head; 18
206; E-pah-son-tsa; M; Head; 51

207; Shon-kah-tsa-a; M; Head; 38
208; Polly Earl; F; Daut; 15

209; Gra-to-moie; M; Head; 64
210; Ke-ah-som-pah; F; Wife; 55
211; Me-gra-to-me; F; Daut; 16
212; Me-gra-to-me; F; Daut; 15
213; Hlu-ah-wah-kon-tah; M; Son; 12
214; Shah-kah-wah-pe; M; Son; 9

215; Wah-tsa-a-hah; M; Head; 52
216; Wah-hrah-lum-pah; F; Wife; 28
217; Wah-tsa-moie; M; Son; 10

218; Ethel Bryant; F; Head; 22
219; Shah-wah-pe; M; Head; 38
220; Embrey Gibson; M; Head; 43
221; Tsa-me-tsa; F; Wife; 25
222; Hun-kah-hop-py; M; Son; 13

223; Son-se-grah; M; Head; 60
224; Moh-shon-tsa-e-tah; F; Wife; 60
225; Wah-ko-sah-moie; F; Daut; 12

226; Dudley Haskell; M; Head; 30
227; Son-se-grah; F; Wife; 24
228; Wah-hrah-lum-pah; F; Daut; 5
229; Hlu-ah-wah-kon-tah; M; Son; 3/12
1983;* Me-grah-to-me; F; Daut; 3

230; He-shah-ah-hle; M; Head; 47
231; He-ah-to-me; F; Wife; 40
232; Ah-kah-me; F; Daut; 7

9

Key: NUMBER; NAME; SEX; RELATION; AGE
* An Askerisk will be next to a number if repeated or out of sequence and inserted among a different family.

233; Hlu-ah-gla-she; M; Son; 3

234; Moh-hah-ah-grah; M; Head; 57
235; Wah-kon-tah-he-um-pah; F; Wife; 63
236; He-kin-to-op-pe; F; Ward; 11

237; Peter Clark; M; Head; 23
238; Tom-pah-pe; F; Head; 80

239; Gra-tah-su-ah; F; Head; 39
240; He-he-kin-to-op-pe; F; Daut; 14
241; A-non-to-op-pe; F; Daut; 2
242; Lizzie June; F; Head; 18
243; Richard Kenny; M; Head; 50
244; Lah-tah-sah; F; Head; 44

245; John Kenny; M; Head; 23
246; Wah-hruh-lum-pah; F; Wife; 20
247; Orlando Kenworthy; M; Head; 30
248; Tony Townsend; M; Head; 26

249; Hun-kah-hop-py; M; Head; 37
250; Hun-lah-hop-py; M; S.Son; 15
251; He-ah-to-me; F; Daut; 11
252; Wah-hrah-lum-pah; F; Daut; 9

253; Jack Hartley; M; Head; 30
254; Nah-hah-scah-she; F; Head; 52

255; Wah-tsa-ki-he-kah; M; Head; 35
256; We-heh; F; Daut; 11
257; Wah-to-sah; F; Daut; 5

258; Julia Dunlap; F; Daut; 8
259; Clara Marshall; F; Widow; 20

BIG HILL BAND

260; To-wah-e-he; M; Head; 50

261; Alfred McKinley; M; Head; 18
262; Adelia; F; Wife; 18

263; Daniel McDougan; M; Head; 36

264; Ben Harrison; M; Head; 34

10

Census of the __Osage__ Indians of __Osage__ Agency __Oklahoma__ taken
By __Ret Millard__ , U. S. Indian Agent __June 30, 1906__

Key: NUMBER; NAME; SEX; RELATION; AGE

* An Askerisk will be next to a number if repeated or out of sequence and inserted among a different family.

265; Edna M. Harvey; F; S.Daut; 11
266; Emily Harrison; F; Daut; 8
267; Ben H. Harrison; M; Son; 4
268; Estella M. Harrison; F; Daut; 7/12

269; Ne-kah-e-se-y; M; head; 60
270; Lizzie Q.; F; Wife; 57
271; Me-se-moie; F; Daut; 15
272; Wah-shah-she; F; Daut; 15

273; Mollie Kyle; F; Head; 19
274; Ke-ne-kah; M; Head; 69

275; Ne-kah-o-e-blah; M; Head; 65
276; A-non-to-op-pe; F; Wife; 57
277; Pah-pah-ah-hah; M; Ward; 14
278; Num-pah-se; M; Ward; 5

279; Earnest Roe; M; Head; 34
280; Emery E. Roe; M; Son; 5

281; Alex Marshall; M; Head; 24

282; Perry King; M; Head; 31
283; E-ne-ke-op-pe; F; Wife; 31
284; Sin-tsa-wah-kon-tah; M; Son; 11
285; Min-tsa-kah; M; Son; 7
286; Pun-q-tah; F; Daut; 4
287; Mon-en-gra-tah; M; Son; 2

288; Mum-brum-pah; F; Head; 81

289; Wah-hrah-lum-pah; F; Head; 50
290; Hun-kah-she; F; Daut.; 40

WHITE HAIR BAND.

291; Che-sho-hun-kah; M; Head; 58
292; Cra-to-me-tsa-he; F; Wife; 53
293; Ne-wal-la; M; Son; 15

294; John Claremore; M; Head; 23
295; Amanda; F; Wife; 22

296; Dominio Daniels; M; Head; 23
297; Joseph Daniels; M; Head; 24

11

Census of the **Osage** Indians of **Osage** Agency **Oklahoma** taken
By **Ret Millard**, U. S. Indian Agent **June 30, 1906**

Key: NUMBER; NAME; SEX; RELATION; AGE
* An Askerisk will be next to a number if repeated or out of sequence and inserted among a different family.

298; Wah-she-ho-tsa; M; Head; 43
299; Gra-to-me; F; Wife; 40
300; Hlu-ah-tse-ke; M; Son; 16
301; Wah-ne-a-tah; M; Son; 13
302; Wah-shun-kah-hah; M; Son; 7
303; Wah-shah-hah-me; F; Daut; 7/12

304; E-gro-op-pe; M; Orphan; 17
305; Wah-hruh—lum-pah (D & D); F; Orphan; 11
306; Mo-se-che-he; F; Head; 45
307; E-som-pah; F; Daut; 12
308; Wah-ke-sa-moie; F; Head; 37
309; Lah-tah-sah; F; Daut; 15
310; Ho-tah-me; F; Daut; 9
311; Hun-tsa-moie; M; Son; 6

312; Joseph Mason; M; Head; 19
313; Rose Mason; F; Wife; 21

314; Francis Drexil; M; Head; 29
315; Wah-ko-sa-moie; F; Wife; 30
316; Ne-kah-ah-se; F; Daut.; 8
317; Me-tsa-kah; M; Son; 4
318; Moie-en-gra-tah; M; Son; 3
319; Pun-q-tah; F; Daut; 3/12

320; Pah-se-to-pah; M; Head; 59
321; Wah-shah-she-me-tsa-he; F; Wife; 56

322; Angela Peace; F; Head; 19
323; Paul Peace; M; Head; 20
324; Henry Peace; M; Head; 23

TALL CHIEF BAND.

325; Alex Tall Chief; M; Head; 39
326; Eliza; F; Wife; 34
327; Rosa; F; Wife; 25
328; Hlu-ah-wah-kon-tah; M; Son; 16

329; Che-sah-me; F; Head; 58
330; He-ah-to-me; F; Head; 53

331; Eaves Tall Chief; M; head; 28
332; Wah-shah-e; F; Wife; 26
333; Helen; F; Daut; 8/12

12

Key: NUMBER; NAME; SEX; RELATION; AGE
* An Askerisk will be next to a number if repeated or out of sequence and inserted among a different family.

334; Me-hun-kah; F; Head; 22
335; No-tah-moie; M; Head; 43
336; Wah-shah-hah-me; F; Head; 59
337; Henry Tall Chief; M; Head; 23

338; Nah-she-wal-la; M; Head; 47
339; Wah-shah-she-me-tsa-he; F; Daut; 16
340; Tilton Entokah; M; Head; 26
341; Pah-she-he; F; Wife; 21
342; He-ah-to-me; F; Daut; 1

KO-SHE-WAH-TSE BAND.

343; He-lo-ki-he; M; Head; 68
344; He-se-moie; M; Head; 57
345; Tsa-me-tsa; F; Daut; 7

346; Charles Grant; M; Head; 33

347; Wah-tsa-e-o-she; F; Head; 57
348; George Dunlap; M; Nephew; 11
349; Lo-tah-tse-a; F; Head; 39

350; En-to-kah-wah-ti-an-kah; M; Head; 70
351; Shon-shin-kah; M; Son; 13
352; E-to-hun-kah; M; Son; 6

353; Kah-wah-ho-tsa (Sas-sa-moie); M; Head; 38
354; Wah-ko-ki-he-kah; F; Wife; 40
355; Wah-to-sah-grah; F; Wife; 38
356; Ah-kah-me-tsa-he; F; Daut; 15
357; Lah-su-su-pah; M; Son; 15
358; Ah-kah; M; Son; 12
359; Tah-tsa-hu-hah; M; Son 10
360; Wah-hu-sah; F; Daut; 6

361; Josephine McKinley; F; Head; 18

362; Ne-wal-la (Tsa-shin-kah); M; Head; 40
363; Me-tsa-he; F; Wife; 30
364; Hlu-ah-to-me; F; Daut; 3

365; Son-se-gra; F; Head; 29

366; Wah-ko-ki-he-kah; F; Head; 52
367; Wah-tsa-moie; M; Son; 14

13

Key: NUMBER; NAME; SEX; RELATION; AGE
* An Askerisk will be next to a number if repeated or out of sequence and inserted among a different family.

368;   Wah-ko-sah-moie; F; Daut; 10

369;   Madaline Hunter; F; Head; 18

BLACK DOG BAND.

370;   Black Dog; M; Head; 59
371;   Gra-to-me-tsa-he; F; Wife; 26

372;   Edgar McCarthy; M; Head; 33
373;   Me-tsa-he; F; Wife; 23

374;   To-wah-e-he; M; Head; 82
375;   Moh-shah-hah-me; F; Wife; 68

376;   Amos Hamilton; M; Head; 34
377;   Noah; M; Son; 4
378;   Ira; M; Son; 2

379;   Gra-tah-me-tsa-hah; F; Head; 26
380;   Wah-tsa-a-tah; M; Son; 11
381;   Mah-sah; M; Son; 8
382;   He-ah-to-me; F; Daut; 7

383;   Me-ho-e; M; Head; 67

384;   Allison Webb; M; Head; 22

385;   He-lo-ki-he; M; Head; 39
386;   E-gro-tah; M; Son; 16

387;   Myron Bangs; M; Head; 25
388;   Wah-sop-py; F; Wife; 22

389;   Silas Sanford; M; Head; 29
390;   Anna; F; Wife; 24

391;   Allen Webb; M; Head; 26
392;   Hum-pah-to-kah; F; Wife; 18
393;   Gra-tah-scah; M; Son; 2

394;   Willie McCarthy (Incompetent); M; Head; 25

395;   Andrew Jackson; M; Head; 37
396;   Wah-hrah-lum-pah; F; Wife; 52
397;   Me-tsa-he; F; Daut; 12

14

Census of the **Osage** Indians of **Osage** Agency **Oklahoma** taken
By **Ret Millard** , U. S. Indian Agent **June 30, 1906**

Key: NUMBER; NAME; SEX; RELATION; AGE
* An Askerisk will be next to a number if repeated or out of sequence and inserted among a different family.

SAUCY CHIEF BAND.

398; Lawrence; M; Head; 52
399; Wah-to-sah; F; Wife; 15

400; Wah-hu-sah-e; F; Head; 70
401; Joseph Mills; M; Adpt Son; 17
402; Alex Eagle Feather; M; Head; 33

403; Wah-te-sah; F; Head; 65
404; Gra-to-me-tsa-he; F; Ward; 11

405; Prudie Martin; F; Head; 31

406; James G. Blaine; M; head; 33
407; Walker Blaine; M; Son; 10

408; E-ne-op-pe; F; Wife; 26
409; Eugene Blaine; M; Son; 6
410; Me-shah-e; F; Daut; 4
411; James G. Blaine; M; Son; 2

412; Sophia Choteau; F; Head; 64

413; Hayes Little Bear; M; Head; 21
414; Lo-hah-me; F; Wife; 18

415; Ah-hu-shin-kah; M; Head; 46
416; Nah-hah-sah-me; F; Wife; 59

417; Choteau Augustine; F; Head; 31
418; Strikeaxe Josephine; F; Daut; 12
419; Chouteau Augustus; M; Son; 11
420; Chouteau Charles; M; Son; 8

421; Chouteau Rose; F; Orphan; 15

422; Panther Robert; M; Head; 43
423; Charles; M; Son; 16
424; Clark; M; Son; 14
425; Maude; F; Daut; 9
426; Nettie; F; Daut; 12

427; John Strait; M; Head; 53
428; Mary Pryor; F; Wife; 55

15

Census of the __Osage__ Indians of __Osage__ Agency __Oklahoma__ taken By __Ret Millard__ , U. S. Indian Agent __June 30, 1906__

Key: NUMBER; NAME; SEX; RELATION; AGE
* An Askerisk will be next to a number if repeated or out of sequence and inserted among a different family.

429; Edna Goodbear; F; Head; 34

430; Charles Me-she-tsa-he; M; Head; 47
431; Wah-ko-sah-moie; F; Wife; 52
432; Pah-she-he; F; Daut;10

433; Sarah Dodson; F; Head; 31
434; Ben Mushunkashey; M; Head; 23
435; Hlu-ah-me-tsa-he; F; Wife; 18

436; William Pryor; M; Head; 31
437; Min-kah-she (Mary); F; Wife; 33
438; Josephine; F; Daut; 6
439; John; M; Son; 3
440; Shon-kah; M; S. Son; 10

441; Susie L. Hutchinson; F; Head; 24

442; Ke-le-kom-pah; M; Head; 56

443; Mo-se-che-he; F; Head; 51
444; Wah-kon-te-ah; M; Nephew; 15

445; Paul Albert; M; Head; 37

446; Pah-she-he; F; Head; 46

447; Hum-pah-to-kah; F; Head; 52

448; George Albert; M; Head; 20

449; Wah-shah-she-me-tsa-he; M; Head; 33

450; Me-shah-e; F; Head; 53

451; Harry Kohpay; M; Head; 37
452; Elsie; F; Daut; 7
453; Hugh; M; Son; 6
454; Lizzie; F; Daut; 3
455; A-non-to-pp-pe; F; Head; 73

456; Wy-e-gla-in-kah; M; Head; 52
457; Wah-kon-tah-he-um-pah; F; Wife; 55
458; Wah-tsa-kon-lah; M; S. Son; 14

459; Raymond Redcorn; M; Head; 20

16

Key: NUMBER; NAME; SEX; RELATION; AGE
* An Askerisk will be next to a number if repeated or out of sequence and inserted among a different family.

460;   Tsa-pah-ke-ah; M; Head; 57
461;   Hlu-ah-me-tsa-he; F; Wife; 54
462;   Kah-shin-kah; M; Son; 16

463;   Pearl Hartley: F; Head; 26

464;   Heh-gah-hah-scah; M; Head; 52
465;   Julia; F; Wife; 60
466;   John; M; Ad. Son; 9

467;   John Buffalo; M; Head; 20
468;   Antwine Albert; M; Head; 43

469;   Charles Michelle; M; Head; 38
470;   Mah-sah-e; F; Wife; 34
471;   Ida Michelle; F; Daut; 10

472;   Harry Big Eagle; M; Head; 20
473;   Sylvia Wood; F; Head; 38
474;   Wah-shah-she-me-tsa-he; F; Head; 82

475;   Kah-wah-ho-tsa-ah-ga-ny; M; Head; 51
476;   Mon-kah-he; M; Son; 12

477;   Harry Py-ah-hun-kah; M; Head; 19

478;   Charles Brave; M; Head; 28
479;   Mum-brum-pah; F; Wife; 21
480;   Andrew; M; Son; 5
481;   Louis; M; Son; 6/12

482;   Laban Miles; M; Head; 46
483;   Mo-se-che-he; F; Daut; 16
484;   Wah-shah-ah-pe; F; Daut; 12
485;   Hlu-ah-shu-tsa; M; Son; 17
486;   Pah-pah-ah-ho; M; Son; 12
487;   Wah-shah-she-me-tsa-he; F; Wife; 37
488;   Eddie Penn; M; S. Son; 17
489;   Walker Penn; M; S. Son; 15
490;   Charles Penn; M; S. Son; 10
491;   Laban Miles Jr.; M; Son; 5

492;   John Whitehorn; M; Head; 23
493;   James; M; Son; 8/12

494;   Hu-la-tun-kah; M; Head; 54

17

Key: NUMBER; NAME; SEX; RELATION; AGE
* An Askerisk will be next to a number if repeated or out of sequence and inserted among a different family.

495; Pah-pu-son-tsa; F; Wife; 56
496; Hun-kah-ah-gra; M; S. Son; 16
497; Wah-she-pah; M; S. Son; 14
498; Pah-she-he; F; S. Daut; 11
499; Russell Warrior; M; Head; 22
500; E-stah-o-gre-she; M; Head; 42
501; Shon-blah-scah; F; Wife; 38

BEAVER BAND.

502; Bigheart James; M; Head; 64
503; Rosal L.; F; Daut; 14
504; Sarah A'; F; Daut; 8
505; Belle L.; F; Daut; 3
506; Che-sho-shin-kah; M; Head; 57
507; Rose; F; Wife; 55

508; Paul Red Eagle; M; Head; 26
509; Cecelia; F; Wife; 24
510; Harry; M; Son; 4
511; Louis; M; Son; 1
512; Joseph; M; Son; 1/12

513; Hlu-ah-shu-tsa; M; Head; 30

514; Beg-gah-hah-she (Brave); M; Head; 72
515; Mary; F; Wife; 75

516; Andrew Bighorse; M; Head; 29
517; Hum-pah-to-kah; F; Wife; 35
518; We-neh; F; S. Daut; 14
519; Peter; M; Son; 7
520; Joseph; M; Son; 5
521; Mary; F; Daut; 2
522; Julia; F; Daut; 10/12

523; Charles McDougan; M; Head; 18
524; John Wagoshe; M; Head; 28
525; Wah-shah-she-me-tsa-he; F; Wife; 28
526; George Vest; M; S. Son; 10
527; Charles Wagoshe; M; Son; 2
528; Mo-se-che-he; F; Daut; 4
529; A-non-to-op-pe; F; Daut; 8/12

530; John Lookout; M; Head; 29
531; Heh-kah-mon-kah; F; Wife; 20

18

Key: NUMBER; NAME; SEX; RELATION; AGE
* An Askerisk will be next to a number if repeated or out of sequence and inserted among a different family.

532; Louis Bighorse; M; Head; 41
533; To-op-pe; F; Wife; 26
534; Rosa; F; Daut; 10
535; Lillie; F; Daut; 5
536; Millie; F; Daut; 2

537; Lookout Fred; M; Head; 48
538; Mo-se-che-he; F; Wife; 37
539; Lookout Charles; M; Son; 14
540; Frederick; M; Son; 11
541; Mary; F; Daut; 6
542; Agnes; F; Daut; 3
543; Henry; M; Son; 2/12

544; Paul Buffalo; M; Head; 42
545; Wah-hu-lah-ga-ny; F; Wife; 48

546; Me-sah-e; F; Head; 53
547; Ah-tsa-shin-kah; F; Daut; 8

548; Mo-ho-gla; M; Head; 52
549; Me-tsa-hi-ke; F; Wife; 62
550; Antwine Pryor; M; Head; 26
551; A-non-to-op-pe; F; Wife; 20
552; Ula; F; Daut; 1

553; Henry Coshehe; M; Head; 33
554; Wah-kon-tah-he-um-pah; F; Wife; 30
555; Clem Coshehe; M; Son; 13
556; John; M; Son; 6

557; Hlu-ah-to-me; F; Head; 60

558; Che-she-walla- Evart; M; Son; 10
559; Floyd; M; Son; 7

560; Hlu-ah-me-tsa-he; F; Head; 28
561; Wah-tsa-a-tah; M; Orphan; 15
562; E-he-kin-to-op-pe; F; Orphan; 10

563; John McFall; M; Head; 39
564; Gra-tah-shin-kah; F; Wife; 27
565; Minnie Whitehorn; F; S. in law; 16

566; John Scott; M; Head; 32
567; William Scott; M; Son; 10/12

19

Key: NUMBER; NAME; SEX; RELATION; AGE
* An Askerisk will be next to a number if repeated or out of sequence and inserted among a different family.

568; Mo-se-che-he; F; Head; 66

STRIKE AXE BAND.

569; James Strike Axe; M; Orphan; 12
570; Wy-e-nah-she; M; Head; 58
571; Tsa-shin-kah-wah-ti-an-kah; Head; 62

572; Joseph buffalohide; M; Head; 20
573; Agnes; F; Wife; 19

574; To-op-pe; F; Head; 52

575; Pendleton Strike Axe; M; Head; 25
576; Mo-se-che-he; F; Wife; 18
577; Emma; F; Daut; 2

578; Foster Strike Axe; M; Head; 32
579; Loh-tah-sah; F; Wife; 28
580; Jennie; F; Daut; 10
581; Emma; F; Daut; 8
582; Dora; F; Daut; 5/12

583; Louis Pryor; M; Head; 27
584; Andrew; M; Son; 2/12
585; Nellie Buffalo; F; Head; 21
586; O-sah-ke-pah (Cap. Strikeaxe) M; Head; 48

587; Pah-se-to-pah (Deaf & Dumb); M; Head; 36
588; Me-sah-e; F; Wife; 26
589; Cora; F; Daut; 5
590; Carrie; F; Daut; 3
591; Lena; F; Daut; 6/12

592; Hun-kah-me; (He-ah-to-m); F; Head; 50
593; Hun-kah-me (He-ah-to-me; F; Head; 56
594; Ke-nun-tah; M; Son; 16

595; Pierce St John; M; Head; 30
596; Ke-ah-som-pah; F; Wife; 32
597; Gra-tah-scah; M; Son; 14
598; Dora; F; Daut; 4
599; Herbert; M; Son; 2
600; William; M; Son; 6/12

601; Frank Corndropper; M; Head; 58

Key: NUMBER; NAME; SEX; RELATION; AGE
* An Askerisk will be next to a number if repeated or out of sequence and inserted among a different family.

602; Gra-to-me-tsa-he; F; Wife; 60

603; Peh-tsa-moie; M; Head; 63
604; Wah-tsa-u-sah; F; Wife; 34

605; Richard Firewwalk; M; Head; 22
606; Son-se-grah; F; Wife; 16
607; Lah-blah-wal-la (Crazy); M; Head; 62

608; Wy-u-hah-kah; M; Head; 48
609; Hlu-ah-me-tsa-he; F; Wife; 57

610; John Oberly; M; Head; 26
611; Me-tsa-he; F; Wife; 24
612; Martha; F; Daut; 1
613; John A. Logan; M; Head; 33
614; Mary; F; Wife; 28
615; Joseph; M; Son; 7
616; Oscar; M; Son; 5
617; Rosa; F; Daut; 1

NE-KAH-KE-PAH-HE BAND.

618; A-she-gah-hre; M; Head; 56
619; Gra-to-me-tsa-he; f; Wife; 50
620; Me-tun-kah; F; Daut; 16
621; Va-sah-pah-shin; F; Daut; 7/12
622; Hlu-ah-me; F; Niece; 14

623; Ke-mo-hah; M; Head; 47
624; Lo-tah-sah; F; Wife; 37
625; Me-tsa-he; F; S. Daut; 14
626; J.R. Townsend; M; S. Son; 6
627; Hun-kah-me; F; Daut; 7
628; Heh-mo-sah; M; Son; 6
629; Mo-e-kah-shah; M; Son; 4
630; Ralph; M; Son; 3/12
1984;* Moh-shon-kah-he; M; Son; 2
631; Tsa-e-kon-lah; F; Head; 62

632; Clarence Gray; M; Head; 29
633; E-ne-op-pe; F; Wife; 19
634; Mary; F; Daut; 2

635; Tsapah-shin-kah; M; Head; 32
636; Wah-shah-pe-wah-ke; F; Wife; 56

21

Key: NUMBER; NAME; SEX; RELATION; AGE
* An Askerisk will be next to a number if repeated or out of sequence and inserted among a different family.

637; E-to-wah-hrah-lum-pah; F; Daut; 11

638; Charles Brown; M; Head; 18

639; David Copperfield; M; Head; 30
640; Hun-kah-me-tsa-he; F; Wife; 32
641; Me-tsa-he; F; Daut; 6
642; Hun-kah-she; M; Son; 4
643; Hun-kah-ah-gra; M; Son; 1

644; William Pitts; M; Head; 29
645; Me-tsa-he; F; Wife; 28
646; Wah-to-ah-nah-she; F; Daut; 1

647; Hun-kah-tun-kah; M; Head; 46
648; Pah-she-he; F; Wife; 25
649; Me-tsa-he; F; Daut; 10
650; Tom-pah-pe; F; Daut; 4
651; Wah-tain-du-sah; F; Daut; 1

652; Che-sho-shin-kah; M; Head; 57
653; Hlu-ah-to-me; F; Wife; 59

654; Frank Lahowa; M; Head; 21

655; Wah-kah-lah-tun-kah; M; Head; 64
656; Pah-pu-son-tsa; F; Wife; 66
657; A-hu-scah; M; Son; 17

658; To-op-pe; F; Head; 58
659; Hun-tsa-moie; M; Head; 42
660; Hlu-ah-to-me; F; Wife; 62

661; Mo-se-che-he; F; Head; 88

CLAREMORE BAND

662; Francis Claremore; M; Head; 41
663; Wah-hrah-lum-pah; F; Wife; 35
664; Tsa-pah-ke-ah; M; Son; 13

665; Ah-sin-kah; F; Head; 68

666; John Abbott; M; Head; 25
667; Ne-kah-she-tsa; F; Wife; 22
668; Wah-shah-she-me-tsa-he; F; Daut; 4

22

Key: NUMBER; NAME; SEX; RELATION; AGE
* An Askerisk will be next to a number if repeated or out of sequence and inserted among a different family.

669; Henry Pratt; M; Head; 34
670; Hun-kah-me; F; Wife; 33
671; Helen Pratt; F; Daut; 11
672; Grah-tah-scah; F; Daut; 5
673; Charles; M; Son; 1

674; Me-grah-to-me; F; Head; 50
675; Bishop; Opah; M; Head; 22
676; Pah-hu-gre-she; F; Wife; 18

677; Charles Big Elk; M; Head; 27
678; Mo-se-che-he; F; Wife; 24
679; Mary; F; Daut; 6

680; Gra-she-ah-tse-a; F; Head; 32
681; Shah-pah-tse-a; M; Head; 77
682; Hlu-ah-me; F; Wife; 62
683; E-ah-scah-wal-la; M; Son; 13
684; Mon-kah-hah; M; Son; 8

685; Eugene Ware; M; Head; 30
686; Hum-pah-to-kah; F; Wife; 29
687; Joseph; M; Son; 7
688; Mary; F; Daut; 5
689; Elijah N.; M; Son; 3
690; Daisy L.; F; Daut; 1

691; Henry Roan; M; Head; 23
692; He-ah-to-me; F; Wife; 17

693; Arthur Bonnicastle; M; Head; 29
694; Angie Bonnicastle; F; Wife; 19
695; Maude Thompson; F; Head; 32
696; Mary; F; Daut; 8

697; Jack Wheeler; M; Head; 64
698; Mah-me-tsa-he; F; Wife; 69

699; Rhoda Wheeler; F; Head; 21
700; Ben Wheeler; M; Head; 30

701; Tsa-me-tsa-he; F; Head; 24
702; Hun-gah-hre; M; Son; 5

703; Nannie Naranjo; F; Head; 34
704; Clara; F; Daut; 7

Key: NUMBER; NAME; SEX; RELATION; AGE
* An Askerisk will be next to a number if repeated or out of sequence and inserted among a different family.

705; Mary F; Daut; 3

706; Hlu-ah-shu-tsa; M; Head; 36
707; Hun-kah-me; F; Wife; 28
708; Hlu-ah-shu-tsa; M; Son; 5
709; Alice Red Eagle; F; Daut; 9/12

710; Wah-shah-she-me-tsa-he; F; Head; 47
711; Sophia Spotted Horse; FD; Head; 32

WAH-TI-AN-KAH BAND.

712; Wah-she-hah (Bacon Rind); M; Head; 46
713; Wah-ko-ki-he-kah; F; Wife; 40
714; In-gro-tah; M; Son; 15
715; Ah-tsa-shin-kah; F; Daut; 9
716; mah-hu-sah; M; Son; 5
717; Julia Baconrind; F; Daut; 3

718; Moh-sah-mum-pah; M; Head; 39
719; Hun-kah-me; F; Wife; 33
720; Ki-he-kah-tun-kah; M; Son; 10

721; To-wah-e-he; M; Head; 61
722; Gra-to-se-me; F; Wife; 50

723; She-she; M; Head; 47
724; Ne-kah; F; Wife; 60

725; Simon Henderson; M; Head; 24
726; Louisa; F; Wife; 20
727; He-ah-to-me; F; Daut; 3/12
728; Howard Buffalo; M; Head; 46
729; George Pitts; M; Head; 25
730; Mary; F; Wife; 20
731; Warren; M; Son; 3
732; David; M; Son; 1

733; Son-se-gra; F; Head; 48
734; Ho-ki-ah-se; M; Head; 38
735; Me-tsa-he; F; Wife; 28
736; Wah-shah-she-me-tsa-he; F; Daut; 10
737; To-ho-ah; M; Son; 2

WILLIAM PENN BAND.

24

Census of the __Osage__ Indians of __Osage__ Agency __Oklahoma__ taken
By __Ret Millard__ , U. S. Indian Agent __June 30, 1906__

Key: NUMBER; NAME; SEX; RELATION; AGE
* An Askerisk will be next to a number if repeated or out of sequence and inserted among a different family.

738; Peter C. Bigheart; M; Head; 67
739; Wah-ko-ki-he-kah; F; Wife; 63
740; Hlu-ah-to-me (Deaf & Dumb); F; Ward; 14

741; George Bigheart; M; Head; 30
742; Pah-she-wah; F; Wife; 20
743; Charles; M; Son; 9/12

744; Claude Smith; M; Head; 32
745; Hlu-ah-to-me; F; Wife; 23
746; Wah-tsa-me; M; Son; 4
747; Hum-pah-to-kah; F; Daut; 3
748; Ke-ah-som-pah; F; Daut; 7/12

749; Wah-she-wah-hah; M; Head; 40
750; Hlu-ah-to-me; F; Wife; 37
751; Wah-tsa-tun-kah; M; Son; 17
752; Ne-kah-sto-kah; M; Son; 9
753; Wah-ko-sah-moie; F; Daut; 8
754; Ne-kah-sto-wah; M; Son; 5
755; Kah-scah; M; Son; 2
756; Grah-egrah-in-kah; M; Son; 2/12

757; Edward Bigheart; M; Head; 18

758; O-lo-hah-wal-la; M; Head; 62
759; He-ah-to-me; F; Wife; 45
760; Wah-shah-hah-me; F; Daut; 16
761; Ne-wal-la; M; Son; 14
762; Ah-hu-shin-kah; M; Son; 12
763; A-non-to-op-pe; F; Daut; 8
764; He-kah-mon-kah; F; Daut; 7
765; Tum-pah-pe-she; M; Son; 1

No #766

767;* Laura Lohah; F; Head; 19
768; Samuel Barker; M; Head; 27

769; O-le-hah-moie; M; Head; 48
770; No-se-che-he; F; Wife; 38
771; Hlu-ah-wah-kon-tah; M; Son; 14
772; Wah-tsa-ah-tah; M; Son; 11
773; Wah-hrah-lum-pah; F; Daut; 8
774; Num-pah-q-ah; M; Son; 6
775; Me-gra-to-me; F; Daut; 4

25

Key: NUMBER; NAME; SEX; RELATION; AGE
* An Askerisk will be next to a number if repeated or out of sequence and inserted among a different family.

776; Moie-ke-kah-he; M; Son; 2

777; Tah-hah-gah-hah; M; Head; 42
778; Wah-hu-sah-e; F; Wife; 37
779; Ah-kah-me; F; Wife; 27
780; Shon-kah; M; Son; 9
781; Ah-nah-me-tsa-he; M; Son; 9
782; Wah-shah-she-me-tsa-he; F; Daut; 2
783; Ho-ke-ah-se; M; Son; 2
784; Ross Maker; M; Head; 18
785; Edgar Maker; M; Head; 21
786; Mo-shah-ke-tah; M; Head; 42

787; Tom-pah-pe; F; Head; 60
788; O-hun-pe-ah; M; Son; 16

789; Albert Penn; M; Head; 36
790; Dora Penn; F; Wife; 19
791; Wah-ses-tah; M; Son; 12
792; Wah-te-sah; F; Daur; 11

793; Annie Penn; F; Head; 22

794; Fred Penn; M; Head; 33
795; Leo Penn; M; Son; 9
796; Oscar Penn; M; Son; 7
797; Wayne M. Penn; M; Son; 1

798; O-ke-sah (Tom West); M; Head; 32
799; Me-tsa-he; F; Wife; 33
800; Wah-kon-tah-he-no-pah-pe; (Frank Wood); M; S. Son; 15
801; John Wood; M; S. Son; 12
802; Mo-se-che-he; F; Daut; 2

803; Dan G. West; M; Head; 28
804; Pah-pu-son-tsa; F; Wife; 25
805; He-ah-to-me; F; Daut; 5
806; Mo-se-che-he.; F; Daut; 2
807; Howard M.; M; Son; 2/12

LITTLE CHIEF BAND.

808; Heh-scah-moie; M; Head; 63
809; Charles Whitehorn; M; Son; 16

810; John Whitehorn; M; Head; 18

Key: NUMBER; NAME; SEX; RELATION; AGE
* An Askerisk will be next to a number if repeated or out of sequence and inserted among a different family.

811; James Whitehorn; M; Head; 22
812; Nah-kah-sah-me; F; Wife; 18
813; Mary; F; Daut; 9/12

814; Kan-sah-ah-hre; M; Head; 54
815; Me-she-kah-me; F; Wife; 54

816; Ki-he-kah-nah-she; M; Head; 43
817; Hlu-ah-to-me; F; Wife; 33
818; Wah-shah-she-me-tsa-he; F; Daut; 12
819; Hum-pah-to-kah; F; Daut; 10
820; Mo-ne-pah-she; M; Head; 57

821; He-ah-to-me; F; Head; 54
822; Francis Little Soldier; F; Head; 18
823; Frank Little Soldier; M; Head; 21
824; Me-tsa-he; F; Wife; 16

825; Ellon Spurgeon; F; Head; 25
826; Mary Agnes; F; Head; 24

827; Hlu-ah-wah-tah; M; Head; 40
828; He-to-op-pe; F; Wife; 37
829; Mah-grah-lum-pah; F; Daut; 7
830; Hlu-ah-wah-kon-tah; M; Son; 2

831; Me-tsa-no; F; Head; 50
833;* Alex Mudd; M; Son; 17
Skipped #332
834; Anna Mudd; F; Daut; 8
835; Lucy Lotson; F; Head; 29
836; Lucius; M; Son; 10

837; Albert Mudd; M; Head; 26

838; Aiken Elizabeth; F; Head; 24
839; Aiken John H.; M; Head; 22

840; Alberty Cynthia; F; Head; 50
841; Lizzie; F; Daut; 15
842; Alberty George; M; Head; 19

843; Alexander Levi; M; Head; 25
844; Mary L.; F; Wife; 21
845; Martha I.; F; Daut; 4

27

Key: NUMBER; NAME; SEX; RELATION; AGE
* An Askerisk will be next to a number if repeated or out of sequence and inserted among a different family.

846; Alexander Maggie; F; head; 23
847; Alexander Ida A; F; Minor; 17

848; Allen Emily; F; Head; 42
849; Whalen Charlotte; F; Daut; 17
850; Esthre[sic]; f; Daut; 12
851; Dorothea; F; Daut; 10

852; Anderson Mary; F; Head; 22
853; Anderson J. B.; F; Head; 20
854; Henry P.; M; Son; 4/12

855; Anderson Edward R.; M; Head; 18

856; Anderson Skinner T.; M; Minor; 12
857; Ora D. ;M; Minor; 8
858; Noble M.; M; Minor; 7

859; Appleby Jane; F; Head; 76
860; Captain Peter (Incom'Pt) M; Son; 42
861; Atkin James B.; M; Head; 22
862; Atkin John D. Jr.; M; Head; 19

863; Avant Rosalie; F; Head; 29
864; Theodore R.; M; Son; 8
865; Ellen; F; Daut; 5

866; Barber Ida; F; Head; 24

867; Barber Bridget A.; F; Head; 45
868; Clara M.; F; Daut; 14
869; Edgar E.; M; Son; 11
870; Lawrence L.; M; Son; 8
871; Paul G.; M; Son; 6
872; Lee A.; M; Son; 2

873; Barker Mary J.; F; Head; 51
874; Simms Sonia; F; Daut; 14
875; Cora E.; F; Daut; 12

876; Baker John Thomas; M; Head; 37
877; Monette; F; Wife; 31
878; Myrtle C.; F; Daut; 10
879; Morris A.; M; Son; 6
880; Frank T.; M; Son; 5
881; Martha B.; F; Daut; 2

28

Key: NUMBER; NAME; SEX; RELATION; AGE
* An Askerisk will be next to a number if repeated or out of sequence and inserted among a different family.

882;   Baylis Elizabeth; F; Head; 62
883;   Baylis Charles D; M; Head; 19
884;   Baylis; Harry; M; Head; 22

885;   Bellieu Thomas A.; M; Head; 24
886;   Bellieu Walter S.; M; Head; 19
887;   Bellieu Srella; F; Daut; 14
888;   Leo F; M; Son; 10
889;   Anna; F; Daut; 8
890;   Stephen H. ; M; Son; 6

891;   Bellmard Elisa (nee George); F; Head; 19

892;   Beekman Kate; F; Head; 29
893;   Sybil A; F; Daut; 6/12
894;   Gorman Mary A; F; Daut; 7

895;   Bennett; M; Head; 30
896;   Isabella; F; Wife; 25
897;   William E.; M; Son; 6
898;   Teresa; F; Daut; 2

899;   Bennett Barbra; F; Head; 19
900;   Blackburn Rachel; F; Head; 26

901;   Boulanger Joseph; M; Head; 57
902;   Benjamin H.; M; Son; 16
903;   James; M; Son; 15
904;   Eulalie C.; F; Daut; 12
905;   Anna V.; F; Daut; 11
906;   Charles E.; M; Son; 9

907;   Boulanger Grover; M; Head; 21

908;   Boulanger Stephen E.; Head; 24
909;   Minnie L.; F; Daut; 5
910;   Augustine C.; F; Daut; 3

911;   Boulanger Isaac; M; Head; 27
912;   Charles M.; M; Son; 6
913;   Alta; F; Daut; 4
914;   Lenora; F; Daut; 3
915;   Nellie; F; Daut; 1

916;   Boulanger W.M.; M; Head; 32
917;   Edward Mc.; M; Son; 11

29

Key: NUMBER; NAME; SEX; RELATION; AGE

* An Askerisk will be next to a number if repeated or out of sequence and inserted among a different family.

918; Lottie; F; Daut; 10
919; Evart; M; Son; 6

920; Bockius Dora; F; Head; 23
921; Boren Blanche; F; Head; 20
922; Bowhan Ida M.; F; Head; 25
923; Bowhan Marie B.; F; Head; 20
924; Bowman Rosette; F; Head; 19
925; Brock Lavaria (Nee Wheeler); F; Head; 26

926; Bradshaw Rose E. F; Head; 32
927; Thomas S.; M; Son; 15
928; Harry A.; M; Son; 12
929; Alvin P.; M; Son; 10
930; Sarah A.; F; Daut; 8
931; Greta E.; F; Daut; 6
932; Elva F.; F; Daut; 4
933; Irene A.; F; Daut; 2

934; Brown Charles; M; Head; 45
935; Bernice; F; Daut; 14
936; Treva; F; Daut; 8

937; Brown Edward; M; Head; 39
938; Brown Earnest; M; Head; 34
939; Maude; F; Daut; 11
940; Laura J; F; Daut; 8
941; William P.; M; Son; 7
942; Lula B.; F; Daut; 2

943; Brown A.M.; M; Head; 46
944; William S.; M; Son; 4
945; Frank R.; M; Son; 7/12

946; Brown Mary J.; F; Head; 39
947; Edith; F; Daut; 13
948; Louis M.; M; Son; 11

949; Brunt Rdward[sic]; M; Head; 46
950; George E; M; Son; 15
951; Joseph L.; M; Son; 7
952; Brunt Theodore; M; Head; 20

953; Bruce Elsie F.; F; Head; 36
954; Bessie; F; Daut; 16
955; Louisa; F; Daut; 12

30

Key: NUMBER; NAME; SEX; RELATION; AGE
* An Askerisk will be next to a number if repeated or out of sequence and inserted among a different family.

956; Lena; F; Daut; 10
957; Adelbert; M; Son; 15
958; Bratton Josephine; F; Head; 26

959; Breeding Mary L.; F; Head; 41
960; Letta M.; F; Daut; 11
961; Frances; F; Daut; 9
962; Elsie E.; F; Daut; 6

963; Brooks Philomena; F; Head; 26
964; Sylvester; M; Son; 8
965; Dollretta; F; Daut; 7
966; Ruby A.; F; Daut; 5
967; Delorus; M; Son; 2

968; Bryant Joe; M; Head; 49
969; Frank; M; Son; 12
970; Della M.; F; Daut; 11
971; Carrie M.; F; Daut; 9
972; Cecil; M; Son; 6
973; Arthur; M; Son; 5
974; Anna B.; F; Daut; 3
975; Arona; F; Daut; 7/12

976; Buxbaum Polly; F; Head; 24
977; Burton Roy B.; M; Son; 10

978; Carr Gertrude; F; Head; 26
979; Carr Nelson; M; Son; 10
980; Carr Gussie N.; F; Daut; 6

981; Carpenter Mary E.; F; Head; 36
982; Floyd H.; M; Son; 14
983; Charles E.; M; Son; 11
984; Rose B.; F; Daut; 9
985; Louis C.; M; Son; 7

986; Carter Alva E.; M; Minor; 8
987; Leota M.; F; Minor; 6
988; Barton D. M; Minor; 12
989; Charles B.; M; Minor; 10

990; Callahan Alfred; M; Head; 23
991; Callahan Cornelius; M; Head; 31
992; Callahan Julia; F; Head; 24

31

Census of the __Osage__ Indians of__ Osage __Agency__ Oklahoma __taken
By___ Ret Millard ___, U. S. Indian Agent__ June 30, 1906

Key: NUMBER; NAME; SEX; RELATION; AGE
* An Askerisk will be next to a number if repeated or out of sequence and inserted among a different family.

993;   Callahan William; M; Head; 28
994;   Leo; M; Son; 8
995;   Charles; M; Son; 6
996;   Mary; F; Daut; 5
997;   Gertrude; F; Daut; 3

998;   Canville Clara; F; Minor; 9
999;   J.B.; M; Minor; 5
1000; Agnes L.; F; Minor; 3

1001; Canville Paschal F.; M; Head; 55
1002; Cecil; M; Son; 8
1003; John; Son; 12
1004; Aouda; F; Daut; 2

1005; Carlton Anthony; M; Head; 34
1006; Mary E.; F; Wife; 25
1007; Eva M.; F; Daut; 8
1008; Ethel; F; Daut; 7
1009; Frances; F; Daut; 5

1985;* Carlton George; M; head; 29
1986;* Augustine; F; Daut; 6
1987;* Robert; M; Son; 4
1988;* Mary E.; F; Daut; 2
1010; George; M; Head; 10/12

1011; Cedar William; M; Minor; 10
1012; Cedar Paul; M; Orphan; 8
1013; Childers Nola; F; Orphan; 7
1014; Chouteau Henry; M; Head; 21
1015; Chouteau Stewart; Head; 20
1016; Chouteau Louis P.; M; Head; 18

1017; Clem William; M; Head; 28
1018; William L.; M; Son; 6
1019; John E.; M; Son; 5
1020; James A.; M; Son; 2
1021; Frantz; M; Son; 6/12

1022; Clem James J,; M; Head; 31
1023; Jessie M.; F; Daut; 10
1024; William H.; M; Son; 8
1025; James H.; M; Son; 7
1026; Sallie J.; F; Daut; 3

32

Census of the__**Osage**__Indians of__**Osage**__Agency__**Oklahoma**__taken
By__**Ret Millard**__, U. S. Indian Agent__**June 30, 1906**

Key: NUMBER; NAME; SEX; RELATION; AGE
* An Askerisk will be next to a number if repeated or out of sequence and inserted among a different family.

1027; Clewien Anna; F; Heads; 25
1028; Claribelle; F; Daut; 2

1029; Clawson Josiah G.; M; Head; 18
1030; Clawson Emma C.; F; Minor; 15
1031; Thomas A.; M; Minor; 11
1032; George D.; M; Minor; 9

1033; Cooper Anna L.; F; Head; 24
1034; Connor Woodie; M; Head; 23
1035; Theil; F; Daut; 1

1036; Connor George; M; Head; 36
1037; Adelia; F; Daut; 5
1038; Connor Victor W.; M; Son; 1

1039; Cottinghan Ida; F; Head; 20

1040; Collins Lulu; F; Head; 31
1041; John W.; M; Son; 7
1042; Roy W.; M; Son; 4

1043; Conness Veva; F; Head; 34
1044; Geneva M.; F; Daut; 7
1045; William S.; M; Son; 1
1046; Conway Jane; F; Head; 78

1047; Crouse Isabella Fuller; F; Head; 40
1048; Earl; M; Son; 14
1049; Laura I.; F; Daut; 10
1050; Stephen M.; M; Son; 7

1051; Crouse Dallas; M; Head; 20
1052; Crane Marie; F; Head; 33
1053; Cross Ellen; F; Head; 25

1054; Cunningham Laura; F; Head; 32
1055; Edward R.; M; Son; 7

1056; Cunningham Rose I.; F; Head; 36
1057; Robert B.; M; Son; 7

1058; Cunningham John M.; M; Head; 18

1059; Curtis Mary; F; Head; 49
1060; Farrell Mary; F; Daut; 17

Key: NUMBER; NAME; SEX; RELATION; AGE
* An Askerisk will be next to a number if repeated or out of sequence and inserted among a different family.

1061; Virgil; M; Son; 15
1062; Curtis Lethia B.; F; Daut; 11
1063; Ada; F; Daut; 8

1064; Daniel Sophia; F; Head; 30
1065; Bessie; F; Daut; 12
1066; Vernie; M; Son; 10
1067; Pearl C.; M; Son; 8
1068; Ida A.; F; Daut; 5

1069; Davis Sophia; F; Head; 65
1070; Davis Mary J.; F; Head; 57
1071; LaSarge Minnie E.; F; Daut; 17

1072; Dailey Dora; F; Head; 24

1073; Darnell Rebecca Jane; F; Head; 43
1074; Vadney Anna V.; F; Daut; 15

1075; Dennison Eliza; F; Head; 37
1076; Fugate Frank E.; M; Son; 16
1077; John A.; M; Son; 15
1078; Dennison Nellie; F; Daut; 5
1079; George O.; M; Son; 6/12

1080; Dennison Bert; M; Head; 21

1081; Del Orier Julia; F; Head; 56
1082; Del Orier Virgil L.; F; Head; 21
1083; Louis; M; Son; 4/12

1084; DeNoya Louis; M; Head; 45

1085; De Noya Frederick; M; Son; 14
1086; Clement; M; Son; 12
1087; Josephine; F; Daut; 10
1088; Ruby P.; F; Daut; 8

1089; DeNoya E.A.; M; Head; 19

1090; De Noya Frank; M; Head; 49
1091; E.D. M; Son; 16
1092; Clara; F; Daut; 15
1093; Grace; F; Daut; 13
1094; Raymond; M; Son; 12
1095; Charlotte; F; Daut; 10

34

Census of the __Osage__ Indians of __Osage__ Agency __Oklahoma__ taken
By __Ret Millard__ , U. S. Indian Agent __June 30, 1906__

Key: NUMBER; NAME; SEX; RELATION; AGE
* An Askerisk will be next to a number if repeated or out of sequence and inserted among a different family.

1096; Myrtle C.; F; Daut; 8
1097; Catherine I.; F; Daut; 3
1098; Walter L.; M; Son; 4/12

1099; De Noya Mable; F; Head; 20

1100; De Noya Jacob; M; Head; 27
1101; Belle; F; Wife; 26
1102; Virgil H.; M; Son; 5
1103; Maurice H.; M; Son; 3
1104; Lillian C.; F; Daut; 2
1105; Helen; F; Daut; 3/12

1106; De Noya Joseph; M; Head; 29
1107; Charlotte E.; F; Daut; 2
1108; Margaret I.; F; Daut; 3
1109; Martha M.; F; Daut; 6/12

1110; De Noya Clement; M; Head; 39
1111; Emily; F; Wife; 39
1112; Clement Jr.; M; Son; 16
1113; Wesley; M; Son; 15
1114; Louis; M; Son; 12
1115; Sadie; F; Daut; 10
1116; Elsie; F; Daut; 8
1117; Edna; F; Daut; 5
1118; Elizabeth; F; Daut; 2
1119; Millard; M; Son; 6/12

1120; Deal Joseph; M; Head; 23
1121; Mary J.; F; Wife; 17
1122; James C.; M; Son; 1/12
1123; Deal Julia A.; F; Head; 51
1124; Sherman; M; Son; 15

1125; Dickey James A.; M; Head; 25
1126; Dickey John F.; M; Head; 22

1127; Dial Eliza; F; Head; 46
1128; Penn Augustus; Son; 16
1129; Rosa B.; F; Daut; 14
1130; Huston John R.; M; A. Son; 15
1131; Dial Cora E.; F; Daut; 9
1132; Eva; F; Daut; 7
1133; Charles P.; M; Son; 1

Census of the __Osage__ Indians of __Osage__ Agency __Oklahoma__ taken
By __Ret Millard__, U. S. Indian Agent __June 30, 1906__
Key: NUMBER; NAME; SEX; RELATION; AGE
* An Askerisk will be next to a number if repeated or out of sequence and inserted among a different family.

1134; Donelson Frances; F; Head; 23
1135; Robert L.; M; Son; 5
1136; John L.; M; Son; 7

1137; Doolin Martha; F; Head; 23

1138; Donovan Augustine; F; Head; 54
1139; Charles; M; Son; 17
1140; Jesse C.; M; Son; 13

1141; Ducotey Stanislaus; M; Head; 32
1142; Versa; F; Daut; 8
1143; Manza; F; Daut; 6
1144; Bettie V.; F; Daut; 3
1145; Frank S.; M; Son; 9/12

1146; Dunn Dora; F; Head; 28
1147; Ida M.; F; Daut; 10
1148; Mary A.; F; Daut; 8
1149; Timothy J. M; Son; 3

1150; Dunham Martha; F; Head; 76

1151; Easley Margaret; F; Head; 34
1152; Pearl; F; Daut; 14
1153; George E.; M; Son; 12
1154; Leo B.; M; Son; 10
1155; John W.; M; Son; 8
1156; Mary F.; F; Daut; 5
1157; Clarence A.; M; Son; 2

1158; Edwards Julia; F; Head; 40
1159; Quinton Alex; M; Son; 17
1160; Julia; F; Daut; 14
1161; Agnes; F; Daut; 10
1162; Pearl C.; F; Daut; 8
1163; Elnora; F; Daut; 4

1164; Edminston Frances (Incom'pt); F; Head; 30

1165; Farrel Nathaniel; M; Head; 29
1166; Ruth; F; Daut; 6
1167; Andrew; M; Son; 3

1168; Farrell Charles; M; Head; 24
1169; Mary; F; Daut; 2

36

Key: NUMBER; NAME; SEX; RELATION; AGE
* An Askerisk will be next to a number if repeated or out of sequence and inserted among a different family.

1170;   Farrell Monica; F; Head; 51
1171;   Shaw Charles M.; M; Son; 17
1172;   Moses R.; M; Son; 16

1173;   Fenton Margaret; F; Head; 23

1174;   Fox Susie; F; Head; 44
1175;   Lombard Sylvester; M; Son; 16
1176;   Augustine; F; Daut; 13
1177;   Joseph; M; Son; 11
1178;   Paul; M; Son; 7

1179;   Fronkier Mary E.; F; Head; 59
1180;   Laban A.; M; Son; 16
1181;   Fronkier William; M; Head; 35

1182;   Fronkier Simon; M; Head; 34
1183;   Florence; F; Daut; 10
1184;   Blanche L.; F; Daut; 8
1185;   Benjamin; M; Son; 4

1186;   Fronkier Eliza; F; Head; 57
1187;   Fronkier Phillip; M; Head; 18

1188;   Fronkier Laura; F; Head; 21
1189;   Fronkier Augustus; M; Head; 28
1190;   Fronkier James; M; Head; 27
1191;   Lewis B.; M; Son; 2/12

1192;   Fuller Thomas; M; Head; 25
1193;   Fuller Charles; M; Head; 22
1194;   Fuller Louis; M; Head; 31
1195;   Andrew B.; M; Son; 4

1196;   Gaylor Victoria; F; Head; 41
1197;   Gaylor Mary E.; F; Head; 20

1198;   George James M.; M; Head; 24
1199;   James J.; M; Son; 7/12

1200;   George Sylvester; M; Head; 22
1201;   George Ruby; F; Minor; 17

1202;   Gilmore Mary A.; F; Head; 52
1203;   S.J. M; Son; 15

Census of the __Osage__ Indians of __Osage__ Agency __Oklahoma__ taken
By __Ret Millard__ , U. S. Indian Agent __June 30, 1906__

Key: NUMBER; NAME; SEX; RELATION; AGE
* An Askerisk will be next to a number if repeated or out of sequence and inserted among a different family.

1204; Gilmore; Coeanna; F; Head; 19
1205; Gilmore William H.; M; Minor; 7

1206; Girard Amelia; F; Head; 32
1207; Mary E.C.; F; Daut; 12
1208; Corrine A.; F; Daut; 11
1209; Amelia B.; F; Daut; 10
1210; Leona; F; Daut; 8

1211; Goad Clara; F; Head; 26
1212; Groves Agnes; F; Head; 24
1213; Hall Ida; F; Head; 21

1214; Harruff Margaret; F; Head; 42
1215; Julia M.; F; Daut; 10

1216; Hardy Emily; F; Head; 33
1217; Louis V.; F; Daut; 12
1218; Goldie; F; Daut; 9
1219; ZGeneva; F; Daut; 6
1220; William R.; M; Son; 2

1221; Hardy Ora; F; Head; 26
1222; Orel; M; Son; 2
1223; Hampton Charles; M; Head; 26
1224; Roland; M; Som[sic]; 7/12

1225; Hampton Rosalie; F; Head; 45
1226; Hayes Pearl; F; Head; 26

1227; Harlow Josephine; F; Head; 27
1228; John A.; M; Son; 9

1229; Hayes Elnora; F; Head; 26

1230; Harlow Susan; F; Head; 44
1231; Grace; F; Daut; 15
1232; Belle M.; F; Daut; 12
1233; Charles C.; M; Son; 8

1234; Haynie Mary; F; Head; 21
1235; Willie; M; S. Son; 11

1236; Hackleman Julia Ann; F; Head; 61
1237; Harrellson Mary L. (Incom'pt); F; Head; 26
1238; Harris Mary E. F; Head; 25

38

Key: NUMBER; NAME; SEX; RELATION; AGE
* An Askerisk will be next to a number if repeated or out of sequence and inserted among a different family.

1239; Harvey Adeline; F; Head; 25
1240; Heenan Anna; F; Head; 24
1241; Herard; Paul; M; Head; 38
1242; Herard Eugene; M; Head; 21
1243; Herard Minnie; F; Head; 20

1244; Herridge Myrtle; F; Minor; 17
1245; Joseph; M; Son; 15
1246; Lulu; F; Daut; 12

1247; Hewitt Rosa; F; Head; 20
1248; Valarie; F; Daut; 4/12
1989;* Mary Hill; F; Head; 70
1249; Hildebrand Ellen; F; Head; 59
1250; Hildebrand Susanna; F; Head; 18
1251; Hildebrand George; M; Head; 23
1252; Hildebrand Richard; M; Head; 27

1990;* Hildebrand David; M; Head; 33
1253; Nancy; F; Daut; 5

1254; Hildebrand James; M; Head; 37
1255; Rose; F; Daut; 17
1256; Letitia; F; Daut; 14
1257; Susan; F; Daut; 12
1258; Oranzonia; F; Daut; 11
1259; Dicha; F; Daut; 6
1260; Ruby; F; Daut; 3/12

1261; Joseph Hildebrand; M; Head; 39
1262; Frank; M; Son; 8

1263; Hickman Clementine; F; Head; 30
1264; Homer; M; Son; 10
1265; Edna J.; F; Daut; 7
1266; Franklin; M; Son; 6
1267; Florence; F; Daut; 4
1268; Lillie V.; F; Daut; 2
1269; Bertha C.; F; Daut; 6/12

1270; Holloway Jasper C.; M; Head; 54
1271; Holloway Sarah; F; Head; 18
1272; Holloway Frank; M; Head; 21
1273; Milton; M; Head; 23
1274; Andrew L.; M; Son; 3
1275; Olita M.; F; Daut; 1/12

39

Census of the **Osage** Indians of **Osage** Agency **Oklahoma** taken
By **Ret Millard** , U. S. Indian Agent **June 30, 1906**

Key: NUMBER; NAME; SEX; RELATION; AGE
* An Askerisk will be next to a number if repeated or out of sequence and inserted among a different family.

1276;   Hoots Rosa; F; Head; 37
1277;   Jane; F; Daut; 11
1278;   Hoots Alfred; M; Head; 19

1279;   Hunt Mary A.; F; Head; 36
1280;   Lulu B.; F; Daut; 9
1281;   Mary G.; F; Daut; 7
1282;   Andrew D.; M; Son; 4
1283;   Hunt Antoine; M; Head; 16

1284;   Javine Peter; M; Head; 54
1285;   Benjamin H.; M; Son; 17
1286;   Javine Hasread; M; Son; 15
1287;   Viola M.; F; Daut; 12
1288;   Ople; F; Daut; 6/12

1289;   Javine Roy B.; M; Son; 10
1290;   Javine John; M; Head; 51
1291;   Ollie; F; Daut; 16
1292;   Andrea; F; Daut; 13
1293;   Ore E.; F; Daut; 12
1294;   Joseph; M; Son; 9
1295;   Javine Anthony; M; Head; 19
1296;   Javine John; M; Head; 24
1297;   George M.; M; Son; 2

1298;   James Jesse; M; Head; 18

1299;   Johnson Julia M; F; Head; 51
1300;   John W.; M; Son; 17

1301;   Jones Laura; F; Head; 20

1302;   Kennedy Agnes; F; Head; 30
1303;   James A.; M; Son; 8
1304;   Firest L.; M; Son; 6
1305;   Thelma; F; Daut; 5
1306;   Cordelia A.; F; Daut; 2
1307;   Samuel G.; M; Son; 3/12

1308;   Kennedy Mable; F; Head; 26
1309;   Albert A.; M; S. Son; 12
1310;   Kennedy Adeline; F; Head; 58
1311;   Kennedy; M; Head; 20

1312;   Keeler Blanche; F; Head; 24

40

Key: NUMBER; NAME; SEX; RELATION; AGE
* An Askerisk will be next to a number if repeated or out of sequence and inserted among a different family.

1313; Dixie; M; Son; 2
1314; Alberta M.; F; Daut; 5/12

1315; Kilbie Benedict; M; Head; 20
1316; Krebs Henry; M; Son; 9

1317; Lawrence Maggie; F; Head; 49

1318; Labadie Charles; M; Head; 35
1319; Hazel; F; Daut; 8
1320; Frank; M; Son; 6
1321; Alvin L.; M; Son; 4
1322; Nita; F; Daut; 2

1323; Labadie William H.; M; Head; 21
1324; Labadie Ella; F; Head; 19

1325; Labadie Frederic; M; Minor; 16
1326; Earnie; M; Minor; 15
1327; Joseph; M; Minor; 13

1328; Labadie Edward; M; Head; 40
1329; Milton; M; Son; 8
1330; Rose M.; F; Daut; 5
1331; Robert E.; M; Son; 3
1332; Charles W.; M; Son; 1

1333; Frank; M; Head; 45
1334; G.B.; M; Son; 45[?]
1335; Paul P.; M; Son; 11
1336; Labadie John; M; Head; 19

1337; LaSarge Marie; F; Minor; 12
1338; Louis; M; Minor; 10
1339; Arthur; M; Minor; 9
1340; Charles B.; M; Minor; 7

1341; LaSarge Joseph; M; Head; 37
1342; Ellen; F; Daut; 6

1343; Lane Joseph; M; head; 37
1344; Zella A.; F; Wife; 36
1345; Mary; F; Daut; 12
1345;* Bessie; F; Daut; 8
1346; Joseph C.; M; Son; 3
1347; Roy B.; M; Son; 1

41

Key: NUMBER; NAME; SEX; RELATION; AGE
* An Askerisk will be next to a number if repeated or out of sequence and inserted among a different family.

1348; Leahy Mary L; F; Head; 57

1349; Leahy Bertha; F; Head; 31
1350; Thomas R.; M; Son; 9
1351; Cora W.; F; Daut; 7
1352; Mable A; F; Daut; 3
1353; Edward A.; M; Son; 1

1354; Leahy W.T.; M; Head; 37
1355; Martha; F; Wife; 28
1356; W.T. Jr.; M; Son; 8
1357; Clarence B.T.; M; Son; 7

1358; Lewis Mary; F; Head; 45
1359; Lessert Frank; M; Head; 64
1360; Lessert Walter; M; Head; 21
1361; Lessert Joseph; M; Head; 22
1362; Lessert David; M; Head; 28

1363; Lessert Guy; M; Minor; 10
1364; Millie M.; F; Minor; 8
1365; Charles A.; M; Minor; 6
1366; Hattie; F; Minor; 4

1367; Lessert Frank Jr.; M; Head; 42
1368; Mary J.; F; Daut; 11
1369; Robert A.; M; Son; 9
1370; Grace J.; F; Daut; 5
1371; Ray L.; M; Son; 3
1372; Cora L.; F; Daut; 4/12

1373; Lessert Benjamin; M; Head; 36
1374; William C.; M; Son; 17
1375; Wade; M; Son; 15
1376; Susie; F; Daut; 10
1377; Benjamin L.; M; Son; 3
1378; Fay; F; Daut; 8
1379; Fanny; F; Daut; 4/12
1380; Lessert Charles; M; Head; 39

1381; Liese; Coenia M.; F; Head; 24

1382; Lombard Albert; M; Head; 60
1383; Irene; F; Daut; 14
1384; Bessie; F; Daut; 12
1385; Robert A.; M; Son; 5

42

Census of the **Osage** Indians of **Osage** Agency **Oklahoma** taken
By **Ret Millard** , U. S. Indian Agent **June 30, 1906**

Key: NUMBER; NAME; SEX; RELATION; AGE
* An Askerisk will be next to a number if repeated or out of sequence and inserted among a different family.

1386; Lombard Clara; F; Head; 20
1387; Lombard Nina; F; Head; 18
1388; Lombard John; M; Head; 22
1389; Lombard George W.; M; Head; 27
1390; Lombard John E.; M; Head; 20

1391; Lombard Walter; M; Head; 28
1392; Lucy; F; Daut; 5
1393; Lola; F; Daut; 3
1394; Samie; F; Daut; 2

1395; Lyman Olive G.; F; Head; 43

1396; Lyman Paul S.; M; Head; 40
1397; [Lyman] Agnes; F; Daut; 3
1398; [Lyman] Capitola; F; Daut; 1

1399; Lyman Arthur J.; M; Head; 36

1400; Lynn Mary A.; F; Head; 29
1401; John F.; M; Son; 11
1402; Theresa M.; F; Daut; 7
1403; Patrick; M; Son; 3
1404; Joseph; M; Son; 5
1405; William R,; M; Som; 4/12

1406; Mackey Joseph; M; Head; 28
1407; Eva; F; Daut; 8
1408; Tenne; F; Daut; 4
1409; Grace; F; Daut; 2
1410; Warren F.; M; Son; 1/12

1411; Mackey William B.; M; Head; 23
1412; Cecelia E.; F; Daut; 6
1413; Bertha M.; F; Daut; 1
1414; Mackey Grover; M; Head; 20

1415; Mathews W.S.; M; Head; 58
1416; John J.; M; Son; 12
1417; Mary I.; F; Daut; 9
1418; Lillian B.; F; Daut; 7
1419; Florence; F; Daut; 4

1420; Mathews Sarah J.; F; Head; 18

1421; Mathews W.W.; M; Head; 27

43

Census of the__ **Osage**__ Indians of__ **Osage**__ Agency__ **Oklahoma**__ taken
By__ **Ret Millard**__, U. S. Indian Agent__ **June 30, 1906**
Key: NUMBER; NAME; SEX; RELATION; AGE
* An Askerisk will be next to a number if repeated or out of sequence and inserted among a different family.

1422; Norman S.; M; Son; 1

1423; Mathews J. A.; M; Head; 30
1424; Lorenza; F; Wife; 24
1425; John A.; M; Son; 5
1426; Victoria; F; Daut; 4

1427; Mathews Edward O.; M; Head; 27
1428; Alfred E.; M; Son; 2
1429; Thomas; M; Son; M; Son; 17

1430; Martin Alex; M; Head; 60
1431; Bertha; F; Daut; 11

1432; Martin Lombard; M; Head; 18

1433; Martin Lee; M; head; 29
1434; Dane L.; F; Daut; 8
1435; Edgar E.; M; Son; 5
1436; Lennie F; Daut; 2

1437; Martin Emery; M; Head; 25
1438; John D.; M; Son; 7/12

1439; Martin Richard; M; Head; 32
1440; Martin Claude; M; Son; 9
1441; Martin James; M; Minor; 13
1442; Martin Wilson; M; Minor; 13

1443; McCarthy Lenora; F; Head; 25

1444; McDaniel Ellen; F; Head; 30
1445; Frederick W.; M; Son; 10

1446; McGath Emma; F; Head; 27
1447; John W.; M; Son; 9

1448; McComb Ellen; F; Head; 28
1449; Jessie; F; Daut; 11
1450; William H.; M; Son; 8
1451; Gladys I.; F; Daut; 5
1452; Rachel B.; F; Daut; 3
1453; Naioma A.; F; Daut; 2/12

1454; Mc Guire Mary E.; F; Head; 33
1455; Ethel; F; Daut; 15

44

Key: NUMBER; NAME; SEX; RELATION; AGE
* An Askerisk will be next to a number if repeated or out of sequence and inserted among a different family.

1456; Leo; M; Son; 11
1457; Bird A.; M; Son; 8
1458; William T.; M; Son; 6
1459; Charles A.; M; Son; 4

1460; Mc Laughlin Nancy; F; Head; 42
1461; Mc Laughlin Flora; F; Head; 19

1462; McLintic Mary; F; Head; 29
1463; Aloysia; F; Daut; 7

1464; McLain Minnie; F; Head; 19

1465; Mickels Arania; F; Head; 29
1466; Carr Delilah; F; Daut; 4
1467; Miller Guerney; M; Orphan; 8
1468; Mongrain Rosa; F; Daut; 16
1469; Mongrain Coania; F; Head; 56
1470; Mongrain Stewart; M; Head; 58
1471; [Mongrain] Ernest; M; Son; 17
1472; [Mongrain] Stewart; M; Son; 13

1473; Mongrain Hattie; F; Head; 19
1474; Mosier Thomas; M; Head; 63
1475; Mosier Adeline; F; Wife; 65

1476; Mosier W.T.; M; Head; 38
1477; Louisa; F; Wife; 31
1478; Charles W.; M; Son; 10
1479; John T.; M; Son; 7
1480; Edwin F.; M; Son; 4
1481; Mosier Luther P.; M; Son; 2
1482; Agnes C.; F; Daut; 1

1483; Mosier Jacob; M; Head; 44
1484; Stella; F; Daut; 14
1485; Claude; M; Son; 11
1486; Lione; F; Daut; 8

1487; Mosier Kate; F; Head; 18

1488; Mosier Eugene; F; Head; 31
1489; Mary M.; F; Daut; 10
1490; John J.; M; Son; 4
1491; Ida M.; F; Daut; 2
1492; Walter L.; M; Son; 4/12

45

Census of the **Osage** Indians of **Osage** Agency **Oklahoma** taken
By **Ret Millard**, U. S. Indian Agent **June 30, 1906**

Key: NUMBER; NAME; SEX; RELATION; AGE
* An Askerisk will be next to a number if repeated or out of sequence and inserted among a different family.

1493; Mosier Bismark; M; Head; 23
1494; Clara O.; F; Daut; 2
1495; Thelma V.; F; Daut; 7/12

1496; Moore James W.; M; Head; 20
1497; Moore Eliza; F; Minor; 17
1498; Alice; F; Minor; 15

1499; Moncravie Charles; M; Head; 37
1500; Rosa; F; Wife; 28
1501; Augustine; F; Daut; 7
1502; Virginia M.; F; Daut; 4

1503; Moncravie Fred; M; Head; 31
1504; Moncravie Henry; M; head; 33
1505; Henri E.; F; Daut; 2

1506; Moncravie John; M; Head; 36
1507; Sylvester A.; M; Son; 13
1508; John N.; M; Son; 9
1509; Alexander; M; Son; 7
1510; Barada; M; Son; 5
1511; Vivian L.; F; Daut; 2
1512; Anna; F; Daut; 1/12

1513; Murray Jennie; F; head; 30
1514; Morton J.; M; Son; 8
1515; Ruby M.; F; Daut; 7
1516; Arthur R.; M; Son; 4
1517; Alfred G.; M; Son; 2

1518; Murphy Gertrude; F; Head; 24
1519; Murphy Alice; F; Head; 22
1520; Murphy Elizabeth; F; Head; 20
1521; Murphy Nettie; F; Head; 16

1522; Musgrove William; M; Head; 28
1523; Carl R.; M; Son; 1
1524; Willis E.; F; Daut; 1/12

1525; Newman George; M; Head; 24
1526; Nolegs Larry; M; Head; 51
1527; Owens Ora; F; Head; 23

1528; Pappan Samuel T.; M; Minor; 15
1529; Lee A.; M; Minor; 13

46

Key: NUMBER; NAME; SEX; RELATION; AGE
* An Askerisk will be next to a number if repeated or out of sequence and inserted among a different family.

1530; Oakley; M; Son; 11
1531; Lester; M; Son; 9

1532; Pappin Alex; M; Head; 47
1533; Grace; F; Daut; 16
1534; Herbert; M; Son; 9
1535; Franklin A.; M; Son; 4
1536; Roosevelt; M; Son; 1

1537; Pappin John; M; Head; 48
1538; Jesse L.; M; Son; 16
1539; John L.; M; Son; 14
1540; Jeanette; F; Daut; 11
1541; Joseph L.; M; Son; 9
1542; Jules C.; M; Son; 7
1543; Joshua J.; M; Son; 3
1544; Jeremiah; M; Son; 7/12
1545; Pappin James; M; Head; 22

1546; Palmer John F.; M; Head; 45
1547; Martha; F; Wife; 33
1548; Mable; F; Daut; 17
1549; Mary E.; F; Daut; 12
1550; Clementine; F; Daut; 10

1551; Pease Minnie A.; F; Head; 32
1552; Perrier Joseph; M; Head; 29
1553; Perrier Samuel; M; Head; 38
1554; Perrier Leo; M; Head; 25

1555; Perrier James; M; Head; 35
1556; John T.; M; Son; 12
1557; James F.; M; Son; 6
1558; Perrier Napoleon; M; Head; 48
1559; Louis F.; M; Son; 17
1560; Nina; F; Daut; 15
1561; Leo; M; Son; 12
1562; Peter; M; Son; 9
1563; Lola; F; Daut; 8
1564; Owen; M; Son; 4

1565; Perrier Thomas; M; Head; 22
1566; Roy B.; M; Son; 5/12

1567; Perrier Eugene; M; Head; 23
1568; Ray L.D.; M; Son; 1/12

47

Census of the **Osage** Indians of **Osage** Agency **Oklahoma** taken
By **Ret Millard** , U. S. Indian Agent **June 30, 1906**

Key: NUMBER; NAME; SEX; RELATION; AGE
* An Askerisk will be next to a number if repeated or out of sequence and inserted among a different family.

1569; Pettit S.W.; M; Head; 61
1570; Pettit Nettie M.; F; Head; 19
1571; Pettit Isabella; F; Head; 21

1572; Pettit Charles; M; Head; 33
1573; Hattie; F; Daut; 9
1574; Lela M.; F; 5
1575; Charles W.; M; Son; 4
1576; Lee; M; Son; 2

1577; Pettit George; M; Head; 31
1578; George R.; M; Son; 7
1579; Lula B.; F; Daut; 4

1580; Pettit John; M; Head; 29
1581; Pettit Andrew; M; Head; 28
1582; Perkins Elizabeth; M; Head; 51

1583; Pearson Rosa; F; Head; 43
1584; Madeline; F; Daut; 17
1585; Cordelia C.; F; Daut; 15
1586; Lilian F.; F; Daut; 14
1587; Bertha L.; F; Daut; 12
1588; Kate V.; F; Daut; 9
1589; Willie J.; M; Son; 6
1590; Rosa E.; F; Daut; 3

1591; Pearson October; M; Head; 23
1592; Mary C.; F; Wife; 19
1593; Bernice M.; F; Daut; 1/12

1594; Phillips William; M; Head; 36
1595; Angeline M.; F; Daut; 12
1596; Ida; F; Daut; 10
1597; James; M; Son; 8

1598; Plomondon Clemy; F; Head; 52
1599; Stella; F; Daut; 17
1600; Daniel B.; M; Son; 14
1601; Julia A.; F; Daut; 12
1602; Louisa; F; Daut; 9

1603; Plomondon Louis; M; Head; 21

1604; Plomondon Barnard; M; Head; 36
1605; Ella; F; Wife; 32

48

Key: NUMBER; NAME; SEX; RELATION; AGE
* An Askerisk will be next to a number if repeated or out of sequence and inserted among a different family.

1606; Grace; F; Daut; 14
1606;* Clementine; F; Daut; 12
1607; Moses E.; M; Son; 10
1608; George A.; M; Son; 7

1609; Potter Ethel; F; Head; 28
1610; Francis A.; M; Son; 11
1611; Oliver L.; M; Son; 6
1612; James L.; M; Son; 3

1613; Prudom Charles N.; M; Head; 31
1614; Prudom Nora; F; Head; 23
1615; Prudom Nettie; F; Head; 20
1616; Prudom Frank; M; Head; 40

1617; Prue Henry; M; Head; 31
1618; Maude; F; Wife; 24
1619; Hattie M.; F; Daut; 8
1620; Charles S.; M; Son; 7
1621; Henry E.; M; Son; 5
1622; Floyd B.; M; Son; 2
1623; Anna B.; F; Daut; 5/12

1624; Quinton Franklin; M; Head; 19

1625; Rairton Jane R.; F; Head; 47
1626; Miller Louis; M; Son; 17
1627; Ida J.; F; Daut; 14
1628; Rairton Wendall; M; Son; 6

1629; Reece Elizabeth; F; Head; 22

1630; Revelette James; M; Head; 27
1631; Teresa; F; Daut; 7
1632; William L.; M; Son; 5
1633; Revelette Mary E.; F; Daut; 8/12
1634; Minnie F.; F; Daut; 8/12

1635; Revelette Fred; M; Head; 27
1636; Pauline; F; Daut; 6
1637; Fred L.; M; Son; 4

1638; Revelette Frank; M; Head; 65
1639; Franklin; M; Son; 17

1640; Revelette Charles; M; Head; 33

Key: NUMBER; NAME; SEX; RELATION; AGE
* An Askerisk will be next to a number if repeated or out of sequence and inserted among a different family.

1641; Joseph; M; Son; 3/12

1642; Revard William; M; Head; 41
1643; William E.; M; Son; 5
1644; Della M.; F; Daut; 3
1645; Gladdis; F; Daut; 10/12

1646; Revard Solomon; M; Head; 47
1647; Revard Charles; M; Head; 47
1648; Revard Alex; M; Head; 46
1649; Benjamin; M; Head; 25

1650; Revard Paul; M; Head; 31
1651; Susie; F; Daut; 11

1652; Revard Mary E.; F; Head; 58
1653; Elsie E.; F; Daut; 15

1654; Revard Francis; M; Head; 38
1655; Mack; M; Son; 12
1656; Emanuel M.; M; Son; 7
1657; Pearl P.; F; Daut; 5

1658; Revard John W.; M; Head; 28
1659; Edward L.; M; Son; 8
1660; Evart A.; M; Son; 7

1661; Revard Joseph; M; Head; 76
1662; Susan W.; F; Daut; 16
1663; Clementine; F; Daut; 13
1664; William J.; M; Son; 11
1665; Ronald V.; M; Son; 9

1666; Revard Ralph; M; Head; 18

1667; Revard Franklin; M; Head; 42
1668; Nicholas N.; M; Son; 12
1669; Pearl; F; Daut; 11
1670; Myrta; F; Daut; 3

1671; Revard Mark B.; M; Head; 18

1672; Revard Charles E.; M; Head; 46
1673; Clarence; M; Son; 16
1674; Ed. Clifford; M; Son; 14
1675; Clara; F; Daut; 12

Census of the___**Osage**___Indians of___**Osage**___Agency___**Oklahoma**___taken
By___**Ret Millard**___, U. S. Indian Agent___**June 30, 1906**

Key: NUMBER; NAME; SEX; RELATION; AGE
* An Askerisk will be next to a number if repeated or out of sequence and inserted among a different family.

1676; Carrie; F; Daut; 8
1677; Cora; F; Daut; 8
1678; Nora T.; F; Daut; 7
1679; Mc Guire N.; M; Son; 2
1680; Lean; F; Daut; 1/12

1681; Revard Leonard; M; Head; 48
1682; Lode; F; Daut; 12
1683; Opal A.; F; Daut; 9
1684; Hazel; F; Daut; 6
1685; Minnie; F; Daut; 3
1686; Cleo; M; Son; 6/12

1687; Revard Joseph Jr.; M; Head; 49
1688; Nellie; F; Daut; 5
1689; Edgar T.; M; Son; 6/12
1690; Mary G.; F; Daut; 6/12

1691; Revard Curtis; M; Head; 20
1692; Revard Mable; F; Head; 18

1693; Revard Odell; F; Minor; 16
1694; Aaron T.; M; Son; 14

1695; Riddle Sherman; M; Minor; 14
1696; Joseph; M; Minor; 12
1697; Frank; M; Minor; 10

1698; Ririe Effie; F; Minor; 13
1699; Scott; M; Minor; 10
1700; Otis E.; M; Minor; 6
1701; Nellie I.; F; Minor; 4
1702; Arthur M.; M; Minor; 5/12

1703; Ririe Oscar A.; M; Head; 19

1704; Rodman Antwine;M; Head; 33
1705; Rogers Stephen; M; Head; 35
1706; Rogers Louis; M; Head; 63

1707; Rogers Louis Jr.; M; Head; 21
1708; Wahneta; F; Daut; 1

1709; Rogers Thomas L.; M; Head; 68
1710; Nancy; F; Wife; 58

51

Key: NUMBER; NAME; SEX; RELATION; AGE
* An Askerisk will be next to a number if repeated or out of sequence and inserted among a different family.

1711; Rogers T.L.; M; Head; 20

1712; Rogers Arthur; M; Head; 46
1713; Minerva; F; Wife; 34
1714; Joseph L. M; Son; 7
1715; Ellen E.; F; Daut; 5
1716; John R.; M; Son; 3
1717; William C.; M; Son; 1

1718; Rogers Mary E.; F; Head; 32
1719; Irene; F; Daut; 14
1720; Mary A.; F; Daut; 12
1721; Coania; F; Daut; 8
1722; Elred T.; M; Son; 6

1723; Rogers Ida; F; Head; 24

1724; Rogers Antwine; M; Head; 61
1725; Viola; F; Daut; 14

1726; Rogers Mae; F; Head; 20

1727; Rogers Kenneth; M; Head; 26
1728; Helen; F; Daut; 3
1729; Rogers Antwine; M; Son; 1

1730; Rogers Jasper; M; Head; 36
1731; Rose; F; Wife; 27
1732; Emmet; M; Son; 4;
1733; Cecelia; F; Daut; 5
1734; Maude; F; Daut; 1

1735; Rogers Bertha B.; Minor; 12
1736; Helen C.; F; Minor; 10

1737; Rogers Arthur; M; Head; 26
1738; Rogers Thomas L. Jr.; M; Head; 21
1739; Rogers Granville; M; Head; 18
1740; Rogers Rosa L.; F; Minor; 13
1741; Josephine; F; Minor; 10
1742; John H.; M; Minor; 8

1743; Rogers Nora; F; Head; 22
1744; Richard L.; M; Son; 1

1745; Rogers Lewis A.; M; Head; 31

Census of the __Osage__ Indians of __Osage__ Agency __Oklahoma__ taken
By __Ret Millard__ , U. S. Indian Agent __June 30, 1906__

Key: NUMBER; NAME; SEX; RELATION; AGE
* An Askerisk will be next to a number if repeated or out of sequence and inserted among a different family.

1746; Rogers Isadora; F; Wife; 28
1747; Fred R.; M; son; 5
1748; Frank; M; Son; 1

1749; Roberts Ola; F; Head; 20

1750; Ross John; M; Head; 61
1751; Floyd F.; M; Son; 9

1752; Roach Wilfred D.; M; Head; 26
1753; Bridget A.; F; Daut; 3
1754; Melvin C.; M; Son; 1

1755; Roach Samuel; M; Head; 24
1756; Mikle J.; M; Son; 3
1757; Herman B.; M; Son; 4/12

1758; Roach Mary E.; F; Head; 23
1759; Roach George W.; M; Head; 20
1760; Roach Hattie B.; F; Head; 18

1761; Saxon Cora; F; Head; 32
1762; Vava M.; F; Daut; 2

1763; Scott Estella; F; Minor; 8
1764; Della; F; Minor; 5

1765; Scott George; M; Head; 29
1766; Mary M.; F; Daut; 6/12

1767; Scott Julia Ann; F; Head; F; Head; 26
1768; William J.; M; Son; 1

1769; Selby Georgia; F; Head; 20
1770; Shafer Joanna; M; Head; 26

1771; Shaw Franklin; M; Head; 19
1772; Rosa M.; F; Wife; 18
1773; Shaw Moses; M; Son; 2
1774; John; M; Son; 3/12

1775; Shobe Anna U.; F; Head; 22
1776; Simpson Susan; F; Head; 64

1777; Simkins Mary L.; F; Head; 34
1778; Warren D.; M; Son; 13

Key: NUMBER; NAME; SEX; RELATION; AGE
* An Askerisk will be next to a number if repeated or out of sequence and inserted among a different family.

1779; Mary E.; F; Daut; 12
1780; Vivian P.; F; Daut; 9
1781; Oren E.; M; Son; 8
1782; Edward; M; Son; 6
1783; Virgil; M; Son; 7/12

1784; Slaughter A.B.; M; Head; 22
1785; Slaughter Amanda; M; Head; 19
1786; Slaughter Harry E.; M; Minor; 16
1787; Smith Minnie; F; Head; 23
1788; Smith Anna; F; Head; 27

1789; Soderstrom Gertrude; F; Head; 27
1790; Dickey Alta A.; F; Daut; 8

1791; Soldani Sylvester J.; M; Head; 46
1792; Josephine; F; Wife; 37
1793; Louis E.; M; Son; 17
1794; Myrtle; F; Daut; 15
1795; E.A.; M; Son; 14
1796; Soldani Kate; F; Head; 18
1797; Soldani Ida M.; F; Head; 19
1798; Soldani Agnes; F; Head; 20

1799; Soldani Anthony; M; Head; 44
1800; Amelia K.; F; Wife; 38
1801; Frank E.; M; Son; 15
1802; C.L.; M; Son; 13
1803; Clarence' M; Son; 10
1804; Grace M.; F; Daut; 9
1805; Rosa M.; F; Daut; 7
1806; George H. M; Son; 5

1807; Soldani Mary L.; F; Head; 19

1808; Stevens John H,; M; Head; 40
1809; Mildred V.; F; daut; 2

1810; Stephens Madeline; F; Head; 64
1811; Stephens Mary; F; Daut; 12

1812; Stotts Emma; F; Head; 31
1813; Joseph L.; M; Son; 15
1814; William W.; M; Son; 11
1815; James E.; M; Son; 2

54

Census of the __Osage__ Indians of __Osage__ Agency __Oklahoma__ taken
By __Ret Millard__ , U. S. Indian Agent __June 30, 1906__

Key: NUMBER; NAME; SEX; RELATION; AGE

* An Askerisk will be next to a number if repeated or out of sequence and inserted among a different family.

1816; Stobaugh Alice; F; Head; 35
1817; Riddle John L.; M; Son; 16
1818; Arthur; M; Son; 4

1819; Stewart Leonora; F; Head; 44
1820; Wilkie George; M; Son; 16
1821; Rose E.; F; Daut; 12

1822; Swanson Celestine; F; Head; 24
1823; Addison L.; M; Son; 2
1824; Ora E.; F; Daut; 4

1825; Swinney Oscar E.; F; Orphan; 13

1826; Tapp Belle; F; Head; 42
1827; Chambers James W,; Son; 10
1828; Minnie A.; F; Daut; 7

1829; Taylor James E.; M; Orphan; 13
1830; John F; M; Orphan; 11
1831; Hiram; M; Orphan; 9
1832; Fanny; F; Orphan; 8
1833; Agnes; F; Orphan; 6
1834; Anna; F; Orphan; 2

1835; Tayrien John; M; Head; 24
1836; Mary L.; F; Daut; 2
1837; Agnes; F; Daut; 7/12

1838; Tayrien Charles; M; Head; 31
1839; Edna; F; Daut; 8

1840; Tayrien Thomas; M; Head; 45
1841; George A.; M; Son; 16
1842; Andrew W.; M; Son; 12
1843; Paul; M; Son; 10
1844; Maude J.; F; daut; 2
1845; John C.; M; Son; 1

1846; Tayrien James; M; Head; 21
1847; Alberty; M; Son; 2
1848; Elmer C.; M; Son; 3/12

1849; Tayrien David W.; Head; 18

1850; Tayrien Andrew; M; Head; 32

55

Key: NUMBER; NAME; SEX; RELATION; AGE
* An Askerisk will be next to a number if repeated or out of sequence and inserted among a different family.

1851;   Jeanie; F; Daut; 10
1852;   Viola; F; Daut; 9
1853;   Alfred J.; M; Son; 7
1854;   Violet M.; F; Daut; 6
1855;   William J.; M; Son; 3
1856;   Rosanna; F; Daut; 3

1857;   Tayrien Cyprian; M; Head; 68
1858;   William; M; Son; 16
1859;   Beggs Julia L.; F; Gr. Daut; 16

1860;   Tayrien Lillie; M; Head; 19
1861;   Thompson Leroy; M; Minor; 12

1862;   Thompson Nicholas; M; Head; 48

1863;   Thomas Agnes; F; Head; 24
1864;   Maggie C.; F; Daut; 4
1865;   Julia H.; F; Daut; 1

1866;   Thurman Lola; F; Head; 20

1867;   Tinker Louis; M; Head; 39
1868;   William; M; Son; 15
1869;   Bessie; F; Daut; 12
1870;   Nora; F; Daut; 8
1871;   Ora; F; Daut; 8
1872;   Eva; F; Daut; 6
1873;   Isabella; F; Daut; 3
1874;   Ida; F; Daut; 1

1875;   Tinker George E.; M; Head; 37
1876;   Mary G.; F; Daut; 14
1877;   Sarah Ann; F; Daut; 12
1878;   Nicholas; M; Son; 10
1879;   George E. Jr.; M; Son; 7
1880;   Villa; F; Daut; 3
1881;   Tinker Clarence; M; Head; 18

1882;   Tinker Charley; M; Head; 34
1883;   Mary J.; F; Daut; 15
1884;   Roy B.; M; Son; 12
1885;   Maude; F; Daut; 9
1886;   Lucille; F; Daut; 8
1887;   David W.; M; Son; 5
1888;   Louis H.; M; Son; 1

Census of the __Osage__ Indians of __Osage__ Agency __Oklahoma__ taken
By __Ret Millard__ , U. S. Indian Agent __June 30, 1906__

Key: NUMBER; NAME; SEX; RELATION; AGE
* An Askerisk will be next to a number if repeated or out of sequence and inserted among a different family.

1889; Tinker Frank; M; Head; 45
1890; Mary L.; F; Wife; 45
1891; Norris J.; M; Son; 17
1892; Tom; M; Son; 12
1893; Mary E.; F; Daut; 10
1894; Eliza; F; Daut; 6
1895; Sylvester J.; M; Son; 3

1896; Todd Maude; F; Head; 27

1897; Trumbly Julian; M; Head; 55
1898; Eliza; F; Wife; 50
1899; Harry; M; Son; 16
1900; Tina O.; F; Daut; 14
1901; Charles; M; Son; 13
1902; Theresa; F; Daut; 8

1903; Trumbly Oliver; M; Head; 24

1904; Trumbly Clarence; M; Head; 25
1905; Eliza A.; F; Daut; 4
1906; Gladys; F; Daut; 3
1907; Clarence E.; M; Son; 5/12

1908; Trumbly George; M; Head; 32
1909; Trumbly Andrew; M; Head; 31
1910; Mary; F; Wife; 20

1911; Trumbly J.B.; M; Head; 52
1912; Florence; F; Daut; 17
1913; John F,; M; Son; 15
1914; Elizabeth; F; Daut; 12
1915; Paul P.; M; Son; 6

1916; Tucker Anna; F; Head; 22
1917; Beulah G.; F; Daut; 1

1918; Tucker Angeline; F; Head; 71
1919; Turner Frederick D.; M; Son; 11
1920; Turner Mary B.; F; Head; 24
1921; Tyner Benjamin F.; M; Head; 31
1922; Ethel M.; F; Daut; 7
1923; Roy F.; M; Son; 5
1924; William L.; M; Son; 1

1925; Vesser Eliza; M; Head; 36

57

Key: NUMBER; NAME; SEX; RELATION; AGE
* An Askerisk will be next to a number if repeated or out of sequence and inserted among a different family.

1926; Ruth; F; Daut; 13

1927; Voiles Ora M.; F; Head; 26

1928; Watkins; Rosalie; F; Head; 31
1929; Frances M.; M; Son; 12
1930; James; M; Son; 11
1931; John F.; M; Son; 4

1932; Ware Victoria; F; Head; 55
1933; Del Orier Lillie M.; F; Daut; 17
1934; Edna; F; Daut; 15

1935; Ware Aggie; F; Head; 36
1936; Julia; F; Daut; 12
1937; Nancy; F; Daut; 10
1938; Aggie; F; Daut; 8
1939; Rosa L.; F; Daut; 6
1940; Henry H.; M; Son; 4
1941; David; M; Son; 3

1942; Wade Effie; F; Head; 19
1943; Whiles Elmer; M; Head; 24
1944; Whiles Telina; F; Head; 23
1945; Whiles Delilah; F; Head; 21
1946; Whiles Frances M.; M; Orphan; 17
1947; Wheeler Paul; M; Head; 34
1948; Merrit J.; M; Son; 3
1949; Geneva; F; Daut; 2

1950; Wheeler Elmer; M; Head; 27
1951; Eva E.; F; Wife; 28
1952; Virginia; F; Daut; 2

1953; Wheeler Alma; F; Head; 20
1954; Wheeler Anna; F; Head; 23
1955; Wheeler Susan; F; Head; 29
1956; Wilkie Arnold; M; Head; 23
1957; Wilkie Louis F.; M; Head; 20

1958; Wilson Mary; F; Head; 28
1959; William E.; M; Son; 9
1960; Julia K.; F; Daut; 7
1961; Banie; M; Son; 5
1962; Audry; F; Daut; 2

58

Census of the__**Osage**__Indians of__**Osage**__Agency__**Oklahoma**__taken
By__**Ret Millard**__, U. S. Indian Agent__**June 30, 1906**

Key: NUMBER; NAME; SEX; RELATION; AGE
* An Askerisk will be next to a number if repeated or out of sequence and inserted among a different family.

1963;   Woodring Tena; F; Head; 31
1964;   Carlton; M; Son; 11
1965;   Orville W.; M; Son; 9
1966;   Anna; F; F; Daut; 2

1967;   Woodham Lucy; F; Head; 56

1968;   Wyrick Mary; F; Head; 33
1969;   Jessie; F; Daut; 10
1970;   John H.; M; Son; 9
1971;   Elnora J.; F; Daut; 5
1972;   Elmer; F.; M; Son; 2

1973;   Yeargain Estella; F; Head; 18

1974;   Yeargain Early I.; M; Minor; 15
1975;   Verona C.; F; Minor; 13

1976;   Yeargain Leona; F; Minor; 12

1977;   York Adah M.; F; Head; 20

1978;   Hooper Sallie; F; Head; 35
1979;   Mary; F; Daut; 12

1980;   Siggins Clara; F; Head; 43
1981;   Andrew W.; M; Son; 15

1982;   See page 5
1983;   See page 5
1984;   See page 14
1985   See page 22
1986;   See page 22
1987;   See page 22
1988;   See page 22
1989;   See page 27
1990;   See page 27

Omitted from Little Chief Band
1991;   Me-tsa-he; F; Wife; 40
1992;   Wah-shah-she-me-tsa-he; F; Daut; 5
1993;   Ho-ho; M; S. Son; 11
1994;   Wah-shah-she; F; Daut; 3
Nos. 766 & 832 omitted
Nos. 1345 & 1606 duplicated

59

Census of the __Osage__ Indians of __Osage__ Agency __Oklahoma__ taken
By __Ret Millard__, U. S. Indian Agent __June 30, 1906__

Key: NUMBER; NAME; SEX; RELATION; AGE
* An Askerisk will be next to a number if repeated or out of sequence and inserted among a different family.

RECAPITULATION.

All ages (males, 1008; females, 989)- - - - - - - - -   1994

FULL BLOODS
All ages (males, 425; females 413)- - - - - - - - - -   838
18 years and over (males 256; females, 242)- - - - - - 498
Between 6 and 16 (males, 102; females 89)- - - - - - 191

MIXED BLOODS.
All ages (males, 580; females, 576)- - - - - - - - - - 1156
18 years and over (males, 226; females, 226)- - - - - 452
Between 6 and 16 (males, 211; females, 212)- - - - - 423

**Asterisk * where there's an inserted number
or repeated number. INTRO**

60

Census of the Osage Indians

of

Osage Indian Agency, Oklahoma,

As of 1907

Ret Millard, U. S. Indian Agent

Osage

Census of the __Osage__ Indians of __Osage__ Agency __Oklahoma__ taken By __Ret Millard__, United States Indian Agent, during the First Quarter, 1908**[sic]**(?)**1907?**

Key: NUMBER; Indian Name; English Name; Sex; Relation; Age
* An Askerisk will be next to a number if repeated or out of sequence and inserted among a different family.

1; Pah-hu-scah; Tom Big Chief; M; Head; 48
2; Me-to-op-pe; ---; F; Wife; 34
3; He-ah-to-me; May White; F; Daut; 16
4; Heh-kah-mon-kah; ---; F; Daut; 8
5; Gra-to-me; ---; F; Daut; 4

6; Nah-me-tsa-he; ---; F; Head; 70

7; Mo-she-to-moie; ---; M; Head; 63
8; Mo-se-che-he; ---; F; Wife; 63

9; Richard Rusk; Richard Rusk; M; Head; 25
10; ---; May Rusk; F. Daut; 4
11; Hla-me-tsa-he; ---; F; Daut; 6 mo.

12; Wy-u-tsa-kah-she; ---; M; Head; 73
13; Me-tsa-he; ---; F; Wife; 55
14; Moie-wah-kon-tah; Philip Carson; M; Son; 13
15; Num-pah-wah-kon-tah; Tom Carson; M; Head; 18
16; Hun-kah-me; ---; F; Head; 50
17; To-sho-ho; Charles Whitehorn; M; Son; 11
18; E-nah-min-tsa; ---; M; Son; 3

19; Me-lo-tah-moie; John Furguson; M; Head; 44

20; Fidelis Cheehewahkepah; ---; M; Head; 25
21; Hum-pah-to-kah; ---; F; Wife; 52
22; He-ah-to-me; Agnes Ferguson; F; S. Daut; 6
23; Gra-tah-wah-kah; ---; M; S. Son; 3

24; ---; Howard Russell; M; Head; 19

25; ---; Otis Russell; M; Head; 20

26; ---; Pearl Murray; F; Head; 28
27; Wah-she-ke-pah; Willie Russell; M; Son; 11
28; He-ah-shin-kah; ---; M; Son; 7
29; Min-kah-she; ---; F; Daut; 1

30; ---; Herman McCarthy; M; Head; 28

31; Son-sah-kah-hah; ---; M; Head; 59
32; Hlu-ah-to-me; ---; F; Wife; 60

33; Wah-shah-she-me-tsa-he; ---; F; Head; 74

63

Census of the **Osage** Indians of **Osage** Agency **Oklahoma** taken
By **Ret Millard**, United States Indian Agent, during the First Quarter,
1908[sic](?)**1907?**

Key: NUMBER; Indian Name; English Name; Sex; Relation; Age
* An Askerisk will be next to a number if repeated or out of sequence and inserted among a different family.

34; Wah-sho-shah; ---; M; Head; 45
35; Mo-se-che-he; F; Wife; 38
36; Hlu-ah-me-tsa-he; F; Daut; 9 mo.

37; Mon-kah-sop-py; ---; M; Head; 58
38; He-ah-to-me; ---; F; Wife; 37
39; Wah-tsa-ah-tah; Joe Osage; M; S. Son; 13
40; E-ne-op-pe; Nellie Osage; F; S. Daut; 11
41; Hun-kah-me; ---; F; Daut; 2

42; Wah-hre-she; Charles; M; Head; 44
43; Hlu-ah-to-me; ---; F; Wife; 37
44; Mo-se-che-he; Josephine; F; Daut; 11
45; Mon-kah-hah; ---; M; Son; 6
46; Num-me-tsa-he; ---; F; Daut; 2

47; ---; Luther Harvey; M; Head; 37
48; Ke-ah-som-pah; Mary; F; Wife; 34
49; He-ah-to-me; Minnie; F; Daut; 12
50; Hlu-ah-wah-kon-tah; Walter; M; Son; 9
51; Num-pah-q-tah; Theodore R.; M; Son; 8
52; Wah-tsa-su-sah; ---; M; Son; 4

53; Me-ke-wah-ti-an-kah; ---; M; Head; 43
54; Wah-hrah-lum-pah; ---; F; Wife; 36
55; Kah-he-ah-gra; Louis James; M; Son; 10
56; Me-to-op-pe; ---; F; Daut; 2

57; ---; Roy James; M; Head; 21

58; Me-tsa-he; ---; F; Head; 54

59; ---; Roscoe Conklin; M; Head; 44
60; ---; Edith White; F; Wife; 25
61; ---; Joseph; M; S. Son; 3
62; ---; Abraham; M; S. Son; 1

63; He-ah-to-me; Nellie White; F; Orphan; 11

64; Sho-e-ne-blah (Blind); ---; M; Head; 35

65; Wah-shin-kah-sop-py; ---; M; Head; 60
66; E-ne-op-pe; Mary Bird; F; Daut; 16
67; E-gro-tah; Joseph Bird; M; Son; 14

64

Census of the **Osage** Indians of **Osage** Agency **Oklahoma** taken By **Ret Millard**, United States Indian Agent, during the First Quarter, 1908[sic](?)**1907?**

Key: NUMBER; Indian Name; English Name; Sex; Relation; Age

* An Askerisk will be next to a number if repeated or out of sequence and inserted among a different family.

68; ---; Esther; F; Wife; 20

69; E-gro-kah-shin-kah; ---; M; Head; 47
70; Hum-pah-to-kah; ---; F; Wife; 35
71; We-heh; Margaret Little; F; Daut; 13
72; Wah-sop-py-wah-kah; Mary Pappin; F; Daut; 6

73; Sin-tsa-hu; Ralph Hamilton; M; Head; 18

JOE'S BAND.

74; Shon-kah-mo-lah; ---; M; Head; 61
75; Wah-tsa-me; ---; F; Wife; 53
76; Wah-shin-kah-hu; Joseph; M; Son; 17

77; ---; Daniel West; M; Head; 33
78; Hlu-ah-to-me; ---; F; Wife; 36
79; Kah-shin-kah; ---; M; Son; 6

80; Wah-hah-sah-e; ---; F; Head; 70

81; Wah-ses-tah-shin-kah; John Blackbird; M; Head; 49
82; Hlu-ah-tome; Mary; F; Wife; 32
83; Mon-shon-tsa-e-tah; Maud Blackbird; F; Daut; 12
84; Wah-hrah-lum-pah; Mollie Mantle; F; Ward; 16
85; Che-sho-ki-he-kah; ---; M; Son; 10 da.

86; Pun-kah-shin-kah; ---; M; Head; 42
87; He-ah-to-me; ---; F; Wife; 31
88; Kah-scah; ---; M; Son; 7

89; Kah-wah-o; Yellow Horse; M; Head; 50
90; Ke-ah-som-pah; ---; F; Wife; 40
91; Pah-kah-me-tsa-he; Maggie Bates; F; Daut; 12
92; Ah-kah-hu; John Bates; M; Son; 10
93; Hun-kah-me-tsa-he; ---; F; Daut; 8
94; Kah-ah-sum-pah; ---; F; Daut; 2

95; ---; Joseph Bates; M; Head; 20

96; Wah-hrah-lum-pah; ---; F; Head; 65

97; Hun-tsa-me; ---; F; Head; 63

98; Wah-tsa-moie; ---; M; Head; 28

65

Census of the___**Osage**___Indians of___**Osage**___Agency___**Oklahoma**___taken
By_____**Ret Millard**_____, United States Indian Agent, during the First Quarter,
1908**[sic]**(?)**1907?**

Key: NUMBER; Indian Name; English Name; Sex; Relation; Age
* An Askerisk will be next to a number if repeated or out of sequence and inserted among a different family.

  99; Hun-kah-me-tsa-he; ---; Wife; 24
100; ---; Michel; M; Son; 2

101; Pun-q-tah; ---; F; Head; 56

102; ---; Andrew Berry; M; Head; 20

103; ---; Grace berry; F; Head; 22

104; ---; Esther Berry; F; Head; 22

105; Nun-tsa-wah-hu; ---; M; Head; 55
106; Num-pah-se; Joseph Cannon; M; Son; 16
107; ---; John; M; Son; 5

108; ---; Frank Cannon; M; Head; 22

109; ---; Alex Cannon; M; Head; 24

110; O-pah-su-ah; ---; M; Head; 38
111; Wah-to-sah; ---; F; Wife; 38
112; Pah-pah-ah-hah; Francis; M; Son; 13

113; Tsa-po-in-kah; ---; M; Head; 58
114; Hlu-ah-me-tsa-he; ---; F; Wife; 54

115; ---; Lawrence Gray; M; Head; 21

116; ---; Hazel Gray; F; Head; 23
117; ---; Laura Gray; F; Daut; 5

118; ---; Amos Osage; M; Head; 35
119; Ne-kah-ah-se; Liza; F; Wife; 26
120; He-ah-to-me; Rosa; F; Daut; 8

M O H – E – K A H – M O I E   B A N D .

121;   Moh-e-kah-moie; ---; M; Head; 73
122; Hlu-ah-to-me; ---; F; Wife; 53
123; Tsa-me-hun-kah; Minnie; F; Daut; 17
124; Me-hah-sah-he; Aggie; F; Daut; 17
125; Me-ah-hre; Mary; F; Daut; 13

126; ---; Adair Hickey; M; Head; 31

Census of the __Osage__ Indians of __Osage__ Agency __Oklahoma__ taken
By_____ **Ret Millard**_____, United States Indian Agent, during the First Quarter,
1908**[sic](?)1907?**

Key: NUMBER; Indian Name; English Name; Sex; Relation; Age
* An Askerisk will be next to a number if repeated or out of sequence and inserted among a different family.

127; ---; William Fletcher; M; Head; 36
128; Me-sah-e; ---; F; Wife; 25
129; Gra-to-me-tsa-he; ---; F; S. Daut; 6
130; Gra-to-ah; ---; F; S. Daut; 3
131; Sin-tsa-wah-kon-tah; Charles; M; Son; 10
132; E-to-moie; Anna; F; Daut; 7
133; ---; Frances T. Fletcher; F; Daut; 10

134; Gro-tun-kah; Joseph Fletcher; M; Orphan; 17

135; To-wan-gah-she; ---; M; Head; 48
136; He-ah-to-me; ---; F; Wife; 44
137; Gra-tah-su-ah; Thomas Butler; M; Son; 14

138; ---; Eugene Butler; M; Head; 19

139; Me-gra-to-me; ---; F; Head; 41
140; U-se-tah-wah-hah; ---; M; Head; 75

141; ---; Gilbert Cox; M; Head; 36

142; Me-ti-ah-kah; ---; M; Head; 44
143; Me-se-che-he; ---; F; Wife; 38
144; Ne-wal-la; Edward; M; Son; 11
145; E-he-ke-op-pe; ---; F; Daut; 6
146; Wah-ne-en-kah; ---; F; Daut; 1

147; ---; Bernadette Elkins; F; Head; 19

148; ---; Luther Elkins; M; Head; 21

149; ---; Charles West; M; Head; 24
150; ---; Louisa; F; Daut; 1

151; ---; Don Dickinson; M; Head; 29

152; ---; Herbert Spencer; M; Head; 31
153; ---; Jennie Spencer; F; Wife; 23

154; Gra-tah-su-ah; Donnie Cole; F; Orphan; 16

155; To-wan-gah-he; ---; M; Head; 48
156; Son-se-grah; ---; F; Wife; 34
157; He-ah-to-me; Fanny Frye; F; Daut; 16

67

Census of the __Osage__ Indians of __Osage__ Agency __Oklahoma__ taken
By_____**Ret Millard**_____, United States Indian Agent, during the First Quarter,
1908**[sic]**(?)**1907?**

Key: NUMBER; Indian Name; English Name; Sex; Relation; Age
* An Askerisk will be next to a number if repeated or out of sequence and inserted among a different family.

158; ---; Edward Cox; M; Head; 31
159; A-non-to-op-pe; ---; F; Wife; 20
160; Wah-tsa-ah-tah; Joseph; M; Son; 3
161; ---; Lottie Ione; F; Daut; 1 mo.

162; ---; Clinton Bigheart; M; Head; 36
163; Mon-shon-tsa-e-tah; ---; F; Wife; 25
164; Hum-pah-to-kah; Rose Bigheart; F; S. Daut; 11

165; Wah-kon-tah-he-um-pah; ---; F; Head; 58
166; Ne-wal-la; ---; M; Son; 8

167; ---; Stevens Neal; M; Head; 28
168; ---; Rose; F; Wife; 20
169; Kle-o-tone; ---; F; Daut; 1mo.

170; ---; Wilson Kirk; M; Head; 50
171; ---; Dora Kirk; F; Daut; 6
172; ---; Rosie Kirk; F; Daut; 2

173; Pah-she-he; Mary Cox; F; Orphan; 17

174; ---; Mable Cole; F; Head; 18

N E – K A H – W A H – S H E – T U N – K A H   B A N D .

175; Ne-kah-wah-she-tun-kah; ---; M; Head; 57
176; Wah-hrah-lum-pah; ---; F; Wife; 55

177; ---; Nicholas Webster; M; Head; 32
178; Lo-tah-tse-a; ---; F; Wife; 40

179; E-to-moie; Little Star; M; Head; 38
180; Wah-to-sah-e; ---; F; Wife; 38
181; Gra-tah-ah-kah; John Star; M; Son; 7
182; Tompah-pe; ---; F; Daut; 4
183; E-kah-pah-she; ---; F; Daut; 2

184; Che-sho-wah-ke-pah; ---; M; Head; 37
185; Wah-hrah-lum-pah; F; Wife; 40
186; Hum-pah-to-kah; ---; F; Daut; 10
187; Ke-ah-som-pah; ---; F; Daut; 7
188; ---; Mary; F; Daut; 4

189; ---; Millie Kirk; F; Head; 23

Census of the __Osage__ Indians of __Osage__ Agency __Oklahoma__ taken By_____ __Ret Millard_____, United States Indian Agent, during the First Quarter, 1908[sic](?)**1907?**

Key: NUMBER; Indian Name; English Name; Sex; Relation; Age
* An Askerisk will be next to a number if repeated or out of sequence and inserted among a different family.

190; Hun-wah-ko; ---; F; Head; 71

191; Pun-kah-wah-ti-an-kah; ---; M; Head; 45
192; Wah-hrah-lum-pah; ---; F; Wife; 32
193; Wah-tsa-ah-hah; James Bigheart; M; Son; 11
194; Wah-te-sah; ---; F; Daut; 5
195; Wah-sis-tah; ---; M; Son; 9

196; Pah-nee-wah-with-tah; ---; M; Head; 65
197; Gra-to-me-tsa-he; ---; F; Wife; 46

198; Ne-kah-lum-pah; ---; M; Head; 51
199; Hlu-ah-to-me; ---; F; Wife; 49
200; Hah-moie; Bird Tuman; M; Son; 16

201; ---; Gurney Miller; M; Head; 40
202; ---; Grace; F; Daut; 6
203; ---; Howard; M; Son; 4
204; ---; Chester; M; Son; 10 mo.

205; Ne-ah-tse-pe; ---; F; Head; 65

206; ---; Annie Turpie; F; Head; 20

207; Bro-ki-he-kah; ---; M; Head; 51
208; E-ne-op-pe; Annie Brokey; F; Daut; 13

209; ---; Herbert Brokey; M; Head; 19

210; E-pah-son-tsa; ---; M; Head; 52

211; Shon-kah-tsa-a; ---; M; Head; 39
212; ---; Polly Earl; F; Daut; 16
213; Hun-kah-me-tsa-he; ---; F; Daut; 8 mo.

214; Gra-to-moie; ---; M; Head; 65
215; Ke-ah-som-pah; ---; F; Wife; 56
216; Me-gra-to-me; Helen Scott; F; Daut; 17
217; Me-hun-kah; Rosa Scott; F; F; Daut; 16
218; Hlu-ah-wah-kon-tah; Daniel Scott; M; Son; 13
219; Shah-kah-wah-pe; Walter Scott; M; Son; 10

220; Wah-tsa-ah-hah; ---; M; Head; 53
221; Wah-hrah-lum-pah; ---; F; Wife; 29
222; Wah-tsa-moie; Joseph Watson; M; Son; 11

69

Census of the___Osage___Indians of___Osage___Agency___Oklahoma___taken
By_____Ret Millard_____, United States Indian Agent, during the First Quarter,
1908[sic](?)1907?

Key: NUMBER; Indian Name; English Name; Sex; Relation; Age
* An Askerisk will be next to a number if repeated or out of sequence and inserted among a different family.

223;   ---; Ethel Bryant; F; Head; 23

224;   Shah-wah-pe; ---; M; Head; 39

225;   ---; Embrey Gibson; M; Head; 44
226;   Hun-kah-hop-py; Edward G.; M; Son; 14

227;   Son-se-o-grah; ---; M; Head; 61
228;   Mon-shon-tsa-e-tah; F; Wife; 61
229;   Wah-ko-sah-moie; Mary Clay; F; Daut; 13

230;   ---; Dudley Haskell; M; Head; 31
231;   Son-se-grah; ---; F; Wife; 25
232;   Wah-hrah-lum-pah; ---; F; Daut; 6
233;   Me-gra-to-me; ---; F; Daut; 4
234;   Hlu-ah-wah-kon-tah; ---; M; Son; 1

235;   He-shah-ah-hle; ---; M; Head; 48
236;   He-ah-to-me; ---; F; Wife; 41
237;   Ah-kah-me; ---; F; Daut; 8
238;   Hlu-ah-gla-she; M; Son; 4

239;   Me-hah-ah-gra; ---; M; Head; 58
240;   Wah-kon-tah-he-um-pah; ---; F; Wife; 64
241;   He-kin-to-op-pe; Angelia Hanna; F; Ward; 12

242;   ---; Peter Clark; M; Head; 24

243;   Tom-pah-pe; ---; F; Head; 81

244;   ---; Richard Kenny; M; Head; 51
245;   Gra-tah-su-ah; ---; F; Wife; 40
246;   He-he-kin-to-pope; Mary June; F; Daut; 15
247;   A-non-to-op-pe; ---; F; Daut; 3
248;   Hlu-la-tsa-kah; ---; M; Son; 1 mo.

249;   ---; Lizzie June; F; Head; 19
250;   Hun-kah; ---; M; Son; 10 mo.

251;   Lah-tah-sah; ---; F; Head; 47

252;   ---; John Kenny; M; Head; 24
253;   Wah-hrah-lum-pah; ---; F; Wife; 21

254;   ---; Orlando Kenworthy; M; Head; 31

Census of the __Osage__ Indians of __Osage__ Agency __Oklahoma__ taken By __Ret Millard__, United States Indian Agent, during the First Quarter, 1908[sic](?)**1907?**

Key: NUMBER; Indian Name; English Name; Sex; Relation; Age
* An Askerisk will be next to a number if repeated or out of sequence and inserted among a different family.

255; ---; Nellie Buffalo; F; Wife; 22

256; ---; Tony Townsend; M; Head; 27

257; Hun-kah-hop-py; ---; M; Head; 38
258; Hun-kah-hop-py; William; M; S. Son; 16
259; He-ah-to-me; Mary; F; Daut; 12
260; Wah-hrah-lum-pah; Rosa; F; Daut; 10

261; ---; Jack Hartley; M; Head; 31

262; Nah-hah-scah-she; ---; F; Head; 53

263; Wah-tsa-ki-he-kah (Blind); ---; M; Head; 36
264; We-heh; ---; F; Daut; 12
265; Wah-to-sah; ---; F; Daut; 6

266; ---; Julia Dunlap; F; Daut; 9

BIG HILL BAND.

267; To-wah-e-he; ---; M; Head; 51

268; ---; Alfred McKinley; M; Head; 19
269; ---; Adelia; F; Wife; 19
270; Eu-pah-shon-kah-me; ---; F; Daut; 7

271; ---; Daniel McDougan; M; Head; 37

272; ---; Ben Harrison; M; Head; 35
273; ---; Edna M. Harvey; F; S. Daut; 12
274; ---; Emily Harrison; F; Daut; 9
275; ---; Ben H. Harrison; M; Son; 5
276; ---; Wauneta E.; F; Daut; 2

277; Ne-kah-e-se-y; Jimmy; M; Head; 61
278; ---; Lizzie Q; F; Wife; 58
279; Me-se-moie; Minnie Kyle; F; Daut; 17
280; Wah-shah-she; Rita Kyle; F; Daut; 16

281; ---; Mollie Kyle; F; Head; 20

282; Ke-ne-kah; ---; M; Head; 70

283; A-non-to-op-pe; ---; F; Head; 58

Census of the **Osage** Indians of **Osage** Agency **Oklahoma** taken
By **Ret Millard**, United States Indian Agent, during the First Quarter,
1908[sic](?)**1907?**

Key: NUMBER; Indian Name; English Name; Sex; Relation; Age
* An Askerisk will be next to a number if repeated or out of sequence and inserted among a different family.

284; Pah-pah-ah-hah; Thos. Dorry; M; Ward; 15
285; Num-pah-se; ---; M; Ward; 6

286; ---; Earnest Roe; M; Head; 35

287; ---; Alex Marshall; M; Head; 25

288; ---; Perry King; M; Head; 32
289; E-ne-ke-op-pe; ---; F; Wife; 32
290; Sin-tsa-wah-kon-tah; ---; M; Son; 12
291; Min-tsa-kah; ---; M; Son; 8
292; Pun-q-tah; ---; F; Daut; 5
293; Meh-e-gra-tah; ---; M; Son; 3

294; Mum-brum-pah; ---; F; Head; 82

295; Wah-hrah-lum-pah; ---; F; Head; 51
296; Hun-kah-she; Clementine P. Harris; F; Daut; 11

WHITE HAIR BAND.

297; Gra-to-me-tsa-he; ---; F; Head; 54
298; Ne-wal-la; George W. Allen; M; Son; 16

299; ---; John Claremore; M; Head; 24
300; ---; Amanda; F; Wife; 23
301; Mon-she-ah-she; ---; M; Son; 2 mo.

302; ---; Dominic Daniels; M; Head; 24

303; ---; Joseph Daniels; M; Head; 25

304; Wah-she-ho-tsa; ---; M; Head; 44
305; Gra-to-me; ---; F; Wife; 41
306; Hlu-ah-tsa-ke; John Kenworthy; M; Son; 17
307; Wah-ne-en-tah; William Kenworthy; M; Son; 14
308; Wah-shun-kah-hah; ---; M; Son; 8
309; Wah-shah-hah-me; ---; F; Daut; 2

310; E-gro-op-pe; Hall Goode; M; Head; 18

311; Wah-hrah-lum-pah (D & D); ---; F; Orphan; 12

312; Mo-se-che-he; ---; F; Head; 46
313; E-som-pah; May-Collum; F; Daut; 14

72

Census of the___**Osage**___Indians of___**Osage**___Agency___**Oklahoma**___taken
By___**Ret Millard**___, United States Indian Agent, during the First Quarter,
1908[sic](?)**1907?**

Key: NUMBER; Indian Name; English Name; Sex; Relation; Age
* An Askerisk will be next to a number if repeated or out of sequence and inserted among a different family.

314;   Wah-ke-sah-moie; ---; F; Head; 38
315;   Lah-tah-sah; Clara Collum; F; Daut; 16
316;   Ho-tah-me; Anna Collum; F; Daut; 10
317;   Hun-tsa-moie; ---; M; Son; 7

318;   ---; Joseph Mason; M; Head; 20
319;   ---; Rose; F; Wife; 22
320;   Lo-ton-tse; ---; M; Son; 2 da

321;   ---; Francis Drexil; M; Head; 30
322;   Wah-ko-sah-moie; ---; F; Wife; 31
323;   Ne-kah-ah-se; ---; F; Daut; 9
324;   Ne-tsa-kah; ---; M; Son; 5
325;   Pun-q-tah; ---; F; Daut; 1

326;   Pah-se-to-pah; ---; M; Head; 60
327;   Wah-shah-she-me-tsa-he; ---; Wife; 57

328;   ---; Angela Peace; F; Head; 20

329;   ---; Paul Peace; M; Head; 21
330;   ---; Clara Marshall; F; Wife; 21
331;   Sin-cha-wah-kon-tah; ---; F; Daut; 4 mo.

332;   ---; Henry Peace; M; Head; 24

T A L L   C H I E F   B A N D .

333;   ---; Alex Tall Chief; M; Head; 40
334;   ---; Eliza; F; Wife; 35
335;   ---; Rosa; F; Wife; 26
336;   Hlu-ah-wah-kon-tah; Alex Jr.; M; Son; 17

337;   Che-sah-me; ---; F; Head; 59

338;   He-ah-to-me; Emma; F; Head; 54

339;   ---; Eves Tall Chief; M; Head; 29
340;   Wah-shah-hah-me; ---; F; Wife; 27
341;   ---; Helen; F; Daut; 2
   342;   ---; Henry Tall Chief; M; Son; 1

343;   Me-hun-kah; ---; F; Head; 23
344;   Ho-tah-moie; John Stink; M; Head; 44

73

Census of the __Osage__ Indians of __Osage__ Agency __Oklahoma__ taken
By_____**Ret Millard**_____, United States Indian Agent, during the First Quarter,
1908**[sic]**(?)**1907?**

Key: NUMBER; Indian Name; English Name; Sex; Relation; Age
* An Askerisk will be next to a number if repeated or out of sequence and inserted among a different family.

345; Wah-shah-hah-me; ---; M; Head; 60

346; ---; Henry Tall Chief; M; Head; 24

347; Nah-she-wal-la; ---; M; Head; 48
348; Wah-shah-she-me-tsa-he; Mattie Walsh; F; Daut; 17

349; ---; Tilton Entokah; M; Head; 27
350; Pah-she-he; Grace; F; Wife; 22
351; He-ah-to-me; ---; F; Daut; 2

K O – S H E – W A H – T S E B A N D .

352; He-lo-ki-he; Bare Legs; M; Head; 69

Ko-she-wah-tse Band--

353; He-se-moie; ---; M; Head; 58
354; Tsa-me-tsa; Mary Buffalo; F; Daut; 8

355; ---; Charles Grant; M; Head; 34

356; Wah-tsa-e-c-she; ---; F; Head; 58
357; ---; George Dunlap; M; Nephew; 12

358; En-to-kah-wah-ti-an-kah; ---; M; Head; 71
359; Shon-shin-kah; Bryan Wilson; M; Son; 14
360; E-to-hun-kah; ---; M; Son; 7

361; Kah-wah-ho-tsa (Sassamoie); ---; M; Head; 39
362; Wah-ko-ki-he-kah; ---; F; Wife; 41
363; Wah-to-sah-grah; ---; F; Wife; 39
364; Ah-kah-me-tsa-he; Eva McKinley; F; Daut; 16
365; Lah-su-sah-pah; Henry McKinley; M; Son; 16
366; Ah-kah; James McKinley; M; Son; 13
367; Tah-tsa-hu-hah; William McKinley; M; Son; 11
368; Wah-hu-sah; ---; F; Daut; 7
369; Gre-scah; ---; M; Son; 7 mo
370; Ah-kah-me; ---; F; Daut; 10 da.

371; ---; Josephine McKinley; F; Head; 19

372; Ne-wal-la (Tsa-shin-kah); ---; M; Head; 41
373; Me-tsa-he; ---; F; Wife; 31
374; Hlu-ah-to-me; ---; F; Daut; 4

Census of the___**Osage**___Indians of___**Osage**___Agency___**Oklahoma**___taken
By_____**Ret Millard**_____, United States Indian Agent, during the First Quarter,
1908**[sic]**(?)**1907?**

Key: NUMBER; Indian Name; English Name; Sex; Relation; Age
* An Askerisk will be next to a number if repeated or out of sequence and inserted among a different family.

375; To-wah-e-he; ---; M; Son; 8 mo.

376; Son-se-gra; ---; F; Head; 30

377; Wah-ko-ki-he-kah; ---; F; Head; 53
378; Wah-tsa-moie; John Hunter; M; Son; 15
379; Wah-ko-sah-moie; Mary Hunter; F; Daut; 11

380; ---; Magdaline Hunter; F; Head; 19

BLACK DOG BAND.

381; ---; Black Dog; M; Head; 60
382; Gra-to-me-tsa-he; Louisa; F; Wife; 27

383; ---; Edgar McCarthy; M; Head; 34
384; ---; Nettie; F; Wife; 24

385; To-wah-e-he; ---; M; Head; 83
386; Mo-shah-hah-me; ---; F; Wife; 69

387; ---; Amos Hamilton; M; Head; 35
388; ---; Noah; M; Son; 5
389; ---; Ira; M; Son; 3
390; ---; Otto Hamilton; M; Son; 6 da.

391; Gra-tah-me-tsa-hah; ---; F; Head; 27
392; Wah-tsa-ah-tah; James McKinley; M; Son; 12
393; Mah-sah; Walter McKinley; M; Son; 9
394; He-ah-to-me; ---; F; Daut; 8

395; Me-ho-e; ---; F; Head; 68

396; ---; Allison Webb; M; Head; 23

397; He-lo-ki-he; Long Bow; M; Head; 40
398; E-gro-tah; Charles Pettus; M; Son; 17

399; ---; Myron Bangs; M; Head; 26
400; Wah-sop-py; Lucy Hah-moie; F; Wife; 23
401; ---; Percy Bangs; M; Son; 11 mo.

402; ---; Silas Sanford; M; Head; 30
403; ---; Anna; F; Wife; 25

75

Census of the **Osage** Indians of **Osage** Agency **Oklahoma** taken
By **Ret Millard**, United States Indian Agent, during the First Quarter,
1908**[sic]**(?)**1907?**

Key: NUMBER; Indian Name; English Name; Sex; Relation; Age
* An Askerisk will be next to a number if repeated or out of sequence and inserted among a different family.

404; ---; Allen Webb; M; Head; 27
405; Hum-pah-to-kah; ---; F; Wife; 19
406; Gro-tah-scah; ---; M; Son; 3
407; ---; Bertha Webb; F; Daut; 11 mo.

408; ---; Willie McCarthy (Incompt.); M; Head; 26

409; ---; Andrew Jackson; M; Head; 38
410; Me-tsa-he; Maud Hah-moie; F; Daut; 13

SAUCY CHIEF BAND.

411; ---; Lawrence; M; Head; 53

412; Wah-she-shah; Martha Neal; F; Wife; 16

413; Wah-hu-sah-he; ---; F; Head; 71

414; ---; Joseph Mills; M; Head; 18

415; ---; Alex Eagle Feather; M; Head; 34

416; Wah-te-sah; ---; F; Head; 66
417; Gra-to-me-tsa-he; Ida Gibson; F; Ward; 12

418; ---; Prudie Martin; F; Head; 32
419; ---; Christine; F; Daut; 4
420; ---; Cecil; M; Son; 1

421; ---; James G. Blaine; M; Head; 54
422; ---; Walker Blaine; M; Son; 11

423; E-ne-op-pe; ---; F; Wife; 26
424; ---; Eugene Blaine; M; Son; 7
425; He-shah-he; ---; F; Daut; 5
426; ---; James G. Blaine Jr.; M; Son; 3

427; ---; Sophia Chouteau; F; Head; 65

428; ---; Hayes Little Bear; M; Head; 22
429; Lo-hah-me; ---; F; Wife; 19

430; Ah-hu-shin-kah; ---; M; Head; 47
431; Nah-hah-sah-me; ---; F; Wife; 60

76

Census of the **Osage** Indians of **Osage** Agency **Oklahoma** taken
By **Ret Millard**, United States Indian Agent, during the First Quarter,
1908[sic](?)**1907?**

Key: NUMBER; Indian Name; English Name; Sex; Relation; Age
* An Askerisk will be next to a number if repeated or out of sequence and inserted among a different family.

432; ---; Chouteau Augustine; F; Head; 31
433; ---; Strike Axe, Josephine; F; Daut; 13
434; ---; Chouteau Augustus; M; Son; 12
435; ---; Chouteau, Charles; M; Son; 9

436; ---; Chouteau, Rose; F; Orphan; 16

437; ---; Panther, Robert; M; Head; 44
438; ---; Charles; M; Son; 17
439; ---; Clark; M; Son; 15

440; ---; Panther, Nellie; F; Daut; 13
441; ---; Maude; F; Daut; 10

442; ---; John Strait; M; Head; 54

443; ---; Mary Pryor; F; Wife; 56

444; ---; Edna Goodbear; F; Head; 35

445; Charles Me-she-tsa-he; ---; M; Head; 48
446; Wah-ko-sah-moie; ---; F; Wife; 53
447; Hlu-ah-me; ---; F; Daut; 15
448; Pah-she-he; Emma Hoover; F; Daut; 11

449; ---; Mizer, Sarah; F; Head; 32

450; Ben-Mushunkashey; ---; M; Head; 24
451; Hlu-ah-me-tsa-he; Edna; F; Wife; 19
452; ---; Charley; M; Son; 2 mo.

453; ---; William Pryor; M; Head; 32
454; Min-kah-she; Mary; F; Wife; 34
455; ---; Josephine; F; Daut; 7
456; ---; John; M; Son; 4
457; Shon-kah; Charles Mushunkashey; M; S. Son; 11

458; ---; Susie L. Hutchinson; F; Head; 25
459; ---; Vernie L.; F; Daut; 6
460; ---; Charles V.; M; Son; 4
461; ---; Carlos H; M; Son; 2

462; Ke-lo-kom-pah; ---; M; Head; 57

463; Mo-se-che-he; ---; F; Head; 52

77

Census of the **Osage** Indians of **Osage** Agency **Oklahoma** taken
By **Ret Millard** , United States Indian Agent, during the First Quarter,
1908**[sic]**(?)**1907?**

Key: NUMBER; Indian Name; English Name; Sex; Relation; Age
* An Askerisk will be next to a number if repeated or out of sequence and inserted among a different family.

464; Wah-kon-te-ah; Wakon Iron; M; Nephew; 16

465; ---; Paul Albert; M; Head; 38
466; ---; Annie Albert; F; Wife; 23
467; Hlu-ah-me-tsa-he; ---; F; Daut; 5 mo.

468; Pah-she-he; ---; F; Head; 47

469; Hum-pah-to-kah; ---; F; Head; 53

470; ---; George Albert; M; Head; 21

471; Wah-shah-she-me-tsa-he; Augustine Black; F; Head; 34
472; Hum-me-tsa-he; May; F; Daut; 9 mo.

473; Me-shah-he; ---; F; Head; 54

474; ---; Harry Kohpay; M; Head; 35
475; ---; Elsie; F; Daut; 8
476; ---; Hugh; M; Son; 7
477; ---; Lizzie; F; Daut; 4
478; ---; Loretto; M; Son; 5 mo.

479; Wy-e-gla-in-kah; Red Corn; M; Head; 53
480; Wah-kon-tah-he-um-pah; ---; F; Wife; 56
481; Wah-tsa-kon-lah; Ralph Malone; M; S. Son; 15

482; ---; Raymond Red Corn; M; Head; 21

483; Tsa-pah-ke-ah; ---; M; Head; 58
484; Hlu-ah-me-tsa-he; ---; F; Wife; 55
485; Kah-shin-kah; James Black; M; Son; 17

486; ---; Pearl Hartley; F; Head; 27

487; Heh-gah-hah-scah; Charles WhiteTail; M; Head; 53
488; ---; Julia; F; Wife; 61
489; ---; John Pahsu; M; Adopt. Son; 10

490; ---; Antwine Albert; M; Head; 44
491; Ne-kah-she-he (Blind); ---; F; Wife; 33
492; Wah-pah-ah-hah; Edward Elkins; M; S. Son; 10
493; Gra-to-me; Minnie Elkins; F; S. Daut; 2
494; Com-pox-she; Kate; F; Daut; 4 mo.

Census of the __Osage__ Indians of __Osage__ Agency __Oklahoma__ taken
By_____**Ret Millard**_____, United States Indian Agent, during the First Quarter,
1908**[sic]**(?)**1907?**

Key: NUMBER; Indian Name; English Name; Sex; Relation; Age
* An Askerisk will be next to a number if repeated or out of sequence and inserted among a different family.

495; ---; Charles Michelle; M; Head; 39
496; Me-sah-e; ---; F; Wife; 35
497; ---; Ida; F; Daut; 11

498; ---; Harry Big Eagle; M; Head; 21
499; Wah-shah-hah-me; Elsie; F; Wife; 17
500; Me-tsa-he; ---; F; Daut; 1

501; ---; Sylvia Wood; F; Head; 39

502; Wah-shah-she-me-tsa-he; ---; F; Head; 83

503; Kah-wah-ho-tsa-ah-ga-ny; ---; M; Head; 52

504; ---; Harry Py-ah-hun-kah; M; Head; 20

505; ---; Charles Brave; M; Head; 29
506; Mum-brum-pah; Mary Strike Axe; F; Wife; 22
507; ---; Andrew; M; Son; 6
508; ---; Louis; M; Son; 2

509; ---; Laban Miles; M; Head; 47
510; Mo-se-che-he; Anna; F; Daut; 17
511; Wah-shah-ah-pe; Mary; F; Daut; 13
512; Pah-pah-ah-ho; Leo; M; Son; 13
513; Wah-shah-she-me-tsa-he; ---; F; Wife; 38
514; ---; Walter Penn; M; S. Son; 15
515; ---; Charles Penn; M; S. Son; 11
516; ---; Laban Miles Jr.; M; Son; 6

517; Hlu-ah-shu-tsa; John Miles; M; Head; 18

518; ---; Eddie Penn; M; Head; 18

519; ---; John Whitehorn; M; Head; 24
520; ---; Arthur; M; Son; 2

521; Hu-lah-tun-kah; Big Eagle; M; Head; 55
522; Pah-pu-son-tsa; ---; F; Wife; 57
523; Hun-kah-ah-gra; Robert Warrior; M; S. Son; 17
524; Wah-she-pah; Wash Warrior; M; S. Son; 15
525; Pah-she-he; Mary Warrior; F; S. Daut; 12

526; ---; Russell Warrior; M; Head; 23

Census of the **Osage** Indians of **Osage** Agency **Oklahoma** taken
By **Ret Millard** , United States Indian Agent, during the First Quarter,
1908[sic](?)**1907?**

Key: NUMBER; Indian Name; English Name; Sex; Relation; Age
* An Askerisk will be next to a number if repeated or out of sequence and inserted among a different family.

627;? E-stah-o-e-gre-she; ---; M; Head; 43
528; Shon-blah-scah; ---; F; Wife; 39
529; Mon-kah-he; Frank Pyahhunkah; M; Bro.-in-law; 13

BEAVER BAND.

530; ---; Bigheart James; M; Head; 65
531; ---; Rosa L.; F; Daut; 15
532; ---; Sarah L.; F; Daut; 9
533; ---; Belle L.; Daut; 4

534; Che-sho-shin-kah; Henry Red Eagle; M; Head; 58
535; ---; Rose; F; Wife; 56

536; ---; Paul Red Eagle; M; Head; 27
537; ---; Cecelia; F; Wife; 25
538; ---; Harry; M; Son; 5
539; ---; Louis; M; Son; 2
540; ---; Joseph; M; Son; 1

541; Hlu-ah-shu-tsa; Joseph Red Eagle; M; Head; 31

542; Beg-gah-she; Brave; M; Head; 73
543; ---; Mary; F; Wife; 76

544; ---; Andrew Bighorse; M; Head; 30
545; Hum-pah-to-kah; ---; F; Wife; 36
546; We-heh; Rose McDougan; F; S. Daut; 15
547; ---; Peter Bighorse; M; Son; 8
548; ---; Joseph Bighorse; M; Son; 6
549; ---; Mary Bighorse; F; Daut; 3
550; ---; Edward Bighorse; M; Son; 5

551; ---; Charles McDougan; M; Head; 19

552; ---; John Wagoshe; M; Head; 29
553; Wah-shah-she-me-tsa-he; Agnes Bigheart; F; Wife; 29
554; ---; George Vest; M; S. Son; 3
555; ---; Charles Wagoshe; M; Son; 3
556; A-non-to-op-pe; ---; F; Daut; 2
557; Wah-sah-po; ---; F; Daut; 1 mo.

558; ---; John Lookout; M; Head; 30
559; Heh-kah-mon-kah; ---; F; Wife; 21
2156;* ---; Willie Lookout; M; Son; 1 da.

80

Census of the **Osage** Indians of **Osage** Agency **Oklahoma** taken By **Ret Millard** , United States Indian Agent, during the First Quarter, 1908**[sic]**(?)**1907?**

Key: NUMBER; Indian Name; English Name; Sex; Relation; Age
* An Askerisk will be next to a number if repeated or out of sequence and inserted among a different family.

560; ---; Louis Bighorn; M; Head; 42
561; To-op-pe; Ida; F; Wife; 27
562; ---; Rosa; F; Daut; 11
563; ---; Lillie; F; Daut; 6
564; ---; Minnie; F; Daut; 3

565; ---; Paul Buffalo; M; Head; 43
566; Pah-pu-son-tsa; ---; F; Wife; 49

567; Me-sah-e; ---; F; Head; 54
568; Ah-tsa-shin-kah; Mary Wildcat; F; Daut; 9

569; Mo-ho-gla; ---; M; Head; 53
570; Me-tsa-hi-ke; ---; F; Wife; 63

571; ---; Antwine Pryor; M; Head; 27
572; A-non-to-op-pe; Frances; F; Wife; 21
573; ---; Julia; F; Daut; 2
574; ---; Susie; F; Daut; 4 mo.

575; ---; Henry Coshehe; M; Head; 34
576; Wah-kon-tah-he-um-pah; ---; F; Wife; 31
577; ---; Clem Coshehe; M; Son; 14
578; ---; John Coshehe; M; Son; 7
579; ---; George Coshehe; M; Son; 1

580; Wah-tsa-ah-tah; Ralph On Hand; M; Orphan; 16
581; He-he-kin-to-op-pe; Minnie On Hand; Orphan; 11

582; ---; John McFall; M; Head; 40
583; Gra-tah-shin-kah; Mary; F; Wife; 28
584; ---; Minnie Whitehorn; F; Sister in law; 17

585; ---; George Michelle; M; Head; 33
586; ---; Wesley W. Michelle; M; Son; 2

587; Mo-se-che-he; ---; F; Head; 67

STRIKE AXE BAND.

588; ---; Fred Lookout; M; Head; 49
589; Mo-se-che-he; Julia; F; Wife; 38
590; ---; Charles; M; Son; 15
591; ---; Frederick; M; Son; 12
592; ---; Nora; F; Daut; 7

Census of the **Osage** Indians of **Osage** Agency **Oklahoma** taken By **Ret Millard**, United States Indian Agent, during the First Quarter, 1908**[sic]**(?)**1907?**

Key: NUMBER; Indian Name; English Name; Sex; Relation; Age
* An Askerisk will be next to a number if repeated or out of sequence and inserted among a different family.

593; ---; Henry; M; Son; 1

594; ---; James Strike Axe; M; Orphan; 13

595; Wy-e-nah-she; ---; M; Head; 59

596; Tsa-shin-kah-wah-ti-an-kah; Saucy Calf; M; Head; 63

597; ---; Joseph Buffalohide; M; Head; 21
598; ---; Agnes; F; Wife; 20

599; Tom-pah-pah; ---; F; Head; 53

600; ---; Pendleton Strike Axe; M; Head; 26
601; Mo-se-che-he; ---; F; Wife; 19
602; ---; Emma; F; Daut; 3
603; ---; Ida; F; Daut; 9 mo.

604; ---; Foster Strike Axe; M; Head; 33
605; ---; Cordelia; F; Wife; 29
606; ---; Jennie; F; Daut; 11
607; ---; Emma; F; Daut; 9
608; ---; Dora; F; Daut; 1

609; ---; Louis Pryor; M; Head; 28
610; ---; Andrew; M; Son; 1

611; O-sah-ke-pah; Cap Strike Axe; M; Head; 49

612; Pah-se-to-pah (D & D); ---; M; Head; 37
613; Me-sah-e; Veva; F; Wife; 27
614; ---; Cora; F; Daut; 6
615; ---; Carrie; F; Daut; 4
616; ---; Louis; M; Son; 2

617; Me-hun-kah (He-ah-to-me); ---; Head; 57
618; Ke-nun-tah; William Shah-pah-nah-she; M; Son; 17

619; ---; Pierce St. John; M; Head; 31
620; Ke-ah-som-pah; ---; F; Wife; 33
621; Gra-tah-scah; Jacob Jump; M; S. Son; 15
622; ---; Dora; F; Daut; 5
623; ---; Herbert; M; Son; 3
624; ---; William; M; Son; 1

82

Census of the __Osage__ Indians of __Osage__ Agency __Oklahoma__ taken By____ __Ret Millard____ , United States Indian Agent, during the First Quarter, 1908[sic](?)**1907?**

Key: NUMBER; Indian Name; English Name; Sex; Relation; Age
* An Askerisk will be next to a number if repeated or out of sequence and inserted among a different family.

625;   ---; Frank Corndropper; M; Head; 59
626;   Gra-to-me-tsa-he; ---; F; Wife; 61

627;   Peh-tsa-moie; ---; M; Head; 64
628;   Wah-tsa-u-sah; ---; F; Wife; 35

629;   ---; Richard Firewalk; M; Head; 23
630;   Son-se-grah; May; F; Wife; 17

631;   Lah-blah-wal-la; Three Striker (Crazy); M; Head; 63

632;   Wy-u-hah-kah; ---; M; Head; 49
633;   Hlu-ah-me-tsa-he; ---; F; Wife; 58

634;   ---; John Oberly; M; M; Head; 27
635;   Me-tsa-he; ---; F; Wife; 25
636;   ---; Martha; F; Daut; 2
637;   A-non-to-op-pe; ---; F; Daut; 7 mo.

638;   ---; John A. Logan; M; Head; 34
639;   ---; Mary; F; Wife; 29
640;   ---; Joseph; M; Son; 8
641;   ---; Oscar; M; Son; 6
642;   ---; Rosa; F; Daut; 2

N E – K A H – K E – P A H – N E   B A N D .

643;   Ah-she-gah-hre; Robert; M; Head; 57
644;   Gra-to-me-tsa-he; ---; F; Wife; 51
645;   Me-tun-kah; Susan Killon; F; Daut; 17
646;   Vah-sah-pah-shin; ---; F; Daut; 2

647;   Ke-mo-hah; ---; M; Head; 48
648;   Lo-tah-sah; ---; F; Wife; 32
   649;   Me-tsa-he; Elda Townsend; F; S. Daut; 15
650;   ---; John R. Townsend; M; S. Son; 10
651;   Hun-kah-me; ---; F; Daut; 8
652;   He-mo-sah; ---; M; Son; 7
653;   Mo-e-kah-scah; ---; M; Son; 5
654;   Mon-shon-kah-heh; ---; M; Son; 3
655;   ---; Ralph; M; Son; 1

656;   Tsa-e-kon-lah (Crazy); ---; F; Head; 63

657;   ---; Clarence Gray; M; Head; 30

83

Census of the___**Osage**___Indians of___**Osage**___Agency___**Oklahoma**___taken
By_____**Ret Millard**_____, United States Indian Agent, during the First Quarter,
1908**[sic]**(?)**1907?**

Key: NUMBER; Indian Name; English Name; Sex; Relation; Age
* An Askerisk will be next to a number if repeated or out of sequence and inserted among a different family.

658; He-kin-to-op-pe; ---; F; Wife; 20
659; ---; Mary; F; Daut; 3
660; ---; Clarence Jr.; M; Son; 3 mo.

661; Tsa-pah-shin-kah; John; M; Head; 53
662; Wah-shah-pe-wah-ke; ---; F; Wife; 57
663; E-to-wah-hrah-lum-pah; Mary Brown; F; Daut; 12

664; ---; Charles Brown; M; Head; 19

665; ---; David Copperfield; M; Head; 31
666; Hun-kah-me-tsa-he; Maggie; F; Wife; 33
667; Me-tsa-he; ---; F; Daut; 7
668; Hun-kah-she; ---; M; Son; 5
669; Hun-kah-ah-gra; ---; M; Son; 2
670; Wah-she-pah; ---; M; Son; 1
671; ---; William Pitts; M; Head; 30
672; Me-tsa-he; Isabella; F; Wife; 29
673; ---; George Treadway Pitts; M; Son; 2

674; Hun-kah-tun-kah; Roma Logan; M; Head; 47
675; Pah-she-he; Mary; F; Wife; 26
676; Me-tsa-he; Agnes; F; Daut; 11
677; Tom-pah-pe; ---; F; Daut; 5
678; Wah-tain-du-sah; ---; F; Daut; 2

679; Che-sho-shin-kah; ---; M; Head; 68
680; Hlu-ah-to-me; ---; F; Wife; 60

681; ---; Frank Lohowa; vM; Head; 22

682; Wah-kah-lah-tun-kah; ---; M; Head; 65
683; Me-tsa-he; ---; F; Wife; 67

684; A-hu-scah; Walla Fish; M; Head; 18

685; To-op-pe; ---; F; Head; 59

686; Hun-tsa-moie; ---; M; Head; 43
687; Hlu-ah-to-me; ---; F; Wife; 63

688; Mo-se-che-he; ---; F; Head; 89

Census of the __Osage__ Indians of __Osage__ Agency __Oklahoma__ taken By __Ret Millard__, United States Indian Agent, during the First Quarter, 1908[sic](?)**1907?**

Key: NUMBER; Indian Name; English Name; Sex; Relation; Age
* An Askerisk will be next to a number if repeated or out of sequence and inserted among a different family.

CLAREMORE BAND.

689; ---; Francis Claremore; M; Head; 42
690; Wah-hrah-lum-pah; ---; F; Wife; 36
691; Tsa-pah-ke-ah; Louis; M; Son; 14

692; ---; John Abbott; M; Head; 26
693; Ne-kah-she-tsa; ---; F; Wife; 23
694; Wah-shah-she-me-tsa-he; ---; F; Daut; 5

695; ---; Henry Pratt; M; Head; 35
696; Hun-kah-me; Josephine; F; Wife; 34
697; ---; Helen; F; Daut; 12
698; Gra-tah-scah; George; M; Son; 6
699; ---; Charles; M; Son; 2
700; ---; Thomas; M; Son; 2 mo.

701; Me-gra-to-me; ---; F; Head; 51

702; ---; Bishop Opah; M; Head; 23
703; Pah-hu-gra-she; ---; F; Wife; 19
704; ---; Andrew; M; Son; 8

705; ---; Charles Big Elk; M; Head; 28
706; Mo-se-che-he; Cora; F; Wife; 25
707; ---; Mary; F; Daut; 7
708; ---; Don S.; M; Son; 11

709; Gra-she-ah-tse-a; Grace Big Elk; F; Head; 33

710; Shah-pah-tse-ah- ---; M; Head; 78
711; Hlu-ah-me; ---; F; Wife; 63
712; E-ah-scah-wal-la; James Browning; M; Son; 14
713; Mon-kah-hah; John Browning; M; Son; 9

714; ---; Eugene Ware; M; Head; 31
715; Hum-pah-to-kah; ---; F; Wife; 30
716; ---; Joseph; M; Son; 8
717; ---; Mary; F; Daut; 6
718; ---; Elijah M; M; Son; 4
719; ---; Daisy L.; F; Daut; 2
720; Num-pe-se; ---; M; Son; 6 mo.

721; ---; Henry Roan; M; Head; 24
722; He-ah-to-me; ---; F; Wife; 18

Census of the __Osage__ Indians of __Osage__ Agency __Oklahoma__ taken
By __Ret Millard__, United States Indian Agent, during the First Quarter,
1908[sic](?)**1907?**

Key: NUMBER; Indian Name; English Name; Sex; Relation; Age
* An Askerisk will be next to a number if repeated or out of sequence and inserted among a different family.

723; ---; Grace; F; Daut; 11 mo.

724; ---; Arthur Bonnicastle; M; Head; 30
725; ---; Angie Bonnicastle; F; Wife; 20

726; ---; Maud Thompson; F; Head; 33
727; ---; Mary; F; Daut; 9

728; ---; Jack Wheeler; M; Head; 65
729; Nah-me-tsa-he; ---; F; Wife; 50

730; ---; Rhoda Wheeler; F; Head; 22

731; ---; Ben Wheeler; M; Head; 31

732; Tsa-me-tsa-he; Fanny Wheeler; F; Wife; 25
733; Hun-kah-hre; Fred; M; Son; 6
734; Me-tsa-he; ---; F; Daut; 10 mo.

735; ---; Nannie Naranjo; F; Head; 45
736; ---; Clara; F; Daut; 8

737; Hlu-ah-shu-tsa; Joe Red Eagle; M; Head; 37
738; Hun-kah-me; Dora; F; Wife; 29
739; Hlu-ah-shu-tsa; Frederick; M; Son; 6
740; ---; Alice Red Eagle; F; Daut; 2

741; Wah-shah-me-tsa-he; ---; F; Head; 48

742; ---; Sophia Spotted Horse; F; Head; 33

W A H – T I – A N – K A H   B A N D .

743; Wah-she-hah; Bacon Rind; M; Head; 47
744; Wah-ko-ki-he-kah; ---; F; Wife; 41
745; In-gro-tah; George Bacon; M; Son; 16
746; Ah-tsa-shin-kah; Louise; F; Daut; 10
747; Mah-hu-scah; Moses Bacon; M; Son; 6
748; ---; Julia Bacon Rind; F; Daut; 4
749; Mo-sah-mum-pah; ---; M; Head; 40
750; Hun-kah-me; ---; F; Wife; 34
751; Ki-he-kah-tun-kah; ---; M; son; 11

752; To-wah-e-he; ---; M; Head; 62

86

Census of the __Osage__ Indians of __Osage__ Agency __Oklahoma__ taken By ____Ret Millard____, United States Indian Agent, during the First Quarter, 1908[sic](?)**1907?**

Key: NUMBER; Indian Name; English Name; Sex; Relation; Age
* An Askerisk will be next to a number if repeated or out of sequence and inserted among a different family.

753; Gra-to-se-me; ---; F; Wife; 51

754; She-she; ---; M; Head; 48
755; Ne-kah; ---; F; Aife[sic]; 61

756; ---; Simon Henderson; M; Head; 25
757; ---; Louisa; F; Wife; 21
758; He-ah-to-me; ---; F; Daut; 1
759; Mon-sha-tsa-e-tah; ---; F; Daut; 1 mo.

760; ---; Howard Buffalo; M; Head; 47

761; ---; George Pitts; M; Head; 26
762; ---; Mary; F; Wife; 21
763; ---; Warren; M; Son; 4
764; ---; David; M; Son; 2
765; ---; Elizabeth; F; Daut; 1 mo.

766; Son-se-gra; ---; F; Head; 49

767; Ho-ki-ah-se; ---; M; Head; 39
768; Me-tsa-he; Louisa; F; Wife; 29
769; Wah-shah-she-me-tsa-he; Louisa; F; Daut; 11
770; To-ho-hah; ---; M; Son; 3
771; Wah-shah-me-tsa-he; ---; F; Daut; 10

WM. PENN BAND.

772; ---; Peter C. Bigheart; M; Head; 68
773; Wah-ko-ki-he-kah; ---; F; Wife; 64
774; Hlu-ah-to-me; (D & D); ---; F; Ward; 15

775; ---; George Bigheart; M; Head; 31
776; Pah-me-she-wah; ---; F; Wife; 21
777; ---; Charles; M; Son; 2
778; Um-pah-to-kah; ---; F; Daut; 7 mo.

779; ---; Claude Smith; M; Head; 33
780; Hlu-ah-to-me; Mamie; F; Wife; 24
781; Wah-tsa-me; ---; M; Son; 5
782; Hum-pah-to-kah; ---; F; Daut; 4
783; Ke-ah-som-pah; ---; F; Daut; 2

784; Wah-she-wah-hah; John Bigheart; M; Head; 41
785; Hlu-ah-to-me; ---; F; Wife; 38

Census of the **Osage** Indians of **Osage** Agency **Oklahoma** taken By **Ret Millard**, United States Indian Agent, during the First Quarter, 1908[sic](?)**1907?**

Key: NUMBER; Indian Name; English Name; Sex; Relation; Age
* An Askerisk will be next to a number if repeated or out of sequence and inserted among a different family.

786; Ne-kah-sto-kah; John; M; Son; 10
787; Wah-ko-sah-moie; ---; F; Daut; 9
788; Ne-kah-sto-wah; ---; M; Son; 6
789; Kah-scah; ---; M; Son; 3
790; Grah-e-grah-in-kah; ---; M; Son; 1

791; Wah-tsa-tun-kah; Joseph Bigheart; M; Head; 18

792; ---; Edward Bigheart; M; Head; 19

793; O-lo-hah-wal-la; ---; M; Head; 63
794; He-ah-to-me; ---; F; Wife; 46
795; Ne-wal-la; Henry Lohah; M; Son; 15
796; Ah-hu-shin-kah; Albert Lohah; M; Son; 13
797; A-non-to-op-pe; Ellen; F; Daut; 9
798; He-kah-mon-kah; Mary; F; Daut; 8
799; Tom-pah-pe-she; ---; M; Son; 2

800; ---; Laura Lohah; F; Head; 20

801; ---; Samuel Barker; M; Head; 28

802; O-lo-hah-moie; ---; M; Head; 49
803; Mo-se-che-he; ---; F; Wife; 39
804; Hlu-ah-wah-kon-tah; Robert; M; Son; 15
805; Wah-tsa-ah-tah; George; M; Son; 12
806; Wah-hrah-lum-pah; ---; F; Daut; 9
807; Num-pah-q-ah; ---; M; Son; 7
808; Me-gra-to-me; ---; F; Daut; 5
809; Moie-ke-kah-she; ---; Son; 3

810; Tah-hah-gah-hah; ---; M; Head; 43
811; Wah-hu-sah-he; ---; F; Wife; 38
812; A-kah-me; ---; F; Wife; 28
813; Shon-kah; James Maker; M; Son; 10
814; A-nah-me-tsa-he; Roy Maker; M; Son; 10
815; Ho-ke-ah-se; ---; M; Son; 3

816; ---; Ross Maker; M; Head; 19

817; ---; Edgar Maker; M; Head; 22

818; Mo-shah-ke-tah; ---; M; Head; 43

819; Tom-pah-pe; ---; M; Head; 61

88

Census of the___**Osage**___Indians of___**Osage**___Agency___**Oklahoma**___taken By_____**Ret Millard**_____, United States Indian Agent, during the First Quarter, 1908**[sic]**(?)**1907?**

Key: NUMBER; Indian Name; English Name; Sex; Relation; Age
* An Askerisk will be next to a number if repeated or out of sequence and inserted among a different family.

820; O-hun-pe-ah; John Bruce; M; Son; 17

821; ---; Albert Penn; M; Head; 37
822; ---; Dora Penn; F; Wife; 20
823; Wah-see-tah; Andrew; M; Son; 13
824; Wah-te-sah; Grace; F; Daut; 12
825; ---; Mary Penn; F; Daut; 10 mo.

826; ---; Fred Penn; M; Head; 34

827; O-ke-sah; Tom West; M; Head; 33
828; Me-tsa-he; ---; F; Wife; 34
829; ---; Frank Wood; M; S. Son; 16
830; ---; John Wood; M; S. Spn; 13
831; Mo-se-che-he; ---; F; Daut; 3
832; Hlu-ah-tse-ke; ---; M; Son; 10 mo.

833; ---; Dan G. West; M; Head; 29
834; Pah-pu-son-tsa; Fanny; F; Wife; 26
835; He-ah-to-me; Lucy; F; Daut; 6
836; ---; Howard; M.; M; Son; 1

LITTLE CHIEF BAND.

837; ---; Charles Whitehorn; M; Orphan; 17

838; ---; John Whitehorn; M; Head; 19

839; ---; James Whitehorn; M; Head; 23
840; Nah-kah-sah-me; Kate; F; Wife; 19
841; ---; Mary; F; Daut; 8
842; Hom-pah-to-kah; ---; F; Daut; 5 mo.

843; Kan-sah-ah-hre; ---; M; Head; 55
844; Wah-shah-kah-me; ---; F; Wife; 55

845; Ki-he-kah-nah-she; ---; M; Head; 44
846; Hlu-ah-to-me; Frances; F; Wife; 34
847; Wah-shah-me-tsa-he; Magella Whitehorn; F; Daut; 13
848; Hum-pah-to-kah; Tresa Whitehorn; F; Daut; 11
849; Monk-she-hop-pe; ---; M; Son; 4 mo.

850; Me-tsa-he; ---; F; Head; 41
851; Wah-shah-she-me-tsa-he; ---; F; Daut; 6
852; Ho-ho; Clarence Daniel; M; Son; 12

89

Census of the___**Osage**___Indians of___**Osage**___Agency___**Oklahoma**___taken
By_____**Ret Millard**_____, United States Indian Agent, during the First Quarter,
1908**[sic]**(?)**1907?**

Key: NUMBER; Indian Name; English Name; Sex; Relation; Age
* An Askerisk will be next to a number if repeated or out of sequence and inserted among a different family.

853; Wah-shah-she; ---; F; Daut; 4

854; He-ah-to-me; ---; F; Head; 55

855; ---; Frances Little Soldier; F; Head; 19

856; ---; Frank Little Soldier; M; Head; 22
857; Me-tsa-he; ---; F; Wife; 17

858; ---; Ellen Spurgeon; F; Head; 26

859; ---; Mary Agnes; F; Head; 25

860; Hlu-ah-wah-tah; ---; M; Head; 41
861; He-to-op-pe; ---; F; Wife; 38
862; Mah-grah-lum-pah; ---; F; Daut; 8
863; Hlu-ah-wah-kon-tah; ---; M; Son; 3
864; Wah-sha-me-tsa-he; ---; F; Daut; 2 mo.

865; Me-tsa-no; Mary Mudd; F; Head; 51
866; ---; Anna Mudd; F; Daut; 9

867; ---; Alex Mudd; M; Head; 18

868; ---; Lucy Lotson; F; Head; 30
869; ---; Lucius; M; Son; 11

870; ---; Albert Mudd; M; Head; 27

871; -- See #558 [James Lookout]

"A's" See Pages 87 & 88; [Note; For some reason the census taker placed above note in
the middle of the 1907's census for reference to a grouping of names starting once more with,
"A" on the last two pages of the census.]

871; Anderson, Skinner T.; M; Son; 13
872; ---; Ora D.; F; Daut; 9
873; ---; Noble H.; M; Son; 8

874; ---; Anderson Florence (nee Trumbly); F; Head; 18
875; ---; Appleby, Jane; F; Head;77
876; ---; Captain, Peter (Incompt); M; Son; 43

877; ---; Atkin, John D, Jr.; M; Head; 20

90

Census of the __Osage__ Indians of __Osage__ Agency __Oklahoma__ taken
By ____Ret Millard____, United States Indian Agent, during the First Quarter,
1908[sic](?)1907?

Key: NUMBER; Indian Name; English Name; Sex; Relation; Age
* An Askerisk will be next to a number if repeated or out of sequence and inserted among a different family.

878; ---; Avant, Rosalie; F; Head; 30
879; ---; Theodore R.; M; Son; 9
880; ---; Ethel; F; Daut; 6

881; ---; Barber, Ida; F; Head; 25
882; ---; Augustus; M; Son; 4
883; ---; Morris G.; M; Son; 9 mo.

884; ---; Barber, Bridget A.; F; Head; 46
885; ---; Clara M.; F; Daut; 15
886; ---; Edgar E.; M; Son; 12
887; ---; Lawrence L.; Son; 10
888; ---; Paul G.; M; Son; 7
889; ---; Lee H.; M; Son; 3

890; ---; Barker, Mary J.; F; Head; 52
891; ---; Simms, Coaina; F; Daut; 15
892; ---; Simms, Cora E.; F; Daut; 13

893; ---; Baker, John Thomas; M; Head; 38
894; ---; Monette; F; Wife; 32
895; ---; Myrtle C.; F; Daut; 11
896; ---; Morris A.; M; Son; 7
897; ---; Frank T.; M; Son; 6
898; ---; Martha B.; F; Daut; 3
899; ---; John Thomas Jr.; M; Son; 6 mo.

900; ---; Baylis, Elizabeth; F; Head; 63

901; ---; Baylis, Harry; M; Head; 23

902; ---; Bellieu, Thomas A.; M; Head; 25

903; ---; Bellieu, Walter S.; M; Head; 20
904; ---; Emmet; M; Son; 10

905; ---; Bellieu, Stella; F; Daut; 15
906; ---; Leo- F.; M; Son; 11
907; ---; Anna; F; Daut; 9
908; ---; Stephen H.; M; Son; 7

909; ---; Belmard, Eliza; F; Head; 20
910; ---; Clarence; M; Son; 7

911; ---; Beekman, Kate; F; Head; 30

91

Census of the **Osage** Indians of **Osage** Agency **Oklahoma** taken
By **Ret Millard** , United States Indian Agent, during the First Quarter,
1908**[sic]**(?)**1907?**

Key: NUMBER; Indian Name; English Name; Sex; Relation; Age
* An Askerisk will be next to a number if repeated or out of sequence and inserted among a different family.

912; ---; Sybil F.; F; Daut; 2
913; ---; Gorman, Mary A.; F; Daut; 8

914; ---; Bennett, William; M; Head; 31
915; ---; Isabella; F; Wife; 26
916; ---; William E.; M; Son; 7
917; ---; Teresa; F; Daut; 3
918; ---; Irene; F; Daut; 5

919; ---; Bennett, Barbara; F; Head; 20

920; ---; Blackburn, Rachel; F; Head; 27
921; ---; Oliver O.; M; Son; 7
922; ---; Luther A.; M; Son; 2

923; ---; Boulanger, Joseph; M; Head; 58
924; ---; Benjamin H.; M; Son; 17
925; ---; James V.; M; Son; 16
926; ---; Eulalie C.; F; Daut; 13
927; ---; Anna V.; F; Daut; 12
928; ---; Charles F.; M; Son; 10

929; ---; Boulanger, Grover; M; Head; 22

930; ---; Boulanger, Stephen E.; M; Head; 25
931; ---; Minnie L.; F; Daut; 6
932; ---; Augustine C.; F; Daut; 4

933; ---; Boulanger, Isaac; M; Head; 28
934; ---; Charles M.; M; Son; 7
935; ---; Alta; F; Daut; 5
936; ---; Lenora; F; Daut; 4
937; ---; Nellie; F; Daur; 2
938; ---; Sarah G.; F; Daut; 7

939; ---; Boulanger, W.J.; M; Head; 33
940; ---; Edward Mc.; M; Son; 12
941; ---; May; F; Daut; 11
942; ---; Evart; M; Son; 7

943; Bockius, Dora; F; Head; 24
944; ---; Cyril D.; M; Son; 9
945; ---; Earnest F.; M; Son; 6
946; ---; Mary B.; F; Daut; 4
947; ---; Milton J.; M; Son; 9

Census of the **Osage** Indians of **Osage** Agency **Oklahoma** taken
By **Ret Millard** , United States Indian Agent, during the First Quarter,
1908**[sic]**(?)**1907?**

Key: NUMBER; Indian Name; English Name; Sex; Relation; Age
* An Askerisk will be next to a number if repeated or out of sequence and inserted among a different family.

948; ---; Boren Blanche; F; Head; 21
949; ---; Kathleen; F; Daut; 2
950; ---; Evaleen; F; Daut; 2

951; ---; Bowhan, Ida M.; F; Head; 26
952; ---; Francis D.; M; Son; 6
953; ---; Sewel C.; M; Son; 3
954; ---; Erin S.; M; Son; 1

955; ---; Bowhan, Marie B.; F; Head; 21
956; ---; John C.; M; Son; 2

957; ---; Bowman, Rosetta; F; Head; 20
958; ---; Mildred L.; F; Daut; 3
959; ---; Ben; M; Son; 1

960; ---; Brock, Lavaria; F; Head; 27
961; ---; Winona V.; F; Daut; 4 mo.

962; ---; Bradshaw, Rose E.; F; 33
963; ---; Thomas S.; M; Son; 16
964; ---; Harry A.; M; Son; 13
965; ---; Alvin S.; M; Son; 11
966; ---; Sarah A.; F; Daut; 9
967; ---; Greta E.; F; Daut; 7
968; ---; Alva F; F; Daut; 5
969; ---; Irene A.; F; Daut; 3
970; ---; George W.; M; Son; 10 mo.

971; ---; Brown, Mable; F; Head; 21

972; ---; Brown, Charles; M; Head; 46
973; ---; Bernice; F; Daut; 15
974; ---; Treva; F; Daut; 9

975; ---; Brown, Edward; M; Head; 40

976; ---; Brown, Earnest; M; Head; 35
977; ---; Maude; F; Daut; 12
978; ---; Laura J.; F; Daut; 9
979; ---; William P.; M; Son; 8
980; ---; Lula B.; F; Daut; 3
981; ---; Helen M.; F; Daut; 6 MO.

982; ---; Brown, A.H.; M; Head; 47

Census of the__Osage__Indians of__Osage__Agency__Oklahoma__taken
By_____Ret Millard_____, United States Indian Agent, during the First Quarter,
1908[sic](?)1907?

Key: NUMBER; Indian Name; English Name; Sex; Relation; Age
* An Askerisk will be next to a number if repeated or out of sequence and inserted among a different family.

983;   ---; William S.; M; Son; 5
984;   ---; Frank R.; M; Son; 2

985;   ---; Brown, Mary J.; F; Head; 40
986;   ---; Edith; F; Daut; 14
987;   ---; Louis M.; M; Son; 12

988;   ---; Brunt Edward; M; Head; 47
989;   ---; George E.; M; Son; 16
990;   ---; Joseph L.; M; Son; 8

991;   ---; Brunt, Theodore; M; Head; 21

992;   ---; Bruce, Elsie F.; F; Head; 37
993;   ---; Bessie; F; Daut; 17
994;   ---; Louisa; F; Daut; 13
995;   ---; Lena; F; Daut; 11

996;   ---; Bruce, Adelbert; M; Son; 16

997;   ---; Bratton, Josephine; F; Head; 27
998;   ---; William E.; M; Son; 8
999;   ---; Edmund S.; M; Son; 5
1000;   ---; John I.; M; Son; 2

1001;   ---; Breeding, Mary L.; F; Head; 42
1002;   ---; Leta M.; F; Daut; 12
1003;   ---; Frances; F; Daut; 10
1004;   ---; Elsie E.; F; Daut; 7

1005;   ---; Brooks, Philomina; F; Head; 27
1006;   ---; Sylvester; M; Son; 9
1007;   ---; Dollretta; F; Daut; 8
1008;   ---; Ruby A.; F; Daut; 6
1009;   ---; Del Orier; M; Son; 3

1010;   ---; Bryant, Joe; M; Head; 55
1011;   ---; Frank; M; Son; 13
1012;   ---; Della M.; F; Daut; 12
1013;   ---; Carrie M.; F; Daut; 10
1014;   ---; Cecil; M; Son; 8
1015;   ---; Arthur; M; Son; 7
1016;   ---; Anna B.; F; Daut; 4
1017;   ---; Arena; F; Daut; 2

Census of the __Osage__ Indians of __Osage__ Agency __Oklahoma__ taken By __Ret Millard__, United States Indian Agent, during the First Quarter, 1908[sic](?)1907?

Key: NUMBER; Indian Name; English Name; Sex; Relation; Age

* An Askerisk will be next to a number if repeated or out of sequence and inserted among a different family.

1018; ---; Burton, Roy B.; M; Son; 11

1019; ---; Carr, Nelson; M; Son; 11
1020; ---; Gussie M.; F; Daut; 7

1021; ---; Carr, Gertrude; F; Head; 27

1022; ---; Carpenter, Mary E.; F; Head; 37
1023; ---; Floyd H.; M; Son; 15
1024; ---; Charles E.; M; Son; 12
1025; ---; Rose B.; F; Daut; 10
1026; ---; Louis S.; M; Son; 8

1027; ---; Carter, Alva E.; M; Son; 9
1028; ---; Leota M.; F; Daut; 7
1029; ---; Barton D.; M; Son; 13
1030; ---; Charles A.; M; Son; 11

1031; ---; Callahan, Alfred; M; Head; 24

1032; ---; Callahan, Cornelius; M; Head; 32

1033; ---; Callahan, Julia; F; Head; 25
1034; ---; Rosemary; F; Daut; 1

1035; ---; Callahan, William; M; Head; 29

1036; ---; Callahan, Leo; M; Son; 9
1037; ---; Charles; M; Son; 7
1038; ---; Mary; F; Daut; 6
1039; ---; Gertrude; F; Daut; 4

1040; ---; Canville, Clara; F; Daut; 10
1041; ---; John B.; M; Son; 6
1042; ---; Agnes L.; F; Daut; 4

1043; ---; Canville, Pascal; M; Head; 56
1044; ---; Cecil; M; M; Son; 9
1045; ---; John; M; Son; 13
1046; ---; Aouda; F; Daut; 3

1047; ---; Carlton, Anthony; M; Head; 35
1048; ---; Mary E; F; Wife; 26
1049; ---; Eva M.; F; Daut; 9
1050; ---; Ethel; F; Daut; 8

Census of the **Osage** Indians of **Osage** Agency **Oklahoma** taken
By **Ret Millard** , United States Indian Agent, during the First Quarter,
1908**[sic]**(?)**1907?**

Key: NUMBER; Indian Name; English Name; Sex; Relation; Age
* An Askerisk will be next to a number if repeated or out of sequence and inserted among a different family.

1051; ---; Frances; F;Daut; 6

1052; ---; Carlton, George; M; Head; 30
1053; ---; Augustine; F; Daut; 7
1054; ---; Robert; M; Son; 5
1055; ---; Mary E.; F; Daut; 3
1056; ---; George Jr.; M; Son; 2
1057; ---; Ella; F; Daut; 2 mo.

1058; ---; Cedar, William; M; Son; 11

1059; ---; Cedar, Paul; M; Orphan; 9

1060; ---; Cheshewalla, Evart; M; Son; 11
1061; ---; Floyd; M; Son; 8

1062; ---; Childers, Nola; F; Orphan; 8

1063; ---; Chouteau, Henry; M; Head; 22
1064; ---; Edward G.; M; Son; 6 mo.

1065; ---; Chouteau, Stewart; M; Head; 21

1066; ---; Chouteau, Louis P.; M; Head; 19

1067; ---; Clem, William; M; Head; 29
1068; ---; William L.; M; Son; 7
1069; ---; John E.; M; Son; 6
1070; ---; James A.; M; Son; 3
1071; ---; Frantz: M; Son; 2

1072; ---; Clem, James J.; M; Head; 32

1073; ---; Clem Jessie M.; M[sic]; Daut; 11
1074; ---; William H.; M; Son; 9
1075; ---; James N.; M; Son; 8
1076; ---; Sallie J.; F; Daut; 4

1077; ---; Clewien, Anna; F; Head; 26
1078; ---; Clarabelle; F; Daut; 3
1079; ---; Frances; F; Daut; 5 MO
1080; ---; Clawson, Josiah G.; M; Head; 19

1081; ---; Clawson, Emma C.; F; Daut; 16

96

Census of the __Osage__ Indians of __Osage__ Agency __Oklahoma__ taken
By_____ __Ret Millard_____, United States Indian Agent, during the First Quarter,
1908[sic](?)1907?

Key: NUMBER; Indian Name; English Name; Sex; Relation; Age
* An Askerisk will be next to a number if repeated or out of sequence and inserted among a different family.

1082; ---; Thomas A.; M; Son; 12
1083; ---; George B.; M; Son; 10

1084; ---; Collins, Mary (nee Hill); F; Head; 71

1085; ---; Cooper, Ann L.; F; Head; 25
1086; ---; William O.; M; Son; 7
1087; ---; Francis; M; Son; 4
1088; ---; Edward E.; M; Son; 11 mo.

1089; ---; Connor, Woodie; M; Head; 24
1090; ---; Theil L.; F; Daut; 2

1091; ---; Cooper, George; M; Head; 37
1092; ---; Adelia; F; Daut; 6
1093; ---; Victor W.; M; Son; 2
1094; ---; Daniel I.; M; Son; 4 mo.

1095; ---; Cottingham, Ida; F; Head; 21
1096; ---; Vera L.; F; Daut; 4
1097; ---; Logan; M; Son; 2

1098; ---; Collins, Lula; F; Head; 32
1099; ---; John W.; M; Son; 8
1100; ---; Roy W.; M; Son; 8

1101; ---; Conness, Veva; F; Head; 35
1102; ---; Geneva; F; Daut; 8
1103; ---; William B.; M; Son; 2

1104; ---; Conway, Jane; F; Head; 79

1105; ---; Crouse, Isabella Fuller; F; Head; 41
1106; ---; Earl; M; Son; 15
1107; ---; Laura I; F; Daut; 11
1108; ---; Stephen M; M; Son; 8

1109; ---; Crouse, Dallas; M; Head; 21

1110; ---; Crane, Marie; F; Head; 34
1111; ---; Frankie M.; F; Daut; 8 mo.

1112; ---; Cross, Ellen; F; Head; 26
1113; ---; Lou M.; F; Daut; 7
1114; ---; Charles L.; M; Son; 4

97

Census of the___Osage___Indians of___Osage___Agency___Oklahoma___taken
By___Ret Millard___, United States Indian Agent, during the First Quarter,
1908[sic](?)1907?

Key: NUMBER; Indian Name; English Name; Sex; Relation; Age
* An Askerisk will be next to a number if repeated or out of sequence and inserted among a different family.

1115; ---; Candie J.; F; Daut; 4 mo.

1116; ---; Cunningham, Laura; F; Head; 33
1117; ---; Edward R.; M; Son; 8

1118; ---; Cunningham, Rose I.; F; Head; 37
1119; ---; Robert B.; M; Son; 8

1120; ---; Cunningham, John M.; M; Head; 19

1121; ---; Curtis, Mary; F; Head; 50
1122; ---; Farrell, Virgil; M; Son; 16
1123; ---; Curtis, Lethia B.; F; Daut; 12
1124; ---; Ada; F; Daut; 9

1125; ---; Daniel, Sophia; F; Head; 31
1126; ---; Bessie; F; Daut; 13
1127; ---; Vernie; M; Son; 11
1128; ---; Pearl C.; M; Son; 9
1129; ---; Ida I.; F; Daut; 6

1130; ---; Davis, Sophia; F; Head; 66

1131; ---; Davis, Mary J.; F; Head; 58

1132; ---; Dailey, Dora; F; Head; 25
1133; ---; Dial, Elsie A.; F; Daut; 8
1134; ---; Lawton W.; M; Son; 6

1135; ---; Darnell, Rebecca J.; F; Head; 44
1136; ---; Vadney, May V.; F; Daut; 16

1137; ---; Dennison, Eliza; F; Head; 38
1138; ---; Fugate, Frank E.; M; Son; 17
1139; ---; John A.; M; Son; 16
1140; ---; Dennison, Nellie; F; Daut; 6
1141; ---; George O.; M; Son; 2

1142; ---; Dennison, Bert; M; Head; 22
1143; ---; Florence L.; F; Daut; 3 mo.

1144; ---; Del Orier, Julia; F; Head; 57

1145; ---; Del Orier, Virgil L.; M; Head; 22
1146; ---; Louis; M; Son; 1

98

Census of the __ **Osage** __ Indians of __ **Osage** __ Agency __ **Oklahoma** __ taken
By __ **Ret Millard** __, United States Indian Agent, during the First Quarter,
1908[sic](?)**1907?**

Key: NUMBER; Indian Name; English Name; Sex; Relation; Age
* An Askerisk will be next to a number if repeated or out of sequence and inserted among a different family.

1147; ---; DeNoya, Louis; M; Head; 46
1148; ---; Frederick; M; Son; 15
1149; ---; Clement; M; son; 13
1150; ---; Josephine; F; Daut; 11
1151; ---; Ruby P.; F; Daut; 9

1152; ---; Denoya, Everett A.; M; Head; 20

1153; ---; DeNoya, Frank; M; Head; 50
1154; ---; James E.D.; M; Son; 17
1155; ---; Clara; F; Daut; 16
1156; ---; Grace; F; Daut; 14
1157; ---; Alfred Raymond; M; Son; 13
1158; ---; Charlotte; F; Daut; 11
1159; ---; Myrtle; F; Daut; 9
1160; ---; Catherine I.; F; Daut; 4
1161; ---; Walter; M; Son; 1

1162; ---; DeNoya, Jacob; M; Head; 28
1163; ---; Belle; F; Wife; 27
1164; ---; Virgil H.; M; Son; 6
1165; ---; Maurice H.; M; Son; 4
1166; ---; Lillian C.; F; Daut; 3
1167; ---; Helen; F; Daut; 1

1168; ---; DeNoya, Joseph; M; Head; 30
1169; ---; Charlotte; F; Daut; 3
1170; ---; Margaret I.; F; Daut; 4
1171; ---; Martha M.; F; Daut; 2

1172; ---; DeNoya, Clement; M; Head; 40
1173; ---; Emily; F; Wife; 36
1174; ---; Clement Jr.; M; Son; 17
1175; ---; Wesley; M; Son; 16
1176; ---; Louis; M; Son; 13
1177; ---; Sadie; F; Daut; 11
1178; ---; Elsie; F; Daut; 9
1179; ---; Edna; F; Daut; 6
1180; ---; Elizabeth; F; Daut; 3
1181; ---; Millard; M; Son; 2

1182; ---; Deal, Joseph; M; Head; 24
1183; ---; Mary J.; F; Wife; 18
1184; ---; James C.; M; Son; 1

Census of the __Osage__ Indians of __Osage__ Agency __Oklahoma__ taken By __Ret Millard__ , United States Indian Agent, during the First Quarter, 1908**[sic]**(?)**1907?**

Key: NUMBER; Indian Name; English Name; Sex; Relation; Age
* An Askerisk will be next to a number if repeated or out of sequence and inserted among a different family.

1185; ---; Deal, Julia A.; F; Head; 52
1186; ---; Harrelson, Mary L. (Incompt); Daut; 27
1187; ---; Emerine; F; G. Daut; 9
1188; ---; Deal, Sherman; M; Son; 16

1189; ---; Dickey, James A.; M; Head; 26

1190; ---; Dickey, John T.; M; Head; 23

1191; ---' Dial, Eliza; F; Head; 47
1192; ---; Penn, Augustus; M; Son; 17
1193; ---; Rose E.; F; Daut; 15
1194; ---; Dial, Cora E.; F; Daut; 10
1195; ---; Eva; F; Daut; 8
1196; ---; Charles P.; M; Son; 2
1197; ---; Huston, J.R.; M; Adpt. Son; 16

1198; ---; Donelson, Frances; M; Head; 24
1199; ---; James L.; M; Son; 8
1200; ---; Robert L.; M; Son; 6

1201; ---; Doolin, Martha; F; Head; 24
1202; ---; Alta Josephine; F; Daut; 1 mo.

1203; ---; Donovan, Augustine; F; Head; 55
1204; ---; Jesse; M; Son; 14

1205; ---; Donovan, Charles; M; Head; 18

1206; ---; Ducotey, Stanislus; M; Head; 33
1207; ---; Versa; F; Daut; 9
1208; ---; Manza; F; Daut; 7
1209; ---; Bettie V.; F; Daut; 4
1210; ---; Frank S.; M; Son; 2

1211; ---; Dunn, Dora; F; Head; 29
1212; ---; Ida M.; F; Daut; 11
1213; ---; Mary A.; F; Daut; 9
1214; ---; Timothy J.; M; Son; 4

1215; ---; Dunham, Martha; F; Head; 77

1216; ---; Easley, Margaret; F; Head; 35
1217; ---; Pearl; F; Daut; 15
1218; ---; George E.; M; Son; 13

Census of the **Osage** Indians of **Osage** Agency **Oklahoma** taken
By **Ret Millard** , United States Indian Agent, during the First Quarter,
1908[sic](?)**1907?**

Key: NUMBER; Indian Name; English Name; Sex; Relation; Age
* An Askerisk will be next to a number if repeated or out of sequence and inserted among a different family.

1219; ---; Leo B.; M; Son; 11
1220; ---; John W.; M; Son; 9
1221; ---; Mary E.; F; Daut; 6
1222; ---; Clarence A.; M; Son; 3
1223; ---; Robert J.; M; Son; 4 mo.

1224; ---; Edwards, Julia; F; Head; 41
1225; ---; Quinton, Lillie; F; Daut; 15
1226; ---; Agnes; F; Daut; 11
1227; ---; Pearl C.; F; Daut; 9
1228; ---; Elnora; F; Daut; 5
1229; ---; Edwards, Theodore; M; Son; 2 mo.

1330; ---; Edmiston, Frances (Imcompt[sic]); F; Head; 31

1231; ---; Edmiston, Bessie E.; F; Daut; 5

1232; ---; Evans, Mary (nee Gaylor); F; Head; 21

1233; ---; Farrell, Nathaniel; M; Head; 30
1234; ---; Ruth; F; Daut; 7
1235; ---; Andrew; M; Son; 4

1236; ---; Farrell, Charles; M; Head; 25
1237; ---; Mary; F; Daut; 3
1238; ---; Pearl; F; Daut; 4 mo.

1239; ---; Farrell, Monica; F; Head; 52
1240; ---; Moses R.; M; Son; 17

1241; ---; Farrell, Mary; F; Head; 18

1242; ---; Fenton, Margaret; F; Head; 24
1243; ---; Sylvester R.; M; Son; 6
1244; ---; Louis L.; M; Son; 5
1245; ---; Curtis D.; M; Son; 2

1246; ---; Fox, Susie; F; Head; 45
1247; ---; Lombard, Sylvester; M; Son; 17
1248; ---; Augustine; F; Daut; 14
1249; ---; Joseph; M; Son; 12
1250; ---; Paul; M; Son; 8
1251; ---; Fox, Alexander; M; Son; 10 mo.

1252; ---; Fronkier, Laban A.; M; Orphan; 17

Census of the___**Osage**___Indians of___**Osage**___Agency___**Oklahoma**___taken
By___**Ret Millard**___, United States Indian Agent, during the First Quarter,
1908**[sic]**(?)**1907?**

Key: NUMBER; Indian Name; English Name; Sex; Relation; Age
* An Askerisk will be next to a number if repeated or out of sequence and inserted among a different family.

1253; ---; Fronkier, William; M; Head; 36

1254; ---; Fronkier, Simon; M; Head; 35
1255; ---; Florence; F; Daut; 11
1256; ---; Blanche L.; F; Daut; 9
1257; ---; Benjamin; M; Son; 5

1258; ---; Fronkier, Philip; M; Head; 19

1259; ---; Fronkier, Augustus; M; Head; 29

1260; ---; Fronkier, James; M; Head; 28
1261; ---; Louis B.; M; Son; 1

1262; ---; Fuller, Thomas; M; Head; 26

1263; ---; Fuller, Louis; M; Head; 32
1264; ---; Andrew B.; M; Son; 5

1265; ---; Fuller, Charles; M; Head; 23

1266; ---; Gaylor, Victoria; F; Head; 42

1267; ---; George, James M.; M; Head; 24
1268; ---; James I.; M; Son; 2

1269; ---; George, Sylvester; M; Head; 23

1270; ---; George, Ruby; F; Head; 18

1271; ---; Gilmore, Mary A.; F; Head; 53
1272; ---; S.J.; M; Son; 16

1273; ---; Gilmore, William H.; M; Son; 10

1274; ---; Girard, Amelia; F; Head; 33
1275; ---; Corine A.; F; Daut; 12
1276; ---; Mary E.C.; F; Daut; 13
1277; ---; Amelia V.; F; Daut; 11
1278; ---; Leona; F; Daut; 9

1279; ---; Goad, Clara; F; Head; 27
1280; ---; Cecil J.; M; Son; 5
1281; ---; Ethel; F; Daut; 8

Census of the __Osage__ Indians of __Osage__ Agency __Oklahoma__ taken
By_____ __Ret Millard_____, United States Indian Agent, during the First Quarter,
1908**[sic]**(?)**1907?**

Key: NUMBER; Indian Name; English Name; Sex; Relation; Age
* An Askerisk will be next to a number if repeated or out of sequence and inserted among a different family.

1282; ---; Groves, Agnes; F; Head; 25
1283; ---; Mural W.; M; Son; 5
1284; ---; Mary L.; F; Daut; 3
1285; ---; Harry L.; M; Son; 4 mo.

1286; ---; Hall, Ida; F; Head; 22
1287; ---; Alfred; M; Son; 3

1288; ---; Harruff, Margaret; F; Head; 43
1289; ---; Julia M.; F; Daut; 11

1290; ---; Hardy, Emily; F; Head; 34
1291; ---; Louisa V.; F; Daut; 13
1292; ---; Goldie; F; Daut; 10
1293; ---; Geneva; F; Daut; 7
1294; ---; William R.; M; Son; 3

1295; ---; Hardy, Ora; F; Head; 27
1296; ---; Orel; M; Son; 3
1297; ---; Mary I.; F; Daut; 7 mo.

1298; ---; Hampton, Charles; M; Head; 27
1299; ---; Roland; M; Son; 2

1300; ---; Hampton, Rosalie; F; Head; 46

1301; ---; Hayes, Pearl; F; Head; 27
1302; ---; Olivia; F; Daut; 3
1303; ---; Elizabeth, F; Daut; 3
1304; ---; Margaret; F; Daut; 3

1305; ---; Harlow, Josephine; F; Head; 28
1306; ---; John N.; M; Son; 10

1307; ---; Hayes, Elnora; F; Head; 27
1308; ---; Lawrence L.; M; Son; 2

1309; ---; Harlow, Susan; F; Head; 45
1310; ---; Grace; F; Daut; 16
1311; ---; Belle; F; Daut; 13
1312; ---; Charles C.; M; Son; 9

1313; ---; Haynie, Mary; F; Head; 22
1314; ---; Willie; M; S. Son; 12
1315; ---; John C.; M; Son; 2

Census of the___Osage___Indians of___Osage___Agency___Oklahoma___taken
By_____Ret Millard_____, United States Indian Agent, during the First Quarter,
1908[sic](?)1907?

Key: NUMBER; Indian Name; English Name; Sex; Relation; Age
* An Askerisk will be next to a number if repeated or out of sequence and inserted among a different family.

1316; ---; Emma; F; Daut; 1

1317; ---; Hackleman, Julia Ann; F; Head; 62

1318; ---; Harris, Mary E.; F; Head; 26
1319; ---; Slaughter; M; Son; 9 mo.

1320; ---; Harvey, Adeline; F; Head; 26

1321; ---; Heenan; Anna; F; Head; 25
1322; ---; Beatrice M.; F; Daut; 3

1323; ---; Herard, Paul; M; Head; 39

1324; ---; Herard, Eugene; M; Head; 22

1325; ---; Herard, Minnie; F; Head; 21

1326; ---; Herridge, Myrtle; F; Head; 18
1327; ---; Herridge, Joseph; M; Son; 16
1328; ---; Lulu; F; Daut; 13

1329; ---; Hewitt, Rosa; F; Head; 21
1330; ---; Valaria; F; Daut; 1
1331; ---; Loretta M.; F; Daut; 2 mo.

1332; ---; Hildebrand, Ellen; F; Head; 60

1333; ---; Hildebrand, Susanna; F; Head; 19

1334; ---; Hildebrand, George; M; Head; 24

1335; ---; Hildebrand, Richard; M; Head; 28

1336; ---; Hildebrand, David; M; Head; 34
1337; ---; Nancy; F; Daut; 6

1338; ---; Hildebrand, James; M; Head; 38
1339; ---; Letitia; F; Daut; 15
1340; ---; Susan; F; Daut; 13
1341; ---; Orangonia B.; F; Daut; 12
1342; ---; Dica; F; Daut; 7

1343; ---; Hildebrand, Joseph; M; Head; 40
1344; ---; Frank, M; Son; 9

Census of the__**Osage**__Indians of__**Osage**__Agency__**Oklahoma**__taken
By____**Ret Millard**____, United States Indian Agent, during the First Quarter,
1908[sic](?)1907?

Key: NUMBER; Indian Name; English Name; Sex; Relation; Age
* An Askerisk will be next to a number if repeated or out of sequence and inserted among a different family.

1345; ---; Hickman, Clementine; F; Head; 31
1346; ---; Homer; M; Son; 11
1347; ---; Edna J.; F; Daut; 8
1348; ---; Franklin; M; Son; 7
1349; ---; Florence; F; Daut; 5
1350; ---; Lillie V.; F; Daut; 3
1351; ---; Bertha C.; F; Daut; 2

1352; ---; Holloway, Jasper C.; M; Head; 55

1353; ---; Holloway, Frank; M; Head; 22

1354; ---; Holloway, Milton; M; Head; 24
1355; ---; Andrew L.; M; Son; 4
1356; ---; Olita M.; F; Daut; 1

1357; ---; Horn, Polly; F; Head; 28
1358; ---; Buxbaum, Vernon E.; M; Son; 7

1359; ---; Hoots, Rosa; F; Head; 38
1360; ---; Agnes; F; Daut; 12

1361; ---; Hoots, Alfred; M; Head; 20

1362; ---; Hunt, Mary A.; F; Head; 37
1363; ---; Lulu B.; F; Daut; 10
1364; ---; Mary G.; F; Daut; 8
1365; ---; Andrew D.; M; Son; 5
1366; ---; Robert M.; M; Son; 4 mo.

1367; ---; Hunt, Antione[sic]; M; Head; 19

1368; ---; Hunt, Harold R.; M; Son; 5 mo.

1369; ---; Javine, Peter; M; Head; 55
1370; ---; Hasread; M; Son; 16
1371; ---; Viola M.; F; Daut; 13
1372; ---; Opie; F; Daut; 1

1373; ---; Javine, Benjamin H.; M; Head; 18

1374; ---; Javine, Roy V.; M; Son; 11

1375; ---; Javine, John Sr.; M; Head; 52
1376; ---; Ollie; F; Daut; 17

Census of the __Osage__ Indians of __Osage__ Agency __Oklahoma__ taken
By __Ret Millard__, United States Indian Agent, during the First Quarter,
1908[sic](?)1907?

Key: NUMBER; Indian Name; English Name; Sex; Relation; Age
* An Askerisk will be next to a number if repeated or out of sequence and inserted among a different family.

1377; ---; Audra; F; Daut; 14
1378; ---; Ora E.; F; Daut; 13
1379; ---; Joseph; M; Son; 10

1380; ---; Javine, Anthony; M; Head; 20

1381; ---; Javine, John Jr.; M; Head; 25
1382; ---; George M.; M; Son; 3
1383; ---; Earl T.; M; Son; 11 mo.

1384; ---; James, Jesse; M; Head; 19

1385; ---; Johnson, Julia M.; F; Head; 52

1386; ---; Johnson, John W.; M; Head; 18

1387; ---; Jones, Laura; F; Head; 21
1388; ---; James F.; M; Son; 2
1389; ---; Lillian Mae; F; Daut; 2 mo.

1390; ---; Kennedy, Agnes; F.; Head; 31
1391; ---; James A.; M; Son; 9
1392; ---; Forest L.; M; Son; 7
1393; ---; Thelma; F; Daut; 6
1394; ---; Cordelia A.; F; Daut; 3
1395; ---; Samuel G.; M; Son; 1

1396; ---; Kennedy, Mable; M; Head; 27
1397; ---; Albert A.; M; S. Son; 13

1398; ---; Kennedy, Adeline; F; Head; 59

1399; ---; Kennedy, Samuel; M; Head; 21

1400; ---; Keeler, Blanche; F; Head; 25
1401; ---; Dixie; M; Son; 3
1402; ---; Alberta M.; F; Daut; 1

1403; ---; Kilbie, Benedict; M; Head; 21
1404; ---; John A.; M; Son; 10 mo.

1405; ---; Krebs, Henry; M; Son; 10

1406; ---; Lawrence, Maggie; F; Head; 50

106

Census of the __Osage__ Indians of __Osage__ Agency __Oklahoma__ taken
By __Ret Millard__, United States Indian Agent, during the First Quarter,
1908**[sic]**(?)**1907?**

Key: NUMBER; Indian Name; English Name; Sex; Relation; Age
* An Askerisk will be next to a number if repeated or out of sequence and inserted among a different family.

1407; ---; Labadie, Charles; M; Head; 36
1408; ---; Hazel; F; Daut; 9
1409; ---; Frank; M; Son; 7
1410; ---; Alvin L.; Son; 5
1411; ---; Nita; F; Daut; 3
1412; ---; Arthur Milton; M; Son; 2 mo.

1413; ---; Labadie, William H.; M; Head; 22

1414; ---; Labadie, Ella; F; Head; 20

1415; ---; Labadie, Frederick; M; Son; 17
1416; ---; Earnie; M; Son; 16
1417; ---; Joseph; M; Son; 14

1418; ---; Labadie, Edward; M; Head; 41
1419; ---; Milton; M; Son; 9
1420; ---; Rose M.; F; Daut; 6
1421; ---; Robert E.; M; Son; 4
1422; ---; Charles W.; M; Son; 2

1423; ---; Labadie, Frank; M; Head; 46
1424; ---; G.V.; M; Son; 15
1425; ---; Paul F.; M; Son; 12

1426; ---; Labadie, John; M; Head; 20

1427; ---; LaBarge, Marie; F; Daut; 13
1428; ---; Louis; M; Son; 11
1429; ---; Arthur; M; Son; 10
1430; ---; Charles V.; M; Son; 8

1431; ---; LaBarge, Joseph; M; Head; 38
1432; ---; Ellen; F; Daut; 7
1433; ---; Harold L.; M; Son; 7 mo.

1434; ---; Lane, Joseph; M; Head; 38
1435; ---; Zella A.; F; Wife; 37
1436; ---; Mary; F; Daut; 13
1437; ---; Bessie; F; Daut; 9
1438; ---; Joseph C.; M; Son; 4
1439; ---; Roy B.; M; Son; 2

1440; ---; LaSarge, Minnie E.; F; Head; 18

Census of the___**Osage**___Indians of__**Osage**___Agency___**Oklahoma**___taken
By_____**Ret Millard**_____, United States Indian Agent, during the First Quarter,
1908**[sic]**(?)**1907?**

Key: NUMBER; Indian Name; English Name; Sex; Relation; Age
* An Askerisk will be next to a number if repeated or out of sequence and inserted among a different family.

1441; ---; Leahy, Mary L.; F; Head; 58

1442; ---; Leahy, Bertha; F; Head; 32
1443; ---; Thomas R.; M; Son; 10
1444; ---; Cora W.; F; Daut;8
1445; ---; Mable A.; F; Daut; 4
1446; ---; Edward A.; M; Son; 2

1447; ---; Leahy, W.T.; M; Head; 38
1448; ---; Martha; F; Wife; 29
1449; ---; William T. Jr.; M; Son; 9
1450; ---; B. Thomas; M; Son; 8

1451; ---; Lewis, Mary; F; Head; 46

1452; ---; Lessert, Frank; M; Head; 65

1453; ---; Lessert, Walter; M; Head; 22

1454; ---; Lessert, Joseph; M; Head; 23

1455; ---; Lessert; David; M; Head; 29

1456; ---; Lessert, Guy; M; Son; 11
1457; ---; Millie M.; M; Son; 9
1458; ---; Charles A.; M; Son; 7
1459; ---; Hattie; F; Daut; 5

1460; ---; Lessert, Frank Jr.; M; Head; 43
1461; ---; Mary J.; F; Daut; 12
1462; ---; Robert A.; M; Son; 10
1463; ---; Grace J.; F; Daut; 6
1464; ---; Ray L.; M; Son; 4
1465; ---; Cora L.; F; Daut; 1

1466; ---; Lessert, Benjamin; M; Head; 36
1467; ---; Wade; M; Son; 16
1468; ---; Susie; F; Daut; 11
1469; ---; Benjamin L.; M; Son; 4
1470; ---; Fay; F; Daut; 9
1471; ---; Fanny; F; Daut; 1

1472; ---; Lessert, William K.; M; Head; 18

1473; ---; Lessert, Charles; M; Head; 40

Census of the __Osage__ Indians of __Osage__ Agency __Oklahoma__ taken By_____Ret Millard_____, United States Indian Agent, during the First Quarter, 1908[sic](?)1907?

Key: NUMBER; Indian Name; English Name; Sex; Relation; Age

* An Askerisk will be next to a number if repeated or out of sequence and inserted among a different family.

1474; ---; Liese, Coenia M.; F; Head; 25
1475; ---; Washaki; M; Son; 2

1476; ---; Lohman, Nettie (nee Prudom); F; Head; 21

1477; ---; Lombard, Albert; M; Head; 61
1478; ---; Irene; F; Daut; 15
1479; ---; Bessie; F; Daut; 13
1480; ---; Robert; M; Son; 6

1481; ---; Lombard, Clara; F; Head; 21

1482; ---; Lombard, Nina; F; Head; 19

1483; ---; Lombard, John; M; Head; 23

1484; ---; Lombard, George W.; M; Head; 28

1485; ---; Lombard, John E.; M; Head; 21

1486; ---; Lombard, Walter; M; Head; 29
1487; ---; Lucy; F; Daut; 6
1488; ---; Lois; F; Daut; 4
1489; ---; Samie; F; Daut; 3

1490; ---; Lyman, Olive G.; F; Head; 44

1491; ---; Lyman, Paul S.; M; Head; 41
1492; ---; Agnes; F; Daut; 4
1493; ---; Capitola; F; Daut; 2
1494; ---; Pauline; F; Daut; 2 mo.

1495; ---; Lyman, Arthur J.; M; Head; 37

1496; ---; Lynn, Mary A.; F; Head; 30
1497; ---; John F.; M; Son; 12
1498; ---; Theresa M.; F; Daut; 8
1499; ---; Patrick; M; Son; 4
1500; ---; Joseph; M; Son; 6
1501; ---; William R.; M; Son; 1

1502; ---; Mackey, Joseph; M; Head; 29
1503; ---; Eva; F; Daut; 9
1504; ---; Tenne; F; Daut; 5
1505; ---; Agnes L.; F; Daut; 3

Census of the __Osage__ Indians of __Osage__ Agency __Oklahoma__ taken By_____**Ret Millard**_____, United States Indian Agent, during the First Quarter, 1908**[sic]**(?)**1907?**

Key: NUMBER; Indian Name; English Name; Sex; Relation; Age
* An Askerisk will be next to a number if repeated or out of sequence and inserted among a different family.

1506; ---; Warren F.; M; Son; 1

1507; ---; Mackey, William B.; M; Head; 24
1508; ---; Cecelia E.; F; Daut; 7
1509; ---; Bertha M.; F; Daut; 2

1510; ---; Mackey, Grover; M; Head; 21

1511; ---; Mann, Stella (nee Plomondon); F; Head; 18

1512; ---; Mathews, W.S.; M; Head; 59
1513; ---; John J.; M; Son; 13
1514; ---; Mary I.; F; Daut; 10
1515; ---; Lillian B.; F; Daut; 8
1516; ---; Florence; F; Daut; 5

1517; ---; Mathews, Sarah J.; F; Head; 19

1518; ---; Mathews, W.W.; M; Head; 28
1519; ---; Norman S.; M; Son; 2
1520; ---; Anna M.; F; Daut; 5 mo.

1521; ---; Mathews, John A.; M; Head; 31
1522; ---; Lorenza; F; Wife; 25
1523; ---; John A. Jr.; M; Son; 6
1524; ---; Victoria; F; Daut; 5

1525; ---; Mathews, Edward O.; M; Head; 28
1526; ---; Alfred E.; M; Son; 3

1527; ---; Mathes, Thomas S.; M; Head; 18

1528; ---; Marshall, Sarah (nee Holloway); Head; 19

1529; ---; Martin, Alex; M; Head; 61
1530; ---; Bertha; F; Daut; 12

1531; ---; Martin, Lombard; M; Head; 19

1532; ---; Martin, Lee; M; Head; 30
1533; ---; Dane L.; F; Daut; 9
1534; ---; Edgar E.; M; Son; 6
1535; ---; Linnie N.; F; Daut; 3

1536; ---; Martin, Emery; M; Head; 26

110

Census of the___**Osage**___Indians of___**Osage**___Agency___**Oklahoma**___taken
By_____**Ret Millard**_____, United States Indian Agent, during the First Quarter,
1908**[sic]**(?)**1907?**

Key: NUMBER; Indian Name; English Name; Sex; Relation; Age
* An Askerisk will be next to a number if repeated or out of sequence and inserted among a different family.

1537; ---; John D.; M; Son; 2
1538; ---; Delmas E.; M; Son; 2 mo.

1539; ---; Martin, Richard; M; Head; 33
1540; ---; Nannie V.; F; Daut; 2 mo.

1541; ---; Martin, Claude; M; Son; 10

1542; ---; Martin, James; M; M; Son; 14

1543; ---; Martin, Wilson; M; Son; 14

1544; ---; McCarthy, Lenora; F; Head; 26
1545; ---; William H.; M; Son; 6
1546; ---; Solomon; M; Son; 5
1547; ---; Edna V.; F; Daut; 2
1548; ---; Charles W.; Son; 6 mo.

1549; ---; McCoy, Lillie; F; Head; 20
1550; ---; Richard M.; M; Son; 2 mo.

1551; ---; McDaniel, Ellen; F; Head; 31
1552; ---; Frederick W.; Son; 11

1553; ---; McGath; Emma; Head; 28
1554; ---; John W.; M; Son; 10

1555; ---; McGuire, Mary E.; F; Head; 34
1556; ---; Ethel; F; Daut; 16
1557; ---; Leo; M; Son; 12
1558; ---; Bird A.; M; Son; 9
1559; ---; William T.; M; Son; 7
1560; ---; Charles A.; M; Son; 5

1561; ---; McCombs, Ellen; F; Head; 29
1562; ---; Jessie; F; Daut; 12
1563; ---; William N.; M; Son; 9
1564; ---; Gladys I.; F; Daut; 6
1565; ---; Rachel B.; F; Daut; 4
1566; ---; Naioma; F; Daut; 1

1567; ---; McLaughlin, Nancy; F; Head; 43

1568; ---; McLaughlin, Flora; F; Head; 20

Census of the__**Osage**___Indians of___**Osage**___Agency__**Oklahoma**___taken
By____**Ret Millard**____, United States Indian Agent, during the First Quarter,
1908**[sic]**(?)**1907?**

Key: NUMBER; Indian Name; English Name; Sex; Relation; Age
* An Askerisk will be next to a number if repeated or out of sequence and inserted among a different family.

1569; ---; McLintic, Mary; F; Head; 30
1570; ---; Aloysia; F; Daut; 8

1571; ---; McLain, Minnie; F; Head; 20
1572; ---; Roy S.; M; Son; 2

1573; ---; Michelle, Estella; F; Daut; 9
1574; ---; Della; F; Daut; 6

1575; ---; Mickels, Arania; F; Head; 30
1576; ---; Carr, Delilah; F; Daut; 5
1577; ---; Mickels, Clarence D.; F; Son; 2

1578; ---; Miller, Gurney; M; Orphan; 9

1579; ---; Miller, Louis S.; M; Head; 18

1580; ---; Mongrain, Rosa; F; Daut; 17

1581; ---; Mongrain, Coaina; F; Head; 57

1582; ---; Mongrain, Stewart; M; Head; 59
1583; ---; Stewart Jr.; M; Son; 14

1584; ---; Mongrain, Ernest; M; Head; 18

1885; ---; Mongrain, Hattie; F; Head; 20

1586; ---; Mosier, Thomas; M; Head; 64

1587; ---; Mosier, Adeline; F; Head; 66

1588; ---; Mosier, W.T.; M; Head; 39
1589; ---; Louisa; F; Wife; 32
1590; ---; Charles P.; M; Son; 11
1591; ---; John T.; M; Son; 8
1592; ---; Edwin P.; M; Son; 5
1593; ---; Luther P.; M; Son; 3
1594; ---; Agnes C.; F; Daut; 2

1595; ---; Mosier, Jacob; M; Head; 45
1596; ---; Mosier, Stella; F; Daut; 15
1597; ---; Claude; M; Son; 12
1598; ---; Lione; F; Daut; 9

Census of the___**Osage**___Indians of___**Osage**___Agency___**Oklahoma**___taken
By_____**Ret Millard**_____, United States Indian Agent, during the First Quarter,
1908**[sic]**(?)**1907?**

Key: NUMBER; Indian Name; English Name; Sex; Relation; Age
* An Askerisk will be next to a number if repeated or out of sequence and inserted among a different family.

1599;   ---; Mosier, Kate; F; Head; 19

1600;   ---; Mosier, Eugene; M; Head; 32
1601;   ---; Mary M.; F; Daut; 11
1602;   ---; John J.; M; Son; 5
1603;   ---; Ida M.; F; Daut; 3
1604;   ---; Walter L.; M; Son; 1

1605;   ---; Mosier, Bismark; M; Head; 24
1606;   ---; Clara O.; F; Daut; 3
1607;   ---; Thelma V.; F; Daut; 2

1608;   ---; Moore, James W.; M; Head; 2

1609;   ---; Moore, Eliza; F; Head; 18

1610;   ---; Moore, Alice; F; Daut; 16

1611;   ---; Moncravie, Charles; M; Head; 38
1612;   ---; Rosa; F; Wife; 29
1613;   ---; Augustine; F; Daut; 8
1614;   ---; Virginia M.; F; Daut; 5

1615;   ---; Moncravie, Fred; M; Head; 32

1616;   ---; Moncravie, Henry; M; Head; 34
1617;   ---; Henri E.; F; Daut; 3

1618;   ---; Moncravie, John; M; Head; 37
1619;   ---; Sylvester A.; M; Son; 14
1620;   ---; John N.; M; Son; 10
1621;   ---; Alexander C.; M; Son; 8
1622;   ---; Barada J.; M; Son; 6
1623;   ---; Vivian L.; F; Daut; 3
1624;   ---; Anna A.; F; Daut; 1

1625;   ---; Murray, Jennie; F; Head; 31
1626;   ---; Martin J.; M; Son; 9
1627;   ---; Ruby M.; F; Daut; 8
1628;   ---; Arthur R.; M; Son; 5
1629;   ---; Alfred G.; M; Son; 3
1630;   ---; Maurice C.; M; Son; 7 mo.

1631;   ---; Murphy, Gertrude; F; Head; 25

Census of the___**Osage**___Indians of___**Osage**___Agency___**Oklahoma**___taken
By_____**Ret Millard**_____, United States Indian Agent, during the First Quarter,
1908**[sic]**(?)**1907?**

Key: NUMBER; Indian Name; English Name; Sex; Relation; Age
* An Askerisk will be next to a number if repeated or out of sequence and inserted among a different family.

1632;   ---; Murphy, Alice; F; Head; 23

1633;   ---; Murphy, Elizabeth; F; Head; 21

1634;   ---; Murphy, Amy; F; Head; 45
1635;   ---; Nettie; F; Daut; 17

1636;   ---; Musgrove, William; M; Head; 29
1637;   ---; Carl R.; M; Son; 2
1638;   ---; Willis E.; F; Daut; 11 mo

1639;   --; Newman, George; M; Head; 25

1640;   ---; Noble, Ida; F; Head; 25

1641;   ---; Nokegs, Larry; M; Head; 52

1642;   ---; Odell, Isabella; F; Head; 22

1643;   ---; Owens, Catherine; F; Daut; 3 mo.

1644;   ---; Pappan, Samuel T.; M; Son; 16
1645;   ---; Lee A.; M; Son; 14
1646;   ---; Oakley; M; Son; 12
1647;   ---; Lester; M; Son; 10

1648;   ---; Pappin, Alex; M; Head; 48
1649;   ---; Grace; F; Daut; 17
1650;   ---; Herbert; M; Son; 10
1651;   ---; Franklin A.; M; Son; 5
1652;   ---; Roosevelt; M; Son; 2

1653;   ---; Pappin, John; M; Head; 49
1654;   ---; Jesse L.; M; Son; 17
1655;   ---; John L.; M; Son; 15
1656;   ---; Jeanette; F; Daut; 12
1657;   ---; Joseph L.; M; Son; 10
1658;   ---; Jules C.; M; Son; 8
1659;   ---; Joshua J.; M; Son; 4
1660;   ---; Jeremiah; M; Son; 2

1661;   ---; Pappin, James; M; Head; 23

1662;   ---; Palmer, John F.; M; Head; 46
1663;   ---; Mrtha[sic]; F; Wife; 34

114

Census of the **Osage** Indians of **Osage** Agency **Oklahoma** taken By **Ret Millard**, United States Indian Agent, during the First Quarter, 1908[sic](?)**1907?**

Key: NUMBER; Indian Name; English Name; Sex; Relation; Age
* An Askerisk will be next to a number if repeated or out of sequence and inserted among a different family.

1664;   ---; Mary E.; F; Daut; 13
1665;   ---; Clementine; F; Daut; 11
1666;   ---; Martha M.; F; Daut; 4 mo.
1667;   ---; Mable; F; Daut; 17

1668;   ---; Pease, Minnie A.; F; Head; 33
1669;   ---; Marion H.; M; Son; 2

1670;   ---; Perrier, Joseph; M; Head; 30

1671;   ---; Perrier, Samuel; M; Head; 39

1672;   ---; Perrier, Leo; M; Head; 26
1673;   ---; Clifford R.; M; Son; 9 mo.

1674;   ---; Perrier, James; M; Head; 36
1675;   ---; John T.; M; Son; 13
1676;   ---; James R.; M; Son; 7

1677;   ---; Perrier, Napoleon; M; Head; 49
1678;   ---; Nina; F; Daut; 16
1679;   ---; Leo; M; Son; 13
1680;   ---; Peter; M; Son; 10
1681;   ---; Lola; F; Daut; 9
1682;   ---; Owen; M; Son; 5

1683;   ---; Perrier, Louis F.; M; Head; 18

1684;   ---; Perrier, Thomas; M; Head; 23
1685;   ---; Roy B.; M; Son; 1

1686;   ---; Perrier, Eugene; M; Head; 24
1687;   ---; Ray L.D.; M; Son; 1

1688;   ---; Penn, Leo; M; Son; 10
1689;   ---; Oscar; M; Son; 8
1690;   ---; Wayne M.; M; Son; 2

1691;   ---; Pettit, S.W.; M; Head; 62

1692;   ---; Pettit, Nette M.; F; Head; 20

1693;   ---; Pettit, Charles; M; Head; 34
1694;   ---; Hattie B.; F; Daut; 10
1695;   ---; Lele M.; F; Daut; 6

115

Census of the __Osage__ Indians of __Osage__ Agency __Oklahoma__ taken
By ____ __Ret Millard__ ____, United States Indian Agent, during the First Quarter,
1908**[sic]**(?)**1907?**

Key: NUMBER; Indian Name; English Name; Sex; Relation; Age
* An Askerisk will be next to a number if repeated or out of sequence and inserted among a different family.

1696; ---; Charles W.; M; Son; 5
1697; ---; Leo Samuel; M; Son; 3

1698; ---; Pettit, George; M; Head; 32
1699; ---; George R.; M; Son; 8
1700; ---; Lula B.; F; Daut; 5
1701; ---; William A.; M; Son; 4 mo.

1702; ---; Pettit, John; M; Head; 30

1703; ---; Pettit, Andrew; M; Head; 29

1704; ---; Perkins, Elizabeth; F; Head; 52

1705; ---; Peters, James M.; M; Son; 8

1706; ---; Pearson, Rosa; F; Head; 44
1707; ---; Cordelia C.; F; Daut; 16
1708; ---; Lillian F.; F; Daut; 15
1709; ---; Bertha L.; F; Daut; 13
1710; ---; Kate V.; F; Daut; 10
1711; ---; Willie J.; M; Son; 7
1712; ---; Rose E.; F; Daut; 4

1713; ---; Pearson, Madeline; F; Head; 18

1714; ---; Pearson; October; M; Head; 24
1715; ---; Mary C.; F; Wife; 20
1716; ---; Bernice M.; F; Daut; 1

1717; ---; Phillips, William; M; Head; 37
1718; ---; Angeline; F; Daut; 13
1719; ---; Iva M.; F; Daut; 11
1720; ---; James W.; M; Son; 10

1721; ---; Plomondon, Clemy; F; Head; 53
1722; ---; Daniel B.; M; Son; 15
1723; ---; Julia A; F; Daut; 13
1724; ---; Louisa; F; Daut; 9

1725; ---; Plomondon, Louis; M; Head; 22
1726; ---; Kathleen; F; Daut; 7 mo.

1727; ---; Plomondon, Barnard; M; Head; 37
1728; ---; Ella; F; Wife; 33

116

Census of the___**Osage**___Indians of___**Osage**___Agency___**Oklahoma**___taken
By_____**Ret Millard**_____, United States Indian Agent, during the First Quarter,
1908[sic](?)**1907?**

Key: NUMBER; Indian Name; English Name; Sex; Relation; Age
* An Askerisk will be next to a number if repeated or out of sequence and inserted among a different family.

1729; ---; Grace; F; Daut; 15
1730; ---; Clementine; F; Daut; 13
1731; ---; Moses E.; M; Son; 11
1732; ---; George A.; M; Son; 8

1733; ---; Potter, Ethel; F; Head; 29
1734; ---; Frances A.; M; Son; 12
1735; ---; Oliver L.; M; Son; 7
1736; ---; James L.; M; Son; 4
1737; ---; Zelma; F; Daut; 2 mo.

1738; ---; Prudom, Charles N.; M; Head; 52

1739; ---; Prudom, Nore; F; Head; 24

1740; ---; Prudom, Frank; M; Head; 41

1741; ---; Prue, Henry; M; Head; 32
1742; ---; Maude; F; Wife; 25
1743; ---; Hattie M; F; Daut; 9
1744; ---; Charles F.; M; Son; 8
1745; ---; Henry E.; M; Son; 6
1746; ---; Floyd B.; M; Son; 3
1747; ---; Anna B.; F; Daut; 1

1748; ---; Quinton, Franklin; M; Head; 20

1749; ---; Quinton, Alex; M; Head; 18

1750; ---; Rairdon, Jane R.; F; Head; 48
1751; ---; Wendall H.; M; Son; 7
1752; ---; Miller, Ida J.; F; Daut; 15

1753; ---; Reece, Elizabeth; F; Head; 23
1754; ---; Hallie; F; Daut; 5
1755; ---; Ethel; F; Daut; 3

1756; ---; Revelette, James; M; Head; 30
1757; ---; Teresa; F; Daut; 8
1758; ---; William L.; M; Son; 6
1759; ---; Mary E.; F; Daut; 2
1760; ---; Minnie F.; Daut; 2

1761; ---; Revelette, Fred; M; Head; 28
1762; ---; Pauline; F; Daut; 7

Census of the___Osage___Indians of___Osage___Agency___Oklahoma___taken
By___Ret Millard___, United States Indian Agent, during the First Quarter,
1908[sic](?)1907?

Key: NUMBER; Indian Name; English Name; Sex; Relation; Age
* An Askerisk will be next to a number if repeated or out of sequence and inserted among a different family.

1763; ---; Fred L.; M; Son; 5

1764; ---; Revelette, Frank; M; Head; 66

1765; ---; Revelette, Franklin; M; Head; 18

1766; ---; Revelette, Charles; M; Head; 34
1767; ---; Joseph; M; Son; 1

1768; ---; Revard, William; M; Head; 42
1769; ---; William E.; M; Son; 6
1770; ---; Della M.; F; Daut; 4
1771; ---; Gladis; F; Daut; 2

1772; ---; Revard, Solomon; M; Head; 48

1773; ---; Revard, Charles; M; Head; 47

1774; ---; Revard, Alex; M; Head; 47

1775; ---; Revard, Benjamin; M; Head; 26

1776; ---; Revard, Paul; M; Head; 32
1777; ---; Susie; F; Daut; 12

1778; ---; Revard, Mary E.; F; Head; 59

1779; ---; Revard, Elsie E.; F; Daut; 16
1780; ---; Maynard; M; Son; 12

1781; ---; Revard, Francis; M; Head; 39
1782; ---; Mack; M; Son; 13
1783; ---; Emanuel M; Son; 8
1784; ---; Pearl I.; F; Daut; 6
1785; ---; Ethel E.; F; Daut; 10 mo.

1786; ---; Revard, John W.; M; Head; 29
1787; ---; Edward L.; M; Son; 9
1788; ---; Evart A.; M; Son; 8

1789; ---; Revard, Joseph; M; Head; 77
1790; ---; Ursula; F; Daut; 17
1791; ---; Clementine; F; Daut; 14
1792; ---; William J.; M; Son; 12
1793; ---; Renald V.; M; Son; 10

118

Census of the __Osage__ Indians of __Osage__ Agency __Oklahoma__ taken
By __Ret Millard__ , United States Indian Agent, during the First Quarter,
1908[sic](?)**1907?**

Key: NUMBER; Indian Name; English Name; Sex; Relation; Age
* An Askerisk will be next to a number if repeated or out of sequence and inserted among a different family.

1794; ---; Revard, Ralph; M; Head; 19

1795; ---; Revard, Franklin; M; Head; 43
1796; ---; Nicholas N.; M; Son; 13
1797; ---; Pearl; F; Daut; 12
1798; ---; Myrta; F; Daut; 4
1799; ---; Katheryn; F; Daut; 2 mo.

1800; ---; Revard, Mark S.; M; Head; 19

1801; ---; Revard, Charles E.; M; Head; 47
1802; ---; Clarence; M; Son; 17
1803; ---; Ed. Clifford; M; Son; 15
1804; ---; Clara; F; Daut; 13
1805; ---; Carrie; F; Daut; 9
1806; ---; Cora; F; Daut; 9
1807; ---; Nora T; F; Daut; 8
1808; ---; McGuire N.; M; Son; 3
1809; ---; Lean; F; Daut; 1

1810; ---; Revard, Leonard; M; Head; 49
1811; ---; Lode; F; Daut; 13
1812; ---; Opal A.; F; Daut; 10
1813; ---; Hazel; F; Daut; 7
1814; ---; Minnie; F; Daut; 4
1815; ---; Cleo; F; Daut; 2

1816; ---; Revard, Joseph Jr.; M; Head; 50

1817; ---; Revard, Nellie; F; Daut; 6
1818; ---; Edgar T.; M; Son; 3
1819; ---; Mary G.; F; Daut; 1

1820; ---; Revard, Curtis; M; Head; 21

1821; ---; Revard, Mae Belle; F; Head; 19

1822; ---; Revard, Odell; F; Daut; 17
1823; ---; Aaron T.; M; Son; 15

1824; ---; Riddle, Sherman; M; Son; 151[sic]
1825; ---; Joseph; M; Son; 13
1826; ---; Frank; M; Son; 11

1827; ---; Ririe, Effie E.; F; Daut; 14

119

Census of the **Osage** Indians of **Osage** Agency **Oklahoma** taken
By **Ret Millard** , United States Indian Agent, during the First Quarter,
1908**[sic]**(?)**1907?**

Key: NUMBER; Indian Name; English Name; Sex; Relation; Age
* An Askerisk will be next to a number if repeated or out of sequence and inserted among a different family.

1828; ---; Scott F.; M; Son; 11
1829; ---; Otis E.; M; Son; 7
1830; ---; Nellie I.; F; Daut; 5
1831; ---; Arthur M.; M. Son; 1

1832; ---; Ririe, Oscar A.; M; Head; 20
1833; ---; Edith J.; F; Daut; 2 mo.

1834; ---; Rodman, Antwine; M; Head; 20
1835; ---; Loyd; M; Son; 2 mo.

1836; ---; Rogers, Stephen; M; Head; 26

1837; ---; Rogers, Louis; M; Head; 64

1838; ---; Rogers, Louis Jr.; M; Head; 22

1839; ---; Rogers, Wahneta; F; Daut; 2

1840; ---; Rogers, Thomas L.; M; Head; 69
1841; ---; Nancy; F; Wife; 59

1842; ---; Rogers, T.L.; M; Head; 21

1843; ---; Rogers, Arthur; M; Head; 47
1844; ---; Minerve; F; --; --
1845; ---; Joseph L.; M; Son; 8
1846; ---; Ellen E.; F; Daut; 6
1847; ---; John R.; M; Son; 4
1848; ---; William C.; M; Son; 2
1849; ---; Isabell; F; Daut; 4 mo.

1850; ---; Rogers, Mary E.; F; Head; 33
1851; ---; Irene; F; Daut; 15
1852; ---; Mary A.; F; Daut; 13
1853; ---; Coaina; F; Daut; 9
1854; ---; Eldred T.; M; Son; 7

1855; ---; Rogers, Antwine; M; Head; 62
1856; ---; Viola; F; Daut; 15

1857; ---; Rogers, May; F; Head; 21

1858; ---; Rogers, Kenneth; M; Head; 27
1859; ---; Ellen; F; Daut; 4

Census of the___Osage___Indians of___Osage___Agency___Oklahoma___taken
By_____Ret Millard_____, United States Indian Agent, during the First Quarter,
1908[sic](?)1907?

Key: NUMBER; Indian Name; English Name; Sex; Relation; Age
* An Askerisk will be next to a number if repeated or out of sequence and inserted among a different family.

1860; ---; Antwine; M; Son; 2

1861; ---; Rogers, Jasper; M; Head; 37
1862; ---; Rosa; F; Wife; 28
1863; ---; Emmett; M; Son; 5
1864; ---; Cecelia; F; Daut; 6
1865; ---; Maude; F; Daut; 2
1866; ---; Flora; F; Daut; 1 mo.

1867; ---; Rogers, Bertha D.; Daut; 13
1868; ---; Helen C.; M; Daut; 11

1869; ---; Rogers, Arthur; M; Head; 27
1870; ---; Willie L.; M; Son; 8 mo.

1871; ---; Rogers, Thomas L. Jr.; M; Head; 22

1872; ---; Rogers, Granville; M; Head; 19

1873; ---; Rogers, Rosa L.; F; Daut; 14
1874; ---; Josephine; F; Daut; 11
1875; ---; John H.; M; Son; 9

1876; ---; Rogers, Nora; F; Head; 23
1877; ---; Richard L.; M; Son; 2

1878; ---; Rogers, Lewis A.; M; Head; 32

1879; ---; Rogers, Isadore; F; Wife; 29
1880; ---; Fred R.; M; Son; 6
1881; ---; Frank; M; Son; 2

1882; ---; Roberts, Ola; F; Head; 21

1883; ---; Ross, John; M; Head; 62
1884; ---; Floyd F.; M; Son; 10

1885; ---; Roach, Wilfred D; M; Head; 27
1886; ---; Bridget A.; F; Daut; 4
1887; ---; Melvin C.; M; Son; 2
1888; ---; Wilfred D. Jr.; M; Son; 2 mo.

1889; ---; Roach, Samuel; M; Head; 25
1890; ---; Mikie J.; M; Son; 4
1891; ---; Herman B.; Son; 1

Census of the **Osage** Indians of **Osage** Agency **Oklahoma** taken By **Ret Millard**, United States Indian Agent, during the First Quarter, 1908[sic](?)**1907?**

Key: NUMBER; Indian Name; English Name; Sex; Relation; Age
* An Askerisk will be next to a number if repeated or out of sequence and inserted among a different family.

1892; ---; Roach, Mary E.; F; Head; 24

1893; ---; Roach, George W.; Head; 21

1894; ---; Roach, Hattie B.; F; Head; 19

1895; ---; Saxon, Cora; F; Head; 33
1896; ---; Veva M.; F; Daut; 3
1897; ---; Harry H.; M; Son; 9 mo.

1898; ---; Scott, George; M; Head; 30
1899; ---; Mary M.; F; Daut; 2

1900; ---; Scott, Julia Ann; F; Head; 27
1901; ---; William J.; M; Son; 2
1902; ---; Violet; F; Daut; 2 mo.

1903; ---; Selby, Georgia; F; Head; 21

1904; ---; Shafer, Joanna; F; Head; 27
1905; ---; Flippin, Nettie B.; F; Daut; 9

1906; ---; Sheriff, Coeanna (nee Gilmore); F; Head; 20

1907; ---; Shaw, Franklin; M; Head; 19
1908; ---; Rose M.; F; Wife; 19
1909; ---; Moses; M; Son; 3
1910; ---; John; M; Son; 1

1911; ---; Shobe, Anna U.; F; Head; 23

1912; ---; Shaw, Charles M; Head; 18

1913; ---; Simpson, Susan; F; Head; 65

1914; ---; Simpkins, Mary L.; F; Head; 35
1915; ---; Warren D.; M; Son; 14
1916; ---; Mary E.; F; Daut; 13
1917; ---; Vivian P.; F; Daut; 10
1918; ---; Oren F.; M; Son; 9
1919; ---; Edward; M; Son; 7
1920; ---; Virgil; M; Son; 2

1921; ---; Slaughter, A.B.; M; Head; 23

122

Census of the___**Osage**___Indians of___**Osage**___Agency___**Oklahoma**___taken
By_____**Ret Millard**_____, United States Indian Agent, during the First Quarter,
1908**[sic]**(?)**1907?**

Key: NUMBER; Indian Name; English Name; Sex; Relation; Age
* An Askerisk will be next to a number if repeated or out of sequence and inserted among a different family.

1922;   ---; Slaughter, Amanda; F; Head; 20

1923;   ---; Slaughter, Harry E.; M; Son; 17

1924;   ---; Smith, Minnie; F; Head; 24
1925;   ---; George B.; M; Son; 8
1926;   ---; Genevieve; F; Daut; 5
1927;   ---; Samuel; M; Son; 7 mo.

1928;   ---; Smith, Anna; F; Head; 28

1929;   ---; Soderstrom, Gertrude; F; Head; 28
1930;   ---; Dickey, Alta E.; F; Daut; 9
1931;   ---; Soderstrom, Hanna N.; F; Daut; 6

1932;   ---; Soldani, Sylvester J.; M; Head; 47
1933;   ---; Josephine; F; Wife; 38
1934;   ---; Myrtle; F; Daut; 16
1935;   ---; Emmerty A.; M; Son; 15

1936;   ---; Soldani, Louis E.; M; Head; 18

1937;   ---; Soldani, Kate P.; F; Head; 19

1938;   ---; Soldani; Ida M.; F; Head; 20

1939;   ---; Soldani, Agnes; F; Head; 21

1940;   ---; Soldani, Anthony; M; Head; 45
1941;   ---; Amelia K.; F; Wife; 39
1942;   ---; Frank E.; M; Son; 16
1943;   ---; Charles L.; M; Son; 14
1944;   ---; Clarence; M; Son; 11
1945;   ---; Grace M.; F; Daut; 10
1946;   ---; Rose M.; F; Daut; 8
1947;   ---; George H.; M; Son; 6

1948;   ---; Soldani, Mary L.; F; Head; 20

1949;   ---; Souligny, Laura; F; Head; 22
1950;   ---; Mildred; F; Daut; 3

1951;   ---; Stevens, John H.; M; Head; 41
1952;   ---; Mildred V.; F; Daut; 3
1953;   ---; Gilbert J.; M; Son; 7 mo.

123

Census of the **Osage** Indians of **Osage** Agency **Oklahoma** taken
By **Ret Millard**, United States Indian Agent, during the First Quarter,
1908**[sic]**(?)**1907?**

Key: NUMBER; Indian Name; English Name; Sex; Relation; Age
* An Askerisk will be next to a number if repeated or out of sequence and inserted among a different family.

1954; ---; Stephens, Madeline; F; Head; 65

1955; ---; Stephens, Mary; F; Daut; 13

1956; ---; Stotts, Emma; F; Head; 32
1957; ---; Joseph L.; M; Son; 15
1958; ---; William W.; M; Son; 12
1959; ---; James E.; M; Son; 3

1960; ---; Stobaugh, Alice; F; Head; 36
1961; ---; Riddle, John L.; M; Son; 17
1962; ---; Arthur; M; Son; 5

1963; ---; Stewart, Lenora; F; Head; 45
1964; Wilkie, George L.; M; Son; 17
1965; ---; Rose E.; F; Daut; 13

1966; ---; Swanson, Celestine; F; Head; 25
1967; ---; Addison L.; M; Son; 3
1968; ---; Ora E.; F; Daut; 5
1969; ---; Joseph N.; M; Son; 2

1970; ---; Swain, Rose; F; Head; 16

1971; ---; Swinney, Oscar E.; M; Orphan; 14

1972; ---; Tall Chief, Enoch; M; Son; 1

1973; ---; Tapp, Belle; F; Head; 43
1974; ---; Chambers, James W.; M; Son; 11
1975; ---; Minnie A.; F; Daut; 8

1976; ---; Taylor, James E.; M; Orphan; 14
1977; ---; John F.; M; Orphan; 12
1978; ---; Hiram; M; Orphan; 10
1979; ---; Fanny; F; Orphan; 9
1980; ---; Agnes; F; Orphan; 7
1981; ---; Anna; F; Orphan; 3

1982; ---; Tayrien, John; M; Head; 25
1983; ---; Mary L.; F; Daut; 3
1984; ---; Agnes; F; Daut; 2
1985; ---; Gladys; F; Daut; 8 mo.

1986; ---; Tayrien, Charles; M; Head; 32

Census of the__Osage__Indians of__Osage__Agency__Oklahoma__taken
By____Ret Millard____, United States Indian Agent, during the First Quarter,
1908[sic](?)1907?

Key: NUMBER; Indian Name; English Name; Sex; Relation; Age
* An Askerisk will be next to a number if repeated or out of sequence and inserted among a different family.

1987; ---; Edna; F; Daut; 9

1988; ---; Tayrien, Thomas; M; Head; 46
1989; ---; George A.; M; Son; 17
1990; ---; Andrew W.; M; Son; 13
1991; ---; Paul; M; Son; 11
1992; ---; Maude J.; F; Daut; 3
1993; ---; John C.; M; Son; 2

1994; ---; Tayrien, James; H; Head; 22
1995; ---; Alberty; F; Daut; 3
1996; ---; Elmer C.; M; Son; 1

1997; ---; Tayrien, David W.; M; Head; 19

1998; ---; Tayrien, Andrew; M; Head; 33
1999; ---; Jennie; F; Daut; 11
2000; ---; Viola; F; Daut; 10
2001; ---; Alfred J.; M; Son; 8
2002; ---; Violet M; F; Daut; 7
2003; ---; William J.; M; Son; 4
2004; ---; Rose Ann; F; Daut; 4

2005; ---; Tayrien, Cyprian; M; Head; 69
2006; ---; William; M; Son; 17
2007; ---; Beggs, Rena L.; F; G. Daut; 17

2008; ---; Thompson, Leroy; M; Son; 13
2009; ---; Roe, Emery E.; M; Son; 6

2010; ---; Thompson, Nicholas; M; Head; 49

2011; ---; Thomas, Agnes; F; Head; 25
2012; ---; Maggie C.; F; Daut; 5
2013; ---; Julia H.; F; Daut; 2

2014; ---; Thurman, Lola; F; Head; 21
2015; ---; Geneva; F; Daut; 1

2016; ---; Tinker, Louis; M; Head; 40
2017; ---; William; M; Son; 16
2018; ---; Bessie; F; Daut; 13
2019; ---; Nora; F; Daut; 9
2020; ---; Ora; F; Daut; 9
2021; ---; Eva; F; Daut; 7

Census of the **Osage** Indians of **Osage** Agency **Oklahoma** taken By **Ret Millard**, United States Indian Agent, during the First Quarter, 1908[sic](?)**1907?**

Key: NUMBER; Indian Name; English Name; Sex; Relation; Age
* An Askerisk will be next to a number if repeated or out of sequence and inserted among a different family.

2022; ---; Isabella; F; Daut; 4
2023; ---; Rose; F; Daut; 2
2024; ---; Cora; F; Daut; 3 mo.

2025; ---; Tinker, Geo. E.; M; Head; 38
2026; ---; Mary G.; F; Daut; 15
2027; ---; Sarah Anna; F; Daut; 13
2028; ---; Nicholas A.T.; M; Son; 11
2029; ---; George E. Jr.; M; Son; 8
2030; ---; Villa; F; Daut; 4

2031; ---; Tinker, Clarence; M; Head; 19

2032; ---; Tinker, Charley; M; Head; 35
2033; ---; Mary J.; F; Daut; 16
2034; ---; Roy B.; M; Son; 13
2035; ---; Maude; F; Daut; 10
2036; ---; Lucille; F; Daut; 9
2037; ---; Davis W.; M; Son; 6
2038; ---; Louis H.; M; Son; 2

2039; ---; Tinker, Frank; M; Head; 46
2040; ---; Mary L.; F; Wife; 46
2041; ---; Tom; M; Son; 13
2042; ---; Mary E.; F; Daut; 11
2043; ---; Eliza; F; Daut; 7
2044; ---; Sylvester J.; M; Son; 4

2045; ---; Tinker, Norris J.; M; Head; 18

2046; ---; Todd, Maud; F; Head; 28
2047; ---; Harold; M; Son; 2
2048; ---; Gerald J.; M; Son; 6

2049; ---; Trumbly, Jilian; M; Head; 56
2050; ---; Eliza; F; Wife; 51
2051; ---; Henry; M; Son; 17
2052; ---; Tina O.; F; Daut; 15
2053; ---; Charles; M; Son; 14
2054; ---; Theresa; F; Daut; 9

2055; ---; Trumbly, Oliver; M; Head; 25

2056; ---; Trumbly, Clarence; M; Head; 26
2057; ---; Gladys; F; Daut; 4

Census of the **Osage** Indians of **Osage** Agency **Oklahoma** taken
By **Ret Millard** , United States Indian Agent, during the First Quarter,
1908[sic](?)**1907?**

Key: NUMBER; Indian Name; English Name; Sex; Relation; Age
* An Askerisk will be next to a number if repeated or out of sequence and inserted among a different family.

2058; ---; Clarence E.; M; Son; 2

2059; ---; Trumbly, George; M; Head; 33

2060; ---; Trumbly, Andrew; M; Head; 32
2061; ---; Mary; F; Wife; 21
2062; ---; Oscar; M; Son; 10 mo.

2063; ---; Trumbly, J.B.; M; Head; 53
2064; ---; John F.; M; Son; 16
2065; ---; Elizabeth; F; Daut; 13
2066; ---; Paul P.; M; Son; 7

2067; ---; Tucker, Anna; F; Head; 23
2068; ---; Beulah C.; F; Daut; 2
2069; ---; Stephen Jr.; M; Son; 1 mo.

2070; ---; Tucker, Angeline; F; Head; 72

2071; ---; Turner, Frederick D.; M; Son; 12

2072; ---; Turner, Mary B.; F; Head; 25

2073; ---; Tyner, Benjamin F.; M; Head; 32
2074; ---; Ethel M.; F; Daut; 8
2075; ---; Roy F.; M; Son; 6
2076; ---; William L.; M; Son; 2

2077; ---; Vesser, Ruth; F; Daut; 14

2078; ---; Voils, Ora M.; F; Head; 27
2079; ---; Kathleen N.; F; Daut; 8
2080; ---; Elsie L.; F; Daut; 10

2081; ---; Watkins, Rosalie; F; Head; 32
2082; ---; Francis M.; M; Son; 13
2083; ---; James; M; Son; 12
2084; ---; John F.; M; Son; 5

2085; ---; Ware, Victoria; F; Head; 56
2086; ---; Del Orier, Edna; F; Daut; 16
2087; ---; Lillie M.; F; Daut; 17

2088; ---; Ware, Aggie; F; Head; 37
2089; ---; Julia; F; Daut; F; 13

Census of the **Osage** Indians of **Osage** Agency **Oklahoma** taken
By **Ret Millard**, United States Indian Agent, during the First Quarter,
1908**[sic]**(?)**1907?**

Key: NUMBER; Indian Name; English Name; Sex; Relation; Age
* An Askerisk will be next to a number if repeated or out of sequence and inserted among a different family.

2090; ---; Nancy; F; Daut; 11
2091; ---; Bulah; F; Daut; 9
2092; ---; Rosa L.; F; Daut; 7
2093; ---; Henry H.; M; Son; 5
2094; ---; David; M; Son; 4

2095; ---; Ware, Effie; F; Head; 20
2096; ---; Merle C.; M; Son; 2

2097; ---; Waters, Telina; F; Head; 24

2098; ---; Whalen, Charlotte; F; Head; 18

2099; ---; Whiles, Elmer; M; Head; 25

2100; ---; Whiles, Delilah; F; Head; 22

2101; ---; Whiles, Francis M.; M; Head; 18

2102; ---; Wheeler, Paul; M; Head; 35
2103; ---; Merrit J.; M; Son; 4
2104; ---; Geneva; F; Daut; 3
2105; ---; Louisa; F; Daut; 6 mo.

2106; ---; Wheeler, Elmer; M; Head; 28
2107; ---; Eva E.; F; Wife; 29
2108; ---; Virginia; F; Daut; 3

2109; ---; Wheeler, Alma; F; Head; 21

2110; ---; Wheeler, Anna; F; Head; 24

2111; ---; Wheeler, Susan; F; Head; 30
2112; ---; Morris E.; M; Son; 6

2113; ---; Wilkie, Louie F.; M; Head; 21
2114; ---; Andrew E.; M; Son; 9 mo.

2115; ---; Wilson, Mary; F; Head; 29
2116; ---; William E.; M; Son; 10
2117; ---; Julia K.; F; Daut; 8
2118; ---; Banie; M; Son; 6
2119; ---; Audry; F; Daut; 3
2120; ---; Howard; M; Son; 7 mo.

128

Census of the __Osage__ Indians of __Osage__ Agency __Oklahoma__ taken
By __Ret Millard__, United States Indian Agent, during the First Quarter,
1908[sic](?)**1907?**

Key: NUMBER; Indian Name; English Name; Sex; Relation; Age
* An Askerisk will be next to a number if repeated or out of sequence and inserted among a different family.

2121; ---; Woodring, Tena; F; Head; 32
2122; ---; Carlton W.; M; Son; 12
2123; ---; Orville W.; M; Son; 10
2124; ---; Anna; F; Daut; 6

2125; ---; Woodham, Lucy; F; Head; 57

2126; ---; Wyrick, Mary; F; Head; 34
2127; ---; Jessie W.; F; Daut; 11
2128; ---; John H.; M; Son; 10
2129; ---; Elnora J.; F; Daut; 6
2130; ---; Elmer F.; M; Son; 3

2131; ---; Yeargain, Estella; F; Head; 19

2132; ---; Yeargain, Early I.; M; Son; 16
2133; ---; Verona C.; F; Daut; 14
2134; ---; Leona; F; Daut; 13

2135; ---; York. Adah M.; F; Head; 21

2136; ---; Hooper, Sallie; F; Head; 36
2137; ---; Mary; F; Daut; 13

2138; ---; Siggins, Clara; F; Head; 44
2139; ---; Andrew W.; M; Son; 16

2140; ---; Aiken, Elizabeth; F; Head; 25

2141; ---; Aiken, John H.; M; Head; 23

2142; ---; Alberty, Cynthia; F; Head; 51
2143; ---; Lizzie; F; Daut; 10

2144; ---; Alberty, George; M; Head; 20

2145; ---; Alexander, Levi; M; Head; 26
2146; ---; Marthe L.; F; Daut; 5

2147; ---; Alexander, Maggie; F; Head; 24

2148; ---; Alexander, Ida A.; F; Head; 18

2149; ---; Allen, Emily; F; Head; 43
2150; ---; Whalen, Esther; F; Daut; 13

129

Census of the **Osage** Indians of **Osage** Agency **Oklahoma** taken
By **Ret Millard**, United States Indian Agent, during the First Quarter,
1908**[sic]**(?)**1907?**

Key: NUMBER; Indian Name; English Name; Sex; Relation; Age
* An Askerisk will be next to a number if repeated or out of sequence and inserted among a different family.

2151; ---; Dorethea; F; Daut; 11

2152; ---; Anderson, Mary; F; Head; 23

2153; ---; Anderson, John B.; M; Head; 21
2154; ---; Henry P.; M; Son; 1
2155; ---; Anderson, Edward R.; M; Head; 19
2156; # Enrolled with #558 BEAVER BAND.

RECAPITULATION:

All ages (males, 1096; females, 989)	2156
Full-Bloods:	
All ages (males, 435; females 436)	871
18 years and over (males 244; females, 241)	485
Between 6 and 16 (males, 101; females 100)	201
Mixed-Bloods:	
All ages (males, 661; females, 624)	1285
18 years and over (males, 244; females, 228)	472
Between 6 and 16 (males, 236; females, 228)	464

Census of the Osage Indians

of

Osage Indian Agency, Oklahoma,

As of 1909

Hugh Pitzer, Supt. & Sp'l. Disb'g. Agent

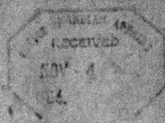

CENCUS OF OSAGE INDIANS

of

OSAGE AGENCY, OKLAHOMA,

Taken during the 4th
quarter, 1909.

DEPARTMENT OF THE INTERIOR,

UNITED STATES INDIAN SERVICE

Annual census
Osages.

The Osage Indian Agency,

Pawhuska, Okla., Nov. 1, 1909.

The Honorable
    Commissioner of Indian Affairs,
        Washington, D. C.

Sir:-

Replying to Office letter Land-Population Circular No.
309, "Annual Census", I am transmitting under separate cover
the annual census of Osage Indians.

Very respectfully,

Hugh L. Pitzer

Superintendent.

LaM.

133

Census of the **Osage Indians** Indians of **Osage Indians** Agency **Oklahoma,** taken by **Hugh Pitzer, Supt. & Sp'l. Disb'g. Agent** , United States Indian Agent, during the 4th quarter, **1909**

Key: NUMBER; Indian Name; English Name; Sex; Relation; Age
* An Askerisk will be next to a number if repeated or out of sequence and inserted among a different family.

1; Pah-hu-scah; Tom Big Chief; M; Head; 50
2; Me-to-op-pe; ---; F; Wife; 36
3; He-ah-to-me; May White; F; Daut; 18
4; Heh-kah-mon-kah; ---; F; Daut; 10
5; Gra-to-me; ---; F; Daut; 6

6; Mo-she-to-moie; ---; M; Head; 65
7; Mo-se-che-he; ---; F; Wife; 65

8; Richard Rusk; Richard Rusk; M; Head; 27
9; Gra-tah-me-tsa-hah; ---; F; Wife; 29
10; Wah-tsa-ah-tah; James McKinley; M; S. Son; 14
11; Mah-sah; Walter McKinley; M; S. Son; 11
12; He-ah-to-me; ---; F; S. Daut; 10
13; ---; May Rusk; F; Daut; 6
14; Hla-me-tsa-he; ---; F; Daut; 3

15; Wy-u-tsa-kah-she; ---; M; Head; 74
16; Moie-wah-kon-tah; Phillip Carson; M; Son; 15
17; Num-pah-wah-kon-tah; Tom Carson; M; Son; 20

18; Hun-kah-me; ---; F; Head; 52
19; To-sho-ho; Charles Whitehorn; M; Son; 13
20; E-nan-min-tsa; ---; M; Son; 5

21; ---; Fidelis Cheshowahkepah; M; Head; 27
22; Hum-pah-to-kah; ---; F; Wife; 54
23; He-ah-to-me; Agnes Ferguson; F; S. Daut; 8
24; Gra-tah-wah-kah; ---; M; S. Son; 5

25; ---; Howard Russell; M; Head; 21

26; ---; Otis Russell; M; Head; 22
27; ---; Angella Russell; F; Wife; 22
28; He-ah-to-me; ---; F; Daut; 2

29; ---; Howard Buffalo; M; Head; 49
30; ---; Pearl Buffalo; F; Wife; 30
31; Wah-she-ke-pah; Willie Russell; M; S. Son; 13
32; Min-kah-she; ---; F; S. Daut; 3

33; ---; Herman McCarthy; M; Head; 30
34; ---; Martha Neal; F; Wife; 18

35; Son-sah-kah-hah; ---; M; Head; 61

135

Census of the __Osage Indians__ Indians of __Osage Indians__ Agency __Oklahoma,__
taken by __Hugh Pitzer, Supt. & Sp'l. Disb'g. Agent__ , United States Indian Agent,
during the 4th quarter, 1909

Key: NUMBER; Indian Name; English Name; Sex; Relation; Age
* An Askerisk will be next to a number if repeated or out of sequence and inserted among a different family.

36; Hlu-ah-to-me; ---; F; Wife; 62

37; Wah-ahah-she-me-tse-he; ---; F; Head; 76

38; Wah-she-shah; ---; M; Head; 47
39; Mo-se-che-he; ---; F; Wife; 40
40; Hlu-ah-me-tsa-he; ---; F; Daut; 3

41; Mon-kah-sop-py; ---; M; Head; 60
42; He-ah-to-me; ---; F; Wife; 39
43; Wah-tsa-ah-tah; Joe Osage; M; S. Son; 15
44; E-ne-op-pe; Nellie Osage; F; S. Daut; 13
45; Hun-kah-me; ---; F; Daut; 4
46; Heh-sah-hah; ---; M; Son; 2

47; Wah-hre-she-he; Charles; M; Head; 45
48; Hlu-ah-me; ---; F; Wife; 39
49; Mo-se-che-he; Josephine Wahhreshe; F; Daut; 13
50; Mon-kah-hah; ---; M; Son; 8
51; Nah-me-tsa-he; ---; F; Daut; 4

52; ---; Luther Harvey; M; Head; 39
53; Ke-ah-som-pah; Mary Harvey; F; Wife; 36
54; He-ah-to-me; Minnie Harvey; F; Daut; 14
55; Hlu-ah-wah-kon-tah; Walter Harvey; M; Son; 11
56; Num-pah-q-ah; Theodore R. Harvey; M; Son; 10
57; Wah-tsa-su-sah; ---; M; Son; 6
58; ---; Luther Harvey Jr.; M; Son; 2

59; Me-ke-wah-ti-an-kah; ---; M; Head; 52
60; Wah-hrah-lum-pah; ---; F; Wife; 38
61; Kah-he-ah-gra; Louis James; M; Son; 12
62; Me-to-op-pe; ---; F; Daut; 4

63; ---; Roy James; M; Head; 23
64; ---; Laura James; F; Wife; 22

65; ---; Roscoe Conklin; M; Head; 46
66; ---; Edith White; F; Wife; 27
67; ---; Joseph White; M; S. Son; 5
68; ---; Abraham White; M; S. Son; 3
69; Wah-shah-ke-pah; ---; M; Son; 2

70; He-ah-to-me; Nellie White; F; Orphan; 13

Census of the **Osage Indians** Indians of **Osage Indians** Agency **Oklahoma,**
taken by **Hugh Pitzer, Supt. & Sp'l. Disb'g. Agent**, United States Indian Agent,
during the 4th quarter, **1909**

Key: NUMBER; Indian Name; English Name; Sex; Relation; Age
* An Askerisk will be next to a number if repeated or out of sequence and inserted among a different family.

71; Sho-e-ne-lah; ---; M; Head; 37

72; Wah-shin-kah-sop-py; ---; M; Head; 62
73; To-op-pe; ---; F; Wife; 61
74; E-gro-tah; Joseph Bird; M; Son; 16

75; E-gron-kah-shin-kah; ---; M; Head; 49
76; Hum-pah-to-kah; ---; F; Wife; 37
77; We-heh; Margaret Little; F; Daut; 15
78; Wah-sop-py-wah-kah; Mary Pappin; F; Daut; 8
79; Sin-tsa-hu; Ralph Hamilton; M; Son; 20

80; Shun-kahomo-lah; ---; M; Head; 63
81; Wah-tsa-me; ---; F; Wife; 55
82; Wah-shin-kah-hu; Joseph Shunkahmolah; M; Son; 19

83; ---; Daniel West; M; Head; 35
84; Hlu-ah-to-me; ---; F; Wife; 38
85; Kah-shin-kah; ---; M; Son; 8

86; Wah-hah-sah-e; ---; F; Head; 72

87; Wah-ses-tah-shin-kah; John Blackbird; M; Head; 51
88; Hlu-ah-to-me; Mary Blackbird; F; Wife; 34
89; Mon-shon-tsa-e-tah; Maud Blackbird; F; Daut; 14
90; Che-sho-ki-he-kah; ---; M; Son; 2

91; Wah-hrah-lum-pah; Mollie Mantle; F; Orphan; 18

92; ---; Mollie Kyle; F; Head; 22
93; He-ah-to-me; ---; F; Head; 33
94; Kah-scah; Charles Antwine; M; Son; 9

95; Kah-wah-o; Yellow Horse; M; Head; 52
96; Ke-ah-som-pah; ---; F; Wife; 42
97; Pun-kah-me-tsa-he; Maggie Bates; F; Daut; 14
98; Ah-kah-hu; John Bates; M; Son; 12
99; Hun-kah-me-tsa-he; ---; F; Daut; 10
100; Kah-ah-sum-pah; ---; F; Daut; 4

101; ---; Joseph Bates; M; Head; 23
102; ---; Lizzie June; F; Wife; 21
103; Hun-kah; ---; M; Son; 3

104; Hun-tsa-me; ---; F; Head; 65

Census of the **Osage Indians** Indians of **Osage Indians** Agency **Oklahoma,**
taken by **Hugh Pitzer, Supt. & Sp'l. Disb'g. Agent**, United States Indian Agent,
during the 4th quarter, 1909

Key: NUMBER; Indian Name; English Name; Sex; Relation; Age
* An Askerisk will be next to a number if repeated or out of sequence and inserted among a different family.

105; Wah-tsa-moie; ---; M; Head; 30
106; Hun-kah-me-tsa-he; ---; F; Wife; 26
107; ---; Michel Wah-tsa-moie; M; Son; 4
108; --; Frank Wah-tsa-moie; M; Son; 2

109; Pun-q-tah; ---; F; Head; 58

110; ---; Andfew[sic] Berry; M; Head; 22

111; ---; Esther Smith; F; Head; 24

112; Nun-tsa-wah-hu; ---; M; Head; 56
113; Num-pah-se; Joseph Cannon; M; Son; 18
114; ---; John Cannon; M; Son; 7

115; ---; Frank Cannon; M; Head; 24

116; ---; Alex Cannon; M; Head; 26

117; O-pah-su-ah; ---; M; Head; 40
118; Wah-to-sah; ---; F; Wife; 40
119; Pah-pah-ah-hah; Francis O-pah-su-ah; M; Son; 15

120; Tsa-po-in-kah; ---; M; Head; 60

121; ---; Lawrence Gray; M; Head; 23

122; ---; Amos Osage; M; Head; 37
123; ---; Liza Osage; F; Wife; 28
124; He-ah-to-me; Rosa Osage; F; Daut; 10

MOH-E-KAH-MOIE BAND.

125; Moh-e-kah-moie; ---; M; Head; 75
126; Hlu-ah-me; ---; F; Wife; 55
127; Mah-hah-sah-e; Aggie Mohekahmoie; F; Daut; 19
128; Me-ah-hre; Mary Mohekahmoie; F; Daut; 15

129; ---; Adair Hickey; M; Head; 33

130; ---; William Fletcher; M; Head; 38
131; Me-sah-e; ---; F; Wife; 27
132; Gra-to-me-tsa-he; ---; F; S. Daut; 8
133; Gra-to-ah; ---; F; S. Daut; 5
134; Sin-tsa-wah-kon-tah; Charles Fletcher; S; Son; 12

138

Census of the **Osage Indians** Indians of **Osage Indians** Agency **Oklahoma,** taken by **Hugh Pitzer, Supt. & Sp'l. Disb'g. Agent** , United States Indian Agent, during the 4th quarter, **1909**

Key: NUMBER; Indian Name; English Name; Sex; Relation; Age
* An Askerisk will be next to a number if repeated or out of sequence and inserted among a different family.

135; E-to-moie; Anna Fletcher; F; Daut; 9
136; ---; Frances T. Fletcher; F; Daut; 3

137; Gro-tun-kah; Joseph Fletcher; M; Orphan; 19

138; To-wah-gah-she; ---; M; Head; 50
139; He-ah-to-me; ---; F; Wife; 46
140; Gra-tah-su-ah; Thomas Butler; M; Son; 16

141; ---; Eugene Butler; M; Head; 21
142; ---; Grace Butler; F; Wife; 24

143; Me-gra-to-me; ---; F; Head; 43

144; U-ses-tah-wah-hah; ---; M; Head; 76

145; ---; Gilbert Cox; M; Head; 38

146; Me-ti-an-kah; ---; M; Head; 46
147; Mo-se-che-he; ---; F; Wife; 40
148; Ne-wal-la; Edward Elkins; M; Son; 13
149; E-he-ke-op-pe; ---; F; Daut; 8
150; Wah-ne-en-kah; ---; F; Daut; 3

151; Luther Elkins; Luther Elkins; M; Head; 23

152; ---; Charles West; M; Head; 26
153; ---; Louisa West; F; Dau; 2

154; ---; Don Dickinson; M; Head; 31

155; ---; Herbert Spencer; M; Head; 33
156; ---; Jennie Spencer; F; Wife; 25

157; Gra-tah-su-ah; Donnie Cole; F; Orphan; 18

158; To-wah-gah-he; ---; M; Head; 50
159; Son-se-grah; ---; F; Wife; 36
160; He-ah-to-me; Fanny Frye; F; Daut; 18

161; ---; Edward Cox; M; Head; 33
162; A-non-to-op-pe; ---; F; Wife; 22
163; Wah-tsa-ah-tah; Joseph Cox; M; Son; 4
164; ---; Lottie Ione Cox; F; Daut; 2
165; ---; Mary Cox; F; Daut; 6 mo

Census of the **Osage Indians** Indians of **Osage Indians** Agency **Oklahoma,** taken by **Hugh Pitzer, Supt. & Sp'l. Disb'g. Agent**, United States Indian Agent, during the 4th quarter, **1909**

Key: NUMBER; Indian Name; English Name; Sex; Relation; Age
* An Askerisk will be next to a number if repeated or out of sequence and inserted among a different family.

166; ---; Clinton Bigheart; M; Head; 38
167; Mon-shon-tsa-e-tah; ---; F; Wife; 28
168; Hum-pah-to-kah; Rose Bigheart; F; S. Daut; 13

169; Ne-wal-la; Oscar Neal; M; Orphan; 10

170; ---; Stevens Neal; M; Head; 30
171; ---; Rose Neal; F; Wife; 22
172; ---; Clara May Neal; F; Daut; 1

173; ---; Wilson Kirk; M; Head; 52
174; ---; Dora Kirk; F; Daut; 8
175; ---; Rosa Kirk; F; Daut; 4
176; ---; Charles Kirk; M; Son; 2
177; Pah-she-he; Mary Cox; F; Orphan; 19

178; Hun-tsa-me; Mable Cole; F; Head; 21

NE KAH WAH SHE TUN KAH BAND.

179; Ne-kah-wah-she-tun-kah; ---; M; Head; 69
180; Wah-hrah-lum-pah; ---; F; Wife; 57

181; ---; Nicholas Webster; M; Head; 34
182; Lo-tah-tse-a; ---; F; Wife; 42

183; E-to-moie; Little Star; M; Head; 40
184; Wah-to-sah-e; ---; F; Wife; 40
185; Gra-tah-ah-kah; John Star; M; Son; 9
186; Tom-pah-pe; ---; F; Daut; 6
187; E-kah-pah-she; ---; M; Son; 3
188; Me-tsa-ah-tah; ---; F; Daut; 1

189; Che-sho-wah-ke-pah; ---; M; Head; 39
190; Wah-hrah-lum-pah; ---; F; Wife; 42
191; Hum-pah-to-kah; ---; F; Daut; 12
192; Ke-ah-som-pah; ---; F; Daut; 9
193; ---; Mary Cheshowahkepah; F; Daut; 6

194; ---; Millie Kirk; F; Head; 25
196;* Ke-ah-som-pah; ---; F; Daut; 1 [Skipped #195.]

197; Hun-wah-ko; ---; F; Head; 73

198; Pun-kah-wah-ti-an-kah; ---; M; Head; 47

140

Census of the **Osage Indians** Indians of **Osage Indians** Agency **Oklahoma,** taken by **Hugh Pitzer, Supt. & Sp'l. Disb'g. Agent** , United States Indian Agent, during the 4th quarter, **1909**

Key: NUMBER; Indian Name; English Name; Sex; Relation; Age
* An Askerisk will be next to a number if repeated or out of sequence and inserted among a different family.

199; Wah-hrah-lum-pah; ---; F; Wife; 24
200; Wah-tsa-ah-hah; James Bigheart; M; Son; 13
201; Wah-te-sah; ---; F; Daut; 7
202; Wah-sis-tah; ---; M; Son; 3

203; Pah-nee-wah-with-tah; ---; M; Head; 67
204; Gra-tah-me-tsa-he; ---; F; Wife; 48
205; Ne-kah-lum-pah; ---; M; Head; 53
206; Hah-moie; Bird Tuman; M; Son; 18

207; ---; Gurney Miller; M; Head; 42
208; ---; Grace Miller; F; Daut; 8
209; ---; Howard Miller; M; Son; 6
210; ---; Chester Miller; M; Son; 3
211; ---; Joseph Miller; M; Son; 1

212; Ne-ah-tse-pe; ---; F; Head; 67

213; ---; Annie Turpie; F; Head; 22

214; Bro-ki-he-kah; ---; M; Head; 53
215; Wah-tsa-eo-she; ---; F; Wife; 60
216; E-ne-op-pe; Annie Brokey; F; Daut; 15

217; ---; Herbert Brokey; M; Head; 21

218; E-pah-son-tsa; ---; M; Head; 54

219; Shon-kah-tsa-a; ---; M; Head; 41
220; ---; Polly Earl; F; Daut; 18

221; Ke-ah-som-pah; ---; F; Head; 58
222; Me-hun-kah; Rosa Scott; F; Daut; 18
223; Hlu-ah-wah-kon-tah; Daniel Scott; M; Son; 15
224; Shah-kah-wah-pe; Walter Scott; M; Son; 12

225; Wah-tsa-ah-hah; ---; M; Head; 55
226; Wah-hrah-lum-pah; ---; F; Wife; 31
227; Wah-tsa-moie; Joseph Watson; M; Son; 13

228; Ethel Bryant; Ethel Bryant; F; Head; 25

229; Shah-wah-pe; ---; M; Head; 41

230; ---; Embrey Gibson; M; Head; 46

Census of the **Osage Indians** Indians of **Osage Indians** Agency **Oklahoma,** taken by **Hugh Pitzer, Supt. & Sp'l. Disb'g. Agent** , United States Indian Agent, during the 4th quarter, **1909**

Key: NUMBER; Indian Name; English Name; Sex; Relation; Age
* An Askerisk will be next to a number if repeated or out of sequence and inserted among a different family.

231; Hun-kah-hop-py; Edward G. Gibson; M; Son; 16

232; Son-se-o-grah; Ropemaker; M; Head; 63
233; Mon-shon-tsa-e-tah; ---; F; Wife; 63
234; Wah-ko-aah-moie; Mary Clay; F; Daut; 15

235; ---; Dudley Haskell; M; Head; 33
236; Son-se-grah; ---; F; Wife; 27
237; Wah-hrah-lum-pah; ---; F; Daut; 8
238; Me-gra-to-me; ---; F; Daut; 6
239; Hlu-ah-wah-kon-tah; ---; M; Son; 3

240; He-shah-ah-hle; ---; M; Head; 50
241; He-ah-to-me; ---; F; Wife; 43
242; Ah-kah-me; ---; F; Daut; 10
243; Hlu-ah-gla-she; ---; M; Son; 6
244; Hun-kah-me-tsa-he; ---; F; Daut; 2

245; Mo-hah-ah-gra; ---; M; Head; 60
246; Wah-kon-tah-he-um-pah; ---; F; Wife; 66
247; He-kin-to-op-pe; Angella Hanna; F; Orphan; 14

248; ---; Peter Clark; M; Head; 26
249; ---; Madeline Clark; F; Wife; 20

250; Tom-pah-pe; ---; F; Head; 83

251; ---; Richard Kenny; M; Head; 53
252; Gra-tah-su-ah; ---; F; Wife; 42
253; He-kin-to-op-pe; Mary June; F; Daut; 17
254; A-non-to-op-pe; ---; F; Daut; 5
255; Hlu-lah-tsa-keh; ---; M; Son; 2

256; ---; John Kenny; M; Head; 26
257; Wah-hrah-lum-pah; ---; F; Wife; 24

258; ---; Orlando Kenworthy; M; Head; 33

259; ---; Tony Townsend; M; Head; 29

260; Hun-kah-hop-py; ---; M; Head; 40
261; He-ah-to-me; Mary Hunkahhoppy; F; Daut; 14
262; Wah-hrah-lum-pah; Rosa Hunkahhoppy; F; Daut; 12
263; ---; Lucy Hunkahhoppy; F; Daut; 1

142

Key: NUMBER; Indian Name; English Name; Sex; Relation; Age
* An Askerisk will be next to a number if repeated or out of sequence and inserted among a different family.

264; Hun-kah-hop-py; William Stepson; M; Orphan; 18

265; ---; Jack Hartley; M; Head; 33

266; Nah-hah-scah-she; ---; F; Head; 55

267; Wah-tsa-ki-he-kah; Charles Drum; M; Head; 38
268; We-heh; Agnes Drum; F; Daut; 14
269; Wah-to-sah; Lucy Drum; F; Daut; 8

270; ---; Julia Dunlap; F; Son[sic]; 11

BIG HILL BAND.

271; To-wah-e-he; ---; M; Head; 53
272; Che-sah-me; ---; F; Wife; 61

273; Hun-kah; Alfred McKinley; M; Head; 21
274; Eu-pah-shon-kah-me; ---; F; Daut; 2

275; ---; Daniel McDougan; M; Head; 39

276; ---; Ben Harrison; M; Head; 37
277; ---; Edna M. Harvey; F; S. Daut; 14
278; ---; Emily Harrison; F; Daut; 11
279; ---; Ben H. Harrison; M; Son; 7
280; ---; Wauneta E. Harrison; F; Daut; 4

281; Ne-kah-e-se-y; Jimmy; M; Head; 63
282; ---; Lizzie Q.; F; Wife; 60
283; Wah-shah-she; Rita Kyle; F; Daut; 18

284; Minnie Smith; Minnie Smith; F; Head; 22

285; Ke-ne-kah; ---; M; Head; 72

286; A-non-to-op-pe; ---; F; Head; 60

287; Pah-pah-ah-hah; Thomas Dorry; M; Orphan; 17

288; Num-pah-se; Philip Brokey; M; Son; 8

289; ---; Earnest Roe; M; Head; 37

290; ---; Perry King; M; Head; 34

Census of the **Osage Indians** Indians of **Osage Indians** Agency **Oklahoma,** taken by **Hugh Pitzer, Supt. & Sp'l. Disb'g. Agent**, United States Indian Agent, during the 4th quarter, **1909**

Key: NUMBER; Indian Name; English Name; Sex; Relation; Age
* An Askerisk will be next to a number if repeated or out of sequence and inserted among a different family.

291; E-ne-ke-op-pe; ---; F; Wife; 34
292; Min-tsa-kah; Walter King; M; Son; 10
293; Pun-q-tah; Mary King; F; Daut; 7
294; Cha-hun-kah-me; ---; F; Daut; 2

295; Moh-en-gra-tah; ---; M; Son; 5

296; Mum-brum-pah; ---; F; Head; 84

297; Wah-hrah-lum-pah; ---; F; Head; 53
298; Hun-kah-she; Clementine P. Harris; F; Daut; 13

WHITEHAIR BAND.

299; ---; John Claremore; M; Head; 26
300; ---; Amanda Claremore; F; Wife; 25
301; Mon-shah-ah-she; ---; M; Son; 2

302; Gra-to-me-tsa-he; ---; F; Head; 56
303; Ne-wal-la; George W. Allen; M; Son; 16

304; ---; Dominic Daniels; M; Head; 26

305; ---; Joseph Daniels; M; Head; 27

306; Gra-to-me; ---; F; Head; 43
307; Hlu-ah-tse-ke; John Kenworthy; M; Son; 19
308; Wah-ne-ah-tah; William Kenworthy; M; Son; 16
309; Wah-shun-kah-hah; ---; M; Son; 10
310; Wah-shah-hah-me; ---; F; Daut; 4

311; E-gro-op-pe; Hall Goode; M; Orphan; 20

312; Wah-hrah-lum-pah (D&D); ---; F; Orphan; 14

313; Mo-se-che-he; ---; F; Head; 48
314; E-som-pah; May Collum; F; Daut; 15

315; Wah-ko-sah-moie; ---; F; Head; 40
316; Eah-tah-sah; Clara Collum; F; Daut; 18
317; Ho-tah-me; Anna Collum; F; Daut; 12
318; Hun-tsa-moie; ---; M; Son; 11

319; ---; Joseph Mason; M; Head; 22
320; ---; Rose Mason; F; Wife; 24

144

Census of the **Osage Indians** Indians of **Osage Indians** Agency **Oklahoma,** taken by **Hugh Pitzer, Supt. & Sp'l. Disb'g. Agent** , United States Indian Agent, during the 4th quarter, 1909

Key: NUMBER; Indian Name; English Name; Sex; Relation; Age
* An Askerisk will be next to a number if repeated or out of sequence and inserted among a different family.

321; ---; Frank Mason; M; Son; 1

322; ---; Francis Drexil; M; Head; 32
323; Wah-ko-sah-moie; --; F; Wife; 33
324; Ne-kah-ah-se; ---; F; Daut; 11
325; Me-tsa-kah; ---; M; Son; 7

326; Pah-se-to-pah; ---; M; Head; 62
327; Wah-sha-she-me-tsa-he; ---; F; Wife; 59

328; ---; Paul Peace; M; Head; 23
329; ---; Clara Marshall; F; Wife; 23

330; ---; Henry Peace; M; Head; 26

TALL CHIEF BAND.

331; ---; Alex Tall Chief; M; Head; 42
332; ---; Eliza Tall Chief; F; Wife; 37
333; Hlu-ah-wah-kon-tah; Alex Tall Chief Jr.; M; Son; 19

334; ---; Rosa Tall Chief; F; Wife; 28

335; He-ah-to-me; Emma; F; Head; 56

336; ---; Eves Tall Chief; M; Head; 31
337; Wah-shah-hah-me; ---; F; Wife; 29
338; ---; Helen Tall Chief; F; Daut; 4
339; ---; Henry Tall Chief; M; Son; 2

340; Me-hun-kah; ---; F; Head; 25

341; Ho-tah-moie; John Stink; M; Head; 46

342; Wah-shah-hah-me; ---; F; Head; 62

343; ---; Hanry Tall Chief; M; Head; 26

344; Nah-she-wal-la; ---; M; Head; 50
345; Wah-shah-she-me-tsa-he; Mattie Walsh; F; Daut; 19

346; Pah-she-he; Grace Entokah; F; Head; 24
347; He-ah-to-me; ---; F; Daut; 4
348; ---; Louis Entokah; M; Son; 1

145

Census of the **Osage Indians** Indians of **Osage Indians** Agency **Oklahoma,** taken by **Hugh Pitzer, Supt. & Sp'l. Disb'g. Agent** , United States Indian Agent, during the 4th quarter, **1909**

Key: NUMBER; Indian Name; English Name; Sex; Relation; Age
* An Askerisk will be next to a number if repeated or out of sequence and inserted among a different family.

KO SHE WAH TSE BAND.

349; He-lo-li-he; Bare Legs; M; Head; 71

350; He-se-moie; ---; M; Head; 60
351; Tsa-me-tsa; Mary Buffalo; F; Daut; 10

352; ---; Charles Grant; M; Head; 36

353; ---; George Dunlap; M; Son; 14

354; E-to-kah-wan-ti-an-kah; ---; M; Head; 73
355; Shon-shin-kah; Bryan Wilson; M; Son; 16
356; E-to-hun-kah; ---; M; Son; 9

357; Kah-wah-ho-tsa (Sassamoie); ---; M; Head; 41
358; Wah-ko-ki-he-kah; ---; F; Wife; 43
359; Ah-kah; James McKinley; M; Son; 15
360; Tah-tsa-hu-hah; William McKinley; M; Son; 13
361; Wah-hu-sah; ---; F; Daut; 9

362; Wah-to-sah-grah; ---; F; Wife; 41
363; Ah-kah-me-tsa-he; Eva McKinley; F; Daut; 18
364; Lah-su-sah-pah; Henry McKinley; M; Son; 18

365; ---; Josephine McKinley; F; Head; 21

366; Ne-wal-la; (Tsa-shin-kah); ---; M; Head; 43
367; Me-tsa-he; ---; F; Wife; 33
368; Hlu-ah-to-me; ---; F; Daut; 6
369; To-wah-e-he; ---; M; Son; 2

370; Son-se-gra; ---; F; Head; 32

371; Wah-ko-ki-he-kah; ---; F; Head; 55
372; Wah-tsa-moie; John Hunter; M; Son; 17
373; Wah-ko-sah-moie; Mary Hunter; F; Daut; 13

BLACK DOG BAND.

374; ---; Black Dog; M; Head; 62
375; Gra-to-me-tsa; Louisa Black Dog; F; Wife; 29

376; ---; Edgar McCarthy; M; Head; 36
377; Me-tsa-he; Nettie McCarthy; F; Wife; 26

146

Key: NUMBER; Indian Name; English Name; Sex; Relation; Age
* An Askerisk will be next to a number if repeated or out of sequence and inserted among a different family.

378; To-wah-e-he; ---; M; Head; 85
379; Son-se-gra; ---; F; Wife; 51

380; ---; Amos Hamilton; M; Head; 37
381; ---; Noah Hamilton; M; Son; 7
382; ---; Ira Hamilton; M; Son; 5
383; ---; Otto Hamilton; M; Son; 2

384; Me-ho-e ---; F; Head; 70

385; ---; Allison Webb; M; Head; 25
386; ---; Grace Webb; F; Wife; 35

387; He-lo-ki-he; Long Bow; M; Head; 42
388; E-gro-tah; Charles; M; Son; 19

389; Wah-sop-py; Lucy Hahmoie Bangs; F; Head; 25
390; ---; Myron Bangs Jr.; M; Son; 1

391; ---; Silas Sanford; M; Head; 32
392; ---; anna Sanford; F; Wife; 27

393; ---; Allen Webb; M; Head; 29
394; Hum-pah-to-kah; ---; F; Wife; 21
395; ---; Bertha Webb; F; Daut; 3
396; ---; Charles M. Webb; M; Son; 3

397; ---; Willie McCarthy (Incompetent); M; Head; 28

398; ---; Andrew Jackson; M; Head; 40
399; Me-tsa-he; Maude Hahmoie; F; Daut; 15

SAUCY CHIEF BAND.

400; ---; Lawrence; M; Head; 55

401; ---; Joseph Mills; M; Orphan; 20

402; ---; Alex Eagle Feather; M; Head; 36

403; Wah-te-sah; ---; F; Head; 68

404; Gra-to-me-tsa-he; Ida Gibson; F; Orphan; 14

405; ---; Prudie Martin; F; Head; 34

Key: NUMBER; Indian Name; English Name; Sex; Relation; Age
* An Askerisk will be next to a number if repeated or out of sequence and inserted among a different family.

406; ---; Christine Martine; F; Daut; 6
407; ---; Cecil martin; M; Son; 3

408; ---; James G. Blaine; M; Head; 36
409; ---; Hazel Blaine; F; Wife; 25
410; ---; Laura Gray; F; S. Daut; 7
411; ---; Walker Blaine; M; Son; 13

412; E-ne-op-pe; ---; F; Head; 28
413; ---; Eugene Blaine; M; Son; 9
414; Me-shah-e; ---; F; Daut; 7
415; ---; James G. Blaine Jr.; M; Son; 5

416; ---; Hayes Little Bear; M; Head; 24
417; Lo-hah-me; Dora Little Bear; F; Wife; 21

418; Ah-hu-shin-kah; ---; M; Head; 49
419; Nah-hah-sah-me; ---; F; Wife; 62

420; ---; Augustine Crowe; F; Head; 34
421; ---; Josephine Strike Axe; F; Daut; 15
422; ---; Augustus Chouteau; M; Son; 14
423; ---; Charles Chouteau; M; Son; 11

424; ---; Robert Panther; M; Head; 46
425; ---; Charles Panther; M; Son; 19
425;* ---; Clark Panther; M; Son; 17 [Two #425's.]
426; ---; Nettie Panther; F; Daut; 15
427; ---; Maud Panther; F; Daut; 12

428; ---; Mary Pryor; F; Head; 58

429; ---; Edna Good Bear; F; Head; 37

430; Charles Me-she-tsa-he; ---; M; Head; 50
431; Wah-ko-aah-moie; ---; F; Wife; 55
432; Hlu-ah-me; Eva Bean; F; Daut; 17
433; Pah-she-he; Emma Hoover; F; Daut; 13

434; ---; Ben Mushunkashey; M; Head; 26
435; Hlu-ah-me-tsa-he; Edna Mushunkashey; F; Wife; 21
436; ---; Charley Mushunkashey; M; Son; 2

437; ---; William Pryor; M; Head; 34
438; Min-kah-she; Mary Pryor; F; Wife; 36

148

Census of the **Osage Indians** Indians of **Osage Indians** Agency **Oklahoma,** taken by **Hugh Pitzer, Supt. & Sp'l. Disb'g. Agent** , United States Indian Agent, during the 4th quarter, **1909**

Key: NUMBER; Indian Name; English Name; Sex; Relation; Age
* An Askerisk will be next to a number if repeated or out of sequence and inserted among a different family.

439; ---; Josephine Pryor; F; Daut; 9
440; Shon-kah; Charles Mushunkashey; M; S. Son; 13

441; ---; Susie L. Hutchinson; F; Head; 27
442; ---; Vernie L. Hutchinson; F; Daut; 8
443; ---; Charles V. Hutchinson; M; Son; 6
444; ---; Carlos H. Hutchinson; M; Son; 4
445; ---; Genvis Hutchinson; F; Daut; 2

446; Ke-le-kom-pah; ---; M; Head; 59
447; Mo-se-che-he; ---; F; Wife; 54

448; Wah-kon-te-ah; Wakon Iron; M; Son; 18

449; ---; Paul Albert; M; Head; 40
450; ---; Annie Albert; F; Wife; 25

451; Pah-she-he; ---; F; Head; 49

452; Hum-pah-to-kah; ---; F; Head; 55

453; Wah-shah-she-me-tsa-he; Augustine Black; F; Head; 36
454; ---; John P. White Tail; M; Son; 12
455; Hom-me-tsa-he; May Black; F; Daut; 3

456; Me-shah-e; ---; F; Head; 56

457; ---; Harry Kohpay; M; Head; 37
458; ---; Elsie Kohpay; F; Daut; 10
459; ---; Hugh Kohpay; M; Son; 9
460; ---; Loretto Kohpay; M; Son; 2

461; Wy-e-gla-in-kah; Red Corn; M; Head; 55
462; Wah-kon-tah-he-um-pah; ---; F; Wife; 58
463; Wah-tsa-kon-lah; Ralph Malone; M; S. Son; 17

464; ---; Raymond Red Corn; M; Head; 23

465; Tsa-pah-ke-ah; ---; M; Head; 60
466; Hlu-ah-me-tsa-he; ---; F; Wife; 67

467; ---; Pearl Hartley; F; Head; 29

468; ---; Julia White Tail; F; Head; 63

Census of the **Osage Indians** Indians of **Osage Indians** Agency **Oklahoma,** taken by **Hugh Pitzer, Supt. & Sp'l. Disb'g. Agent** , United States Indian Agent, during the 4th quarter, **1909**

Key: NUMBER; Indian Name; English Name; Sex; Relation; Age
* An Askerisk will be next to a number if repeated or out of sequence and inserted among a different family.

469;   ---; Antwine Albert; M; Head; 46
470;   Ne-kah-she-he (Blind); ---; F; Wife; 35
471;   Wah-pah-ah-hah; Edward Elkins; M; S. Son; 12
372;* Gra-to-me; Minnie Elkins; F; S. Daut; 4 [Wrong #.]
473;   Com-pox-she; Kate Albert; F; Daut; 2

474;   ---; Charles Michelle; M; Head; 41
475;   Me-sah-e; ---; F; Wife; 37
476;   ---; Ida Michelle; F; Daut; 13

477;   ---; Harry Big Eagle; M; Head; 23
478;   Wah-shah-hah-me; Elsie Big Eagle; F; Wife; 19
479;   Me-tsa-he; Metsa Big Eagle; F;

480;   ---; Sylvia Wood; F; Head; 40

481;   Wah-shah-she-me-tsa-he; ---; F; Head; 85
482;   ---; Harry Pyahhunkah; M; Head; 22

483;   ---; Charles Brave; M; Head; 31
484;   Mum-brum-pah; Mary Strike Axe Brave; F; Wife; 24
485;   ---; Andrew Brave; M; Son; 8
486;   ---; Louis Brave; M; Son; 3

487;   ---; Laban Miles; M; Head; 49
488;   Mo-se-che-he; Anna Miles; F; Daut; 19
489;   Wah-shah-ah-pe; Mary Miles; F; Daut; 15
490;   Pah-pah-ah-ho; Leo Miles; M; Son; 15
491;   Hlu-ah-shu-tsa; John Miles; M; Son; 20

492;   Wah-shah-she-me-tsa-he; ---; F; Head; 40
493;   ---; Walker Penn; M; Son; 18
494;   ---; Laban Miles Jr.; M; Son; 8
495;   ---; Eddie Penn; M; Son; 20

496;   ---; John Whitehorn; M; Head; 26
497;   ---; Arthur Whitehorn; M; Son; 4

498;   Hu-lah-tun-kah; Big Eagle; M; Head; 57
499;   Pah-pu-son-tsa; ---; F; Wife; 59
500;   Wah-she-pah; Wash Warrior; M; S. Son; 17
501;   Pah-she-he; Mary Warrior; F; S. Daut; 14

502;   Hun-kah-ah-gra; Robert Warrior; M; Head; 19
503;   Tsa-me-hun-kah; Mamie Warrior; F; Wife; 19

150

Census of the **Osage Indians** Indians of **Osage Indians** Agency **Oklahoma,** taken by **Hugh Pitzer, Supt. & Sp'l. Disb'g. Agent** , United States Indian Agent, during the 4th quarter, **1909**

Key: NUMBER; Indian Name; English Name; Sex; Relation; Age
* An Askerisk will be next to a number if repeated or out of sequence and inserted among a different family.

504;   ---; Russell Warrior; M; Head; 25

505;   E-stah-o-gre-she; --; M; Head; 45
506;   Shon-blah-scah; ---; F; Wife; 41

507;   Mon-kah-he; Frank Pyahhunkah; M; Orphan; 15

BEAVER BAND.

508;   ---; Rose L. Bigheart; F; Daut; 17
509;   ---; Sarah L' Bigheart; F; Daut; 11
510;   ---; Belle L. Bigheart; F; Daut; 6

511;   Che-sho-shin-kah; Henry Red Eagle; M; Head; 50
512;   ---; Rosa Red Eagle; F; Wife; 58

513;   ---; Paul Red Eagle; M; Head; 29
514;   ---; Cecelia Red Eagle; F; Wife; 27
515;   ---; Harry Red Eagle; M; Son; 7
516;   ---; Louis Red Eagle; M; M; Son; 4
518;* ---; Joseph Red Eagle; M; Son; 3 [Skipped #417.]
519;   ---; May Louise Red Eagle; F; Daut; 1
520;   ---; Henry Red Eagle; M; Son; 3mo

521;   Hlu-ah-shu-tsa (D&D); Joseph Red Eagle; M; Head; 33

522;   Beg-gah-hah-she; Brave; M; Head; 75
523;   ---; Mary Brave; F; Wife; 78

524;   ---; Andrew Bighorse; M; Head; 32
525;   Hum-pah-to-kah; ---; F; Wife; 38
526;   We-heh; Rose McDougal; F; S. Daut; 17
527;   ---; Peter Bighorse; M; Son; 10
528;   ---; Joseph Bighorse; M; Son; 8
529;   ---; Mary Bighorse; F; Daut; 5
530;   ---; Edward Bighorse; M; Son; 2

531;   ---; Charles McDougan; M; Head; 21

532;   ---; John Wagoshe; M; Head; 31
533;   Wah-shah-she-me-tsa-he; Agnes Bigheart; F; Wife; 31
534;   ---; George Vest; M; S. Son; 13
535;   ---; Charles Wagoshe; M; Son; 5
536;   A-non-to-op-pe; ---; F; Daut; 3
537;   Wah-sah-po; ---; F; Daut; 2

151

Census of the **Osage Indians** Indians of **Osage Indians** Agency **Oklahoma,** taken by **Hugh Pitzer, Supt. & Sp'l. Disb'g. Agent** , United States Indian Agent, during the 4th quarter, 1909

Key: NUMBER; Indian Name; English Name; Sex; Relation; Age
* An Askerisk will be next to a number if repeated or out of sequence and inserted among a different family.

538; ---; John Lookout; M; Head; 32
539; Heh-kah-mon-kah; ---; F; Wife; 23
540; ---; William Lookout; M; Son; 2

541; ---; Louis Bighorse; M; Head; 44
542; To-op-pe; Ida Bighorse; F; Wife; 29
543; ---; Rose Bighorse; F; Daut; 13
544; ---; Lillie Bighorse; F; Daut; 8
545; ---; Minnie Bighorse; F; Daut; 5
546; ---; Louise Bighorse; F; Daut; 2

547; ---; Paul Buffalo; M; Head; 45
548; pah-pu-s-n-tsa; ---; F; Wife; 51

549; Ah-tsa-shin-kah; Mary Wild Cat; F; Orphan; 11

550; Mo-ho-gla; ---; M; Head; 55
551; Me-tsa-hi-ke; ---; F; Wife; 65

552; ---; Antwine Pryor; M; Head; 29
553; A-non-to-op-pe; Frances Pryor; F; Wife; 23
554; ---; Julia Pryor; F; Daut; 4
555; ---; Susie Pryor; F; Daut; 2

556; ---; Henry Coshehe; M; Head; 36
557; Wah-kon-tah-he-um-pah; ---; F; Wife; 33
558; ---; Clem Coshehe; M; Son; 16
559; ---; John Coshehe; M; Son; 9
560; ---; George Coshehe; M; Son; 3

561; Wah-tsa-ah-tah; Ralph On Hand; M; Orphan; 18

562; He-he-kin-to-op-pe; Minnie On Hand; F; Orphan; 13

563; ---; John McFall; M; Head; 42
564; Gra-tah-shin-kah; Mary McFall; F; Wife; Orphan; 30

565; ---; Minnie Whitehorn; F; Orphan; 19

566; ---; George Michelle; M; Head; 35
567; ---; Wesley W. Michelle; M; Son; 4

568; Mo-se-che-he; ---; F; Head; 69

Census of the **Osage Indians** Indians of **Osage Indians** Agency **Oklahoma,** taken by **Hugh Pitzer, Supt. & Sp'l. Disb'g. Agent** , United States Indian Agent, during the 4th quarter, **1909**

Key: NUMBER; Indian Name; English Name; Sex; Relation; Age
* An Askerisk will be next to a number if repeated or out of sequence and inserted among a different family.

STRIKE AXE BAND.

569; ---; Fred Lookout; M; Head; 51
570; Mo-se-che-he; Julia Lookout; F; Wife; 40
571; ---; Charles Lookout; M; Son; 17
572; ---; Frederick Lookout; M; Son; 14
573; ---; Nora Lookout; F; Daut; 9
574; ---; Henry Lookout; M; Son; 3
575; ---; James Strike Axe; M; Orphan; 15

576; Wy-e-nah-she; ---; M; Head; 61

577; Tsa-shin-kah-wah-ti-an-kah; Saucy Calf; M; Head; 65
578; ---; Sophia Chouteau; F; Wife; 67

579; ---; Joseph Buffulohide; M; Head; 23
580; Agnes Buffalohide; F; Wife; 22

581; Tom-pah-pah; ---; F; Head; 55

582; ---; Pendleton Strike Axe; M; Head; 28
583; Mo-se-che-he; ---; F; Wife; 21
584; ---; Emma Strike Axe; F; Daut; 5
585; ---; Ida Strike Axe; F; Daut; 3

586; ---; Foster Strike Axe; M; Head; 35
587; Lo-tah-sah; Cordelia Strike Axe; F; Wife; 31
588; ---; Jennie Strike Axe; F; Daut; 13
589; ---; Emma Strike Axe; F; Daut; 11
590; ---; Dora Strike Axe; F; Daut; 3

591; ---; Louis Pryor; M; Head; 30
592; ---; Andrew Pryor; M; Son; 3

593; O-sah-ke-pah; Cap Strike Axe; M; Head; 51

594; Pah-se-to-pah (D&D); ---; M; Head; 39
595; Me-sah-e; Veva Pahsetopah; F; Wife; 29
596; ---; Cora Pahsetopah; F; Daut; 8
597; ---; Carrie Pahsetopah; F; Daut; 6
598; ---; Louis Pahsetopah; M; Son; 4

599; Me-hun-kah (He-ah-to-me); ---; F; Head; 59
600; Ke-nun-tah; William Shahpahnahshe; M; Son; 19

Census of the **Osage Indians** Indians of **Osage Indians** Agency **Oklahoma,** taken by **Hugh Pitzer, Supt. & Sp'l. Disb'g. Agent**, United States Indian Agent, during the 4th quarter, **1909**

Key: NUMBER; Indian Name; English Name; Sex; Relation; Age
* An Askerisk will be next to a number if repeated or out of sequence and inserted among a different family.

601; ---; Pierce St. John; M; Head; 33
602; Ke-ah-som-pah; ---; F; Wife; 35
603; Gra-tah-scah; Jacob Jump; M; S. Son; 17
604; ---; Dora St. John; F; Daut; 7
605; ---; Herbert St. John; M; Son; 5
606; ---; William St. John; M; Son; 3
607; ---; Anna St. John; F; Daut; 2

608; ---; Frank Corndropper; M; Head; 61
609; Gra-tah-me-tsa-he; ---; F; Wife; 63

610; Peh-tsa-moie; ---; M; Head; 66
611; Wah-tsa-u-sah; ---; F; Wife; 37

612; ---; Richard Firewalk; M; Head; 25
613; Son-se-grah; May Firewalk; F; Wife; 19

614; Lah-blah-wal-la; Three Striker (Incompetent); M; Head; 65

615; Wy-u-hah-kah; ---; M; Head; 51
616; Hlu-ah-me-tsa-he; ---; F; Wife; 60

617; ---; John Oberly; M; Head; 29
617;* Me-tsa-he; ---; F; Wife; 27
618; ---; Martha Oberly; F; Daut; 4
619; A-non-to-op-pe; ---; F; Daut; 2
620; Pah-pah-ah-he; ---; M;Son; 1

621; ---; John A. Logan; M; Head; 36
622; ---; Mary Logan; F; Wife; 31
623; ---; Joseph Logan; M; Son; 10
624; ---; Rosa Logan; F; Daut; 4
625; ---; Oscar Logan; M; Son; 8
626; Tom-pah-pah; ---; F; Daut; 2

NE-KAH-KEE-PAH-NEE BAND.

627; ---; Robert A-she-gah-hre; M; Head; 59
628; Gra-to-me-tsa-he; ---; F; Wife; 53
629; Me-tun-kah; Susan Killon; F; Daut; 19
630; Vah-sah-pah-shin; ---; F; Daut; 4
631; Sho-tsa; ---; M; Son; 2

632; Ke-mo-hah; ---; M; Head; 50
633; Loh-tah-sah; ---; F; Wife; 34

154

Census of the **Osage Indians** Indians of **Osage Indians** Agency **Oklahoma,**
taken by **Hugh Pitzer, Supt. & Sp'l. Disb'g. Agent** , United States Indian Agent,
during the 4th quarter, **1909**

Key: NUMBER; Indian Name; English Name; Sex; Relation; Age
* An Askerisk will be next to a number if repeated or out of sequence and inserted among a different family.

634; Me-tsa-he; Elda Townsend; F; S. Daut; 17
635; ---; John R. Townsend; M; S. Son; 12
636; Hun-kah-me (D&D); ---; F; Daut; 10
637; Heh-mo-sah; ---; M; Son; 9
638; Moh-e-kah-shah; ---; M; Son; 7
639; Mon-shon-kah-hah; ---; M; Son; 5

640; Tsa-e-kon-lah (Crazy); Mrs. Womack; F; Head; 65

641; ---; Clarence Gray; M; Head; 32
642; He-kin-to-op-pe; Jennie Gray; F; Wife; 22
643; ---; Mary Gray; F; Daut; 5
644; ---; Clarence Gray Jr.; M; Son; 2

645; Tsa-pah-shin-kah; John; M; Head; 55
646; Wah-shah-pe-wah-ko; ---; F; Wife; 59
647; E-to-wah-hrah-lum-pah; Mary Brown; F; Daut; 14

648; Shon-kah; Charles Brown; M; Head; 21

649; ---; David Copperfield; M; Head; 33
650; Hun-kah-me-tsa-he; Maggie Copperfield; F; Wife; 35
651; Me-tsa-he; ---; F; Daut; 9
652; Hun-kah-she; ---; F; Son; 7
653; Hun-kah-ah-gra; ---; M; Son; 4
654; Wah-she-pah; ---; M; Son; 2
655; ---; William Pitts; M; Head; 32
656; Me-tsa-he; Isabella Pitts; F; Wife; 31
657; ---; George T. Pitts; M; Son; 2

658; Hun-kah-tun-kah; Roman Logan; M; Head; 49
659; Pah-she-he; Mary Logan; F; Wife; 28
660; Me-tsa-he; Agnes Logan; F; Daut; 13
661; Tom-pah-pe; ---; F; Daut; 7

662; Che-she-shin-kah; ---; M; Head; 70
663; Hlu-ah-to-me; ---; F; Wife; 62

664; ---; Frank Lohowa; M; Head; 24
665; ---; Mary Lohowa; F; Wife; 27

666; Wah-kah-lah-tun-kah; ---; M; Head; 67
667; Me-tsa-he; ---; F; Wife; 69

668; Ah-hu-scah; Walla Fish; M; Head; 20

155

Census of the **Osage Indians** Indians of **Osage Indians** Agency **Oklahoma,** taken by **Hugh Pitzer, Supt. & Sp'l. Disb'g. Agent**, United States Indian Agent, during the 4th quarter, **1909**

Key: NUMBER; Indian Name; English Name; Sex; Relation; Age
* An Askerisk will be next to a number if repeated or out of sequence and inserted among a different family.

669; E-no-op-pe; Mary Fish; F; Wife; 18

670; Hun-tsa-moie; ---; M; Head; 45
671; Hlu-ah-to-me; ---; F; Wife; 65

672; Mo-se-che-he; ---; F; Head; 91

CLAREMORE BAND.

673; ---; Francis Claremore; M; Head; 44
674; Wah-hrah-lum-pah; ---; F; Wife; 38
675; Tsa-pah-ke-ah; Louis Claremore; M; SWon; 16

676; ---; John Abbott; M; Head; 28
677; Ne-kah-she-tsa; ---; F; Wife; 25
678; Wah-shah-she-me-tsa-he; ---; F; Daut; 7
679; ---; Margurite Abbott; F; Daut; 2

680; ---; Henry Pratt; M; Head; 37
681; Hun-kah-me; Josephine Pratt; F; Wife; 36
682; ---; Helen Pratt; F; Daut; 14
683; Gra-tah-scah; George Pratt; M; Son; 8
684; ---; Charles Pratt; M; Son; 4

685; Me-gra-to-me; ---; F; Head; 53

686; Pah-hu-gre-she; ---; F; Head; 21
687; ---; Andrew Opah; M; Son; 3
688   ---; Charles Big Elk; M; Head; 30
689; Mo-se-che-he; Cora Big Elk; F; Wife; 27
690; ---; Mary Big Elk; F; Daut; 9
691   ---; Don S. Big Elk; M; Son; 3

692; Hlu-ah-me; ---; F; Head; 65
693; E-ah-scah-wal-la; James Browning; M; Son; 16
694; Mon-kah-hah; John Browning; M; Son; 11

695; ---; Eugene Ware; M; Head; 33
696; Hum-pah-to-kah; ---; F; Wife; 32
697; ---; Joseph Ware; M; Son; 10
698; ---; Mary Ware; F; Daut; 8
699; ---; Elijah N. Ware; M; Son; 6
700; ---; Daisy L. Ware; F; Ware; F; Daut; 4

701; ---; Henry Roan; M; Head; 26

156

Census of the **Osage Indians** Indians of **Osage Indians** Agency **Oklahoma,** taken by **Hugh Pitzer, Supt. & Sp'l. Disb'g. Agent** , United States Indian Agent, during the 4th quarter, **1909**

Key: NUMBER; Indian Name; English Name; Sex; Relation; Age
* An Askerisk will be next to a number if repeated or out of sequence and inserted among a different family.

702; He-ah-to-me; ---; F; Wife; 20
703; ---; Grace Roan; F; Daut; 3

704; ---; Arthur Bonnicastle; M; Head; 32
705; ---; Angie Bonnicastle; F; Wife; 22

706; ---; Maud Supernaw; F; Head; 35
707; ---; Mary Thompson; F; Daut; 11

708; ---; Jack Wheeler; M; Head; 67
709; Nah-me-tsa-he; ---; F; Wife; 62

710; ---; Rhoda Wheeler; F; Head; 24

711; ---; Ben Wheeler; M; Head; 33
712; Tsa-me-tsa-he; Fanny Wheeler; F; Wife; 27
713; Hun-kah-hre; Fred Wheeler; M; Son; 8
714; Me-tsa-he; ---; F; Daut; 3
715; ---; Shah-kah-pah-he; ---; M; Son; 1

716; ---; Nannie Naranjo; M; Head; 37
717; ---; Clara Naranjo; F; Daut; 10

718; Hlu-ah-shu-tsa; Joe Red Eagle; M; Head; 39
719; Hun-kah-me; Dora Red Eagle; F; Wife; 31
720; ---; Alice Red Eagle; F; Daut; 4

721; Wah-shah-she-me-tsa-he; ---; F; Head; 50

722; ---; Sophia Greenback; F; Head; 35

WAH TI AN KAH BAND.

723; Wah-she-hah; Bacon Rind; M; Head; 49
724; Wah-ko-ki-h-e-kah; Rosa Bacon Rind; F; Wife; 45
725; In-gro-tah; George Baconrind[sic]; M; Son; 18
726; Ah-tsa-shin-kah; Louisa Baconrind; F; Daut; 12
727; Mah-hu-sah; Moses Baconrind; M; Son; 8
728; ---; Julia Baconrind; F; Daut; 6

729; Mo-sah-mum-pah; ---; M; Head; 42
730; Hun-kah-me; ---; F; Wife; 36
731; Ki-he-kah-tun-kah; ---; M; Son; 13

732; To-wah-e-he; ---; M; Head; 64

157

Census of the **Osage Indians** Indians of **Osage Indians** Agency **Oklahoma,** taken by **Hugh Pitzer, Supt. & Sp'l. Disb'g. Agent** , United States Indian Agent, during the 4th quarter, **1909**

Key: NUMBER; Indian Name; English Name; Sex; Relation; Age
* An Askerisk will be next to a number if repeated or out of sequence and inserted among a different family.

733; Gra-tose-me; ---; F; Wife; 53

734; She-she; ---; M; Head; 50
735; Ne-kah; ---; F; Wife; 53

736; ---; Simon Henderson; M; Head; 27
737; ---; Louisa Henderson; F; Wife; 23
738; He-ah-to-me; ---; F; Daut; 3

739; ---; George Pitts; M; Head; 28
740; ---; Mary Pitts; F; Wife; 23
741; ---; Warren Pitts; M; Son; 6
742; ---; David Pitts; M; Son; 4
743; ---; Elizabeth Pitts; F; Daut; 2

744; Ho-ki-ah-se; ---; M; Head; 41
745; Me-tsa-he; Louisa Hokiahse; F; Wife; 31
746; Wah-shah-she-me-tsa-he; Louisa Hokiahse; F; Daut; 13
747; To-ho-ah; ---; M; Son; 5
748; E-nan-me-tsa-tun; ---; M; Son; 1

WM. PENN BAND.

749; ---; Peter G. Bigheart; M; Head; 70
750; Wah-ko-ki-he-kah; ---; F; Wife; 66

751; Hlu-ah-to-me (D&D); ---; F; Orphan; 17

752; ---; George Bigheart; M; Head; 33
753; Pah-me-she-wah; ---; F; Wife; 23
754; ---; Charles Bigheart; M; Son; 4
755; Um-pah-to-kah; ---; F; Daut; 2
756; Wah-ko-sah-moie; ---; F; Daut; 9mo

757; ---; Claude Smith; M; Head; 35
758; Hlu-ah-to-me; Mamie Smith; F; Wife; 26
759; Wah-tsa-me; ---; M; Son; 7
760; Hum-pah-to-kah; ---; F; Daut; 6
761; Ke-ah-som-pah; ---; F; Daut; 3
762; Wah-ko-sah-moie; ---; F; Daut; 2

763; Wah-she-wah-hah; John Bigheart; M; Head; 43
764; Hlu-ah-to-me; Grace Bigheart; F; Wife; 40
765; Ne-kah-sto-kah; John Bigheart; M; Son; 12
766; Wah-ko-sah-moie; ---; F; Daut; 11
767; Ne-kah-sto-wah; ---; M; Son; 8

Census of the **Osage Indians** Indians of **Osage Indians** Agency **Oklahoma,** taken by **Hugh Pitzer, Supt. & Sp'l. Disb'g. Agent** , United States Indian Agent, during the 4th quarter, **1909**

768; Kah-scah; ---; M; Son; 5
769; Grah-e-grah-in-kah; ---; M; Son; 3
770; Wah-tsa-tun-kah; Joseph Bigheart; M; Son; 20

771; ---; Edward Bigheart; M; Head; 21
772; ---; Rose Bigheart; F; Wife; 18

773; O-lo-hah-wal-la; ---; M; Head; 65
774; He-ah-to-me; ---; F; Wife; 48
775; Ne-wal-la; Henry Lohah; M; Son; 17
776; Ah-hu-shin-kah; Albert Lohah; M; Son; 15
777; A-non-to-op-pe; Ellen Lohah; F; Daut; 11
778; Heh-kah-mon-kah; Mary Lohah; F; Daut; 10
779; Tompahpeshe; ---; M; Son; 4

780; ---; Samuel Barker; M; Head; 30
781; ---; Frances Barker; F; Wife; 21
782; ---; James Barker; M; Son; 1

783; O-lo-hah-moie; ---; M; Head; 51
784; Mo-se-che-he; ---; F; Wife; 41
785; Hlu-ah-wah-lon-tah; Robert Olohahmoie; M; Son; 17
786; Wah-tsa-a-tah; George Olohahmoie; M; Son; 14
787; Wah-hrah-lum-pah; ---; F; Daut; 11
788; Num-pah-q-ah; ---; M; Son; 9
789; Mepgra-to-me; ---; F; Daut; 7
790; Moie-ke-kah-she; ---; M; Son; 5

791; Tah-hah-gah-hah; ---; M; Head; 45
792; Wah-hu-sah-e; ---; F; Wife; 40
793; Ah-nah-me-tsa-he; Roy Maker; M; Son; 12
794; Ho-ke-ah-se; George Maker; M; Son; 5

795; ---; Ross Maker; M; Head; 21

796; Ah-kah-me; ---; F; Wife; 30
797; Shon-kah; James Maker; M; Son; 12

798; ---; Edgar Maker; M; Head; 24
799; ---; Helen Maker; F; Wife; 19
800; ---; Theodore Maker; M; Son; 1

801; Mo-shah-ke-tah; ---; M; Head; 45

802; Tom-pah-pe; ---; M; Head; 63

Census of the **Osage Indians** Indians of **Osage Indians** Agency **Oklahoma,** taken by **Hugh Pitzer, Supt. & Sp'l. Disb'g. Agent** , United States Indian Agent, during the 4th quarter, **1909**

Key: NUMBER; Indian Name; English Name; Sex; Relation; Age
* An Askerisk will be next to a number if repeated or out of sequence and inserted among a different family.

803; O-hun-pe-ah; John Bruce; M; Son; 19

804; ---; Albert Penn; M; Head; 39
805; ---; Dora Penn; F; Wife; 22
806; Wah-ses-tah; Andrew Penn; M; Son; 15
807; Wah-te-sah; Grace Penn; F; Daut; 14
808; ---; Mary Penn; F; Daut; 3

809; ---; Fred Penn; M; Head; 36

810; O-ke-sah; Tom West; M; Head; 35
811; Me-tsa-he; Rosa West; F; Wife; 36
812; ---; John Wood; M; S. Son; 15
813; Mo-se-che-he; ---; F; Daut; 5
814; Hlu-ah-tse-ke; ---; M; Son; 3

815; ---; Dan G. West; M; Head; 31
816; Pah-pu-son-tsa; Fanny West; F; Wife; 25
817; He-ah-to-me; Lucy West; F; Daut; 8
818; ---; Howard M. West; M; Son; 3

LITTLE CHIEF BAND.

819; ---; Charles Whitehorn; M; Orphan; 19

820; ---; John Whitehorn; M; Head; 21

821; Nah-kah-sah-me; Kate Whitehorn; F; Head; 21

822; Wah-shah-hah-me; ---; F; Head; 57

823; Ki-he-kah-nah-she; ---; M; Head; 46
824; Hlu-ah-to-me; Frances Kihekahnahshe; F; Wife; 36
825; Wah-shah-she-me-tsa-he; Magella Whitehorn; F; Daut; 15
826; Hum-pah-to-kah; Tresa Whitehorn; F; Daut; 13
827; Monk-she-hah-pe; ---; M; Son; 2

828; Me-tsa-he; ---; F; Head; 43
829; Wah-shah-she-me-tsa-he; ---; F; Daut; 8
830; Ho-ho; Clarence Daniel; M; Son; 14
831; Wah-ahah-she; ---; F; Daut; 6

832; He-ah-to-me; ---; F; Head; 57

833; ---; Frank Little Soldier; M; Head; 24

160

Census of the **Osage Indians** Indians of **Osage Indians** Agency **Oklahoma,** taken by **Hugh Pitzer, Supt. & Sp'l. Disb'g. Agent** , United States Indian Agent, during the 4th quarter, **1909**

Key: NUMBER; Indian Name; English Name; Sex; Relation; Age
* An Askerisk will be next to a number if repeated or out of sequence and inserted among a different family.

834; ---; Esther Little Soldier; F; Wife; 23

835; Me-tsa-he; ---; F; Head; 19
836; Wah-shah-e-no-pah; ---; M; Son; 1

837; ---; Ellen Spurgeon; F; Head; 28

838; Hlu-ah-wah-tah; ---; M; Head; 43
839; He-to-op-pe; ---; F; Wife; 40
840; Mah-grah-lum-pah; ---; F; Daut; 10
841; Hlu-ah-wah-kon-tah; ---; M; Son; 5
842; Wah-shah-me-tsa-he; Lillie Hlu-ah-wah-tah; F; Daut; 2

843; Me-tsa-no; Mary Mudd; F; Head; 53
844; ---; Anna Mudd; F; Daut; 11
845; ---; Alex Mudd; M; Son; 20

846; ---; Lucy Lotson; F; Head; 32
847; ---; Lucious Lotson; M; Son; 13

848; ---; Cleatess Mudd; F; Daut; 2
849; ---; Dorothy Mudd; F; Daut; 2

849-1/3; (Son of 437) ---; John Pryor; M; Son; 6
849-2/3; (Son of 696) ---; Charles Ware; M; Son; 3
850; (Son of 718) ---; Frederick Red Eagle; M; Son; 8

HALF BREED BAND.

850-1/2; ---; Aiken, Elizabeth; F; Head; 27

851; ---; Aiken, John; M; Head; 25

852; ---; Alberty, Cynthia; F; Head; 53
853; ---; Alberty Lizzie; F; Daut; 18

854; ---; Alberty, George; M; Head; 22
855; ---; Alberty Flora; F; Wife; 22

856; ---; Alexander, Levi; M; Head; 28
857; ---; Alexander Martha I.; F; Daut; 7

858; ---; Alexander, Ida A.; F; Daut; 20

859; ---; Allen, Emily; F; Head; 45

161

Key: NUMBER; Indian Name; English Name; Sex; Relation; Age
* An Askerisk will be next to a number if repeated or out of sequence and inserted among a different family.

860; ---; Whalen, Esther; F; Daut; 15
861; ---; Whalen Dorothea; F; Daut; 13
862; ---; Whalen Charlotte; F; Daut; 20

863; ---; Anderson, Mary; F; Head; 25

864; ---; Anderson, John B.; M; Head; 23
865; ---; Anderson Henry P.; M; Son; 3
866; ---; Anderson Viretta; F; Daut; 2

867; ---; Anderson, Edward R.; M; Head; 21

868; ---; Anderson; Skinner T.; M; Son; 15
869; ---; Anderson Ora D.; F; Daut; 11
870; ---; Anderson Noble M.; M; Son; 10

871; ---; Anderson, Florence; F; Head; 20

872; ---; Appleby, Jane; F; Head; 78
873; ---; Captain, Peter; (Incompetent); M; Son; 45

874; ---; Atkin, John D. Jr.; M; Head; 22

875; ---; Avant, Rosalie; F; Head; 32
876; ---; Avant Theodore R.; M; Son; 11
877; ---; Avant Ethel; F; Daut; 8

878; ---; Barber, Ida; F; Head; 27
879; ---; Barber; Augustus; M; Son; 6
880; ---; Barber; Morris G.; M; Son; 3

881; ---; Barber, Bridget A.; F; Head; 48
882; ---; Barber Clara M.; F; Daut; 17
883; ---; Barber Edgar E.; M; Son; 14
884; ---; Barber Lawrence L.; M; Son; 12
885; ---; Paul G.; M; Son; 9
886; ---; Lee R.; M; Son; 5

887; ---; Barker, Mary J.; F; Head; 54
888; ---; Simms, Cora E.; F; Daut; 15

889; ---; Baker, John Thomas; Head; 40
890; ---; Baker Monette; F; Wife; 34
891; ---; Baker Myrtle C.; F; Daut; 13
892; ---; Baker Morris A.; M; Son; 9

Census of the **Osage Indians** Indians of **Osage Indians** Agency **Oklahoma,** taken by **Hugh Pitzer, Supt. & Sp'l. Disb'g. Agent** , United States Indian Agent, during the 4th quarter, **1909**

Key: NUMBER; Indian Name; English Name; Sex; Relation; Age
* An Askerisk will be next to a number if repeated or out of sequence and inserted among a different family.

893; ---; Baker Frank T.; M; Son; 8
894; ---; Baker Martha B.; F; Daut; 5
895; ---; Baker, John Thomas Jr.; M; Son; 2

896; ---; Baker, Myrtle; F; Head; 20

897; ---; Baylis, Elizabeth; F; Head; 65

898; ---; Baylis, Harry; M; Head; 25

899; ---; Bellieu, Thomas A.; M; Head; 27

900; ---; Bellieu, Walter S.; M; Head; 22
901; ---; Bellieu Emmet; M; Son; 3

902; ---; Bellieu, Stella; F; Daut;17
903; ---; Bellieu Leo F.; M; Son; 13
904; ---; Bellieu Anna H.; F; Daut; 11
905; ---; Stephen M.; M; Son; 9

906; ---; Bellmard, Eliza; F; Head; 22
907; ---; Bellmard Clarence; M; Son; 2

908; ---; Bennett, William; M; Head; 33
909; ---; Bennett Isabella; F; Wife; 28
910; ---; Bennett William E.; M; Son; 9
911; ---; Bennett Teresa; F; Daut; 5
912; ---; Bennett Irene; F; Daut; 2

913; ---; Blackburn, Rachel; F; Head; 29
914; ---; Blackburn Oliver O.; M; Son; 9
915; ---; Blackburn Luther A.; M; Son; 4

916; ---; Boulanger, Joseph; M; Head; 60
917; ---; Boulanger Benjamin H.; M; Son; 19
918; ---; Boulanger James V.; M; Son; 18
919; ---; Boulanger Eulalie C.; F; Daut; 15
920; ---; Boulanger Anna V.; F; Daut; 14
921; ---; Charles F.; M; Son; 12

922; ---; Boulanger, Grover; M; Head; 24
923; ---; Boulanger, Stephen E.; M; Head; 27
924; ---; Boulanger Minnie L.; F; Daut; 8
925; ---; Boulanger Augustine C.; F; Daut; 6

163

Census of the **Osage Indians** Indians of **Osage Indians** Agency **Oklahoma,** taken by **Hugh Pitzer, Supt. & Sp'l. Disb'g. Agent** , United States Indian Agent, during the 4th quarter, **1909**

Key: NUMBER; Indian Name; English Name; Sex; Relation; Age
* An Askerisk will be next to a number if repeated or out of sequence and inserted among a different family.

926; ---; Boulanger, Isaac; M; Head; 30
927; ---; Boulanger Charles M.; M; Son; 9
928; ---; Boulanger Alta; F; Daut; 7
929: ---; Boulanger Lenora; F; Daut; 6
930; ---; Boulanger Nellie; F; Daut; 4

931; ---; Boulanger, W.J.; M; Head; 35
932; ---; Boulanger Edward Mc; M; Son; 14
933; ---; Boulanger May; F; Daut; 13
934; ---; Boulanger Evart; M; Son; 9

935; ---; Bookius; Dora; F; Head; 26
936; ---; Bookius Cyril D.; M; Son; 11
937; ---; Bookius Earnest F.; M; Son; 8
938; ---; Bookius Mary B.; F; Daut; 6
939; ---; Bookius Milton J; M; Son; 2

940; ---; Boren, Blanche; F; Head; 23
941; ---; Boren Kathleen; F; Daut; 4
942; ---; Boren Evaleen; F; Daut; 4

943; ---; Bowhan, Ida M.; F; Head; 28
944; ---; Bowhan Francis D.; M; Son; 8
945; ---; Bowhan Sewel C.; M; Son; 5
946; ---; Bowhan Erin S.; M; Son; 3

947; ---; Bowhan, Marie B.; F; Head; 23
948; ---; Bowhan John C.; M; Son; 4
949; ---; Bowhan Harry; M; Son; 1

950; ---; Bowman, Rosetta; F; Head; 22
951; ---; Bowman Mildred L.; F; Daut; 5
952; ---; Ben; M; Son; 3

953; ---; Brock, Lavaria; F; Head; 29
954; ---; Brock Winona V.; F; Daut; 2

955; ---; Bray, Emma; F; Head; 30
956; ---; McGath, John W.; M; Son; 12

957; ---; Bradshaw, Rose E.; F; Head; 35
958; ---; Bradshaw Thomas S.; M; Son; 18
959; ---; Bradshaw Harry A.; M; Son; 15
960; ---; Bradshaw Alvin S.; M; Son; 13
961; ---; Bradshaw Sarah A.; F; Daut; 11

164

Key: NUMBER; Indian Name; English Name; Sex; Relation; Age
* An Askerisk will be next to a number if repeated or out of sequence and inserted among a different family.

962; ---; Bradshaw Greta E.; F; Daut; 9
963; ---; Bradshaw Alva F.; F; Daut; 7
964; ---; Irene A.; F; Daut; 5
965; ---; Bradshaw George W.; M; Son; 3
966; ---; Bradshaw Courtland A.; M; Son; 1

967; ---; Brown, Mable; F; Head; 23

968; ---; Brown, Charles; M; Head; 48
969; ---; Brown Bernice; F; Daut; 17
970; ---; Brown Treva; F; Daut; 11

971; ---; Brown, Edward; M; Head; 42

972; ---; Brown, Earnest; M; Head; 37
973; ---; Brown Maude; F; Daut; 14
974; ---; Brown Laura J.; F; Daut; 11
975; ---; Brown William P.; M; Son; 10
976; ---; Brown Lula B.; F; Daut; 5
977; ---; Brown Helen M.; F; Daut; 2

978; ---; Brown, A.H.; M; Head; 49
979; ---; Brown William S.; M; Son; 7
980; ---; Brown Louis M.; M; Son; 14

981; ---; Brown, Mary J.; F; Head; 42
982; ---; Brown Edith; F; Daut; 16
983; ---; Brown Louis M.; M; Son; 14

984; ---; Brown, Hattie B.; F; Head; 21

985; ---; Brunt, Edward; M; Head; 49
986; ---; Brunt George E.; M; Son; 18
987; ---; Brunt Joseph L.; M; Son; 10

988; ---; Brunt, Theodore; M; Head; 23

989; ---; Bruce, Elsie F,; F; Head; 39
990; ---; Bruce, Louisa; F; Daut; 15
991; ---; Bruce Lena; F; Daut; 13
992; ---; Adelbert; M; Son; 18

993; ---; Bratton, Josephine; M; Head; 29
994; ---; Bratton William E.; M; Son; 10
995; ---; Edmund S.; M; Son; 7

Census of the **Osage Indians** Indians of **Osage Indians** Agency **Oklahoma,** taken by **Hugh Pitzer, Supt. & Sp'l. Disb'g. Agent** , United States Indian Agent, during the 4th quarter, **1909**

Key: NUMBER; Indian Name; English Name; Sex; Relation; Age
* An Askerisk will be next to a number if repeated or out of sequence and inserted among a different family.

996; ---; John I.; M; Son; 4

997; ---; Breeding, Mary L.; F; Head; 44
998; ---; Breeding Leta M.; F; Daut; 14
999; ---; Breeding Francis; M; Son; 12
1000; ---; Breeding Elsie E.; F; Dau; 9

1001; ---; Brooks. Philomena; F; Head; 29
1002; ---; Brooks Sylvester; M; Son; 11
1003; ---; Brooks Dellretta; F; Daut; 10
1004; ---; Brooks Ruby A.; F; Daut; 8
1005; ---; Brooks Del Orier; M; Son; 5

1006; ---; Bryant, Joe; M; Head; 57
1007; ---; Bryant Frank; M; Son; 15
1008; ---; Bryant Della M.; F; Daut; 14
1009; ---; Bryant Carrie M; F; Daut; 12
1010; ---; Bryant Cecil; M; Son; 10
1011; ---; Bryant Arthur; M; Son; 9
1012; ---; Bryant Anna B.; F; Daut; 6
1013; ---; Bryant Arena; F; Daut; 3

1014; ---; Burton, Roy B.; M; Son; 13

1015; ---; Carr, Nelson; M; Son; 13
1016; ---; Carr Gussie M.; F; Daut; 9

1017; ---; Carpenter, Mary E.; F; Head; 39
1018; ---; Carpenter Floyd H.; M; Son; 18
1019; ---; Carpenter Charles E.; M; Son; 14
1020; ---; Carpenter Rose B.; F; Daut; 12
1021; ---; Carpenter Louis S.; M; Son; 10

1022; ---; Carter, Alva E.; M; Son; 11
1023; ---; Lecta M.; F; Daut; 9
1024; ---; Barton D.; M; Son; 15
1025; ---; Charles A.; M; Son; 13

1026; ---; Callahan, Alfred; M; Head; 26

1027; ---; Callahan, Cornelius; M; Head; 34

1028; ---; Callahan, Julia; F; Head; 27
1029; ---; Callahan Rosemary; F; Daut; 3

Census of the **Osage Indians** Indians of **Osage Indians** Agency **Oklahoma,** taken by **Hugh Pitzer, Supt. & Sp'l. Disb'g. Agent** , United States Indian Agent, during the 4th quarter, **1909**

Key: NUMBER; Indian Name; English Name; Sex; Relation; Age
* An Askerisk will be next to a number if repeated or out of sequence and inserted among a different family.

1030; ---; Callahan, William; M; Head; 31

1031; ---; Callahan, Leo; M; Son; 11
1032; ---; Callahan Charles; M; Son; 9
1033; ---; Callahan Mary; F; Daut; 8
1034; ---; Callahan Gertrude; F; Daut; 6

1035; ---; Canville, Clara; F; Daut; 12
1036; ---; Canville John B.; M; Son; 8
1037; ---; Canville Agnes L.; F; Daut; 6

1038; ---; Canville, Cecil; M; Son; 11
1039; ---; Canville John; M; Son; 15
1040; ---; Canville Acuda; F; Daut; 5

1041; ---; Carlton, Anthony; M; Head; 37
1042; ---; Carlton Mary E.; F; Wife; 28
1043; ---; Carlton Eva M.; F; Daut; 11
1044; ---; Carlton Ethel; F; Daut; 10
1045; ---; Carlton Frances; F; Daut; 8

1046; ---; Carlton, George; M; Head; 32
1047; ---; Carlton Augustine; F; Daut; 9
1048; ---; Carlton Robert; M; Son; 7
1049; ---; Carlton Mary E.; F; Daut; 9
1050; ---; Carlton George Jr.; M; Son; 4
1051; ---; Carlton Ella; F; Daut; 2

1052; ---; Cedar, William; M; Son; 13

1053; ---; Cedar, Paul; M; Orphan; 11

1054; ---; Cheshewalla, Evart; M; Son; 13
1055; ---; Cheshewalla Floyd; M; Son; 10

1056; ---; Childers, Nola; F; Orphan; 10

1057; ---; Chouteau, Henry; M; Head; 24

1058; ---; Chouteau, Stewart; M; Head; 22

1059; ---; Chouteau, Louis P.; M; Head; 21

1060; ---; Clem, William; M; Head; 31
1061; ---; Clem William L.; M; Son; 9

167

Census of the **Osage Indians** Indians of **Osage Indians** Agency **Oklahoma,**
taken by **Hugh Pitzer, Supt. & Sp'l. Disb'g. Agent** , United States Indian Agent,
during the 4th quarter, **1909**

Key: NUMBER; Indian Name; English Name; Sex; Relation; Age
* An Askerisk will be next to a number if repeated or out of sequence and inserted among a different family.

1062; ---; Clem John E.; M; Son; 8
1063; ---; Clem James A.; M; Son; 4
1064; ---; Clem Frantz; M; Son; 3
1065; ---; Clem May M.; F; Daut; 3mo

1066; ---; Clem, James J.; M; Head; 34
1067; ---; Clem Jessie M.; F; Daut; 13
1067 ½; ---; Clem William H.; M; Son; 11
1068; ---; Clem James N.; M; Son; 8
1069; ---; Clem Sallie J.; F; Daut; 6

1070; ---; Clewien, Anna; F; Head; 28
1071; ---; Clewien, Clarabell; F; Daut; 4
1072; ---; Clewien Frances; F; Daut; 2

1073; ---; Clawson, Josiah G.; M; Head; 21

1074; ---; Clawson, Emma C.; F; Daut; 18
1075; ---; Clawson Thomas A.; M; Son; 14
1076; ---; Clawson Geore B.; M; Son; 12

1077; ---; Collins, Mary; F; Head; 73

1078; ---; Colby, Ora; F; Head; 29
1079; ---; Hardy, Orel; M; Son; 5
1080; ---; Hardy, Mary I.; F; Daut; 2

1081; ---; Cooper, Anna L.; F; Head; 27
1082; ---; Cooper William O.; M; Son; 9
1083; ---; Cooper Francis; M; Son; 6
1084; ---; Cooper Edward E.; M; Son; 3

1085; ---; Connor, Woodie; M; Head; 26
1086; ---; Connor, Theil L.; F; Daut; 4

1087; ---; Connor, George; M; Head; 38
1088; ---; Connor Adelia; F; Daut; 8
1089; ---; Connor Victoria W.; M; Son; 4
1090; ---; Connor Daniel I.; M; Son; 2

1091; ---; Cottingham, Ida; F; Head; 23
1092; ---; Cottingham Vera L.; F; Daut; 6
1093; ---; Cottingham Logan; M; Son; 4

1094; ---; Collins, Lula; F; Head; 34

Census of the **Osage Indians** Indians of **Osage Indians** Agency **Oklahoma,** taken by **Hugh Pitzer, Supt. & Sp'l. Disb'g. Agent** , United States Indian Agent, during the 4th quarter, **1909**

Key: NUMBER; Indian Name; English Name; Sex; Relation; Age
* An Askerisk will be next to a number if repeated or out of sequence and inserted among a different family.

1095; ---; Collins John W.; M; Son; 10
1096; ---; Collins William S.; M; Son; 4

1097; ---; Conness, Veva; F; Head; 37
1098; ---; Conness Geneva M.; F; Daut; 10
1099; ---; Conness William S.; M; Son; 4

1100; ---; Conway, Jane; F; Head; 81

1101; ---; Crouse, Isabella Fuller; F; Head; 43
1102; ---; Crouse Earl; M; Son; 17
1103; ---; Crouse Laura I.; F; Daut; 13
1104; ---; Crouse Stephen M.; Son; 10

1105; ---; Crouse, Dallas; M; Head; 23

1106; ---; Crane, Marie; F; Head; 36
1107; ---; Crane Frankie M.; F; Daut; 2

1108; ---; Cross, Ellen; F; Head; 28
1109; ---; Cross Lou M.; F; Daut; 9
1110; ---; Cross Charles L.; M; Son; 6
1111; ---; Cross Candis J.; F; Daut; 2

1112; ---; Cunningham, Laura; F; Head; 35
1113; ---; Cunningham Edward R.; M; Son; 10

1114; ---; Cunningham, Rose I.; F; Head; 39
1115; ---; Cunningham Robert B.; M; Son; 10

1116; ---; Cunningham, John M.; M; Head; 21

1117; ---; Curtis, Mary; F; Head; 52
1118; ---; Farrell, Virgil L.; M; Son; 16
1119; ---; Curtis, Lethia B.; F; Daut; 14
1120; ---; Curtis Ada; F; Daut; 11

1121; ---; Daniel, Sophia; F; Head; 33
1122; ---; Daniel Bessie; F; Daut; 15
1123; ---; Daniel Vernie; F[?]; Son[?]; 13
1124; ---; Daniel Pearl[?] C.; M[?]; Son[?]; 11
1125; ---; Ida I.; F; Daut; 8

1126; ---; Davis, Sophia; F; Head; 68

Census of the **Osage Indians** Indians of **Osage Indians** Agency **Oklahoma,** taken by **Hugh Pitzer, Supt. & Sp'l. Disb'g. Agent**, United States Indian Agent, during the 4th quarter, **1909**

Key: NUMBER; Indian Name; English Name; Sex; Relation; Age
* An Askerisk will be next to a number if repeated or out of sequence and inserted among a different family.

1127; ---; Davis, Mary J.; F; Head; 60
1128; ---; LaBarge, Minnie E.; F; Daut; 20

1129; ---; Daily, Dora; F; Head; 27
1130; ---; Dial Elsie A.; F; Daut; 10
1131; ---; Dial Lawton M.; M; Son; 8

1132; ---; Darnell, Rebecca J; F; Head; 46
1133; ---; Vadney, Amy V., F; Daut; 18

1134; ---; Dennison, Eliza; F; Head; 40
1135; ---; Fugate, Frank E.; M; Son; 19
1136; ---; Fugate John A.; M; Son; 18
1137; ---; Dennison Nellie; F; Daut; 8
1138; ---; Dennison George O.; M; Son; 3

1139; ---; Dennison, Bert; M; Head; 24
1140; ---; Dennison Florence L.; F; Daut; 2

1141; ---; Del Orier, Julia; F; Head; 59
1142; ---; Del Orier, Louis; M; Son; 3

1143; ---; DeNoya, Louis; M; Head; 48
1144; ---; DeNoya Frederick; M; Son; 17
1145; ---; DeNoya Clement; M; Son; 15
1146; ---; DeNoya Josephine; F; Daut; 13
1147; ---; DeNoya Ruby P.; F; Daut; 11

1148; ---; DeNoya, Frank; M; Head; 52
1149; ---; DeNoya James E.D.; M; Son; 19
1150; ---; DeNoya Clara; F; Daut; 19
1151; ---; DeNoya Grace; F; Daut; 16
1152; ---; DeNoya Alfred R.; M; Son; 15
1153; ---; DeNoya Charlotte; F; Daut; 13
1154; ---; DeNoya Myrtle C.; F; Daut; 11
1155; ---; DeNoya Catherine L.; F; Daut; 6
1156; ---; DeNoya Walter L.; M; Son; 3

1157; ---; DeNoya, Jacob; M; Head; 30
1158; ---; DeNoya Belle; F; Wife; 29
1159; ---; DeNoya Virgil H.; M; Son; 8
1160; ---; DeNoya Maurice H.; M; Son; 6
1161; ---; DeNoya Lillian C.; F; Daut; 5
1162; ---; DeNoya Helen D.; F; Daut; 3

Census of the **Osage Indians** Indians of **Osage Indians** Agency **Oklahoma,** taken by **Hugh Pitzer, Supt. & Sp'l. Disb'g. Agent** , United States Indian Agent, during the 4th quarter, **1909**

Key: NUMBER; Indian Name; English Name; Sex; Relation; Age
* An Askerisk will be next to a number if repeated or out of sequence and inserted among a different family.

1163; ---; DeNoya, Joseph; M; Head; 32
1164; ---; DeNoya Charlotte E.; F; Daut; 5
1165; ---; DeNoya Margaret I.; F; Daut; 6
1166; ---; DeNoya Martha M.; F; Daut; 3

1167; ---; DeNoya, Clement; M; Head; 42
1168; ---; DeNoya, Emilly; F; Wife; 38
1169; ---; DeNoya Clement Jr.; M; Son; 19
1170; ---; DeNoya Louis; M; Son; 15
1171; ---; DeNoya Sadie; F; Daut; 13
1172; ---; DeNoya Elsie; F; Daut; 11
1173; ---; DeNoya Edna; F; Daut; 7
1174; ---; DeNoya Elizabeth; F; Daut; 5
1175; ---; DeNoya Millard; M; Son; 3

1176; ---; DeNoya, Wesley; M; Head; 18
1177; ---; DeNoya; Odell; F; Wife; 19

1178; ---; DeNoya, Everette A.; M; Head; 22

1179; ---; Deal, Joseph; M; Head; 26
1180; ---; Deal Mary J.; F; Wife; 20
1181; ---; Deal James C.; M; Son; 3
1182; ---; William M.; M; Son; 1

1183; ---; Deal, Julia A.; F; Head; 54
1184; ---; Deal Sherman; M; Son; 18

1185; ---; Dickey, James A.; M; Head; 28

1186; ---; Dickey, John T.; M; Head; 25

1187; ---; Dial, Elisa; F; Head; 49
1188; ---; Penn, Augustus; M; Son; 19
1189; ---; Penn Rose E.; F; Daut; 17
1190; ---; Dial, Cora E.; F; Daut; 12
1191; ---; Dial Eva; F; Daut; 10
1192; ---; Dial Charles P.; M; Son; 4
1193; ---; Huston. John R.; M; Adpt. Son; 18

1194; ---; Donelson, Frances; F; Head; 26
1195; ---; Donelson Robert L.; M; Son; 8
1196; ---; Donelson James L.; M; Son; 10

1197; ---; Doolin, Martha; F; Head; 26

Census of the **Osage Indians** Indians of **Osage Indians** Agency **Oklahoma,** taken by **Hugh Pitzer, Supt. & Sp'l. Disb'g. Agent** , United States Indian Agent, during the 4th quarter, 1909

Key: NUMBER; Indian Name; English Name; Sex; Relation; Age
* An Askerisk will be next to a number if repeated or out of sequence and inserted among a different family.

1198;　---; Alta J.; F; Daut; 2

1199;　---; Donovan, Augustine; F; Head; 57
1200;　---; Donovan Jesse C.; M; Son; 16
1201;　---; Donovan Charles; M; Son; 20

1202;　---; Ducotey, Stanislaus; M; Head; 35
1203;　---; Ducotey Versa; F; Daut; 11
1204;　---; Ducotey Manza; F; Daut; 9
1205;　---; Ducotey Bettie V.; F; Daut; 6
1206;　---; Ducotey Frank S.; M; Son; 4

1207;　---; Dunn, Dora; F; Head; 31
1208;　---; Dunn Ida M.; F; Daut; 13
1209;　---; Dunn Mary A.; F; Daut; 11
1210;　---; Dunn Timothy J.; M; Son; 5

1211;　---; Dunham, Martha; F; Head; 79

1212;　---; Dunn, Nettie M.; F; Head; 22

1213;　---; Easley, Margaret; F; Head; 37
1214;　---; Easley Pearl; F; Daut; 17
1215;　---; Easley George E.; M; Son; 15
1216;　---; Easley Leo B.; M; Son; 13
1217;　---; Easley John W.; M; Son; 11
1218;　---; Easley Mary E.; F; Daut; 8
1219;　---; Easley Clarence A.; M; Son; 5
1220;　---; Easley Robert J.; M; Son; 2

1221;　---; Edwards, Julia; F; Head; 43
1222;　---; Quinton, Agnes; F; Daut; 13
1223;　---; Quinton Pearl C.; F; Daut; 11
1224;　---; Quinton Elnora; F; Daut; 7
1225;　---; Edwards, Theodore; M; Son; 2
1226;　---; Quinton, Alex; M; Son; 20

1227;　---; Edmiston, Frances (Incompt); F; Head; 32
1228;　---; Edmiston, Bessie E.; F; Daut; 7

1228;* ---; Evans, Mary E.; F; Head; 23 [#1228 entered twice.]

1229;　---; Essley, Irene; F; Head 17

1230;　---; Farrell, Nathaniel; M; Head; 32

172

Census of the **Osage Indians** Indians of **Osage Indians** Agency **Oklahoma,** taken by **Hugh Pitzer, Supt. & Sp'l. Disb'g. Agent** , United States Indian Agent, during the 4th quarter, **1909**

Key: NUMBER; Indian Name; English Name; Sex; Relation; Age
* An Askerisk will be next to a number if repeated or out of sequence and inserted among a different family.

1231; ---; Farrell Ruth; F; Daut; 9
1232; ---; Farrell Andrew; M; Son; 6

1233; ---; Farrell, Mary; F; Head; 21

1234; ---; Farrell, Charles; M; Head; 27
1235; ---; Farrell Mary; F; Daut; 5
1236; ---; Farrell Pearl; F; Daut; 2

1237; ---; Farrell, Monica; F; Head; 54
1238; ---; Shaw, Moses R.; M; Son; 19
1239; ---; Shaw Charles M.; Son; 20

1240; ---; Fenton, Margaret; F; Head; 26
1241; ---; Fenton Sylvester R.; M; Son; 8
1242; ---; Fenton Louis L.; M; Son; 7
1243; ---; Fenton Curtis D.; M; Son; 4
1244; ---; Fenton Lenora; F; Daut; 1

1245; ---; Fox, Susie; F; Head; 47
1246; ---; Lombard, Sylvester; M; Son; 19
1247; ---; Lombard Augustine; F; Daut; 16
1248; ---; Lombard Joseph; M; Son; 14
1249; ---; Lombard Paul; M; Son; 10
1250; ---; Fox, Alexander; M; Son; 7

1251; ---; Fronkier, Laban A.; M; Orphan; 19

1252; ---; Fronkier, William; M; Head; 38

1253; ---; Fronkier, Simon; M; Head; 37
1254; ---; Fronkier Florence; F; Daut; 13
1255; ---; Fronkier Blanche L.; F; Daut; 11
1256; ---; Fronkier Benjamin; M; Son; 7

1257; ---; Fronkier, Philip; M; Head; 21

1258; ---; Fronkier Augustus; M; Head; 31

1259; ---; Fronkier, James; M; Head; 30
1260; ---; Fronkier Louis B.; M; Son; 1

1261; ---; Fuller, Thomas; M; Head; 28

1262; ---; Fuller, Louis; M; Head; 34

173

Key: NUMBER; Indian Name; English Name; Sex; Relation; Age
* An Askerisk will be next to a number if repeated or out of sequence and inserted among a different family.

1263; ---; Fuller Andrew B.; M; Son; 7

1264; ---; Fuller, Charles; M; Head; 25
1265; ---; Fish, Eliza; F; Head; 20

1266; ---; Gaylor, Victoria; F; Head; 44

1267; ---; George, James M.; M; Head; 29
1268; ---; George James L.; M; Son; 3

1269; ---; George, Sylvester; M; Head; 25

1270; ---; Gilmore, Mary A.; F; Head; 55
1271; ---; Gilmore S.J.; M; Son; 18

1272; ---; Gilmore, William H.; M; Son; 12

1273; ---; Girard, Amelia; F; Head; 35
1274; ---; Girard Mary E.C.; F; Daut; 15
1275; ---; Girard Corine A.; F; Daut; 14
1276; ---; Girard Amelia V.; F; Daut; 13
1277; ---; Girard Leona; F; Daut; 11

1278; ---; Grammer, Maggie; F; Head; 26

1279; ---; Goad, Clara; F; Head; 29
1280; ---; Goad Cecil J.; M; Son; 7
1281; ---; Goad Ethel; F; Daut; 2

1282; ---; Groves, Agnes; F; Head; 27
1283; ---; Groves Mural W.; M; Son; 7
1284; ---; Groves Mary L.; F; Daut; 5
1285; ---; Groves Harry L.; M; Son; 2

1286; ---; Harrelson, Mary L. (Incompt); F; Head; 29
1287; ---; Harrelson Emerine; F; Daut; 11

1288; ---; Hall, Ida; F; Head; 24
1289; ---; Hall Alfred; M; Son; 5

1290; ---; Harruff, Margaret; F; Head; 45
1291; ---; Harruff Julia; F; Daut; 13

1292; ---; Hardy, Emily; Head; 36
1293; ---; Hardy Louisa V.; F; Daut; 15

Census of the **Osage Indians** Indians of **Osage Indians** Agency **Oklahoma,** taken by **Hugh Pitzer, Supt. & Sp'l. Disb'g. Agent** , United States Indian Agent, during the 4th quarter, **1909**

Key: NUMBER; Indian Name; English Name; Sex; Relation; Age
* An Askerisk will be next to a number if repeated or out of sequence and inserted among a different family.

1294; ---; Hardy Goldie; F; Daut; 12
1295; ---; Hardy Geneva; F; Daut; 9
1296; ---; Hardy William R.; M; Son; 5

1297; ---; Hampton, Charles; M; Head; 29
1298; ---; Hampton Roland C.; M; Son; 3

1299; ---; Hampton, Rosalie; F; Head; 48

1300; ---; Hayes, Pearl; F; Head; 29
1301; ---; Hayes Olivia; F; Daut; 5
1302; ---; Hayes Elizabeth; F; Daut; 5
1303; ---; Hayes Margaret; F; Daut; 2

1304; ---; Harlow, Josephine; F; Head; 30
1304 1/2; ---; Harlow John N.; M; Son; 12
1305; ---; Hayes, Lawrence L.; M; Son; 4

1306; ---; Harlow, Susan; F; Head; 47
1307; ---; Akers, Grace; F; Daut; 18
1308; ---; Gilcrease, Belle M.; F; Daut; 15
1309; ---; Harlow, Charles C.; M; Son; 11

1310; ---; Haynie, Mary; F; Head; 24
1311; ---; Haynie Willie; M; S. Son; 14
1312; ---; Haynie John C.; M; Son; 4
1313; ---; Haynie Emma; F; Daut; 3

1314; ---; Hackleman; Julia Ann; F; Head; 64

1315; ---; Harris, Mary E.; F; Head; 28

1316; ---; Harvey, Adeline; F; Head; 28

1317; ---; Heenan, Anna; F; Head; 27
1318; ---; Heenan Beatrice M.; F; Daut; 5

1319; ---; Herard, Paul; M; Head; 41

1320; ---; Herard, Eugene; M; Head; 24

1321; ---; Herridge, Joseph; M; Son; 18
1322; ---; Herridge Lulu; F; Daut; 15

1323; ---; Hewitt, Rosa; F; Head; 23

175

Key: NUMBER; Indian Name; English Name; Sex; Relation; Age
* An Askerisk will be next to a number if repeated or out of sequence and inserted among a different family.

1324; ---; Hewitt Valaria; F; Daut; 3
1325; ---; Hewitt Loretta M.; F; Daut; 2

1326; ---; Hildebrand, George; M; Head; 26

1327; ---; Hildebrand, Richard; M; Head; 30

1328; ---; Hildebrand, David; M; Head; 36
1329; ---; Hildebrand Nancy; F; Daut; 8

1330; ---; Hildebrand, James; M; Head; 40
1331; ---; Hildebrand Oragonia; F; Daut; 14
1332; ---; Hildebrand Dica; F; Daut; 9
1333; ---; Hildebrand Susan; F; Daut; 15

1334; ---; Hildebrand, Joseph; M; Head; 42
1335; ---; Hildebrand Frank; M; Son; 11

1336; ---; Hickman, Clementine; F; Head; 33
1337; ---; Hickman Homer; M; Son; 13
1338; ---; Hickman Edna J.; F; Daut; 10
1339; ---; Hickman Franklin; M; Son; 9
1340; ---; Hickman Florence; F; Daut; 7
1341; ---; Hickman Lillie V.; F; Daut; 5
1342; ---; Hickman Bertha C.; F; Daut; 3
1343; ---; Hickman Roy N.; M; Son; 2

1344; ---; Holloway. Jasper C.; M; Head; 57

1345; ---; Holloway, Frank; M; Head; 24

1346; ---; Holloway, Milton; M; Head; 26
1347; ---; Holloway Andrew L.; M; Son; 6
1348; ---; Holloway Olita M.; F; Daut; 3

1349; ---; Horn, Polly; F; Head; 27
1350; ---; Buxbaum, Vernon E.; M; Son; 8

1351; ---; Hoots, Rosa; F; Head; 40
1352; ---; Hoots Agnes; F; Daut; 14

1353; ---; Hoots, Alfred; M; Head; 22

1354; ---; Hunt, Mary A.; F; Head; 39
1355; ---; Hunt Lula B.; F; Daut; 12

Census of the **Osage Indians** Indians of **Osage Indians** Agency **Oklahoma,** taken by **Hugh Pitzer, Supt. & Sp'l. Disb'g. Agent** , United States Indian Agent, during the 4th quarter, **1909**

Key: NUMBER; Indian Name; English Name; Sex; Relation; Age

* An Askerisk will be next to a number if repeated or out of sequence and inserted among a different family.

1356; ---; Hunt Mary G.; F; Daut; 10
1357; ---; Hunt Andrew D.; M; Son; 7
1358; ---; Hunt Robert M. Jr.; M; Son; 2

1359; ---; Hunt, Antwine; M; Head; 21

1360; ---; James, Jesse; M; Head; 21

1361; ---; Javine, Peter; M; Head; 57
1362; ---; Javine Hasread; M; Son; 18
1363; ---; Javine Viola M.; F; Daut; 15
1364; ---; Javine Opal; F; Daut; 3
1365; ---; Javine; Benjamin H.; M; Son; 20
1366; ---; Javine Howard Taft; M; Son; 1

1367; ---; Javine, Roy V.; M; Son; 13

1368; ---; Javine, John; M; Head; 54
1369; ---; Javine Ollie; F; Daut; 19
1370; ---; Javine Audra; F; Daut; 16
1371; ---; Javine Ora E.; F; Daut; 15
1372; ---; Javine Joseph; M; Son; 12

1373; ---; Javine, Anthony; M; Head; 22

1374; ---; Javine, John; M; Head; 27
1375; ---; Javine George M.; M; Son; 5
1376; ---; Javine Earl T.; M; Son; 3
1377; ---; Javine Ella C.; F; Daut; 1

1378; ---; Johnson, Julia M.; F; Head; 54
1379; ---; Johnson John W.; M; Son; 20

1380; ---; Jones, Laura; F; Head; 23
1381; ---; Jones James F.; M; Son; 4

1382; ---; Kennedy, Agnes; F; Head; 33
1383; ---; Kennedy James A. M; Son; 11
1384; ---; Kennedy Forrest L.; M; Son; 9
1385; ---; Kennedy Thelma; F; Daut; 8
1386; ---; Kennedy Cordelia A.; F; Daut; 5
1387; ---; Kennedy Samuel G.; M; Son; 3

1388; ---; Kennedy, Mable; F; Head; 29
1389; ---; Kennedy Albert A.; M; S.Son; 15

Census of the **Osage Indians** Indians of **Osage Indians** Agency **Oklahoma,** taken by **Hugh Pitzer, Supt. & Sp'l. Disb'g. Agent**, United States Indian Agent, during the 4th quarter, **1909**

Key: NUMBER; Indian Name; English Name; Sex; Relation; Age
* An Askerisk will be next to a number if repeated or out of sequence and inserted among a different family.

1390; ---; Kennedy, Samuel; M; Head; 23
1391; ---; Kennedy Don C.; M; Son; 2

1392; ---; Keeler, Blanche; F; Head; 27
1393; ---; Keeler Dixie; M; Son; 5
1394; ---; Keeler Alberta M.; F; Daut; 3

1395; ---; Kilbie, Benedict; M; Head; 23
1396; ---; Kilbie John A.; M; Son; 3

1397; ---; Krebs, Henry; M; Ward; 12

1398; ---; Lawrence, Maggie; F; Head; 52

1399; ---; Labadie, Charles; M; Head; 38
1400; ---; Labadie Hazel; F; Daut; 11
1401; ---; Labadie Frank; M; Son; 9
1402; ---; Labadie Alvin L.; M; Son; 7
1403; ---; Labadie Nita; F; Daut; 5
1404; ---; Labadie Ralph; M; Son; 9mo

1405; ---; Labadie, William H.; Head; 24
1406; ---; Labadie Mary Ellen; F; Daut; 1

1407; ---; Labadie, Ella; F; Head; 22

1408; ---; Labadie, Frederick; M; Son; 19
1409; ---; Labadie Earnie; M; Son; 18
1410; ---; Labadie Joseph; M; Son; 16

1411; ---; Labadie, Edward; M; Head; 43
1412; ---; Labadie Milton; M; Son; 11
1413; ---; Labadie Rose M.; F; Daut; 8
1414; ---; Labadie Robert E.; M; Son; 6
1415; ---; Labadie Charles W.; M; Son; 4
1416; ---; Labadie William H.; M; Son; 1

1417; ---; Labadie, Frank; M; Head; 48
1418; ---; Labadie G.V.; M; Son; 17
1419; ---; Labadie Paul F.; M; Son; 14

1420; ---; Labadie, John; M; Head; 22

1421; ---; LaSarge, Marie; F; Daut; 15
1422; ---; LaSarge Louis; M; Son; 13

178

Census of the **Osage Indians** Indians of **Osage Indians** Agency **Oklahoma,** taken by **Hugh Pitzer, Supt. & Sp'l. Disb'g. Agent** , United States Indian Agent, during the 4th quarter, **1909**

Key: NUMBER; Indian Name; English Name; Sex; Relation; Age
* An Askerisk will be next to a number if repeated or out of sequence and inserted among a different family.

1423; ---; LaSarge Arthur; M; Son; 12
1424; ---; LaSarge Charles V.; M; Son; 10

1425; ---; LaSarge, Joseph; M; Head; 40
1426; ---; LaSarge Ellen; F; Daut; 9
1427; ---; LaSarge Harold L.; M; Son; 2

1428; ---; Lane, Joseph; M; Head; 40
1429; ---; Lane Zella A.; F; Wife; 39
1430; ---; Lane Mary; F; Daut; 15
1431; ---; Lane Bessie; F; Daut; 11
1432; ---; Lane Joseph C.; M; Son; 6
1433; ---; Lane Roy B.; M; Son; 4

1434; ---; Leahy, Mary L.; F; Head; 60

1435; ---; Leahy, Bertha; F; Head; 34
1436; ---; Leahy Thomas R.; Son; 12
1437; ---; Leahy Cora W.; F; Daut; 10
1438; ---; Leahy Mable A.; F; Daut; 6
1439; ---; Leahy Edward A.; M; Son; 4

1440; ---; Leahy, W.T.; M; Head; 40
1441; ---; Leahy Martha: F; Wife; 31
1442; ---; Leahy William T. Jr.; M; Son; 11
1443; ---; Leahy B. Thomas; M; Son; 10

1444; ---; Lewis, Mary; F; Head; 48

1445; ---; Lessert, Frank; M; Head; 67

1446; ---; Lessert, Walter; M; Head; 24

1447; ---; Lessert, Joseph; M; Head; 25

1448; ---; Lessert, David; M; Head; 31
1449; ---; Lessert, Guy; M; Son; 13
1450; ---; Millie M.; F; Daut; 11
1451; ---; Charles A.; M; Son; 9
1452; ---; Hattie; F; Daut; 7

1453; ---; Lessert, Frank Jr.; M; Head; 45
1454; ---; Lessert Mary J.; F; Daut; 14
1455; ---; Lessert Robert A.; M; Son; 12
1456; ---; Lessert Grace J.; F; Daut; 8

Census of the **Osage Indians** Indians of **Osage Indians** Agency **Oklahoma,** taken by **Hugh Pitzer, Supt. & Sp'l. Disb'g. Agent**, United States Indian Agent, during the 4th quarter, **1909**

Key: NUMBER; Indian Name; English Name; Sex; Relation; Age
* An Askerisk will be next to a number if repeated or out of sequence and inserted among a different family.

1457; ---; Lessert Ray L.; M; Son; 6
1458; ---; Lessert Cora L.; F; Daut; 3

1459; ---; Lessert, Benjamin; M; Head; 38
1460; ---; Lessert Wade; M; Son; 18
1461; ---; Lessert Susie; F; Daut; 13
1462; ---; Lessert Benjamin L.; M; Son; 6
1463; ---; Lessert Fay; F; Daut; 11
1464; ---; Lessert Fanny; F; Daut; 3
1465; ---; Lessert William K.; M; Son; 20

1466; ---; Lessert, Charles; M; Head; 42

1467; ---; Liese, Coaina M.; F; Head; 27
1468; ---; Liese Washaki; M; Son; 4

1469; ---; Lohmann, Nettie; F; Head; 23

1470; ---; Lombard, Albert; M; Head; 63
1471; ---; Lombard Bessie; F; Daut; 15
1472; ---; Lombard Robert A.; M; Son; 8

1473; ---; Lombard, Nina; F; Head; 21

1474; ---; Lombard, Clara; F; Head; 23

1475; ---; Lombard; John; M; Head; 25

1476; ---; Lombard, George W.; M; Head; 30
1477; ---; Lombard Frank H.; M; Son; 1

1478; ---; Lombard, John E.; M; Head; 23

1479; ---; Lombard, Walter; M; Head; 31
1480; ---; Lombard Lucy; F; Daut; 8
1481; ---; Lombard Lois; F; Daut; 6
1482; ---; Lombard Samie; F; Daut; 5

1483; ---; Lyman, Olive G.; F; Head; 46

1484; ---; Lyman, Paul S.; M; Head; 43
1485; ---; Lyman Agnes; F; Daut; 6
1486; ---; Lyman Capitola; F; Daut; 4
1487; ---; Lyman Pauline; F; Daut; 2

Census of the **Osage Indians** Indians of **Osage Indians** Agency **Oklahoma,** taken by **Hugh Pitzer, Supt. & Sp'l. Disb'g. Agent** , United States Indian Agent, during the 4th quarter, **1909**

Key: NUMBER; Indian Name; English Name; Sex; Relation; Age
* An Askerisk will be next to a number if repeated or out of sequence and inserted among a different family.

1488; ---; Lyman, Arthur J.: M; Head; 39

1489; ---; Lynn, Mary A.; F; Head; 32
1490; ---; Lynn John F.; M; Son; 14
1491; ---; Lynn Theresa M.; F; Daut; 10
1492; ---; Lynn Patrick; M; Son; 6
1493; ---; Lynn Joseph; M; Son; 8
1494; ---; Lynn William R.; M; Son; 3

1495; ---; Logan, Ruby; F; Head; 20

1496; ---; Linley, Susanna; F; Head; 21

1497; ---; Lockwood, Adeline; F; Head; 41

1498; ---; Lavely, Anna; F; Head; 30

1499; ---; Mackey, Joseph; M; Head; 31
1500; ---; Mackey Eva; F; Daut; 11
1501; ---; Mackey Tenne; F; Daut; 7
1502; ---; Mackey Agnes L.; F; Daut; 5
1503; ---; Mackey Warren F.; M; Son; 3

1504; ---; Mackey, William B.; M; Head; 26
1505; ---; Mackey Cecelia E.; F; Daut; 9
1506; ---; Mackey Bertha M.; F; Daut; 4

1507; ---; Mackey, Grover; M; Head; 23

1508; ---; Mann, Stella; F; Head; 20

1509; ---; Mathews, W.S.; M; Head; 61
1510; ---; Mathews, John J.; M; Son; 15
1511; ---; Mathews Mary I.; F; Daut; 12
1512; ---; Mathews Lillian B.; F; Daut; 10
1513; ---; Mathews Florence; F; Daut; 7

1514; ---; Mathews, Sarah J.; F; Head; 21

1515; ---; Mathews, W.W.; M; Head; 30
1516; ---; Mathews, Norman S.; M; Son; 4
1517; ---; Mathews Anna M.; F; Daut; 2

1518; ---; Mathews, John A.; M; Head; 33
1519; ---; Mathews Lorenza; F; Wife; 27

181

Key: NUMBER; Indian Name; English Name; Sex; Relation; Age
* An Askerisk will be next to a number if repeated or out of sequence and inserted among a different family.

1520; ---; John A. Jr.; M; Son; 8
1521; ---; Victoria; F; Daut; 7

1522; ---; Mathews, Edward O.; M; Head; 30
1523; ---; Mathews Alfred E.; M; Son; 5

1524; ---; Mathes, Thomas S.; M. Son; 20

1525; ---; Marshall, Sarah; F; Head; 21

1526; ---; Martin, Alex; M; Head; 63
1527; ---; Martin Bertha; F; Daut; 14

1528; ---; Martin, Lombard; M; Head; 21

1529; ---; Martin, Lee; M; Head; 32
1530; ---; Martin Dane L.; F; Daut; 11
1531; ---; Martin Edgar E.; M; Son; 8
1532; ---; Martin Linnie N.; F; Daut; 5

1533; ---; Martin, Emery; M; Head; 28
1534; ---; Martin John D.; M; Son; 3
1535; ---; Martin Delmas E.; M; Son; 2

1536; ---; Martin, Richard; M; Head; 35
1537; ---; Martin Nannie V.; F; Daut; 2
1538; ---; Martin Claude; M; Son; 12

1539; ---; Martin, James; M; Son; 16

1540; ---; Martin, Wilson; M; Son; 16

1541; ---; Martin, Joeanna; F; Head; 29
1542; ---; Flippin, Nettie B.; F; Daut; 11

1543; ---; McCarty, Lenora; F; Head; 28
1544; ---; McCarty William H.; M; Son; 8
1545; ---; McCarty Solomon; M; Son; 7
1546; ---; McCarty Edna V.; F; Daut; 4
1547; ---; McCarty Charles V.; M; Son; 4
1548; ---; McCarty Charles W.; M; Son; 2

1549; ---; McCoy, Lillei[sic]; F; Head; 22
1550; ---; McCoy Richard M.; M; Son; 2

Census of the **Osage Indians** Indians of **Osage Indians** Agency **Oklahoma,**
taken by **Hugh Pitzer, Supt. & Sp'l. Disb'g. Agent** , United States Indian Agent,
during the 4th quarter, **1909**

Key: NUMBER; Indian Name; English Name; Sex; Relation; Age
* An Askerisk will be next to a number if repeated or out of sequence and inserted among a different family.

1551; ---; McDaniel, Ellen; F; Head; 33
1552; ---; McDaniel Frederick W.; M; Son; 13

1553; ---; McGuire, Mary E.; F; Head; 36
1554; ---; McGuire Ethel; F; Daut; 18
1555; ---; McGuire Leo; M; Son; 14
1556; ---; McGuire Bird A.; M; Son; 11
1557; ---; McGuire William T.; M; Son; 9
1558; ---; McGuire Charles A.; M; Son; 7

1559; ---; McComb, Ellen; F; Head; 31
1560; ---; McComb Jessie; F; Daut; 14
1561; ---; McComb William N.; M; Son; 11
1562; ---; McComb Gladys I.; F; Daut; 8
1563; ---; McComb Rachel B.; F; Daut; 6
1564; ---; McComb Naioma; F; Daut; 3

1565; ---; McLaughlin, Nancy; F; Head; 45

1566; ---; McLintic, Mary; F; Head; 32
1567; ---; McLintic Aloysia; F; Daut; 10

1568; ---; McLain, Minnie; F; Head; 22
1569; ---; McLain Ray S.; M; Son; 4

1570; ---; McCowan, Bessie; F; Head; 19

1571; ---; Michelle, Estella; F; Daut; 11
1572; ---; Michelle Delia; F; Daut; 8

1573; ---; Mickels, Arania; F; Head; 32
1574; ---; Carr, Delilah; F; Daut; 7
1575; ---; Mickels, Clarence D.; M; Son; 4
1576; ---; Mickels Blanche O.; F; Daut; 1

1577; ---; Miller, Gurney; M; Orphan; 11

1578; ---; Mongrain, Rosa; F; Daut; 19

1579; ---; Mongrain, Stewart; M; Head; 61
1580; ---; Mongrain Srewart Jr.; M; Son; 16
1581; ---; Mongrain Ernest; M; Son; 20

1582; ---; Mongrain, Hattie; F; Head; 22

Census of the **Osage Indians** Indians of **Osage Indians** Agency **Oklahoma,** taken by **Hugh Pitzer, Supt. & Sp'l. Disb'g. Agent**, United States Indian Agent, during the 4th quarter, **1909**

Key: NUMBER; Indian Name; English Name; Sex; Relation; Age
* An Askerisk will be next to a number if repeated or out of sequence and inserted among a different family.

1583; ---; Mosier, Thomas; M; Head; 66

1584; ---; Mosier, Adeline; F; Head; 68

1585; ---; Mosier, W.T.; M; Head; 41
1586; ---; Mosier Louisa; F; Wife; 34
1587; ---; Mosier Charles P.; M; Son; 13
1588; ---; Mosier John T.; M; Son; 10
1589; ---; Mosier Edwin P.; M; Son; 7
1590; ---; Mosier Luther P.; M; Son; 4
1591; ---; Mosier Agnes C.; F; Daut; 4
1592; ---; Mosier James R.; M; Son; 2

1593; ---; Mosier, Jacob; M; Head; 47
1594; ---; Mosier Stella; F; Daut; 17
1595; ---; Mosier Claude; M; Son; 14
1596; ---; Mosier Lione; F; Daut; 11

1597; ---; Mosier, Kate; F; Head; 21

1598; ---; Mosier, Eugene; M; Head; 34
1599; ---; Mosier Mary M.; F; Daut; 13
1600; ---; Mosier John J.; M; Son; 7
1601; ---; Mosier Ida M.; F; Daut; 5
1602; ---; Mosier Walter L.; M; Son; 3

1603; ---; Mosier, Bismark; M; Head; 26
1604; ---; Mosier Clara O.; F; Daut; 5
1605; ---; Mosier Thelma V.; F; Daut; 3

1606; ---; Moore, James W.; M; Head; 23

1607; ---; Moore, Alice; F; Daut; 18

1608; ---; Moncravie, Charles; M; Head; 40
1609; ---; Moncravie Rosa; F; Wife; 30
1610; ---; Moncravie Augustine; F; Daut; 10
1611; ---; Moncravie Virginia M.; F; Daut; 7

1612; ---; Moncravie; Fred; M; Head; 34

1613; ---; Moncravie, Henry; M; Head; 36
1614; ---; Moncravie Henri E.; F; Daut; 5

1615; ---; Moncravie, John; M; Head; 39

184

Census of the **Osage Indians** Indians of **Osage Indians** Agency **Oklahoma,** taken by **Hugh Pitzer, Supt. & Sp'l. Disb'g. Agent** , United States Indian Agent, during the 4th quarter, **1909**

Key: NUMBER; Indian Name; English Name; Sex; Relation; Age
* An Askerisk will be next to a number if repeated or out of sequence and inserted among a different family.

1616; ---; Moncravie Sylvester A.; M; Son; 16
1617; ---; Moncravie John N.; M; Son; 12
1618; ---; Moncravie Alexander C.; M; Son; 10
1619; ---; Moncravie Barada J.; M; Son; 8
1620; ---; Moncravie Vivian L.; F; Daut; 5
1621; ---; Moncravie Anna A.; F; Daut; 3

1622; ---; Murray, Jennie; F; Head; 33
1623; ---; Murray Morton J.; M; Son; 11
1624; ---; Murray Ruby M.; F; Daut; 10
1625; ---; Murray Arthur R.; M; Son; 7
1626; ---; Alfred G.; M; Son; 5
1627; ---; Maurice C.; M; Son; 2

1628; ---; Murphy, Gertrude; F; Head; 27

1629; ---; Murphy, Alice; F; Head; 25

1630; ---; Murphy, Elizabeth; F; Head; 23

1631; ---; Murphy, Amy; F; Head; 47
1632; ---; Nettie; F; Daut; 19

1633; ---; Musgrove, William; M; Head; 31
1634; ---; Musgrove Carl R.; M; Son; 4
1635; ---; Musgrove Willis E.; F; Daut; 3

1636; ---; Newman, George; M; Head; 27

1637; ---; Noble, Ida; F; Head; 27

1638; ---; Nolegs, Larry; M; Head; 54

1639; ---; Odell, Clyde; M; Son; 2

1640; ---; Owens, Catherine; F; Daut; 2

1641; ---; Pappan, Samuel T.; M; Son; 18
1642; ---; Pappan Lee A.; M; Son; 16
1643; ---; Pappan Oakley; M; Son; 14
1644; ---; Pappan Lester; M; Son; 12

1645; ---; Pappin, Alex; M; Head; 50
1646; ---; Pappin Herbert; M; Son; 12
1647; ---; Pappin Franklin A.; M; Son; 7

Census of the **Osage Indians** Indians of **Osage Indians** Agency **Oklahoma,** taken by **Hugh Pitzer, Supt. & Sp'l. Disb'g. Agent** , United States Indian Agent, during the 4th quarter, **1909**

Key: NUMBER; Indian Name; English Name; Sex; Relation; Age
* An Askerisk will be next to a number if repeated or out of sequence and inserted among a different family.

1648; ---; Pappin Roosevelt; M; Son; 4
1649; ---; Pappin Nora I.; F; Daut; 2

1650; ---; Pappin, Jesse L.; M; Son; 19
1651; ---; Pappin John L.; M; Son; 17
1652; ---; Pappin Jeanette; F; Daut; 14
1653; ---; Pappin Joseph L.; M; Son; 12
1654; ---; Pappin Jules C.; M; Son; 10
1655; ---; Joshua J.; M; Son; 6

1656; ---; Pappin, James; M; Head; 25

1657; ---; Palmer, John F.; M; Head; 48
1658; ---; Palmer Martha; F; Wife; 36
1659; ---; Palmer Mary E.; F; Daut; 15
1660; ---; Palmer Clementine; F; Daut; 13
1661; ---; Palmer Martha M.; F; Daut; 2
1662; ---; Palmer Mable; F; Daut; 19

1663; ---; Park, Estella; F; Head; 21

1664; ---; Pease, Minnie A.; F; Head; 35
1665; ---; Pease Marion H.; M; Son; 4

1666; ---; Perrier, Joseph; M; Head; 32

1667; ---; Perrier, Samuel; M; Head; 41

1668; ---; Perrier, Leo; M; Head; 28
1669; ---; Perrier Clifford R.; M; Son; 3

1670; ---; Perrier, James; M; Head; 38
1671; ---; Perrier John T.; M; Son; 15
1672; ---; Perrier James R.; M; Son; 9

1673; ---; Perrier, Napoleon; M; Head; 51
1674; ---; Perrier Nina; F; Daut; 18
1675; ---; Perrier Leo; M; Son; 15
1676; ---; Perrier Peter; M; Son; 12
1677; ---; Perrier Lola; F; Daut; 11
1678; ---; Perrier Owen; M; Son; 7
1679; ---; Perrier Louis F.; M; Son; 20

1680; ---; Perrier, Thomas; M; Head; 25
1681; ---; Perrier Roy B.; M; Son; 3

Census of the **Osage Indians** Indians of **Osage Indians** Agency **Oklahoma,**
taken by **Hugh Pitzer, Supt. & Sp'l. Disb'g. Agent**, United States Indian Agent,
during the 4th quarter, **1909**

Key: NUMBER; Indian Name; English Name; Sex; Relation; Age
* An Askerisk will be next to a number if repeated or out of sequence and inserted among a different family.

1682; ---; Perrier, Eugene; M; Head; 26
1683; ---; Perrier Ray L.D.; M; Son; 3
1684; ---; Perrier Kenneth L.; M; Son; 1

1685; ---; Penn, Leo; M; Son; 12
1686; ---; Penn Oscar; M; Son; 10
1687; ---; Penn Wayne M.; M; Son; 4

1688; ---; Pettit, S.W.; M; Head; 64

1689; ---; Pettit, Charles; M; Head; 36
1690; ---; Pettit Hattie B.; F; Daut; 12
1691; ---; Pettit Lela M.; F; Daut; 8
1692; ---; Pettit Charles W.; M; Son; 7

1693; ---; Pettit, George; M; Head; 34
1694; ---; Pettit George R.; M; Son; 10
1695; ---; Pettit Lula B.; F; Daut; 7
1696; ---; Pettit William A.; M; Son; 2

1697; ---; Pettit, John; M; Head; 32

1698; ---; Perkins, Elizabeth; F; Head; 54

1699; ---; Peters, James M.; M; Son; 10

1700; ---; Pearson, Rosa; F; Head; 46
1701; ---; Kent, Cordelia; F; Daut; 18
1702; ---; Pearson Lillian F.; F; Daut; 17
1703; ---; Pearson Bertha L.; F; Daut; 15
1704; ---; Pearson Kate V.; F; Daut; 12
1705; ---; Pearson Willie J.; M; Son; 9
1706; ---; Pearson Rose E.; F; Daut; 6

1707; ---; Pearson, October; M; Head; 26
1708; ---; Pearson Mary C.; F; Wife; 22
1709; ---; Pearson Bernice M.; F; Daut; 3

1710; ---; Phillips, William; M; Head; 39
1711; ---; Phillips Angeline M.; F; Daut; 15
1712; ---; Phillips Iva M.; F; Daut; 13
1713; ---; Phillips James W.; M; Son; 11

1714; ---; Plomondon, Clemy; F; Head; 55
1715; ---; Plomondon Daniel B.; M; Son; 17

Key: NUMBER; Indian Name; English Name; Sex; Relation; Age
* An Askerisk will be next to a number if repeated or out of sequence and inserted among a different family.

1716; ---; Plomondon Julia A.; F; Daut; 15
1717; ---; Plomondon Louisa; F; Daut; 12

1718; [Skipped.]

1719; ---; Plomondon, Louis; M; Head; 24

1720; ---; Plomondon, Barnard; M; Head; 39
1720 ½; ---; Plomondon Ella; F; Wife; 35
1721; ---; Plomondon Brace; F; Daut; 17
1722; ---; Plomondon Clementine; F; 15
1723; ---; Plomondon Moses E.; M; Son; 13
1724; ---; Plomondon George A.; M; Son; 10

1725; ---; Potter, Ethel; F; Head; 31
1726; ---; Potter Francis A.; M; Son; 14
1727; ---; Potter Oliver L.; M; Son; 9
1728; ---; Potter James L.; M; Son; 6
1729; ---; Potter Zelma; F; Daut; 2

1730; ---; Prudom, Charles N.; M; Head; 54

1731; ---; Prudom, Nora; F; Head; 26

1732; ---; Prudom, Frank; M; Head; 43

1733; ---; Prue, Henry; M; Head; 34
1734; ---; Prue Maude; F; Wife; 27
1735; ---; Prue Hattie M.; F; Daut; 11
1736; ---; Prue Charles F.; M; Son; 10
1737; ---; Prue Henry E.; M; Son; 8
1738; ---; Prue Floyd B.; M; Son; 5
1739; ---; Prue Anna B.; F; Daut; 3

1740; ---; Quinton, Franklin; M; Head; 22

1741; ---; Rairdon, Jane R.; F; Head; 50
1742; ---; Miller, Ida J.; F; Daut; 17
1743; ---; Rairdon, Wendall H.; M; Son; 9
1744; ---; Miller, Louis S.; M; Son; 20

1745; ---; Rapp, Barbara; F; Head; 23

1746; ---; Reece, Elizabeth; F; Head; 25
1747; ---; Reece Hallie; F; Daut; 7

Census of the **Osage Indians** Indians of **Osage Indians** Agency **Oklahoma,** taken by **Hugh Pitzer, Supt. & Sp'l. Disb'g. Agent** , United States Indian Agent, during the 4th quarter, **1909**

1748; ---; Reece Ethel; F; Daut; 5

1749; ---; Revelette, James; M; Head; 32
1750; ---; Revelette Teresa; F; Daut; 10
1751; ---; Revelette William L.; M; Son; 8
1752; ---; Revelette Mary E.; F; Daut; 3
1753; ---; Revelette Minnie F.; F; Daut; 3

1754; ---; Revelette, Fred; M; Head; 30
1755; ---; Revelette Pauline; F; Daut; 9
1756; ---; Revelette Fred L.; M; Son; 7

1757; ---; Revelette, Frank; M; Head; 68
1758; ---; Revelette Franklin; M; Son; 20

1759; ---; Revelette, Charles; M; Head; 36
1760; ---; Revelette Joseph; M; Son; 3

1761; ---; Revard, William; M; Head; 44
1762; ---; Revard William E.; M; Son; 8
1763; ---; Revard Della M.; F; Daut; 6
1764; ---; Revard Gladis; F; Daut; 4

1765; ---; Revard, Solomon; M; Head; 50

1766; ---; Revard, Charles; M; Head; 50

1767; ---; Revard, Alex; M; Head; 49

1768; ---; Revard, Benjamin; M; Head; 28

1769; ---; Revard, Paul; M; Head; 34
1770; ---; Revard Susie; F; Daut; 14

1771; ---; Revard. Mary E.; F; Head; 61

1772; ---; Revard, Elsie E.; F; Daut; 17
1773; ---; Revard Maynard; M; Son; 14

1774; ---; Revard, Francis; M; Head; 41
1775; ---; Revard Mack; M; Son; 15
1776; ---; Revard Emanuel M.; M; Son; 10
1777; ---; Revard Pearl I.; F; Daut; 7
1778; ---; Revard Ethel E.; F; Daut; 3

Census of the **Osage Indians** Indians of **Osage Indians** Agency **Oklahoma,** taken by **Hugh Pitzer, Supt. & Sp'l. Disb'g. Agent** , United States Indian Agent, during the 4th quarter, **1909**

Key: NUMBER; Indian Name; English Name; Sex; Relation; Age
* An Askerisk will be next to a number if repeated or out of sequence and inserted among a different family.

1779; ---; Revard, John W.; M; Head; 30
1780; ---; Revard Edward L.; M; Son; 11
1781; ---; Revard Evart A.; M; Son; 10

1782; ---; Revard Joseph; M; Head; 79
1783; ---; Revard Ursula; F; Daut; 19
1784; ---; Revard Clementine; F; Daut; 16
1785; ---; Revard William J.; M; Son; 14
1786; ---; Revard Renald V.; M; Son; 12

1787; ---; Revard, Ralph; M; Head; 21

1788; ---; Revard, Franklin; M; Head; 45
1789; ---; Revard Nicholas N.; M; Son; 15
1790; ---; Revard Pearl; F; Daut; 14
1791; ---; Revard Myrta; F; Daut; 6
1792; ---; Revard Kathryn L.; F; Daut; 2

1793; ---; Revard, Mark S.; M; Head; 21

1794; ---; Revard Charles E.; M; Head; 49
1795; ---; Revard Clarence; M; Son; 19
1796; ---; Revard Ed Clifford; M; Son; 17
1797; ---; Revard Clara; F; Daut; 15
1798; ---; Revard; Carrie; F; Daug; 11
1799; ---; Revard Cora; F; Daut; 11
1800; ---; Revard Nora T.; F; Daut; 10
1801; ---; Revard McGuire N.; M; Son; 5
1802; ---; Revard Lena; F; Daut; 3

1803; ---; Revard, Leonard; M; Head; 51
1804; ---; Revard Lode; F; Daut; 15
1805; ---; Revard Opal A.; F; Daut; 12
1806; ---; Revard Hazel; F; Daut; 9
1807; ---; Revard Minnie; F; Daut; 6
1808; ---; Revard Cleo; F; Daut; 3
1809; ---; Revard Victoria; F; Daut; 1

1810; ---; Revard, Joseph Jr.; M; Head; 52

1811; ---; Revard, Nellie; F; Daut; 8
1812; ---; Revard Edgar T.; M; Son; 5
1813; ---; Revard Mary C.; F; Daut; 3

1814; ---; Revard, Curtis; M; Head; 23

Census of the **Osage Indians** Indians of **Osage Indians** Agency **Oklahoma,**
taken by **Hugh Pitzer, Supt. & Sp'l. Disb'g. Agent** , United States Indian Agent,
during the 4th quarter, **1909**

Key: NUMBER; Indian Name; English Name; Sex; Relation; Age
* An Askerisk will be next to a number if repeated or out of sequence and inserted among a different family.

1815; ---; Revard, Aaron T.; M; Son; 17

1816; ---; Riddle, Sherman; M; Son; 17
1817; ---; Riddle Joseph; M; Son; 15
1818; ---; Riddle Frank; M; Son; 13

1819; ---; Ririe, Effie E.; F; Daut; 16
1820; ---; Ririe Scott F.; M; Son; 13
1821; ---; Ririe Otis E.; M; Son; 9
1822; ---; Ririe Nettie I.; F; Daut; 7
1823; ---; Ririe Arthur M.; M; Son; 3

1824; ---; Ririe, Oscar A.; M; Head; 22

1825; ---; Rodman, Antwine; M; Head; 36

1826; ---; Rogers, Stephen; M; Head; 28

1827; ---; Rogers, Louis; M; Head; 66

1828; ---; Rogers, Louis Jr.; M; Head; 24
1829; ---; Rogers Wahneta; F; Daut; 4

1830; ---; Rogers, Nancy; F; Head; 51

1831; ---; Rogers, T.L.; M; Head; 23

1832; ---; Rogers, Arthur; M; Head; 49
1833; ---; Rogers Joseph L.; M; Son; 10
1834; ---; Rogers Ellen E.; F; Daut; 8
1835; ---; Rogers John R.; M; Son; 6
1836; ---; Rogers William C.; M; Son; 4
1837; ---; Rogers Isabell; F; Daut; 2

1838; ---; Rogers, Mary E.; F; Head; 35
1839; ---; Rogers Irene; F; Daut; 17
1840; ---; Rogers Mary A.; F; Daut; 15
1841; ---; Rogers Coaina; F; Daut; 11
1842; ---; Rogers Eldred T.; Son; 9

1843; ---; Rogers, Antwine; M; Head; 64

1844; ---; Rogers, Mae; F; Head; 23

1845; ---; Rogers, Kenneth; M; Head; 29

191

Census of the **Osage Indians** Indians of **Osage Indians** Agency **Oklahoma,**
taken by **Hugh Pitzer, Supt. & Sp'l. Disb'g. Agent** , United States Indian Agent,
during the 4th quarter, **1909**

Key: NUMBER; Indian Name; English Name; Sex; Relation; Age
* An Askerisk will be next to a number if repeated or out of sequence and inserted among a different family.

1846; ---; Rogers Helen; F; Daut; 6
1847; ---; Rogers Antwine; M; Son; 4

1848; ---; Rogers, Jasper; M; Head; 39
1849; ---; Rogers Rosa; F; Wife; 30
1850; ---; Rogers Emmet; M; Son; 7
1851; ---; Rogers Cecelia; F; Daut; 8
1852; ---; Rogers Maude; F; Daut; 4
1853; ---; Rogers Flora; F; Daut; 2

1854; ---; Rogers, Bertha D.; F; Daut; 15
1855; ---; Rogers Helen C.; F; Daut; 13

1856; ---; Rogers, Willie L.; M; Son; 2

1857; ---; Rogers, Thomas L. Jr.; M; Head; 24

1858; ---; Rogers, Granville; M; Head; 21
1859; ---; Rogers, Rosa L.; Daut; 16
1860; ---; Rogers Josephine; F; Daut; 13
1861; ---; Rogers John H.; M; Son; 11

1862; ---; Rogers, Nora; F; Head; 25
1863; ---; Rogers Richard L.; Son; 4

1864; ---; Rogers, Lewis A.; M; Head; 34
1865; ---; Rogers Isadore; F; Wife; 31
1866; ---; Rogers Fred R.; M; Son; 8
1867; ---; Rogers Frank; M; Son; 4
1868; ---; Roberts, Ola; F; Daut; 23

1869; ---; Ross, John; M; Head; 66
1870; ---; Ross Floyd F.; M; Son; 12

1871; ---; Roach, Wilfred D.; M; Head; 29
1872; ---; Roach Bridget A.; F; Daut; 6
1873; ---; Roach Melvin C.; M; Son; 4
1874; ---; Roach Wilfred D. Jr.; M; son; 2

1875; ---; Roach, Samuel; M; Head; 27
1876; ---; Roach Mikle J.; M; Son; 6
1877; ---; Roach Herman B.; M; Son; 3

1878; ---; Roach, George W.; M; Head; 23

192

Census of the **Osage Indians** Indians of **Osage Indians** Agency **Oklahoma,** taken by **Hugh Pitzer, Supt. & Sp'l. Disb'g. Agent** , United States Indian Agent, during the 4th quarter, 19**09**

Key: NUMBER; Indian Name; English Name; Sex; Relation; Age
* An Askerisk will be next to a number if repeated or out of sequence and inserted among a different family.

1879; ---; Rutter, Gertrude; F; Head; 29

1880; ---; Rivera, Grace; F; Head; 19
1881; ---; Rivera Alex; M; Son; 1

1882; ---; Saxon, Cora; F; Head; 35
1883; ---; Saxon Veva M.; F; Daut; 5
1884; ---; Saxon; Harry H.; M; Son; 3

1885; ---; Scott, George; M; Head; 32
1886; ---; Scott Mary M.; F; Daut; 4

1887; ---; Scott, William J.; M; Son; 4
1888; ---; Scott Violet; F; Daut; 2

1889; ---; Selby, Georgia; F; Head; 23

1890; ---; Sherriff, Coeanna; F; Head; 22

1891; ---; Shaw, Franklin; M; Head; 22
1892; ---; Shaw Rose M.; F; Wife; 21
1893; ---; Shaw Moses; M; Son; 5
1894; ---; Shaw John; M; Son; 3

1895; ---; Shobe, Anna U.; F; Head; 25

1896; ---; Simpson, Susan; F; Head; 67

1897; ---; Simpkins, Mary L.; F; Head; 37
1898; ---; Simpkins Warren D.; M; Son; 16
1899; ---; Simpkins Mary E.; F; Daut; 15
1900; ---; Simpkins Vivian P.; Daut; 12
1901; ---; Simpkins Oren F.; M; Son; 11
1902; ---; Simpkins Edward; M; Son; 9
1903; ---; Simpkins Virgil; M; Son; 3
1904; ---; Simpkins Helen V.; F; Daut; 2

1905; ---; Slaughter, A. B.; M; Head; 25
1906; ---; Slaughter Minnie; F; Wife; 23

1907; ---; Slaughter, Amanda; F; Head; 22

1908; ---; Slaughter, Harry E.; M; Son; 19

1909; ---; Smith, Geore B.; M; Son; 7

Census of the **Osage Indians** Indians of **Osage Indians** Agency **Oklahoma,** taken by **Hugh Pitzer, Supt. & Sp'l. Disb'g. Agent** , United States Indian Agent, during the 4th quarter, **1909**

Key: NUMBER; Indian Name; English Name; Sex; Relation; Age
* An Askerisk will be next to a number if repeated or out of sequence and inserted among a different family.

1910; ---; Smith Genevieve; F; Daut; 10

1911; ---; Soderstrom, Gertrude; F; Head; 30
1912; ---; Dickey, Alta A.; F; Daut; 11
1913; ---; Soderstrom, Hanna N.; F; Daut; 8

1914; ---; Soldani; Sylvester J.; M; Head; 49
1915; ---; Soldani Josephine; F; Wife; 40
1916; ---; Soldani Myrtle; F; Daut; 18
1917; ---; Soldani Emmert A.; M; Son; 17
1918; ---; Soldani Louis E.; M; Son; 20

1919; ---; Soldani, Kate P.; M; Head; 21

1920; ---; Soldani, Ida M.; F; Head; 22
1921; ---; Soldani Agnes; F; Head; 23

1922; ---; Soldani, Anthony; M; Head; 47
1923; ---; Soldani Amelia K.; F; Wife; 41
1924; ---; Soldani Frank E.; M; Son; 18
1925; ---; Soldani Charles L.; M; Son; 16
1926; ---; Soldani Clarence; M; Son; 13
1927; ---; Soldani Grace M.; F; Daut; 10
1927 ½; ---; Soldani Rose M.; F; Daut; 10
1928; ---; Soldani George H.; M; Son; 8

1929; ---; Souligny, Laura; F; Head; 24
1930; ---; Souligny Mildred V.; F; Daut; 5

1931; ---; Stevens, John H.; M; Head; 43
1932; ---; Stevens Mildred V.; F; Daut; 5

1933; ---; Stephens, Madeline; F; Head; 67

1934; ---; Stotts, Emma; F; Head; 34
1935; ---; Stotts Joseh[sic] L.; M; Son; 18
1936; ---; Stotts William W.; M; Son; 14
1937; ---; Stotts James E.; M; Son; 5

1938; ---; Stobaugh, Alice; F; Head; 38
1939; ---; Riddle, John L.; M; Son; 19
1940; ---; Riddle Arthur; M; Son; 7

1941; ---; Srewart, Lenora; F; Head; 47
1942; ---; Wilkie, George L.; M; Son; 19

Census of the **Osage Indians** Indians of **Osage Indians** Agency **Oklahoma,** taken by **Hugh Pitzer, Supt. & Sp'l. Disb'g. Agent** , United States Indian Agent, during the 4th quarter, **1909**

Key: NUMBER; Indian Name; English Name; Sex; Relation; Age
* An Askerisk will be next to a number if repeated or out of sequence and inserted among a different family.

1943;   ---; Wilkie Rose E.; F; Daut; 15

1944;   ---; Swanson, Celestine; F; Head; 27
1945;   ---; Swanson Addison L.; 5[sic]; Son; 5
1946;   ---; Swanson Joseh[sic] N.; M; Son; 4

1947;   ---; Sweeney, Oscar E.; M; Son; 15

1948;   ---; Slamans, Mary E.; F; Head; 26
1949;   ---; Tall Chief, Enoch; M; Son; 3

1950;   ---; Tapp, Belle; F; Head; 45
1951;   ---; Chambers, James W.; M; Son; 13
1952;   ---; Chambers Minnie A.; F; Daut; 10
1953;   ---; Tapp, Ruby; F; Daut; 2

1954;   ---; Taylor, James E.; M; Orphan; 16
1955;   ---; Taylor John F.; M; Orphan; 14
1956;   ---; Taylor Hiram; M; Orphan; 12
1957;   ---; Taylor Fanny; F; Orphan; 11
1958;   ---; Taylor Agnes; F; Orphan; 9
1959;   ---; Taylor Anna; F; Orphan; 5

1960;   ---; Tayrien, John; M; Head; 27
1961;   ---; Tayrien Mary L.; F; Daut; 5
1962;   ---; Tayrien Agnes; F; Daut; 4
1963;   ---; Tayrien Gladys; F; Daut; 2

1964;   ---; Tayrien, Charles; M; Head; 34
1965;   ---; Tayrien Edna; F; Daut; 11

1966;   ---; Tayrien Thomas; M; Head; 48
1967;   ---; Tayrien George A.; M; Son; 17
1968;   ---; Tayrien Andrew J.; M; Son; 15
1969;   ---; Tayrien Paul; M; Son; 13
1970;   ---; Tayrien Maud J.; F; Daut; 5
1971;   ---; Tayrien John C.; M; Son; 4

1972;   ---; Tayrien David W.; M; Head; 21

1973;   ---; Tayrien, James; M; Head; 24
1974;   ---; Tayrien Alberty; F; Daut; 5
1975;   ---; Tayrien Elmer C.; M; Son; 3

1976;   ---; Tayrien, Andrew; M; Head; 35

Census of the **Osage Indians** Indians of **Osage Indians** Agency **Oklahoma,** taken by **Hugh Pitzer, Supt. & Sp'l. Disb'g. Agent** , United States Indian Agent, during the 4th quarter, **1909**

Key: NUMBER; Indian Name; English Name; Sex; Relation; Age
* An Askerisk will be next to a number if repeated or out of sequence and inserted among a different family.

1977; ---; Tayrien Jennie; F; Daut; 13
1978; ---; Tayrien Viola; F; Daut; 12
1979; ---; Tayrien Alfred J.; M; Son; 10
1980; ---; Tayrien Violet M.; F; Daut; 9
1981; ---; Tayrien William J.; M; Son; 6
1982; ---; Tayrien Rose Anna; F; Daut; 6

1983; ---; Tayrien, Cyprian; M; Head; 71
1984; ---; Tayrien William; M; Son; 19

1985; ---; Toothaker, Rena L.; F; Head; 19

1986; ---; Thompson, Leroy; M; Son; 15
1987; ---; Roe, Emery E.; M; Son; 8

1988; ---; Thompson, Nicholas; M; Head; 51

1989; ---; Thomas, Agnes; F; Head; 27
1990; ---; Thomas Maggie C.; F; Daut; 7
1991; ---; Thomas Julia H.; F; Daut; 4

1992; ---; Thurman, Lola; F; Head; 23
1993; ---; Thurman Geneva; F; Daut; 3

1994; ---; Tinker, Louis; M; Head; 42
1995; ---; Tinker William; M; Son; 18
1996; ---; Tinker Bessie; F; Daut; 15
1997; ---; Tinker Nora; F; Daut; 11
1998; ---; Tinker Ora; F; Daut; 11
1999; ---; Tinker Eva; F; Daut; 9
2000; ---; Tinker Isabella; F; Daut; 6
2001; ---; Tinker Rose; F; Daut; 4
2002; ---; Tinker Cora; F; Daut; 2

2003; ---; Tinker, Geo. E.; M; Head; 40
2004; ---; Tinker Mary G.; F; Daut; 17
2005; ---; Tinker Sarah Anna; F; Daut; 15
2006; ---; Tinker Nicholas A.T.; M; Son; 13
2007; ---; Tinker George E. Jr.; M; Son; 10
2008; ---; Tinker Villa; F; Daut; 6

2009; ---; Tinker, Clarence; M; Head; 21

2010; ---; Tinker, Charley; M; Head; 37
2011; ---; Tinker Mary J.; F; Daut; 18

Key: NUMBER; Indian Name; English Name; Sex; Relation; Age
* An Askerisk will be next to a number if repeated or out of sequence and inserted among a different family.

2012; ---; Tinker Roy B.; M; Son; 15
2013; ---; Tinker Maude; F; Daut; 12
2014; ---; Tinker Lucille; F; Daut; 11
2015; ---; Tinker David; M; Son; 8
2016; ---; Tinker Louis N.; M; Son; 4

2017; ---; Tinker, Frank; M; Head; 48
2018; ---; Tinker Mary L.; F; Wife; 48
2019; ---; Tinker Tom; M; Son; 15
2020; ---; Tinker Mary E.; F; Daut; 13
2021; ---; Tinker Eliza; F; Daut; 9
2022; ---; Tinker Sylvester J.; M; Son; 6
2023; ---; Tinker Norris J.; M; Son; 20

2024; ---; Todd, Maud; F; Head; 50
2025; ---; Todd Harold; M; Son; 4
2026; ---; Todd Gerald J.; M; Son; 8

2027; ---; Trumbly, Julian; M; Head; 58
2028; ---; Trumbly Eliza; F; Wife; 53
2029; ---; Trumbly Henry; M; Son; 19
2030; ---; Trumbly Tina O.; F; Daut; 17
2031; ---; Trumbly Charles; M; Son; 16
2032; ---; Trumbly Theresa; F; Daut; 11

2033; ---; Trumbly, Oliver; M; Head; 27

2034; ---; Trumbly, Clarence; M; Head; 28
2035; ---; Trumbly Gladys; F; Daut; 6
2036; ---; Trumbly Clarence E.; M; Son; 3

2037; ---; Trumbly, George; M; Head; 35

2038; ---; Trumbly, Andrew; M; Head; 34
2039; ---; Trumbly Mary; F; Wife; 23
2040; ---; Trumbly Oscar; M; Son; 3

2041; ---; Trumbly, J.B.; M; Head; 55
2042; ---; Trumbly John F.; M; Son; 18
2043; ---; Trumbly Elizabeth; F; Daut; 15
2044; ---; Trumbly Paul P.; M; Son; 9

2045; ---; Tucker, Anna; F; Head; 25
2046; ---; Tucker Bulah G.; F; Daut; 4
2047; ---; Tucker Stephen J. Jr.; M; Son; 2

Census of the **Osage Indians** Indians of **Osage Indians** Agency **Oklahoma,** taken by **Hugh Pitzer, Supt. & Sp'l. Disb'g. Agent** , United States Indian Agent, during the 4th quarter, **1909**

Key: NUMBER; Indian Name; English Name; Sex; Relation; Age
* An Askerisk will be next to a number if repeated or out of sequence and inserted among a different family.

2048; ---; Tucker, Angeline; F; Head; 74

2049; ---; Turner, Frederick D.; M; Son; 14

2050; ---; Turner, Mary B.; F; Head; 27

2051; ---; Tyner, Benjamin F.; M; Head; 34
2052; ---; Tyner Ethel M.; F; Daut; 10
2053; ---; Tyner Roy F.; M; Son; 8
2054; ---; Tyner William L.; M; Son; 4
2055; ---; Vesser, Ruth; F; Daut; 16

2056; ---; Voils, Kathleen; F; Daut; 7
2057; ---; Voils Elsie L.; F; Daut; 3

2058; ---; Watkins, Rosalie; F; Head; 34
2059; ---; Watkins Francis M.; M; Son; 15
2060; ---; Watkins James; M; Son; 14
2061; ---; Watkins John F.; M; Son; 7

2062; ---; Watson, Viola; F; Head; 17

2063; ---; Ware, Victoria; F; Head; 58
2064; ---; Del Drier, Lillie; F; Daut; 19
2065; ---; Ware, Edna; F; Daut; 18

2066; ---; Ware, Aggie; F; Head; 39
2067; ---; Ware Julia; F; Daut; 15
2068; ---; Ware Nancy; F; Daut; 13
2069; ---; Ware Bulah; F; Daut; 11
2070; ---; Ware Rosa L.; F; Daut; 9
2071; ---; Ware Henry H.; M; Son; 7
2072; ---; Ware David; M; Son; 6

2073; ---; Wade, Effie; F; Head; 23
2074; ---; Wade Merle C.; M; Son; 4

2075; ---; Walker, Letetia; F; Head; 17

2076; ---; Waters, Telina; F; Head; 26
2077; ---; Waters Anna M.; F; Daut; 2

2078; ---; Whiles, Elmer; M; Head; 27

2079; ---; Whiles, Delilah; F; Head; 24

Census of the **Osage Indians** Indians of **Osage Indians** Agency **Oklahoma,** taken by **Hugh Pitzer, Supt. & Sp'l. Disb'g. Agent** , United States Indian Agent, during the 4th quarter, 1909

Key: NUMBER; Indian Name; English Name; Sex; Relation; Age
* An Askerisk will be next to a number if repeated or out of sequence and inserted among a different family.

2080; ---; Whiles, Francis M.; M; Orphan; 20

2081; ---; Wheeler, Paul; M; Head; 37
2082; ---; Wheeler Merrit J.; M; Son; 6
2083; ---; Wheeler Geneva; F; Daut; 5
2084; ---; Wheeler Louise; F; Daut; 2

2085; ---; Wheeler, Elmer; M; Head; 30
2086; ---; Wheeler Eva R.; F; Wife; 31
2087; ---; Wheeler Virginia; F; Daut; 5
2088; ---; Wheeler, Alma; F; Head; 23

2089; ---; Weinrich, Anna; F; Head; 26

2090; ---; Wheeler, Susan; F; Head; 32
2091; ---; Wheeler Morris E.; M; Son; 8

2092; ---; Wilkie, Louis F.; M; Head; 23
2093; ---; Wilkie Andrew E.; M; Son; 3

2094; ---; Willis, Lillie; F; Head; 17

2095; ---; Wilson, Mary; F; Head; 31
2096; ---; Wilson William E.; M; Son; 12
2097; ---; Wilson Julia K.; F; Daut; 10
2098; ---; Wilson Banie; M; Son; 8
2099; ---; Wilson Audry; F; Daut; 5
2100; ---; Wilson Howard; M; Son; 2

2101; ---; Woodring, Tena; F; Head; 34
2102; ---; Woodring Carlton W.; M; Son; 14
2103; ---; Woodring Orville W.; M; Son; 12
2104; ---; Woodring Anna; F; Daut; 8

2105; ---; Woodham, Lucy; F; Head; 59

2106; ---; Woodward, Kate; F; Head; 32
2107; ---; Beckman, Subil[sic] F.; F; Daut; 4
2108; ---; Gorman, Mary A.; F; Daut; 10

2109; ---; Wyrick, Mary; F; Head; 36
2110; ---; Wyrick Jessie W.; F; Daut; 13
2111; ---; Wyrick John H.; M; Son; 12
2112; ---; Wyrick Elnora J.; F; Daut; 8
2113; ---; Wyrick Elmer F.; M; Son; 5

Census of the **Osage Indians** Indians of **Osage Indians** Agency **Oklahoma,**
taken by **Hugh Pitzer, Supt. & Sp'l. Disb'g. Agent**, United States Indian Agent,
during the 4th quarter, **1909**

Key: NUMBER; Indian Name; English Name; Sex; Relation; Age
* An Askerisk will be next to a number if repeated or out of sequence and inserted among a different family.

2114; ---; Wynn, Madeline; F; Head; 20
2115; ---; Yeargain, Early I.; M; Son; 18
2116; ---; Yeargain Verona C.; F; Daut; 16
2117; ---; Yeargain Leona; F; Daut; 15

2118; ---; York, Adah M.; F; Head; 23

2119; ---; Hooper, Sallie; F; Head; 38
2120; ---; Hooper Mary; F; Daut; 15

2121; ---; Siggins, Clara; F; Head; 46
2122; ---; Siggins Andrew W.; M; Son; 18

2123; ---; Stephens, Mary; F; Daut; 15

NOTE: Nos. 849-/3, 849-2/3, 850, 1067 ½, 1304 ½, 1720 ½, and 1927 ½
Are interlined hereon. Total of this roll is 2130
Nos. 425, 617, and 1228 duplicated. Nos. 195, 517 and 695 skipped.

RECAPITULATION:

All ages (Males, 1093; Females, 1037)	2130
Full-bloods:	
All ages (males, 430; females 421)	851
18 years and over (males)	270
Between 6 and 16 (males)	90
14 years and over (female)	274
Between 6 and 16 (females)	106
Mixed-Bloods:	
All ages (males, 663; females 616)	1279
18 years and over (males)	283
Between 6 and 16 (males)	252
14 years and over (female)	312
Between 6 and 16 (females)	241

Census of the Osage Indians

of

Osage Indian Agency, Oklahoma,

As of June 30, 1910

Hugh Pitzer, Supt. & Sp'l. Disb'g. Agent

CENSUS OF OSAGE INDIANS.

Taken during the fourth
quarter, 1910, by

HUGH PITZER, Superintendent.

DEPARTMENT OF THE INTERIOR

UNITED STATES INDIAN SERVICE

Land-
Population
W H G
Circular #448.   Osage Indian Agency,

Annual Census.   Pawhuska, Okla. August 3, 1910.

The Honorable

Commissioner of Indian Affairs,

Washington, D. C.

Sir:

Replying to Office Circular #448, dated June 28,
1910, I respectfully forward herewith the annual census of
Osage Indians for the fiscal year ending June 30, 1910.

Very respectfully,

ELM   Acting Superintendent.

McPherson ?

Key: NUMBER; Indian Name; English Name; Sex; Relation; Age
* An Askerisk will be next to a number if repeated or out of sequence and inserted among a different family.

BIG CHIEF BAND.

1; Pah-hu-scah; Tom Big Chief; Head; 51; M
2; Me-to-op-pe; ---; Wife; 37; F
3; He-ah-to-me; May White; Daut; 19; F
4; Heh-kah-mon-kah; ---; Daut; 11; M
5; Gra-to-me; ---; Daut; 7; F

6; Mo-she-to-moie; ---; Head; 66; M
7; Mo-se-che-he; ---; Wife; 66; F

8; ---; Richard Rusk; Head; 28; M
9; Wah-tsa-ah-tah; James McKinley; S. Son; 15; M
10; Mah-sah; Walter McKinley; S. Son; 12; M
11; ---; May Rusk; Daut; 7; F
12; Hla-me-tsa-he; ---; Daut; 4; F

13; Wy-u-tsa-kah-she; ---; Head; 75; M
14; Moie-wah-kon-tah; Phillip Carson; Son; 16; M

15; Num-pah-wah-kon-tah; Tom Carson; Head; 21; M

16; Hun-kah-me; ---; Head; 53; F
17; To-sho-ho; Charles Whitehorn; Son; 14; M
18; E-nah-min-tsa; ---; Son; 6; M

19; ---; Fidelis Cheshowahkepah; Head; 28; M
20; Hum-pah-to-me; ---; Wfe; 55; F
21; He-ah-to-me; Agnes Ferguson; S. Daut; 9; M
22; Gra-tah-wah-kah; ---; S. Son; 6; M

23; ---; Howard Russell; Head; 22; M

24; ---; Otis Russell; Head; 23; M
25; ---; Angella Russell; Wife; 23; F
26; He-ah-to-me; ---; Daut; 3; F

27; ---; Howard Buffalo; Head; 50; M

28; ---; Pearl Buffalo; Wife; 31; F
29; Wah-she-ke-pah; Willie Russell; Son; 14; M
30; Min-kah-she; ---; Daut; 4; F

31; ---; Herman McCarthy; Head; 31; M
32; ---; Martha Neal; Wife; 19; F

Key: NUMBER; Indian Name; English Name; Sex; Relation; Age
* An Askerisk will be next to a number if repeated or out of sequence and inserted among a different family.

33; Son-sah-kah-hah; ---; Head; 62; M
34; Hlu-ah-to-me; ---; Wife; 63; F

35; Wah-shah-she-me-tsa-he; ---; Head; 77; F

36; Wah-sho-shah; ---; Head; 48; M
37; Mo-se-che-he; ---; Wife; 41; F
38; Hlu-ah-me-tsa-he; ---; Daut; 4; F

39; Mon-kah-sop-py; ---; Head; 61; M
40; He-ah-to-me; ---; Wife; 40; F
41; Wah-tsa-ah-tah; Joe Osage; S. Son; 16; M
42; E-ne-op-pe; Nellie Osage; S. Daut; 14; F
43; Hun-kah-me; ---; Daut; 5; F
44; Heh-sah-hah; ---; Son; 3; M

45; Wah-hre-she; Charles; Head; 46; M
46; Hlu-ah-me; ---; Wife; 40; F
47; Mo-se-che-he; Josephine Wahhreshe; Daut; 14; F
48; Mon-kah-hah; ---; Son; 9; M
49; Nah-me-tsa-he; ---; Daut; 5; F

50; ---; Luther Harvey; Head; 40; M
51; Ke-ah-som-pah; Mary Harvey; Wife; 37; F
52; He-ah-wah-kon-tah; Minnie Harvey; Daut; 15; F
53; Hlu-ah-wah-kon-tah; Walter Harvey; Son; 12; M
54; Num-pah-q-ah; Theodore R. Harvey; Son; 11; M
55; Wah-tsa-su-sah; ---; Son; 7; M
56; ---; Luther Harvey Jr.; Son; 3; M

57; Me-ke-wah-ti-an-kah; ---; Head; 53; M
58; Wah-hrah-lum-pah; ---; Wife; 39; F
59; Kah-he-ah-gra; Louis James; Son; 13; M
60; Me-to-op-pe; ---; Daut; 5; F

61; ---; Roy James; Head; 24; M
62; ---; Laura James; Wife; 23; F

63; ---; Roscoe Conklin; Head; 47; M
64; ---; Edith White; Wife; 28; F
65; ---; Joseph White; S. Son; 6; M
66; ---; Abraham White; S. Son; 4; M
67; Wah-shah-ke-pah; ---; Son; 3; M

68; He-ah-to-me; Nellie White; Orphan; 14; F

206

Key: NUMBER; Indian Name; English Name; Sex; Relation; Age
* An Askerisk will be next to a number if repeated or out of sequence and inserted among a different family.

69; Sho-e-ne-lah; ---; Head; 38; M

70; Wah-shin-kah-sop-py; ---; Head; 63; M
71; To-op-pe; ---; Wife; 62; F
72; E-gro-tah; Joseph Bird; Son; 17; M

73; E-gron-kah-shin-kah; ---; Head; 50; M
74; Hum-pah-to-kah; ---; Wife; 38; F
75; We-heh; Margaret Little; Daut; 16 F
76; Wah-sop-py-wah-kah; Mary Pappin; Daut; 9; F

77; Sin-tsa-hu; Ralph Hamilton; Head; 21; M

78; Shun-kah-mo-lah; ---; Head; 64; M
79; Wah-tsa-me; ---; Wife; 56; F
80; Wah-shin-kah-hu; Joseph Shunkahmolah; Son; 20; M

81; ---; Daniel West; Head; 36; M
82; Hlu-ah-to-me; ---; Wife; 39; F
83; Kah-shin-kah; ---; Son; 9; M

84; Wah-hah-sah-e; ---; Head; 73; F

85; Wah-ses-tah-shin-kah; John Blackbird; Head; 52; M
86; Hlu-ah-to-me; Mary Blackbird; Wife; 35; F
87; Mon-shon-tsa-e-tah; Maud Blackbird; Daut; 15; F
88; Che-sho-ki-he-kah; ---; Son; 3; M

89; Wah-hrah-lum-pah; Mollie Mantel; Orphan; 19; F

90; ---; Mollie Kyle; Head; 23; F

91; He-ah-to-me; ---; Head; 34; F
92; Kah-scah; Charles Antwine; Son; 10; M

93; Kah-wah-o; Yellow Horse; Head; 53; M
94; Ke-ah-som-pah; ---; Wife; 43; F
95; Pun-kah-me-tsa-he; Maggie Bates; Daut; 17; F
96; Ah-kah-hu; John Bates; Son; 13; M
97; Hun-kah-me-tsa-he; ---; Daut; 11; F
98; Kah-ah-sum-pah; ---; Daut; 5; F

99; ---; Joseph Bates; Head; 24
100; ---; Lizzie June; Wife; 22; F
101; Hun-kah; ---; Son; 4; M

Key: NUMBER; Indian Name; English Name; Sex; Relation; Age
* An Askerisk will be next to a number if repeated or out of sequence and inserted among a different family.

102; Hun-kah-me-tsa-he; ---; Head; 27; F
103; ---; Michel Wahtsamoie; Son; 3; M
104; ---; Frank Wahtsamoie; Son; 3; M
105; Ki-he-gra-in-kah; Harry Wahtsamoie; Son; 1; M

106; Pun-q-tah; ---; Head; 59; F

107; ---; Andrew Berry; Head; 23; M

108; ---; Esther Smith; Head; 25; F

109; Nun-tsa-wah-hu; ---; Head; 57; M
110; Num-pah-se; Joseph Cannon; Son; 19; M
111; ---; John Cannon; Son; 8; M

112; ---; Frank Cannon; Head; 25; M

113; ---; Alex Cannon; Head; 27; M

114; O-pah-su-ah; ---; Head; 41; M
115; Wah-to-sah; ---; Wife; 41; F
116; Pah-pah-ah-hah; Francis Opahsuah; Son; 16; M

117; Tsa-po-in-kah; ---; Head; 61; M

118; ---; Lawrence Gray; Head; 24; M

119; ---; Amos Osage; Head; 38; M
120; ---; Liza Osage; Wife; 29; F
121; He-ah-to-me; Rosa Osage; Daut; 11; F

MOH E KAH MOIE BAND

122; Moh-e-kah-moie; ---; Head; 76
123; Hluah-to-me; ---; Wife; 56; F
124; Me-ah-hre; Mary Mohekahmoie; Daut; 16; F

125; ---; Adair Hickey; Head; 34; M

126; ---; William Fletcher; Head; 39; M
127; Me-sah-e; ---; Wife; 28; F
128; Gra-to-me-tsa-he; ---; S. Daut; 9; F
129; Gra-to-ah; ---; S. Daut; 6; F
130; Sin-tsa-wah-kon-tah; Charles Fletcher; Son; 13; M
131; E-to-moie; Anna Fletcher; Daut; 10; F
132; ---; Frances T. Fletcher; Daut; 4; F

Key: NUMBER; Indian Name; English Name; Sex; Relation; Age

* An Askerisk will be next to a number if repeated or out of sequence and inserted among a different family.

133; Gro-tun-kah; Joseph Fletcher; Orphan; 20; M

134; To-wah-gah-she; ---; Head; 51; M
135; He-ah-to-me; ---; Wife; 47;
136; Gra-tah-su-ah; Thomas Butler; Son; 17; M

137; ---; Eugene Butler; Head; 22; M
138; ---; Grace Butler; Wife; 25; F

139; Me-gra-to-me; ---; Head; 44; F

140; U-ses-tah-wah-hah; ---; Head; 444; M

141; ---; Gilbert Fox; Head; 39; M

142; Me-ti-an-kah; ---; Head; 47; M
143; Mo-se-che-he; ---; Wife; 41; F
144; Ne-wal-la; Edward Elkins; Son; 14; M
145; E-he-ke-op-pe; ---; Daut; 9; F
146; Wah-ne-en-kah; ---; Daut; 4; F

147; ---; Luther Elkins; Head; 24; M

148; ---; Charles West; Head; 27; M
149; ---; Louisa West; Daut; 3; F

150; ---; Don Dickinson; Head; 32; M

151; ---; Herbert Spencer; Head; 34; M
152; ---; Jennie Spencer; Wife; 26; F

153; Gra-tah-su-ah; Donnie Cole; Orphan; 19; F

154; To-wah-gah-he; ---; Head; 51; M
155; Son-se-grah; ---; Wife; 37; F
156; He-ah-to-me; Fanny Frye; Daut; 19; F

157; ---; Edward Cox; Head; 34; M
158; A-non-to-op-pe; ---; Wife; 23; F
159; ---; Mary Cox; Daut; 1; F
159 ½; Wah-tsa-ah-tah; Joseph Cox; Son; 5; M

160; ---; Clinton Bigheart; Head; 39; M
161; Mon-shon-tsa-e-tah; ---; Wife; 29; F
162; Hum-pah-to-kah; Rose Bigheart; Daut; 14; F

Key: NUMBER; Indian Name; English Name; Sex; Relation; Age
* An Askerisk will be next to a number if repeated or out of sequence and inserted among a different family.

163; Ne-wal-la; Oscar Neal; Orphan; 11; M

164; ---; Rose Neal; Head; 23; F
165; ---; Clara May Neal; Daut; 2; F

166; ---; Wilson Kirk; Head; 53; M
167; ---; Dora Kirk; Daut; 9; F
168; ---; Rosa Kirk; Daut; 5; F
169; ---; Charles Kirk; Son; 3; M

170; Pah-she-he; Mary Cox; Orphan; 20

171; Hun-tsa-me; Mable Cole; Head; 22; F

NE KAH WAH SHE TUN KAH BAND.

172; Ne-kah-wah-she-tun-kah; ---; Head; 70; M
173; Wah-hrah-lum-pah; ---; Wife; 58; F

174; ---; Nicholas Webster; Head; 35; M

175; E-to-moie; Little Star; Head; 41; M
176; Wah-to-sah-e; ---; Wife; 41; 1
177; Gra-tah-ah-kah; John Star; Son; 10; M
178; Tom-pah-pe; ---; Daut; 7; F
179; E-kah-pah-she; ---; Son; 4; M
180; Me-tsa-ah-tah; ---; Daut; 2; F

181; Che-sho-wah-ke-pah; ---; Head; 40; M
182; Wah-hrah-lum-pah; ---; Wife; 43; F
183; Hum-pah-to-kah; ---; Daut; 13; F
184; Ke-ah-som-pah; ---; Daut; 10; F
185; ---; Mary Cheshowahkepah; Daut; 7; F

186; ---; Millie Kirk; Head; 26; F
187; Ke-ah-som-pah; ---; Daut; 2; F

188; Hun-wah-ko; ---; Head; 74; F

189; Pun-kah-wah-ti-an-kah; ---; Head; 48; M
190; Wah-hrah-lum-pah; ---; Wife; 25; F
191; Wah-tsa-ah-hah; James Bigheart; Son; 14; M
192; Wah-te-sah; ---; Daut; 8; F
193; Wah-sis-tah; ---; Son; 4; M
194; Min-kah-she; ---; Daut; 1; F

Census of the_____**Osage**_____Indians of ___**Osage**___Agency ___**Okla.**___
on ___**June 30, 1910.**___, taken by, ___**Hugh Pitzer, Supt. & Sp'l. Disb'g. Agent**___

Key: NUMBER; Indian Name; English Name; Sex; Relation; Age
* An Askerisk will be next to a number if repeated or out of sequence and inserted among a different family.

195; Pah-nee-wah-with-tah; ---; Head; 68; M
196; Gra-tah-me-tsa-he; ---; Wife; 49; F

197; Ne-kah-lum-pah; ---; Head; 54; M
198; Hah-moie; Bird Tuman; Son; 19; M

199; ---; Gurney Miller; Head; 43; M
200; ---; Grace Miller; Daut; 9; F
201; ---; Howard Miller; Son; 7; M
202; ---; Chester Miller; Son; 4; M
203; ---; Joseph Miller; Son; 2; M

204; Ne-ah-tse-pe; ---; Head; 68; F

205; ---; Annie Daniels, nee Turpie; Head; 23; F

206; Bro-ki-he-kah; ---; Head; 54; M
207; Wah-tsa-e-o-she; ---; Wife; 61; F
208; E-ne-op-pe; Annie Brokey; Daut; 16; F

209; ---; Herbert Brokey; Head; 22;   M

210; E-pah-son-tsa; ---; Head; 55; M

211; Shon-kah-tsa-a; ---; Head; 42; M

212; ---; Polly Jones, nee Earl; Head; 19; F
213; ---; Jesse Earl Jones; Son; 2m; M

214; Ke-ah-som-pah; ---; Head; 59; F
215; Me-hun-kah; Rosa Scott; Daut; 19; F
216; Hlu-ah-wah-kon-tah; Daniel Scott; Son; 16; M
217; Shah-kah-wah-pe; Walter Scott; Son; 13; M

218; Wah-tsa-ah-hah; ---; Head; 56; M
219; Wah-hrah-lum-pah; ---; Wife; 32; F
220; Wah-tsa-moie; Joseph Watson; Son; 14; M

221; Ethel Bryant; Ethel Bryant; Head; 25; F

222; Shah-wah-pe; ---; Head; 42; M

223; Hun-kah-hop-py; Edward G. Gibson; Orphan; 17; M

224; Son-se-o-grah; Ropemaker; Head; 64; M
225; Mon-shon-tsa-e-tah; ---; Wife; 64; F

211

Key: NUMBER; Indian Name; English Name; Sex; Relation; Age
* An Askerisk will be next to a number if repeated or out of sequence and inserted among a different family.

226; Wah-ko-sah-moie; Mary Clay; Daut; 16; F

227; ---; Dudly Haskell; Head; 34; M
228; Son-se-grah; ---; Wife; 28; F
229; Wah-hrah-lum-pah; ---; Daut; 9; F
230; Me-gra-to-me; ---; Daut; 7; F
231; Hlu-ah-wah-kon-tah; ---; Son; 4; M

232; He-shah-ah-hle; ---; Head; 51; M
233; He-ah-to-me; ---; Wife; 44; F
234; Ah-kah-me; ---; Daut; 11; F
235; Hlu-ah-gla-she; ---; Daut; 7; F
236; Hun-kah-me-tsa-he; ---; Daut; 3; F

237; Mo-hah-ah-gra; ---; Head; 61; M
238; Wah-kon-tah-he-umpah; ---; Wife; 67; F
239; He-kin-to-op-pe; Angella Hanna; Orphan; 15; F

240; ---; Peter Clark; Head; 27; M
241; ---; Madeline Clark; Wife; 21; F

242; Tom-pah-pe; ---; Head; 84; F

243; ---; Richard Kenny; Head; 54; M
244; Gra-tah-su-ah; ---; Wife; 43; F
245; He-kin-to-op-pe; Mary June; Daut; 18; F
246; A-non-to-op-pe; ---; Daut; 6; F
247; Hlu-lah-tsa-kah; ---; Son; 3; M

248; ---; John Kenny; Head; 27; M

249; Wah-hrah-lum-pah; Annie Kenny; Head; 25; F

250; ---; Orlando Kenworthy; Head; 34; M

251; ---; Tony Townsend; Head; 30; M

252; Hun-kah-hop-py; ---; Head; 41; M
253; He-ah-to-me; Mary Hunkahhoppy; Daut; 15; F
254; Wah-hrah-lum-pah; Rosa Hunkahhoppy; Daut; 13; F
254 ½; ---; Lucy Hunkahhoppy; Daut; 2; F

255; Hun-kah-hoppy; William Stepson; Orphan; 19; M

256; ---; Jack Hartley; Head; 34; M

212

Census of the _____ **Osage** _____ Indians of _____ **Osage** _____ Agency _____ **Okla.** _____

on _____ **June 30, 1910.** _____, taken by, _____ **Hugh Pitzer, Supt. & Sp'l. Disb'g. Agent** _____

Key: NUMBER; Indian Name; English Name; Sex; Relation; Age

* An Askerisk will be next to a number if repeated or out of sequence and inserted among a different family.

257; Nah-hah-scah-she; ---; Head; 56; F

258; Wah-tsa-ki-he-kah; Charles Drum; Head; 39; M
259; Wa-heh; Agnes Drum; Daut; 15; F
260; Wah-te-sah; Lucy Drum; Daut; 9; F

261; ---; Julia Dunlap; Orphan; 12; F

BIG HILL BAND.

262; To-wah-e-he; ---; Head; 54; M
263; Che-sah-me; ---; Wife; 62; F

264; Hun-kah; Alfred McKinley; Head; 22; M
265; Eu-pah-shon-kah-me; ---; Daut; 3; F

266; ---; Daniel McDougan; Head; 40; M

267; ---; Ben Harrison; Head; 30; M
268; ---; Edna M. Harvey; S. Daut; 15; F
269; ---; Emily Harrison; Daut; 12; F
270; ---; Ben H. Harrison; Son; 8; M
271; ---; Wauneta E. Harrison; Daut; 5; F

272; Ne-kah-e-se-y; Jimmy; Head; 64; M
273; ---; Lizzie Q.; Wife; 61; F
274; Wah-shah-she; Rita Kyle; Daut; 19; F

275; ---; Minnie Smith; Head; 23; F

276; A-non-to-op-pe; ---; Head; 61; F

277; Pah-pah-ah-hah; Thomas Dorry; Orphan; 18; M

278; Num-pah-se; Philip Brokey; Son; 9; M

279; ---; Earnest Roe; Head; 38; M

280; ---; Perry King; Head; 35; M
281; E-ne-ke-op-pe; ---; Wife; 35; F
282; Min-tsa-kah; Walter King; Son; 11; M
283; Pun-q-tah; Mary King; Daut; 8; F
284; Cha-hun-kah-me; ---; Daut; 3; F
285; Moh-en-gra-tah; ---; Son; 6; M

286; Mum-brum-pah; ---; Head; 85; F

213

Census of the ____ **Osage** ____ Indians of ___ **Osage** ____ Agency ___ **Okla.** ___
on ___ **June 30, 1910.** ___, taken by, ___ **Hugh Pitzer, Supt. & Sp'l. Disb'g. Agent** ___

Key: NUMBER; Indian Name; English Name; Sex; Relation; Age
* An Askerisk will be next to a number if repeated or out of sequence and inserted among a different family.

287; Wah-hrah-lum-pah; ---; Head; 54; F
288; Hun-kah-she; Clementine P. Harris; Daut; 14; F

WHITEHAIR BAND.

289; ---; John Claremore; Head; 27; M
290; ---; Amanda Claremore; Wife; 26; F
291; Mon-shonah-she; ---; Son; 3; M
292; Ne-wal-la; George W. Allen; Orphan; 19; M

293; ---; Dominic Daniels; Head; 27

294; ---; Joseph Daniels; Head; 28

295; Gra-to-me; ---; Head; 44
296; Hlu-ah-tse-ke; John Kenworthy; Son; 20; M
297; Wan-ne-ah-tah; William Kenworthy; Son; 17; M
298; Wah-shun-kah-kah-hah; ---; Son; 11; M

299; E-gro-op-pe; Hall Goode; Head; 21; M

300; Wah-hrah-lum-pah (D & D); ---; Orphan; 15; F

301; Mo-se-che-he; ---; Head; 49; F
302; E-som-pah; May Collum; Daut; 16; F

303; Wah-ko-sah-moie; ---; Head; 41; F
304; Lah-tah-sah; Clara Collum; Daut; 19; F
305; Ho-tah-me; Anna Collum; Daut; 13; F
306; Hun-tsa-moie; ---; Son; 12; M

307; ---; Joseph Mason; Head; 23; M
308; ---; Rose Mason; Wife; 25; F
309; ---; Frank Mason; Son; 2; M

310; ---; Francis Drexil; Head; 33; M
311; Wah-ko-sah-moie; ---; Wife; 34; F
312; Ne-kah-ah-se; ---; Daut; 12; F
313; Me-tsa-kah; ---; Son; 8; M

314; Pah-se-to-pah; ---; Head; 63
315; Wah-shah-she-me-tsa-me; ---; Wife; 60; F

316; ---; Paul Peace; Head; 24; M
317; ---; Clara Marshall; Wife; 24; F

214

Key: NUMBER; Indian Name; English Name; Sex; Relation; Age
* An Askerisk will be next to a number if repeated or out of sequence and inserted among a different family.

318; ---; Henry Peace; Head; 27; M

TALL CHIEF BAND.

319; ---; Eliza Tall Chief; Head; 38; F

320; Hlu-ah-wah-kon-tah; Alex Tall Chief Jr.; Son; 20; M

321; ---; Rosa Tall Chief; Head; 29; F

322; He-ah-to-me; Emma; Head; 57; F

323; ---; Eves Tall Chief; Head; 32; M
324; Wah-shah-hah-me; ---; Wife; 30; F
325; ---; Helen Tall Chief; Daut; 5; F
326; ---; Henry Tall Chief; Son; 3; M

327; Me-hun-kah; ---; Head; 26; F

328; Ho-tah-moie; John Stink; Head; 47; M

329; Wah-shah-hah-me; ---; Head; 63; F

330; ---; Henry Tall Chief; Head; 27; M

331; Nah-she-wal-la; ---; Head; 51; M
332; Wah-sha-she-me-tsa-he; Mattie Walsh; Daut; 20; F

333; Pah-she-he; Grace Entokah; Head; 25; F
334; He-ah-to-me; ---; Daut; 5; F
335; ---; Louis Entokah; Son; 2; M

KO SHE WAH TSE BAND.

336; He-lo-ki-he; Bare legs; Head; 72; M

337; He-se-moie; ---; Head; 61; M
338; Tsa-me-tsa; Mary Buffalo; Daut; 11; F

339; ---; Charles Grant; Head; 37; M

340; ---; George Dunlap; Orphan; 15; M

341; E-to-kah-wah-ti-an-kah; ---; Head; 74; M
342; Shon-shin-kah; Bryan Wilson; Son; 17; M
343; E-to-hun-kah; ---; Son; 10; M

Key: NUMBER; Indian Name; English Name; Sex; Relation; Age
* An Askerisk will be next to a number if repeated or out of sequence and inserted among a different family.

344; Kah-wah-ho-tsa (Sassamoie); ---; Head; 42; M
345; Ah-kah; James McKinley; Son; 16; M
346; Wah-tsa-hu-hah; William McKinley; Son; 14; M
347; Wah-hu-sah; ---; Daut; 10; F

348; Wah-to-sah-grah; ---; Wife; 42
349; Ah-kah-me-tsa-he; Eva McKinley; Daut; 19
350; Lah-su-sah-pah; Henry McKinley; Son; 19; M

351; ---; Josephine McKinley; Head; 22; F

352; Ne-wal-la (Tsa-shin-kah); ---; Head; 44; M
353; Hlu-ah-to-me; ---; Daut; 7; F
354; To-wah-e-he; ---; Son; 3; M

355; Son-se-gra; ---; Head; 33; F

356; Wah-ko-ki-he-kah; ---; Head; 56; F
357; Wah-tsa-moie; John Hunter; Son; 18; M
358; Wah-ko-sah-moie; Mary Hunter; Daut; 14; F

BLACK DOG BAND.

359; ---; Black Dog; Head; 63; M
360; Graeto-me-tsa; Louisa Blackdog; Wife; 30; F

361; ---; Edgar McCarthy; Head; 37; M
362; Me-tsa-he; Nettie McCarthy; Wife; 27; F

363; Son-se-gra; ---; Head; 52; F

364; ---; Amos Hamilton; Head; 38; M
365; ---; Noah Hamilton; Son; 8; M
366; ---; Ira Hamilton; Son; 6; M
367; ---; Otto Hamilton; Son; 3; M

368; Me-ho-e; ---; Head; 71; F

369; ---; Allison Webb; Head; 26; M
370; ---; Grace Webb; Wife; 36; F

371; He-lo-ki-he; Long Bow; Head; 43; M
372; E-gro-tah; Charles Pettus; Son; 20; M

373; Wah-sop-py; Lucy Hahmoie Bangs; Head; 26; F
374; ---; Myron Bangs Jr.; Son; 2; M

Census of the **Osage** Indians of **Osage** Agency **Okla.**
on **June 30, 1910.** , taken by, **Hugh Pitzer, Supt. & Sp'l. Disb'g. Agent**

Key: NUMBER; Indian Name; English Name; Sex; Relation; Age
* An Askerisk will be next to a number if repeated or out of sequence and inserted among a different family.

375; ---; Silas Sanford; Head; 33; M
376; ---; Anna Sanford; Wife; 28; F

377; ---; Allen Webb; Head; 30; M
378; Hum-pah-to-kah; ---; Wife; 22; F
379; ---; Bertha Webb; Daut; 4; F
380; ---; Charles M. Webb; Son; 4; M

381; Willie McCarthy (Incompt); Head; 29; M

382; ---; Andrew Jackson; Head; 41; M

SAUCY CHIEF BAND.

383; ---; Lawrence; Head; 55; M

384; ---; Joseph Mills; Head; 21; M

385; ---; Alex Eagle Feather; Head; 37; M

386; Wah-te-sah; ---; Head; 69; F

387; Gra-to-me-tsa-he; Ida Gibson; Orphan; 15; F

388; ---; Prudie Martin; Head; 35; F
389; ---; Christine Martin; Daut; 7; F
390; ---; Cecil Martin; Son; 4; M

391; ---; James G. Blaine; Head; 37; M
392; ---; Hazel Blaine; Wife; 26; F
393; ---; Laura Gray; S. Daut; 8; F
394; ---; Walker Blaine; Son; 14; M

395; E-ne-op-pe; ---; Heaa[sic]; 29; F
396; ---; Eugene Blaine; Son; 10; M
397; Me-shah-e; ---; Daut; 8; F
398; ---; James G. Blaine Jr. Son; 6; M

399; ---; Hayes Little Bear; Head; 25; M

400; Lo-hah-me; Dora Little Bear; Head; 22; M

401; Ah-hu-shin-kah; ---; Head; 50; M
402; Nah-hah-sah-me; ---; Wife; 53; F

403; ---; Augustine Crowe; Head; 35; F

217

Census of the   **Osage**   Indians of   **Osage**   Agency   **Okla.**

on   **June 30, 1910.**   , taken by,   **Hugh Pitzer, Supt. & Sp'l. Disb'g. Agent**

Key: NUMBER; Indian Name; English Name; Sex; Relation; Age

* An Askerisk will be next to a number if repeated or out of sequence and inserted among a different family.

404; ---; Josephine Jump, nee Strike Axe; Daut; 16; F
405; ---; Augustus Chouteau; Son; 15; M
406; ---; Charles Chouteau; Son; 12; M

407; ---; Robert Panther; Head; 47; M
408; ---; Charles Panther; Son; 20; M
409; ---; Clark Panther; Son; 18; M
410; ---; Nettie Panther; Daut; 16; F
411; ---; Maud Panther; Daut; 13; F

412; ---; Mary Pryor; Head; 59; F

413; ---; Edna Labatte; Head; 38; F

414; Charles Me-she-tsa-he; ---; Head; 51; M
415; Wah-ko-sah-moie; ---; Wife; 56; F
416; Hlu-ah-me; Eva Bean; Daut; 18; F
417; Pah-she-he; Emma Hoover; Daut; 14; F

418; ---; Ben Mushunkashey; Head; 27; M
419; Hlu-ah-me-tsa-he; Edna Mushunkashey; Wife; 22; F
420; ---; Charley Mushunkashey; Son; 3; M

421; ---; William Pryor; Head; 35; M
422; Min-kah-she; Mary Pryor; Wife; 37; F
423; ---; Josephine Pryor; Daut; 10; F
424; Shon-kah; Charles Mushunkashey; S. Son; 14; M
424 ½; ---; John Pryor; Son; 7; M

425; ---; Susie L. Hutchinson; Head; 28; F
426; ---; Vernie L. Hutchinson; Daut; 9
427; ---; Charles V. Hutchinson; Son; 7; M
428; ---; Carlos H. Hutchinson; Son; 5; M
429; ---; Genvis Hutchinson; Daut; 3; F

430; Ke-le-kom-pah; ---; Head; 60; M
431; Mo-se-che-he; ---; Wife; 55; F

432; Wah-kon-te-ah; Wakon Iron; Son; 19; M

433; ---; Paul Albert; Head; 41; M

434; Pah-she-he; ---; Head; 50; M

435; Hum-pah-to-kah; ---; Head; 56; F

Key: NUMBER; Indian Name; English Name; Sex; Relation; Age
* An Askerisk will be next to a number if repeated or out of sequence and inserted among a different family.

435 1/2; Wah-shah-she-me-tsa-he; Augustine Black; Head; 37; F
436; ---; John P. White Tail; Son; 13; M
437; Hom-me-tsa-he; May Black; Daut; 4; F

437;* Me-shah-e; ---; Head; 51; F [#437 recorded twice.]

438; ---; Harry Kohpay; Head; 38; M
439; ---; Elsie Kohpay; Daut; 11; F
440; ---; Hugh Kohpay; Son; 10; M
441; ---; Loretto Kohpay; Son; 3; M

442; Wy-e-gla-in-nah; Red Corn; Head; 56; M
443; Wah-kon-tah-he-um-pah; ---; Wife; 59; F
444; Wah-tsa-kon-lah; Ralph Malone; S. Son; 18; M

445; ---; Raymond Red Corn; Head; 24; M

446; ---; Pearl Hartley; Head; 30; F

447; ---; Julia White Tail; Head; 64; F

448; Ne-kah-she-he; ---; Head; 35; F
449; Wah-pah-ah-hah; Edward Elkins; Son; 13; M
450; Gra-to-me; Minnie Elkins; Daut; 5; F
451; Com-pox-she; Kate Albert; Daut; 3; F

452; ---; Charles Michelle; Head; 42; M
453; Me-sah-e; ---; Wife; 38; F
454; ---; Ida Michelle; Daut; 14; F

455; ---; Harry Big Eagle; Head; 24; M
456; Wah-shah-hah-me; Elsie Big Eagle; Wife; 20; F
457; Me-tsa-he; Metsa Big Eagle; Daut; 4; F

458; ---; Sylvia Wood; Head; 41; F

459; Wah-shah-she-me-tsa-he; ---; Head; 86; F

460; ---; Harry Pyahhunkah; Head; 23; M

461; ---; Charles Brave; Head; 32; M
462; Mum-brum-pah; Mary Strike Brave; Wife; 25; F
463; ---; Andrew Brave; Son; 9; M
464; ---; Louis Brave; Son; 4; M

465; Laban Miles; Head; 50; M

Key: NUMBER; Indian Name; English Name; Sex; Relation; Age
* An Askerisk will be next to a number if repeated or out of sequence and inserted among a different family.

466; Mo-se-che-he; Anna Miles; Daut; 20; F
467; Wah-shah-ah-pe; Mary Miles; Daut; 16; F
468; Pap-pah-ah-ho; Lee Miles; Son; 16; M

469; Hlu-ah-shu-tsa; John Miles; Head; 21; M

470; Wah-shah-she-me-tsa-he; ---; Head; 41; F
471; ---; Walker Penn; Son; 19; M
472; ---; Laban Miles Jr.; Son; 9; M

473; ---; Eddie Penn; Head; 21; M

474; ---; John Whitehorn; Head; 27; M
475; ---; Arthur Whitehorn; Son; 5; M

476; Hu-lah-tun-kah; Big Eagle; Head; 58; M
477; Pah-pu-son-tsa; ---; Wife; 60; F
478; Wah-she-pah; Wash Warrior; S. Son; 18; M
479; Pah-she-he; Mary Warrior; S. Daut; 15; F

480; Hun-kah-ah-gra; Robert Warrior; Head; 20; M
481; Tsa-me-hun-kah; Mamie Warrior; Wife; 20; F

482; ---; Russell Warrior; Head; 26; M

483; E-stah-o-gre-she; ---; Head; 46; M
484; Shon-blah-scah; ---; Wife; 42; F

485; Mon-kah-he; Frank Pyahhunkah; Orphan; 16; M

BEAVER BAND.

486; ---; Rose L. Bigheart; Daut; 18; F
487; ---; Sarah L. Bigheart; Daut; 12; F
488; ---; Belle L. Bigheart; Daut; 7; F

489; Che-sho-shin-kah; Henry Red Eagle; Head; 61; M
490; ---; Rosa Red Eagle; Wife; 59; F

491; ---; Paul Red Eagle; Head; 30; M
492; ---; Cecelia Red Eagle; Wife; 28; F
493; ---; Harry Red Eagle; Son; 8; M
494; ---; Louis Red Eagle; Son; 5; M
495; ---; Joseph Red Eagle; Son; 4; M
496; ---; May Louisa Red Eagle; Daut; 2; F
497; ---; Henry Red Eagle; Son; 1; M

Key: NUMBER; Indian Name; English Name; Sex; Relation; Age
* An Askerisk will be next to a number if repeated or out of sequence and inserted among a different family.

498; Hlu-ah-shu-tsa (D & D); Joseph Red Eagle; Head; 34; M

499; Beg-gah-hah-she; Brave; Head; 76; M
500; ---; Mary Brave; Wife; 79; F

501; ---; Andrew Bighorse; Head; 33; M;
502; Hum-pah-to-kah; ---; Wife; 39; F;
503; We-heh; Rose McDougan; S. Daut; 18; F
504; ---; Peter Bighorse; Son; 11; M
505; ---; Joseph Bighorse; Son; 9; M
506; ---; Mary Bighorse; Daut; 6; F
507; ---; Edward Bighorse; Son; 3; M

508; ---; Charles McDougan; Head; 22; M

509; ---; John Wagoshe; Head; 32; M
510; Wah-shah-she-me-tsa-he; Agnes Bigheart; Wife; 32; F
511; ---; George Vest; S. Son; 14; M
512; ---; Charles Wagoshe; Son; 6; M
513; A-non-to-op-pe; ---; Daut; 4; F
514; Wah-sah-po; ---; Daut; 3; F

515; ---; John Lookout; Head; 33; M

516; Heh-kah-mon-kah; ---; Wife; 24; F
517; ---; William Lookout; Son; 3; M

518; ---; Louis Bighorse; Head; 45; M
519; To-op-pe; Ida Bighorse; Wife; 30; F
520; ---; Rose Bighorse; Daut; 14; F
521; ---; Lillie Bighorse; Daut; 9; F
522; ---; Minnie Bighorse; Daut; 6; F
523; ---; Louisa Bighorse; Daut; 3; F

524; ---; Paul Buffalo; Head; 46; M
525; Pah-pu-son-tsa; ---; Wife; 52; F

526; Ah-tsa-shin-kah; Mary Wild Cat; Orphan; 12; F

527; Mo-ho-gla; ---; Head; 56; M
528; Me-tsa-hi-ke; ---; Wife; 66; F

529; ---; Antwine Pryor; Head; 30; M
530; Julia; Julia Pryor; Daut; 5; F
531; ---; Susie Pryor; Daut; 3; F

221

Key: NUMBER; Indian Name; English Name; Sex; Relation; Age
* An Askerisk will be next to a number if repeated or out of sequence and inserted among a different family.

532; ---; Henry Coshehe; Head; 37; M
533; Wah-kon-tah-he-um-pah; ---; Wife; 34; F
534; ---; Clem Coshehe; Son; 18; M
535; ---; George Coshehe; Son; 4; M
535 ½; ---; John Coshehe; Son; 10; M

536; Wah-tsa-ah-tah; Ralph On Hand; Orphan; 19; M

537; He-he-kin-to-op-pe; Minnie On Hand; Orphan; 14; F

538; ---; John McFall; Head; 43; M
539; Gra-tah-shin-kah; Mary McFall; Wife; 31; F

540; ---; Minnie Whitehorn; Orphan; 20; F

541; ---; George Michelle; Head; 36; M
542; ---; Wesley W. Michelle; Son; 5; M

543; Mo-se-che-he; ---; Head; 70; F

STRIKE AXE BAND.

544; ---; Fred Lookout; Head; 52; M
545; Mo-se-che-he; Julia Lookout; Wife; 41; F
546; ---; Charles Lookout; Son; 18 M
547; ---; Frederick Lookout; Son; 15; M
548; ---; Nora Lookout; Daut; 10; F
549; ---; Henry Lookout; Son; 4; M

550; ---; James Strike Axe; Orphan; 16; M

551; Wy-e-nah-she; ---; Head; 62; M

552; Tsa-shin-kah-wah-ti-an-kah; Saucy Calf; Head; 66; M
553; ---; Sophia Chouteau; Wife; 68; F

554; ---; Joseph Buffalohide; Head; 24; M
555; ---; Agnes Buffalohide; Wife; 23; F

556; Tom-pah-pah; ---; Head; 56; F

557; ---; Pendleton Strike Axe; Head; 29; M
558; Mo-se-che-he; ---; Wife; 22; F
559; ---; Emma Strike Axe; Daut; 6; F
560; ---; Ida Strike Axe; Daut; 4; F

Key: NUMBER; Indian Name; English Name; Sex; Relation; Age

* An Askerisk will be next to a number if repeated or out of sequence and inserted among a different family.

561; ---; Foster Strike Axe; Head; 36; M
562; ---; Jennie Strike Axe; Daut; 14; F
563; ---; Emma Strike Axe; Daut; 12; F
564; ---; Dora Strike Axe; Daut; 4; F

565; ---; Louis Pryor; Head; 31; M
566; ---; Andrew Pryor; Son; 4; M

567; O-sah-ke-pah; Cap Strike Axe; Head; 52; M

568; Pah-se-to-pah (D & D); Head; 40; M
569; Me-sah-e; Veva Pahsetopah; Wife; 30; F
570; ---; Cora Pahsetopah; Daut; 9; F
571; ---; Carrie Pahsetopah; Daut; 7; F
572; ---; Louis Pahsetopah; Son; 5; M

573; Me-hun-kah (He-ah-to-me); ---; Head; 60; F
574; Ke-nun-tah; William Shahpahnahshe; Son; 20; M

575; ---; Pierce St. John; Head; 34; M
576; Ke-ah-som-pah; ---; Wife; 36; F
577; Gra-tah-scah; Jacob Jump; S. Son; 18; M
578; ---; Dora St. John; Daut; 8 F
579; ---; Herbert St. John; Son; 6 M
580; ---; William St. John; Son; 4 M
581; ---; Anna St. John; Daut; 3; F

582; ---; Frank Corndropper; Head; 62; M
583; Gra-tah-me-tsa-he; ---; Wife; 38; F

584; Peh-tsa-moie; ---; Head; 57; M
585; Wah-tsa-u-sah; ---; Wife; 38; F

586; ---; Richard Firewalk; Head; 26; M
587; Son-se-grah; May Firewalk; Wife; 20; F

588; Lah-blah-wal-la; Three Striker (Incompt); Head; 66; M

589; Wy-u-hah-kah; ---; Head; 52; M
590; Hlu-ah-me-tsa-he; ---; Wife; 61; F

591; ---; John Oberly; Head; 30; M
592; Me-tsa-he; ---; Wife; 28; F
593; A-non-to-op-pe; ---; Daut; 28; 3
594; Pah-pah-ah-he; ---; Son; 2; M

Census of the   **Osage**   Indians of   **Osage**   Agency   **Okla.**

on   **June 30, 1910.**   , taken by,   **Hugh Pitzer, Supt. & Sp'l. Disb'g. Agent**

Key: NUMBER; Indian Name; English Name; Sex; Relation; Age

* An Askerisk will be next to a number if repeated or out of sequence and inserted among a different family.

595; ---; John A. Logan; Head; 37; M
596; ---; Mary Logan; Wife; 32; F
597; ---; Joseph Logan; Son; 11; M
598; ---; Rosa Logan; Daut; 5; F
599; ---; Oscar Logan: Son; 3; M
600; Tom-pah-pah; ---; Daut; 3; F

NE KAH KE PAH NEE BAND.

601; ---; Robert A-she-gah-hre; Head; 60; M
602; Gra-to-me-tsa-he; ---; Wife; 54; F
603; Me-tun-kah; Susan Killon; Daut; 20; F
604; Vah-sah-pah-shin; ---; Daut; 5; F
605; Sho-tsa; ---; Son; 3; M

606; Ke-mo-hah; ---; Head; 51; M
607; Loh-tah-sah; ---; Wife; 35; F
608; Me-tsa-he; Elda Townsend; S. Daut; 18; F
609; ---; John R. Townsend; S. Son; 13; M
610; Hun-kah-me (D & D); ---; Daut; 11; F
611; Heh-mo-sah; ---; Son; 10; M
612; Moh-e-kah-shah; ---; Son; 8; M
613; Mon-shon-kah-hah; ---; Son; 6; M

614; Tsa-e-kon-lah (Crazy); Mrs. Womack; Head; 66; F

615; ---; Clarence Gray; Head; 33; M
616; He-kin-to-op-pe; Jennie Gray; Wife; 23
617; ---; Mary Gray; Daut; 6; F

618; Tsa-pah-shin-kah; John; Head; 56
619; Wah-shah-pe-wah-ko; ---; Wife; 60
620; E-to-wah-hrah-lum-pah; Mary Brown; Daut; 15

621; Shon-kah; Charles Brown; Head; 22

622; ---; David Copperfield; Head; 34
623; Hun-kah-me-tsa-he; Maggie Copperfield; Wife; 36; F
624; Me-tsa-he; ---; Daut; 10; F
625; Hun-kah-she; ---; Son; 8; M
626; Hun-kah-ah-gra; ---; Son; 5; M
627; Wah-she-pah; ---; Son; 3; M

628; ---; William Pitts; Head; 33; M
629; Me-tsa-he; Isabella Pitts; Wife; 32; F
630; ---; George T. Pitts; Son; 3; M

Key: NUMBER; Indian Name; English Name; Sex; Relation; Age

* An Askerisk will be next to a number if repeated or out of sequence and inserted among a different family.

631; Hun-kah-tun-kah; Roman Logan; Head; 50; M
632; Pah-she-he; Mary Logan; Wife; 29; F
633; Me-tsa-he; Agnes Logan; Daut; 14; F
634; Tom-pah-pe; ---; Daut; 8; F

635; Che-sho-shin-kah; ---; Head; 71; M
636; Hlu-ah-to-me; ---; Wife; 63; F

637; ---; Frank Lohowa; ; 25; M
638; ---; Mary Lohowa; Wife; 28; F

639; Wah-kah-lah-tun-kah; ---; Head; 68; M
640; Me-tsa-he; ---; Wife; 79; F

641; Ah-hu-scah; Walla Fish; Head; 21; M
642; E-ne-op-pe; Mary Fish; Wife; 19; F

643; Hun-tsa-moie; ---; Head; 46; M
644; Hlu-ah-to-me; ---; Wife; 66; F

645; Mo-se-che-he; ---; Head; 92; F

CLAREMORE BAND.

646; ---; Francis Claremore; Head; 45; M
647; Wah-hrah-lum-pah; ---; Wife; 39; F
648; Tsa-pah-ke-ah; Louis Claremore; Son; 17; M

649; ---; John Abbott; Head; 29; M
650; Ne-kah-she-tsa; ---; Wife; 26; F
651; Wah-shah-she-me-tah-he; ---; Daut; 8; F
652; ---; Margurite Abbott; Daut; 3; F

653; ---; Henry Pratt; Head; 38; M
654; Hun-kah-me; Josephine Pratt; Wife; 37; F
655; ---; Helen Pratt; Daut; 15; F
656; Gra-tah-scah; George Pratt; Son; 9; M
657; ---; Charles Pratt; Son; 5; M

658; Me-gra-to-me; ---; Head; 54; F

659; Pah-hu-gre-she; ---; Head; 22; F
660; ---; Andrew Opah; Son; 4; M

661; ---; Charles Big Elk; Head; 31; M
662; Mo-se-che-he; Cora Big Elk; Wife; 28; F

225

Key: NUMBER; Indian Name; English Name; Sex; Relation; Age
* An Askerisk will be next to a number if repeated or out of sequence and inserted among a different family.

663; ---; Mary Big Elk; Daut; 10; F
664; ---; Don S. Big Elk; Son; 4; M

665; E-ah-scah-wal-la; James Browning; Orphan; 17; M
666; Mon-kah-hah; John Browning; Orphan; 12; M

667; ---; Eugene Ware; Head; 34; M
668; Hum-pah-to-kah; ---; Wife; 33; F
669; ---; Joseph Ware; Son; 11; M
670; ---; Mary Ware; Daut; 9; F
671; ---; Elijah N. Ware; Son; 7; M
672; ---; Daisy L. Ware; Daut; 5; F
672 ½; Charles Ware; Son; 4; M

673; ---; Henry Roan; Head; 27; M
674; He-ah-to-me; ---; Wife; 21; F
675; ---; Grace Roan; Daut; 4; F

676; ---; Arthur Bonnicastle; Head; 33
677; ---; Angie Bonnicastle; Wife; 23
678; ---; Kathleen Bonnicastle; Daut; 9m

679; ---; Maud Supernaw; Head; 56
680; ---; Mary Thompson; Daut; 12

681; ---; Jack Wheeler; Head; 68; M
682; Nah-me-tsa-he; ---; Wife; 63; F

683; ---; Rhoda Wheeler; Head; 25; F

684; ---; Ben Wheeler; Head; 34; M
685; Tsa-me-tsa-he; Fanny Wheeler; Wife; 28; F
686; Hun-kah-hre; Fred Wheeler; Son; 9; M
687; Me-tsa-he; ---; Daut; 4; F
688; Shah-kah-pah-he; ---; Son; 2; M

689; ---; Nannie Naranjo; Head; 38; F
690; ---; Clara Naranjo; Daut; 11; F

691; Hlu-ah-shu-tsa; Joe Red Eagle; Head; 40; M
692; Hun-kah-me; Dora Red Eagle; Wife; 32; F
693; ---; Alice Red Eagle; Daut; 5; F
693 ½; Frederick Red Eagle; Son; 9; M

694; Wah-shah-she-me-tsa-he; ---; Head; 51; F

226

Key: NUMBER; Indian Name; English Name; Sex; Relation; Age
* An Askerisk will be next to a number if repeated or out of sequence and inserted among a different family.

695; ---; Sophia Greenback; Head; 36; F

WAH TI AN KAH BAND.

696; Wah-she-hah; Bacon Rind; Head; 50; M
697; Wah-ko-ki-he-kah; Rosa Bacon Rind; Wife; 46; F
698; In-gro-tah; George Bacon Rind; Son; 19; M
699; Ah-tsa-shin-kah; Louisa Bacon Rind; Daut; 13; F
700; Mah-hu-sah; Moses Bacon Rind; Son; 9; M
701; ---; Julia Bacon Rind; Daut; 7; F

702; Mo-sah-mum-pah; ---; Head; 43
703; Hun-kah-me; ---; Wife; 37; F
704; Ki-he-kah-tun-kah; ---; Son; 14; M

705; To-wah-e-he; ---; Head; 65; M

706; She-she; ---; Head; 51; M
707; Ne-kah; ---; Wife; 64; F

708; ---; Simon Henderson; Head; 28; M
709; ---; Louisa Henderson; Wife; 24; F
710; He-ah-to-me; ---; Daut; 4; F

711; ---; George Pitts; Head; 29; M
712; ---; Mary Pitts; 24; F
713; ---; Warren Pitts; Son; 7; M
714; ---; David Pitts; Son; 5; M
715; ---; Elizabeth Pitts; Daut; 3; F

716; Ho-ki-ah-se; ---; Head; 42; M
717; Me-tsa-he; Louisa Hokiahse; Wife; 32; F
718; To-ho-ah; ---; Son; 6; M
719; E-nah-min-tsa-tun; ---; Son; 2; M

WILLIAM PENN BAND.

720; ---; Peter C. Bigheart; Head; 71; M
721; Wah-ko-ki-he-kah; ---; Wife; 67; F

722; Hlu-ah-to-me (D & D); ---; Orphan; 18; F

723; ---; George Bigheart; Head; 34; M
724; Pah-me-she-wah; ---; Wife; 24; F
725; ---; Charles Bigheart; Son; 5; M
726; Um-pah-to-kah; ---; Daut; 3; F

Key: NUMBER; Indian Name; English Name; Sex; Relation; Age
* An Askerisk will be next to a number if repeated or out of sequence and inserted among a different family.

727; Wah-ko-sah-moie; ---; Daut; 2; F

728; ---; Claude Smith; Head; 36; M
729; Hlu-ah-to-me; Mamie Smith; Wife; 27; F
730; Wah-tsa-me; ---; Son; 8; M
731; Hum-pah-to-kah; ---; Daut; 7; F
732; Ke-ah-som-pah; ---; Daut; 4; F
733; Wah-ko-sah-moie; ---; Daut; 3; F

734; Wah-she-wah-hah; John Bigheart; Head; 44; M
735; Hlu-ah-to-me; Grace Bigheart; Wife; 41; F
736; Ne-kah-sto-kah; John Bigheart; Son; 13; M
737; Wah-ko-sah-moie; ---; Daut; 12; F
738; Ne-kah-sto-wah; ---; Son; 9; M
739; Kah-scah; ---; Son; 6; M
740; Grah-e-grah-in-kah; ---; Son; 4; M

741; Wah-tsa-tun-kah; Joseph Bigheart; Head; 21; M

742; ---; Edward Bigheart; Head; 22; M
743; ---; Rose Bigheart; Wife; 19; F

744; He-ah-to-me; ---; Head; 49; F
745; Ne-wal-la; Henry Lohah; Son; 18 M
746; Ah-hu-shin-kah; Albert Lohah; Son; 16; M
747; A-non-to-op-pe; Ellen Lohah; Daut; 12; F
748; Heh-kah-mon-kah; Mary Lohah; Daut; 11; F
749; Tom-pah-pe-she; ---; Son; 5; M

750; ---; Samuel Barker; Head; 31; M
751; ---; Frances Barker; Wife; 22; F
752; ---; James Barker; Son; 2; M

753; O-lo-hah-moie; ---; Head; 52 M
754; Mo-se-che-he; ---; Wife; 42; F
755; Hlu-ah-wah-kon-tah; Robert Olchahmoie; Son; 18; M
756; Wah-tsa-a-tah; George Olchahmoie; Son; 15; M
757; Wah-hrah-lum-pah; ---; Daut; 12; F
758; Num-pah-q-ah; ---; Son; 10; M
759; Me-gra-to-me; ---; Daut; 8; F
760; Moie-ke-kah-she; ---; Son; 6; M

761; Tah-hah-gah-hah; ---; Head; 46; M
762; Wah-hu-sah-e; ---; Wife; 41; F
763; Ah-nah-me-tsa-he; Roy Maker; Son; 13; M
764; Ho-ke-ah-se; George Maker; Son; 6; M

Key: NUMBER; Indian Name; English Name; Sex; Relation; Age
* An Askerisk will be next to a number if repeated or out of sequence and inserted among a different family.

765; ---; Ross Maker; Head; 22; M

766; Ah-kah-me; ---; Wife; 31; F
767; Shon-kah; James Maker; Son; 13; M

768; ---; Edgar Maker; Head; 25; M
769; ---; Helen Maker; Wife; 20; F
770; ---; Theodore Maker; Son; 2; M

771; Mo-shah-ke-tah; ---; Head; 46; M

772; Tom-pah-pe; ---; Head; 64; F
773; O-hun-pe-ah; John Bruce; Son; 20; M

774; ---; Albert Penn; Head; 40; M
775; ---; Dora Penn; Wife; 23
776; Wah-ses-tah; Andrew Penn; Son; 16; M
777; Wah-te-sah; Grace Penn; Daut; 15; F
778; ---; Mary Penn; Daut; 4; F

779; ---; Fred Penn; Head; 37; M

780; O-ke-sah; Tom West; Head; 36; M
781; Me-tsa-he; Rosa West; Wife; 37; F
782; ---; John Wood; S. Son; 16; M
783; Mo-se-che-he; ---; Daut; 6; F

784; ---; Dan G. West; Head; 32; M
785; Pah-pu-son-tsa; Fanny West; Wife; 29; F
786; He-ah-to-me; Lucy West; Daut; 9; F
787; ---; Howard M. West; Son; 4; M

LITTLE CHIEF BAND.

788; ---; Charles Whitehorn; Orphan; 20; M

789; ---; John Whitehorn; Head; 22; M

790; Nah-kah-sah-me; Kate Whitehorn; Head; 22; F

791; Wah-shah-hah-me; ---; Head; 58; F

792; Ki-he-kah-nah-she; ---; Head; 47 M
793; Hlu-ah-to-me; Frances Kihekahnahshe; Wife; 37; F
794; Wahahah-she-me-tsa-he; Magella Whitehorn; Daut; 16; F
795; Hum-pah-to-kah; Tresa Whitehorn; Daut; 14; F

229

Key: NUMBER; Indian Name; English Name; Sex; Relation; Age

* An Askerisk will be next to a number if repeated or out of sequence and inserted among a different family.

796; Monk-she-hah-pe; ---; Son; 3; M

797; Me-tsa-he; ---; Head; 44; F
798; Wah-shah-she-me-tsa-he; ---; Daut; 9; F
799; Ho-ho; Clarence Daniel; Son; 15; M
800; Wah-shah-she; ---; Daut; 7; F

801; He-ah-to-me; ---; Head; 58; F

802; ---; Frank Little Soldier; Head; 25; M
803; ---; Esther Little Soldier; Wife; 24; F

804; Me-tsa-he; ---; Head; 20; F
805; Wah-shah-e-no-pah; ---; Son; 2; M

806; ---; Ellen Spurgeon; Head; 29; F

807; Hlu-ahwah-tah; ---; Head; 44; M
808; He-to-op-pe; ---; Wife; 41; F
809; Mah-grah-lum-pah; ---; Daut; 11; F
810; Hlu-ah-wah-kon-tah; ---; Son; 6; M
811; Wah-shah-me-tsa-he; Lillie Hlu-ah-wah-tah; Daut; 3; F

812; Me-tsa-no; Mary Mudd; Head; 54; F

813; ---; Alex Mudd; Head; 21; M

814; ---; Lucy Lotson; Head; 33; F
815; ---; Lucius Lotson; Son; 14; M

816; ---; Cleatess Mudd; Daut; 3; F
817; ---; Dorothy Mudd; Daut; 3; F

HALF BREED BAND.

818; ---; Aiken, Elizabeth; Head; 28; F

819; ---; Aiken, John H.; Head; 26; M

820; ---; Alberty, Cynthia; Head; 54; F
821; ---; Alberty, Lizzie; Daut; 19; F

822; ---; Alberty, George; Head; 23; M
823; ---; Alberty, Flora; Wife; 23; F

824; ---; Alexander, Levi; Head; 29; M

230

Census of the _____ **Osage** _____ Indians of __ **Osage** __ Agency ___ **Okla.** __

on ___ **June 30, 1910.** ___ , taken by, ___ **Hugh Pitzer, Supt. & Sp'l. Disb'g. Agent** ___

Key: NUMBER; Indian Name; English Name; Sex; Relation; Age

* An Askerisk will be next to a number if repeated or out of sequence and inserted among a different family.

825; ---; Alexander, Martha I.; Daut; 8; F

826; ---; Alexander, Ida A.; Head; 21; F

827; ---; Allen, Emily; Head; 46; F
828; ---; Whalen, Esther; Daut; 16; F
829; ---; Whalen, Dorothea; Daut; 14; F
830; ---; Whalen, Charlotte; Daut; 20; F

831; ---; Anderson, Mary; Head; 27; F

832; ---; Anderson, John B.; Head; 24; M
833; ---; Anderson, Henry P,; Son; 4; M
834; ---; Anderson, Viretta; Daut; 3; F

835; ---; Anderson, Edward R.; Head; 22; M

836; ---; Anderson, Skinner T.; Son; 16; M
837; ---; Anderson, Ora D.; Daut; 12; F
838; ---; Anderson, Noble M.; Son; 11; M

839; ---; Anderson, Florence; Head; 21; F

840; ---; Appleby, Jane; Head; 79; F
841; ---; Captain, Peter (Incompt); Son; 46; M

842; ---; Atkins, John D. Jr.: Head; 23; M

843; ---; Avant, Rosalie; Head; 33; F
844; ---; Avant, Theodore R.; Son; 12; M
845; ---; Avant, Ethel; Daut; 9; F

846; ---; Barber, Ida; Head; 28; F
847; ---; Barber, Augustus; Son; 7; M
848; ---; Barber, Morris G.; Son; 4; M

849; ---; Barber, Bridget A.; Head; 49; F
850; ---; Barber, Clara M.; Daut; 18; F
851; ---; Barber, Edgar E.; Son; 15; M
852; ---; Barber, Lawrence L.; Son; 13; M
853; ---; Barber, Paul G.; Son; 10; M
854; ---; Barber, Lee R.; Son; 6; M

855; ---; Barker, Mary J.; Head; 55; F
856; ---; Simms, Cora E.; Daut; 16; F

231

Key: NUMBER; Indian Name; English Name; Sex; Relation; Age
* An Askerisk will be next to a number if repeated or out of sequence and inserted among a different family.

857; ---; Baker, John Thomas; Head; 41; M
858; ---; Baker, Monette; Wife; 35; F
859; ---; Baker, Myrtle C.; Daut; 14; F
860; ---; Baker, Morris A.; Son; 10; M
861; ---; Baker, Frank T.; Son; 9
862; ---; Baker, Martha B.; Daut; 6; F
863; ---; Baker, John Thomas Jr.; Son; 3; M

864; ---; Baker, Myrtle; Head; 21; F

865; ---; Baylis, Elizabeth; Head; 66; F

866; ---; Baylis, Harry; Head; 26; M

867; ---; Bellieu, Thomas A.; Head; 28; M

868; ---; Bellieu, Walter S.; Head; 23; M

869; ---; Bellieu, Stella; Daut; 18; F
870; ---; Bellieu, Leo F.; Son; 14; M
871; ---; Bellieu, Anna H.; Daut; 12; F
872; ---; Bellieu, Stephen M.; Son; 10; M

873; ---; Bellmard, Eliza; Head; 23; F
874; ---; Bellmard, Clarence; Son; 3; M

875; ---; Bennett, William; Head; 34; M
876; ---; Bennett, Isabella; Wife; 29; F
877; ---; Bennett, William E.; Son; 10; M
878; ---; Bennett, Teresa; Daut; 6; F
879; ---; Bennett, Irene; Daut; 3; F

880; ---; Blackburn, Rachel; Head; 30; F
881; ---; Blackburn, Oliver O.; Son; 10; M
882; ---; Blackburn, Luther A.; Son; 5; M

883; ---; Boulanger, Joseph; Head; 61
884; ---; Boulanger, Benjamin H.; Son; 20
885; ---; Boulanger, James V.; Son; 19
886; ---; Boulanger, Eulalie C.; Daut; 16
887; ---; Boulanger, Anna V.; Daut; 15
888; ---; Boulanger, Charles F.; Son; 13

889; ---; Boulanger, Grover; Head; 25; M

890; ---; Boulanger, Stephen E.; Head; 28; M

Key: NUMBER; Indian Name; English Name; Sex; Relation; Age
* An Askerisk will be next to a number if repeated or out of sequence and inserted among a different family.

891; ---; Boulanger, Minnie L.; Daut; 9; F
892; ---; Boulanger, Augustine C.; Daut; 7; F

893; ---; Boulanger, Isaac; Head; 31; M
894; ---; Boulanger, Charles M.; Son; 10; M
895; ---; Boulanger, Alta; Daut; 8; F
896; ---; Boulanger, Lenora; Daut; 7; F
897; ---; Boulanger, Nellie; Daut; 5; F

898; ---; Boulanger, W.J.; Head; 36; M
899; ---; Boulanger, Edward Mc; Son; 15; M
900; ---; Boulanger, May; Daut; 14; F
901; ---; Boulanger, Evart; Son; 10; M

902; ---; Bockius, Dora; Head; 27; F
903; ---; Bockius, Cyril D.; Son; 12; M
904; ---; Bockius, Earnest F.; Son; 9; M
905; ---; Bockius, Mary B.; Daut; 7; F
906; ---; Bockius, Milton J.; Son; 3; M

907; ---; Boren, Blanche; Head; 24; F
908; ---; Boren, Kathleen; Daut; 5; F
909; ---; Boren, Evaleen; Daut; 5; F

910; ---; Bowhan, Ida M.; Head; 29; F
911; ---; Bowhan, Francis D.; Son; 9; M
912; ---; Bowhan, Sewel C.; Son; 6; m
913; ---; Bowhan, Erin S.; Son; 4; M

914; ---; Bowhan, Marie B.; Head; 24; F
915; ---; Bowhan, John C.; Son; 5; M
916; ---; Bowhan, Harry; Son; 2; M

917; ---; Bowman, Rosetta; Head; 23; F
918; ---; Bowman, Mildred L.; Daut; 6; F
919; ---; Bowman, Ben; Son; 4; M

920; ---; Brock, Lavaria; Head; 30; F
921; ---; Brock, Winona V.; Daut; 3; F

922; ---; Bray, Emma; Head; 31; F
923; ---; McGath, John W.; Son; 13; M

924; ---; Bradshaw, Rose E.; Head; 36; F
925; ---; Bradshaw, Thomas S.; Son; 19; M
926; ---; Bradshaw, Harry A.; Son; 16; M

Key: NUMBER; Indian Name; English Name; Sex; Relation; Age
* An Askerisk will be next to a number if repeated or out of sequence and inserted among a different family.

927; ---; Bradshaw, Alvin S.; Son; 14; M
928; ---; Bradshaw, Sarah A.; Daut; 12; F
929; ---; Bradshaw, Greta E.; Daut; 10; F
930; ---; Bradshaw, Alva F.; Daut; 8; F
931; ---; Bradshaw, Irene A.; Daut; 6; F
932; ---; Bradshaw, George W.; Son; 4; M
933; ---; Bradshaw, Courtland A.; Son; 2; M

933 ½; ---; Brown, Mable; Head; 24; F

934; ---; Brown, Charles; Head; 49; M
935; ---; Brown, Bernice; Daut; 18; F
936; ---; Brown, Treva; Daut; 12; F

937; ---; Brown, Edward; Head; 43; M

938; ---; Brown, Earnest; Head; 38; M
939; ---; Brown, Maude; Daut; 15; F
940; ---; Brown, Laura J.; Daut; 12; F
941; ---; Brown, William P.; Son; 11; M
942; ---; Brown, Lula B.; Daut; 6; F
943; ---; Brown, Helen M.; Daut; 3; F

944; ---; Brown, A.H.; Head; 50; M
945; ---; Brown, William S.; Son; 8; M
946; ---; Brown, Frank R.; Son; 5; M

947; ---; Brown, Mary J.; Head; 43; F
948; ---; Brown, Edith; Daut; 17; F
949; ---; Brown, Louis M.; Son; 15; M

950; ---; Brown, Hattie B.; Head; F

951; ---; Brunt, Edward; Head; 50; M
952; ---; Brunt, George E.; Son; 19; M
953; ---; Brunt, Joseph L.; Son; 11; M

954; ---; Brunt, Theodore; Head; 24; M

955; ---; Bruce, Elsie F.; Head; 40; F
956; ---; Bruce, Louisa; Daut; 16; F
957; ---; Bruce, Lena; Daut; 14; F
958; ---; Bruce, Adelbert; Son; 19; M

959; ---; Nix, Josephine, nee Bratton; Head; 30; F
960; ---; Bratton, William E.; Son; 11; M

234

Key: NUMBER; Indian Name; English Name; Sex; Relation; Age
* An Askerisk will be next to a number if repeated or out of sequence and inserted among a different family.

961; ---; Bratton, Edmund S.; 8; M
962; ---; Bratton, John I.; Son; 5; M

963; ---; Breeding, Mary L.; Head; 45; F
964; ---; Breeding, Leta M.; Daut; 15; F
965; ---; Breeding, Francis; Son; 13; M
966; ---; Breeding, Elsie E.; Daut; 10; F

967; ---; Brooks, Philomena; Head; 30; F
968; ---; Brooks, Sylvester; Son; 12; M
969; ---; Brooks, Dollretta; Daut; 11; F
970; ---; Brooks, Ruby A.; Daut; 9; F
971; ---; Brooks, Del Orier; Son; 6; M

972; ---; Bryant, Joe; Head; 58; M
973; ---; Bryant, Frank; Son; 16; M
974; ---; Bryant, Della M.; Daut; 15; F
975; ---; Bryant, Carrie M.; Daut; 13; F
976; ---; Bryant, Cecil; Son; 11; M
977; ---; Bryant, Arthur; Son; 10; M
978; ---; Bryant, Anna B.; Daut; 7; F
979; ---; Bryant, Arena; Daut; 4; F

980; ---; Burton, Roy B.; Son; 14; M

981; ---; Carr, Nelson; Son; 14; M
982; ---; Carr, Gussie M.; Daut; 10; F

983; ---; Carpenter, Mary E.; Head; 40; F
984; ---; Carpenter, Floyd H.; Son; 19; M
985; ---; Carpenter, Charles E.; Son; 15; M
986; ---; Carpenter, Rose B.; Daut; 13; F
987; ---; Carpenter, Louis S.; Son; 11; M

988; ---; Carter, Alva E.; Son; 12; M
989; ---; Carter, Leota M.; Daut; 10; F
990; ---; Carter, Barton D.; Son; 16; M
991; ---; Carter, Charles A.; Son; 14; M

992; ---; Callahan, Alfred; Head; 27; M

993; ---; Callahan, Cornelius; Head; 35; M

994; ---; Callahan, Julia; Head; 28; F
995; ---; Callahan, Rosemary; Daut; 4; F

235

Key: NUMBER; Indian Name; English Name; Sex; Relation; Age
* An Askerisk will be next to a number if repeated or out of sequence and inserted among a different family.

996;   ---; Callahan, William; Head; 32; M

997;   ---; Callahan, Leo; Son; 12; M
998;   ---; Callahan, Charles; Son; 10; M
999;   ---; Callahan, Mary; Daut; 9; F
1000;   ---; Callahan, Gertrude; Dau; 7; F

1001;   ---; Canville, Clara; Daut; 13; F
1002;   ---; Canville, John B.; Son; 9; M
1003;   ---; Canville, Agnes L.; Daut; 7; F

1004;   ---; Canville, Cecil; Son; 12; M
1005;   ---; Canville, John; Son; 16; M
1006;   ---; Canville, Acuda; Daut; 6; F

1007;   ---; Carlton, Anthony; Head; 38; M
1008;   ---; Carlton, Mary E.; Wife; 29; F
1009;   ---; Carlton, Eva M.; Daut; 12; F
1010;   ---; Carlton, Ethel; Daut; 11; F
1011;   ---; Carlton, Frances; Daut; 9; F

1012;   ---; Carlton, George; Head; 33; M
1013;   ---; Carlton, Augustine; Daut; 10; F
1014;   ---; Carlton, Robert; Son; 8; M
1015;   ---; Carlton, Mary E.; Daut; 10; F
1016;   ---; Carlton, George Jr.; Son; 5; M
1017;   ---; Carlton, Ella; Daut; 3; F

1018;   ---; Cedar, William; Son; 14; M

1019;   ---; Cedar, Paul; Orphan; 12; M

1020;   ---; Cheshewalla, Evart; Son; 14; M
1021;   ---; Cheshewalla, Floyd; Son; 11; M

1022;   ---; Childers, Nola; Orphan; 11; F

1023;   ---; Chouteau, Henry; Head; 25; M
1024;   ---; Chouteau, Robert; Son; 1; M

1025;   ---; Chouteau, Stewart; Head; 23; M

1026;   ---; Chouteau, Louis P.; Head; 22; M

1027;   ---; Clem, William; Head; 32; M
1028;   ---; Clem, William L.; Son; 10; M

236

Key: NUMBER; Indian Name; English Name; Sex; Relation; Age

* An Askerisk will be next to a number if repeated or out of sequence and inserted among a different family.

1029; ---; Clem, John E.; Son; 9

1030; ---; Clem, James A.; Son; 5; M

1031; ---; Clem, Frantz; Son; 4; M

1032; ---; Clem, May M.; Daut; 1; F

1033; ---; Clem, James J.; Head; 35; M

1034; ---; Clem, Jessie M.; Daut; 14; F

1035; ---; Clem, William H.; Son; 12; M

1036; ---; Clem, James N.; Son; 9; M

1037; ---; Clem, Sallie J.; Daut; 7; F

1038; ---; Clewien, Anna; Head; 29; F

1039; ---; Clewien, Clarabell; Daut; 5; F

1040; ---; Clewien, Frances; Daut; 3; F

1041; ---; Clawson, Josiah C.; Head; 22; M

1042; ---; Clawson, Emma C.; Daut; 19; F

1043; ---; Clawson, Thomas A.; Son; 15; M

1044; ---; Clawson, George B.; Son; 13; M

1045; ---; Collins, Mary; Head; 74; F

1046; ---; Colby, Anna L.; Head; 28; F

1047; ---; Hardy, Orel; Son; 6; M

1048; ---; Hardy, Mary I.; Daut; 3; F

1049; ---; Cooper, Anna L.; Head; 28; F

1050; ---; Cooper, William O.; Son; 10; M

1051; ---; Cooper, Francis; Son; 7; M

1052; ---; Cooper, Edward E.; Son; 4; M

1053; ---; Conner, Woodie; Head; 27; M

1054; ---; Conner, Theil L.; Daut; 5; F

1055; ---; Conner, George; Head; 39; M

1056; ---; Conner, Adelia; Daut; 9; F

1057; ---; Conner, Victor W.; Son; M

1058; ---; Conner, Daniel I.; Son; 3; M

1059; ---; Cottingham, Ida; Head; 24; F

1060; ---; Cottingham, Vera L.; Daut; 7; F

1061; ---; Cottingham, Logan; Son; 5; M

1062; ---; Collins, Lula; Head; 35; F

1063; ---; Collins, John W.; Son; 11; M

237

Key: NUMBER; Indian Name; English Name; Sex; Relation; Age
* An Askerisk will be next to a number if repeated or out of sequence and inserted among a different family.

1064; ---; Collins, Roy W.; 8; M

1065; ---; Conness, Veva; Head; 38; F
1066; ---; Conness, Geneva M.; Daut; 11; F
1067; ---; Conness, William S.; Son; 5; M

1068; ---; Conway, Jane; Head; 82; F

1069; ---; Crouse, Isabella Fuller; Head; 44; F
1070; ---; Crouse, Earl; Son; 18; M
1071; ---; Crouse, Laura I.; Daut; 14; F
1072; ---; Crouse, Stephen M.; Son; 11; M

1073; ---; Crouse, Dallas; Head; 24; M

1074; ---; Crane, Marie; Head; 37; F
1075; ---; Crane, Frankie M.; Daut; 3; F

1076; ---; Cross, Ellen; Head; 29; F
1077; ---; Cross, Lou M.; Daut; 10; F
1078; ---; Cross, Charles L.; Son; 7; M
1079; ---; Cross, Candis J.; Daut; 3; F

1080; ---; Cunningham, Laura; Head; 36; F
1081; ---; Cunningham, Edward R.; Son; 11; M

1082; ---; Cunningham, Rose I.; 40; F
1083; ---; Cunningham, Robert B.; Son; 11; M

1084; ---; Cunningham, John M.; Head; 22; M

1085; ---; Curtis, Mary; Head; 53; F
1086; ---; Farrell, Virgil L.; Son; 19; M
1087; ---; Curtis, Lethia B; Daut; 15; F
1088; ---; Curtis, Ada; Daut; 12; F

1089; ---; Daniel, Sophia; Head; 34; F
1090; ---; Daniel, Bessie; Daut; 16; F
1091; ---; Daniel, Vernie; Son; 14; M
1092; ---; Daniel, Pearl C.; Son; 12; M
1093; ---; Daniel, Ida I.; Daut; 9; F

1094; ---; Davis, Sophia; Head; 69; F

1095; ---; Davis, Mary J.; Head; 61; F

Key: NUMBER; Indian Name; English Name; Sex; Relation; Age
* An Askerisk will be next to a number if repeated or out of sequence and inserted among a different family.

1096;   ---; LaSarge, Minnie E.; Head; 21; F

1097;   ---; Daily, Dora; Head; 28; F
1098;   ---; Dial, Lawton M.; Son; 9; M
1099;   ---; Dial, Elsie A.; Daut; 11; F

1100;   ---; Darnell, Rebecca J.; Head; 47; F
1101;   ---; Vadney, Amy V.; Daut; 19; F

1102;   ---; Dennison, Eliza; Head; 41; F
1103;   ---; Fugate, Frank E.; Son; 20; M
1104;   ---; Fugate, John A.; Son; 19; M
1105;   ---; Dennison, Nellie; Daut; 9; F
1106;   ---; Dennison, George O.; Son; 4; M

1107;   ---; Dennison, Bert; Head; 25; M
1108;   ---; Dennison, Florence L.; Daut; 3; F

1109;   ---; Del Orier, Julia; Head; 60; F
1110;   ---; Del Orier, Louis; Son; 4; M

1111;   ---; De Noya, Louis; Head; 49; M
1112;   ---; De Noya, Frederick; Son; 18; M
1113;   ---; De Noya, Clement; Son; 16; M
1114;   ---; De Noya, Josephine; Daut; 14; F
1115;   ---; De Noya, Ruby P.; Daut; 12; F

1116;   ---; De Noya, Frank; Head; 53; M
1117;   ---; De Noya, James E.D.; Son; 20; M
1118;   ---; De Noya, Clara; Daut; 19; F
1119;   ---; De Noya, Grace; Daut; 17; F
1120;   ---; De Noya, Alfred R.; Son; 16; M
1121;   ---; De Noya, Charlotte; Daut; 14; F
1122;   ---; De Noya, Myrtle C.; Daut; 12; F
1123;   ---; De Noya, Catherine I.; Daut; 7; F
1124;   ---; De Noya, Walter L.; Son; 4; M

1125;   ---; De Noya, Jacob; Head; 31; M
1126;   ---; De Noya, Belle; Wife; 30; F
1127;   ---; De Noya, Virgil H.; Son; 9; M
1128;   ---; De Noya, Maurice H.; Son; 7; M
1129;   ---; De Noya, Lillian C.; Daut; 6; F
1130;   ---; De Noya, Helen D.; Daut; 4; F

1131;   ---; De Noya, Joseph; Head; 33; M
1132;   ---; De Noya, Charlotte E.; Daut; 6; F

Key: NUMBER; Indian Name; English Name; Sex; Relation; Age
* An Askerisk will be next to a number if repeated or out of sequence and inserted among a different family.

1133; ---; De Noya, Margaret I.; Daut; 7; F
1134; ---; De Noya, Martha M.; Daut; 4; F

1135; ---; De Noya, Clement; Head; 43; M
1136; ---; De Noya, Emily; Wife; 39; F
1137; ---; De Noya, Clement Jr.; Son; 20; M
1138; ---; De Noya, Louis; Son; 16; M
1139; ---; De Noya, Sadie; Daut; 14; F
1140; ---; De Noya, Edna; Daut; 8; F
1141; ---; De Noya, Elizabeth; Daut; 6; F
1142; ---; De Noya, Millard; Son; 4; M
1142 1/2; ---; De Noya, Elsie; Daut; 12; F

1143; ---; De Noya, Wesley; ; 19; M
1144; ---; De Noya, Odell; Wife; 20; F

1145; ---; De Noya, Everette A.; Head; 23; M

1146; ---; Deal, Joseph; Head; 27; M
1147; ---; Deal, Mary J.; Wife; 21; F
1148; ---; Deal, James C.; Son; 4; M
1149; ---; Deal, William M.; Son; 2; M

1150; ---; Deal, Julia A.; Head; 55; F
1151; ---; Deal, Sherman; Son; 19; M

1152; ---; Dickey, James A.; Head; 29; M

1153; ---; Dickey, John T.; Head; 26; M

1154; ---; Dial, Eliza; Head; 50; F
1155; ---; Penn, Augustus; Son; 20; M
1156; ---; Penn, Rose E.; Daut; 18; F
1157; ---; Dial, Cora E.; Daut; 13; F
1158; ---; Dial, Eva; Daut; 11; F
1159; ---; Dial, Charles P.; Son; 5; M
1160; ---; Huston, John R.; Adot.Son; 19; M

1161; ---; Donelson, Frances; Head; 27; F
1162; ---; Donelson, Robert L.; Son; 9; M
1163; ---; Donelson, James L.; Son; 11; M

1164; ---; Doolin, Martha; Head; 27; F
1165; ---; Doolin, Alta J.; Daut; 3; F

1166; ---; Donovan, Augustine; Head; 58; F

Key: NUMBER; Indian Name; English Name; Sex; Relation; Age

* An Askerisk will be next to a number if repeated or out of sequence and inserted among a different family.

1167; ---; Donovan, Jesse C.; Son; 17; M

1168; ---; Donovan, Charles; Head; 21; M

1169; ---; Ducotey, Stanislaus; Head; 36; M
1170; ---; Ducotey, Versa; Daut; 12; F
1171; ---; Ducotey, Manza; Daut; 10; F
1172; ---; Ducotey, Bettie V.; Daut; 7; F
1173; ---; Ducotey, Frank S.; Son; 5; M

1174; ---; Dunn, Dora; Head; 32; F
1175; ---; Dunn, Ida M.; Daut; 14; F
1176; ---; Dunn, Mary A.; Daut; 12; F
1177; ---; Dunn, Timothy J.; Son; 6; M

1178; ---; Dunham, Martha; Head; 80; F

1179; ---; Dunn, Nettie M.; Head; 23; F

1180; ---; Easley, Margaret; Head; 38; F
1181; ---; Easley, Pearl; Daut; 18; F
1182; ---; Easley, George E. Son; 16; M
1183; ---; Easley, Leo B.; Son; 14; M
1184; ---; Easley, John W.; Son; 12; M
1185; ---; Easley, Mary E.; Daut; 9; F
1186; ---; Easley, Clarence A.; Son; 6; M
1187; ---; Easley, Robert J.; Son; 3; M

1188; ---; Edwards, Julia; Head; 44; F
1189; ---; Quinton, Agnes; Daut; 14; F
1190; ---; Quinton, Pearl C.; Daut; 12; F
1191; ---; Quinton, Elnora; Daut; 8; F
1192; ---; Edwards, Theodore; Son; 3; M

1193; ---; Quinton, Alex; Head; 21; M

1194; ---; Edmiston; Frances (Incompt); Head; 24; F
1195; ---; Edmiston, Bessie E,; Daut; 8; F

1196; ---; Evans, Mary E.; Head; 24; F

1197; ---; Easley, Irene; Head; 18; F

1198; ---; Farrell, Nathaniel; Head; 33; M
1199; ---; Farrell, Ruth; Daut; 10; F
1200; ---; Farrell, Andrew; Son; 7; M

Key: NUMBER; Indian Name; English Name; Sex; Relation; Age
* An Askerisk will be next to a number if repeated or out of sequence and inserted among a different family.

1201; ---; Farrell, Mary; Head; 22; F

1202; ---; Farrell, Charles; Head; 28; F
1203; ---; Farrell, Mary; Daut; 7; F
1204; ---; Farrell, Pearl; Daut; 3; F

1205; ---; Farrell, Monica; Head; 55; F
1206; ---; Shaw, Moses R.; Son; 20; M

1207; ---; Shaw, Charles M.; Head; 21; M

1208; ---; Fenton, Margaret; Head; 27; F
1209; ---; Fenton, Sylvester R.; Son; 9; M
1210; ---; Fenton, Louis L.; Son; 8; M
1211; ---; Fenton, Curtis D.; Son; 5; M
1212; ---; Fenton, Lenora; Daut; 2; F

1213; ---; Fox, Susie; Head; 48; F
1214; ---; Lombard, Sylvester; Son; 20; M
1215; ---; Lombard, Augustine; Daut; 17; F
1216; ---; Lombard, Joseph; Son; 15; M
1217; ---; Lombard, Paul; Son; 11; M
1218; ---; Fox, Alexander; Son; 8; M

1219; ---; Fronkier, Laban A.; Orphan; 20; F[sic]

1220; ---; Fronkier, William; Head; 39; M

1221; ---; Fronkier, Simon; Head; 38; M
1222; ---; Fronkier, Florence; Daut; 14; F
1223; ---; Fronkier, Blanche L.; Daut; 12; F
1224; ---; Fronkier, Benjamin; Son; 8; M

1225; ---; Fronkier, Philip; Head; 22; M

1226; ---; Fronkier, Augustus; Head; 32; M

1227; ---; Fronkier, James; Head; 31; M
1228; ---; Fronkier, Louis B.; Son; 4; M

1229; ---; Fuller, Thomas; Head; 29

1230; ---; Fuller, Louis; Head; 35; F[sic]
1231; ---; Fuller, Andrew B; 8; M

1232; ---; Fuller, Charles; Head; 26; M

242

Census of the ___**Osage**___ Indians of ___**Osage**___ Agency ___**Okla.**___
on ___**June 30, 1910.**___, taken by, ___**Hugh Pitzer, Supt. & Sp'l. Disb'g. Agent**___

Key: NUMBER; Indian Name; English Name; Sex; Relation; Age
* An Askerisk will be next to a number if repeated or out of sequence and inserted among a different family.

1233; ---; Fish, Eliza; Head; 21; F

1234; ---; Gaylor, Victoria; Head; 45

1235; ---; George, James M.; Head; 27; M
1236; ---; George, James I.; Son; 4; M

1237; ---; George, Sylvester; Head; 26; M

1238; ---; Gilmore, Mary A.; Head; 56; F
1239; ---; Gilmore, S.J.; Son; 19; M

1240; ---; Gilmore, William H.; Son; 13

1241; ---; Girard, Amelia; Head; 36; F
1242; ---; Girard, Mary E.C.; Daut; 16; F
1243; ---; Girard, Corine A.; Daut; 15; F
1244; ---; Girard, Aemelia[sic] V.; Daut; 14; F
1245; ---; Girard, Leona; Daut; 12; F

1246; ---; Grammer, Maggie; Head; 27

1247; ---; Goad, Clara; Head; 30; F
1248; ---; Goad, Cecil J.; Son; 8; M
1249; ---; Goad, Ethel; Daut; 3; F

1250; ---; Groves, Agnes; Head; 28; F
1251; ---; Groves, Mural W.; Son; 8; M
1252; ---; Groves,Mary L.; Daut; 6; F
1253; ---; Groves, Harry L.; Son; 3; M

1254; ---; Harrelson, Mary L. (Incompet); Head; 30; F
1255; ---; Harrelson, Emerine; Daut; 12; F

1256; ---; Hall, Ida; Head; 25; F
1257; ---; Hall, Alfred; Son; 6; M

1258; ---; Harruff, Margaret; Head; 46; M[sic] [F]
1259; ---; Harruff, Julia; Daut; 14; F

1260; ---; Hardy, Emily; Head; 37; F
1261; ---; Hardy, Louisa V.; Daut; 16; F
1262; ---; Hardy, Goldie; Daut; 13; F
1263; ---; Hardy, Geneva; Daut; 10; F
1264; ---; Hardy, William R.; Son; 6; M

Census of the   **Osage**   Indians of   **Osage**   Agency   **Okla.**
on   **June 30, 1910.**   , taken by,   **Hugh Pitzer, Supt. & Sp'l. Disb'g. Agent**

Key: NUMBER; Indian Name; English Name; Sex; Relation; Age
* An Askerisk will be next to a number if repeated or out of sequence and inserted among a different family.

1265; ---; Hampton, Charles; Head; 30; M
1266; ---; Hampton, Roland C.; Son; 4; M

1267; ---; Hampton, Rosalie; Head; 49; F

1268; ---; Hayes, Pearl; Head; 30; F
1269; ---; Hayes, Olivia; Daut; 6; F
1270; ---; Hayes, Elizabeth; Daut; 6; F
1271; ---; Hayes, Margaret; Daut; 3; F

1272; ---; Harlow, Josephine; Head; 31; F
1273; ---; Harlow, John N.; Son; 13; M

1274; ---; Hayes, Lawrence L.; Son; 5; M

1275; ---; Harlow, Susan; Head; 48; F
1276; ---; Akers, Grace; Daut; 19; F
1277; ---; Gilcrease, Belle M.; Daut; 16; F
1278; ---; Harlow, Charles C.; Son; 12; M

1279; ---; Haynie, Mary; Head; 25; F
1280; ---; Haynie, Willis; S. Son; 15; M
1281; ---; Haynie, John C.; Son; 5; M
1282; ---; Haynie, Emma; Daut; 4; F

1283; ---; Hackleman, Julia Ann; Head; 65; F

1284; ---; Harris, Mary E.; Head; 29; F

1285; ---; Harvey, Adeline; Head; 28; F

1286; ---; Heeman, Anna; Head; 28; F
1287; ---; Heeman, Beatrice M.; Daut; 6; F

1288; ---; Herard, Paul; Head; 42; M

1289; ---; Herard, Eugene; Head; 25; M

1290; ---; Herridge, Joseph; Son; 19; M
1291; ---; Herridge, Lula; Daut; 16; F

1292; ---; Hewitt, Rosa; Head; 24; F
1293; ---; Herridge, Valaria; Daut; 4; F
1294; ---; Herridge, Loretta M.; Daut; 3; F

1295; ---; Hildebrand, George; Head; 27; M

Census of the____ **Osage**____ Indians of ____ **Osage**____ Agency ___ **Okla.**___
on ____ **June 30, 1910.**____ , taken by, ____ **Hugh Pitzer, Supt. & Sp'l. Disb'g. Agent**

Key: NUMBER; Indian Name; English Name; Sex; Relation; Age
* An Askerisk will be next to a number if repeated or out of sequence and inserted among a different family.

1296; ---; Hildebrand, Richard; Head; 31; M

1297; ---; Hildebrand, David; Head; 37; M
1298; ---; Hildebrand, Nancy; Daut; 9; F

1299; ---; Hildebrand, James; Head; 41; M
1300; ---; Hildebrand, Oragonia; Daut; 15; F
1301; ---; Hildebrand, Dica; Daut; 10; F
1302; ---; Hildebrand, Susan; Daut; 16; F

1303; ---; Hildebrand, Joseph; Head; 43; M
1304; ---; Hildebrand, Frank; Son; 12; M

1305; ---; Hickman, Clementine; Head; 33; F
1306; ---; Hickman, Homer; Son; 14; M
1307; ---; Hickman, Edna J.; Daut; 11; F
1308; ---; Hickman, Franklin; Son; 10; M
1309; ---; Hickman, Florence; Daut; 8; F
1310; ---; Hickman, Lillie V.; Daut; 6; F
1311; ---; Hickman, Bertha C.; Daut; 4; F
1312; ---; Hickman, Roy N.; Son; 3; M

1313; ---; Holloway, Jasper C.; Head; 58; M

1314; ---; Holloway, Milton; Head; 27; M
1315; ---; Holloway, Andrew L.; Son; 7; M
1316; ---; Holloway, Olita M.; Daut; 4; F

1317; ---; Horn, Polly; Head; 28; F
1318; ---; Buxbaum, Vernon E.; Son; 9; M

1319; ---; Hoots, Rosa; Head; 41; F
1320; ---; Hoots, Agnes; Daut; 15; F

1321; ---; Hoots, Alfred; Head; 23; M

1322; ---; Hunt, Mary A.; Head; 40; F
1323; ---; Hunt, Lula B; Daut; 13; F
1324; ---; Hunt, Mary G.; Daut; 11; F
1325; ---; Hunt, Andrew D.; Son; 8; M
1326; ---; Hunt, Robert M. Jr.; Son; 3; M

1327; ---; Hunt, Antwine; Head; 22; M

1328; ---; James, Jesse; Head; 22; M

245

Census of the   **Osage**   Indians of   **Osage**   Agency   **Okla.**

on   **June 30, 1910.**   , taken by, **Hugh Pitzer, Supt. & Sp'l. Disb'g. Agent**

Key: NUMBER; Indian Name; English Name; Sex; Relation; Age

* An Askerisk will be next to a number if repeated or out of sequence and inserted among a different family.

1329; ---; Javine, Peter; Head; 58; M
1330; ---; Javine, Hasread; Son; 19; M
1331; ---; Javine, Viola M.; 16; F
1332; ---; Javine, Opal; Daut; 4; F
1333; ---; Javine, Howard Taft; Son; 2; M

1334; ---; Javine, Benjamin H.; Head; 21; M

1335; ---; Javine, Roy V.; Son; 14; M

1336; ---; Javine, John; Head; 55; M
1337; ---; Javine, Ollie; Daut; 20; F
1338; ---; Javine, Audra; Daut; 17; F
1339; ---; Javine, Ora E.; Daut; 16; F
1340; ---; Javine, Joseph; Son; 13; M

1341; ---; Javine, Anthony; Head; 23; M

1342; ---; Javine, John; Head; 28; M
1343; ---; Javine, George M.; Son; 6; M
1344; ---; Javine, Earl T.; Son; 4; M
1345; ---; Javine, Ella C.; Daut; 2; ZF

1346; ---; Johnson, Julia M.; Head; 55; F
1347; ---; Johnson, John W.; Head; 21; M

1348; ---; Jones, Laura; Head; 24; F
1349; ---; Jones, James F.; Son; 5; M

1350; ---; Kennedy, Agnes; Head; 34; F
1351; ---; Kennedy, James A.; Son; 12; M
1352; ---; Kennedy, Forrest L.; Son; 10; M
1353; ---; Kennedy, Thelma; Daut; 9; F
1354; ---; Kennedy, Cordelia A.; Daut; 6; F
1355; ---; Kennedy, Samuel G.; Son; 4; M

1356; ---; Kennedy, Mable; Head; 30; F
1357; ---; Kennedy, Albert A.; S. Son; 16; M

1358; ---; Kennedy, Samuel; Head; 24; M
1359; ---; Kennedy, Don C.; Son; 3; M

1360; ---; Keeler, Blanche; Head; 28; F
1361; ---; Keeler, Dixie; Son; 6; M
1362; ---; Keeler, Alberta M; Daut; 4; F

Census of the _____ **Osage** _____ Indians of _____ **Osage** _____ Agency _____ **Okla.** _____
on _____ **June 30, 1910.** _____, taken by, _____ **Hugh Pitzer, Supt. & Sp'l. Disb'g. Agent** _____

Key: NUMBER; Indian Name; English Name; Sex; Relation; Age
* An Askerisk will be next to a number if repeated or out of sequence and inserted among a different family.

1363; ---; Kilbie, Benedict; Head; 24; M
1364; ---; Kilbie, John A.; Son; 4; M

1365; ---; Krebs, Henry; Son; 14; M

1366; ---; Lawrence, Maggie; Head; 53; F

1367; ---; Labadie, Charles; Head; 39; M
1368; ---; Labadie, Hazel; Daut; 12; F
1369; ---; Labadie, Frank; Son; 10; M
1370; ---; Labadie, Alvin L.; Son; 8; M
1371; ---; Labadie, Nita; Daut; 5; F
1372; ---; Labadie, Ralph; Son; 2; M

1373; ---; Labadie, William H.; Head; 25; M
1374; ---; Labadie, Mary Ellen; Daut; 2; F

1375; ---; Labadie, Ella; Head; 23; F

1376; ---; Labadie, Frederick; Son; 20; M
1377; ---; Labadie, Earnie; Son; 19; M
1378; ---; Labadie, Joseph; Son; 17; M

1379; ---; Labadie, Edward; Head; 44; M
1380; ---; Labadie, Milton; Son; 12; M
1381; ---; Labadie, Rose M.; Daut; 9; F
1382; ---; Labadie, Robert E.; Son; 7; M
1383; ---; Labadie, Charles W.; Son; 5; M
1384; ---; Labadie, William H.; Son; 2; M

1385; ---; Labadie, Frank; Head; 49; M
1386; ---; Labadie, G.V.; Son; 18; M
1387; ---; Labadie, Paul F.; Son; 15; M

1388; ---; Labadie, John; Head; 23; M

1389; ---; LaSarge, Marie; Daut; 16; F
1390; ---; LaSarge, Louis; Son; 14; M
1391; ---; LaSarge, Arthur; Son; 13; M
1392; ---; LaSarge, Charles V.; Son; 11; M

1393; ---; LaSarge, Joseph; Head; 41; M
1394; ---; LaSarge, Ellen; Daut; 10; F
1395; ---; LaSarge, Harold L.; Son; 3; M

1396; ---; Lane, Joseph; Head; 41; M

Census of the_____**Osage**_____Indians of _____**Osage**_____ Agency _____**Okla.**_____

on _____**June 30, 1910.**_____, taken by, _____**Hugh Pitzer, Supt. & Sp'l. Disb'g. Agent**_____

Key: NUMBER; Indian Name; English Name; Sex; Relation; Age

* An Askerisk will be next to a number if repeated or out of sequence and inserted among a different family.

1397;   ---; Lane, Zella A.; Wife; 40; F
1398;   ---; Lane, Mary; Daut; 16; F
1399;   ---; Lane, Bessie; Daut; 12; F
1400;   ---; Lane, Joseph C.; Son; 7; M
1401;   ---; Lane, Roy B.; Son; 5; M

1402;   ---; Leahy, Mary L.; Head; 61; F

1403;   ---; Leahy, Bertha; Head; 35; F
1404;   ---; Leahy, Thomas R.; Son; 13; M
1405;   ---; Leahy, Cora W.; Daut; 11; F
1406;   ---; Leahy, Mable A.; Daut; 7; F
1407;   ---; Leahy, Edward A.; Son; 5; M

1408;   ---; Leahy, W.T.; Head; 41; M
1409;   ---; Leahy, Martha; Wife; 32; F
1410;   ---; Leahy, William T. Jr.; Son; 12; M
1411;   ---; Leahy, B. Thomas; Son; 11; M

1412;   ---; Lewis, Mary; Head; 49; F

1413;   ---; Lessert, Frank; Head; 68; M

1414;   ---; Lessert, Walter; Head; 25; M

1415;   ---; Lessert, Joseph; Head; 26; M

1416;   ---; Lessert, David; Head; 32; M

1417;   ---; Lessert, Guy; Son; 14; M
1418;   ---; Lessert, Millie M.; Daut; 12; F
1419;   ---; Lessert, Charles A.; Son; 10; M
1420;   ---; Lessert, Hattie; Daut; 8; F

1421;   ---; Lessert, Frank Jr.; Head; 46; M
1422;   ---; Lessert, Mary J.; Daut; 15; F
1423;   ---; Lessert, Robert A.; Son; 13; M
1424;   ---; Lessert, Grace J.; Daut; 9; F
1425;   ---; Lessert, Ray L.; Son; 7; M
1426;   ---; Lessert, Dora L.; Daut; 4; F

1427;   ---; Leasert[sic], Benjamin; Head; 39; M
1428;   ---; Lessert, Wade; Son; 19; M
1429;   ---; Lessert, Susie; Daut; 14; F
1430;   ---; Lessert, Banjamin[sic] L.; Son; 7; M
1431;   ---; Lessert, Fay; Daut; 12; F

Key: NUMBER; Indian Name; English Name; Sex; Relation; Age

* An Askerisk will be next to a number if repeated or out of sequence and inserted among a different family.

1432; ---; Lessert, Fanny; Daut; 4; F

1433; ---; Lessert, William K,; Head; 21; M

1434; ---; Lessert, Charles; Head; 43; M

1435; ---; Liese, Coaina M.; Head; 28; F
1436; ---; Liese, Washaki; Son; 5; M
1437; ---; Liese, Vivian; Daut; 6m; F

1438; ---; Lohmann, Hettie; Head; 24; F

1439; ---; Lombard, Albert; Head; 64; M
1440; ---; Lombard, Bessie; Daut; 16; F
1441; ---; Lombard, Robert A.; Son; 9; M

1442; ---; Lombard, Nina; Head; 22; F

1443; ---; Lombard, Clara; Head; 24; F

1444; ---; Lombard, John; Head; 26; M

1445; ---; Lombard, George W.; Head; 26; M
1446; ---; Lombard, Frank H.; Son; 2; M

1447; ---; Lombard, John E.; Head; 24; M

1448; ---; Lombard, Walter; Head; 32; M
1449; ---; Lombard, Lucy; Daut; 9; F
1450; ---; Lombard, Lois; Daut; 7; F
1451; ---; Lombard, Samie; Daut; 6; F

1452; ---; Lyman, Paul S.; Head; 44; M
1453; ---; Lyman, Agnes; Daut; 7; F
1454; ---; Lyman, Capitola; Daut; 5; F
1455; ---; Lyman, Pauline; Daut; 3; F

1456; ---; Lyman, Arthur J.; Head; 40; M

1457; ---; Lynn, Mary A.; Head; 33; F
1458; ---; Lynn, John F.; Son; 15; M
1459; ---; Lynn, Theresa M.; Daut; 11; F
1460; ---; Lynn, Patrick; Son; 7; M
1461; ---; Lynn, Joseph; Son; 9; M
1462; ---; Lynn, William R.; Son; 4; M

Key: NUMBER; Indian Name; English Name; Sex; Relation; Age
* An Askerisk will be next to a number if repeated or out of sequence and inserted among a different family.

1463;   ---; Logan, Ruby; Head; 21; F

1464;   ---; Linley, Susanna; Head; 22; F

1465;   ---; Lockwood, Adeline; Head; 62; F

1466;   ---; Lavely, Anna; Head; 31; F

1467;   ---; Mackey, Joseph; Head; 32; M
1468;   ---; Mackey, Eva; Daut; 12; F
1469;   ---; Mackey, Tenne; Daut; 8; F
1470;   ---; Mackey, Agnes L.; Daut; 6; F
1471;   ---; Mackey, Warren F.; Son; 4; M

1472;   ---; Mackey, William B.; Head; 27; M
1473;   ---; Mackey, Cecelia E.; Daut; 10; F
1474;   ---; Mackey, Bertha M.; Daut; 5; F

1475;   ---; Mackey, Grover; Head; 24; M

1476;   ---; Mann, Stella; Head; 21; F

1477;   ---; Mathews, W.S.; Head; 62; M
1478;   ---; Mathews, John J.; Son; 16; M
1479;   ---; Mathews, Mary I.; Daut; 13; F
1480;   ---; Mathews, Lillian B.; Daut; 11; F
1481;   ---; Mathews, Florence; Daut; 8; F

1482;   ---; Mathews, Sarah J.; Head; 22; F

1483;   ---; Mathews, W.W.; Head; 31; M
1484;   ---; Mathews, Norman S.; Son; 5; M
1485;   ---; Mathews, Anna M.; Daut; 3; F

1486;   ---; Mathews, John A.; Head; 34; M
1487;   ---; Mathews, Lorenza; Wife; 28; F
1488;   ---; Mathews, John A. Jr.; Son; 9; M
1489;   ---; Mathews, Victoria; Daut; 8; F

1490;   ---; Mathews, Edward O.; Head; 31; M
1491;   ---; Mathews, Alfred E.; Son; 6; M

1492;   ---; Mathes, Thomas S.; Head; 21; M

1493;   ---; Marshall, Sarah; Head; 22; F

Census of the _____**Osage**_____ Indians of _____**Osage**_____ Agency _____**Okla.**_____
on _____**June 30, 1910.**_____, taken by, _____**Hugh Pitzer, Supt. & Sp'l. Disb'g. Agent**_____

Key: NUMBER; Indian Name; English Name; Sex; Relation; Age
* An Askerisk will be next to a number if repeated or out of sequence and inserted among a different family.

1494;   ---; Martin, Alex; Head; 64; M
1495;   ---; Martin, Bertha; Daut; 15; F

1496;   ---; Martin, Lombard; Head; 22; M

1497;   ---; Martin, Lee; Head; 33; M
1498;   ---; Martin, Dane L.; Daut; 12; F
1499;   ---; Martin, Edgar E.; Son; 9; M
1500;   ---; Martin, Linnie N.; Daut; 6; F

1501;   ---; Martin, Emery; Head; 29; M
1502;   ---; Martin, John D.; Son; 4; M
1503;   ---; Martin, Delmas E.; Son; 3; M

1504;   ---; Martin, Richard; Head; 36; M
1505;   ---; Martin, Nannie V.; Daut; 3; F
1506;   ---; Martin, Claude; Son; 13; M

1507;   ---; Martin, James; Son; 17; M

1508;   ---; Martin, Wilson; Son; 17; M

1509;   ---; Martin, Joeanna; Head; 30; F
1510;   ---; Flippin, Nettie B.; Daut; 12; F

1511;   ---; McCarty, Lenora; Head; 29; F
1512;   ---; McCarty, William H.; Son; 9; M
1513;   ---; McCarty, Solomon; Son; 8; M
1514;   ---; McCarty, Edna V.; Daut; 5; F
1515;   ---; McCarty, Charles V.; Son; 5; M

1516;   ---; McCoy, Lillie; Head; 23; F
1517;   ---; McCoy, Richard M.; Son; 3; M

1518;   ---; McDaniel, Ellen; Head; 34; F
1519;   ---; McDaniel, Frederick W.; Son; 14; M

1520;   ---; McGuire, Mary E.; Head; 37; M
1521;   ---; McGuire, Ethel; Daut; 19; F
1522;   ---; McGuire, Leo; Son; 15; M
1523;   ---; McGuire, Bird A.; Son; 12; M
1524;   ---; McGuire, William T.; Son; 10; M
1525;   ---; McGuire, Charles A.; Son; 8; M

1526;   ---; McComb, Ellen; Head; 32; F
1527;   ---; McComb, Jessie; Daut; 15; F

Census of the   **Osage**   Indians of   **Osage**   Agency   **Okla.**

on   **June 30, 1910.**   , taken by,   **Hugh Pitzer, Supt. & Sp'l. Disb'g. Agent**

Key: NUMBER; Indian Name; English Name; Sex; Relation; Age

* An Askerisk will be next to a number if repeated or out of sequence and inserted among a different family.

1528; ---; McComb, William N.; Son; 12; M
1529; ---; McComb, Gladys I.; Daut; 9; F
1530; ---; McComb, Rachel B.; Daut; 7; F
1531; ---; McComb, Naioma; Daut; 4; F

1531 1/2; ---; McLaughlin, Nancy; Head; 46; F

1532; ---; McLintic, Mary; Head; 33; F
1533; ---; McLintic, Aloysia; Daut; 11; F

1534; ---; McLain, Minnie; Head; 23; F
1535; ---; McLain, Ray S.; Son; 5; M

1536; ---; McCowan, Bessie; Head; 20; F

1537; ---; Michelle, Estella; Daut; 12; F
1538; ---; Michelle, Della; Daut; 9; F

1539; ---; Mickels, Arania; Head; 33; F
1540; ---; Carr, Delilah; Daut; 8; F
1541; ---; Mickels, Clarence D.; Son; 5; M
1542; ---; Mickels, Blanche O.; Daut; 2; F

1543; ---; Miller Gurney; Orphan; 12; M

1544; ---; Mongrain, Rosa; Daut; 20; F

1545; ---; Mongrain, Stewart; Head; 62; M
1546; ---; Mongrain, Stewart Jr.; Son; 17; M

1547; ---; Mongrain, Ernest; Head; 21; M

1548; ---; Mongrain, Hattie; Head; 23; F

1549; ---; Mosier, Thomas; Head; 67; M

1550; ---; Mosier, Adeline; Head; 69; F

1551; ---; Mosier, W.T.; Head; 42; M
1552; ---; Mosier, Louisa; Wife; 35; F
1553; ---; Mosier, Charles P.; Son; 14; M
1554; ---; Mosier, John T.; Son; 11; M
1555; ---; Mosier, Edwin P.; Son; 8; M
1556; ---; Mosier, Luther P.; Son; 5; M
1557; ---; Mosier, Agnes C; Daut; 5; F
1558; ---; Mosier, James R.; Son; 3; M

Key: NUMBER; Indian Name; English Name; Sex; Relation; Age
* An Askerisk will be next to a number if repeated or out of sequence and inserted among a different family.

1559;   ---; Mosier, Jacob; Head; 48; M
1560;   ---; Mosier, Stella; Daut; 18; F
1561;   ---; Mosier, Claude; Son; 15; M
1562;   ---; Mosier, Lione; Daut; 12; F

1563;   ---; Mosier, Kate; Head; 22; F

1564;   ---; Mosier, Eugene; Head; 35; M
1565;   ---; Mosier, Mary M.; Daut; 14; F
1566;   ---; Mosier, John J.; Son; 8; M
1567;   ---; Mosier, Ida M.; Daut; 6; F
1568;   ---; Mosier, Walter L.; Son; 4; M

1569;   ---; Mosier, Bismark; Head; 27; M
1570;   ---; Mosier, Clara O.; Daut; 6; F
1571;   ---; Mosier, Thelma V.; Daut; 4; F

1572;   ---; Moore, James W.; Head; 24

1573;   ---; Moore, Alice; Daut; 19; F

1574;   ---; Moncravie, Charles; Head; 41; M
1575;   ---; Moncravie, Rosa; Wife; 31; F
1576;   ---; Moncravie, Augustine; Daut; 11; F
1577;   ---; Moncravie, Virginia M.; Daut; 8; F

1578;   ---; Moncravie, Fred; Head; 35; M

1579;   ---; Moncravie, Henry; Head; 37; M
1580;   ---; Moncravie, Henri E.; Daut; 6; F

1581;   ---; Moncravie, John; Head; 40; M
1582;   ---; Moncravie, Sylvester A.; Son; 17; M
1583;   ---; Moncravie, John N.; Son; 13; M
1584;   ---; Moncravie, Alexander C.; Son; 11; M
1585;   ---; Moncravie, Barada J.; Son; 9; M
1586;   ---; Moncravie, Vivian L.; Daut; 6; F
1587;   ---; Moncravie, Anna A.; Daut; 4; F

1588;   ---; Murray, Jennie; Head; 34; F
1589;   ---; Murray, Morton J.; Son; 12; M
1590;   ---; Murray, Ruby M.; Daut; 11; F
1591;   ---; Murray, Arthur R.; Son; 8; M
1592;   ---; Murray, Alfred G.; Son; 6; M
1593;   ---; Murray, Maurice C.; Son; 3; M

Key: NUMBER; Indian Name; English Name; Sex; Relation; Age
* An Askerisk will be next to a number if repeated or out of sequence and inserted among a different family.

1594; ---; Murphy, Gertrude; Head; 28; F

1595; ---; Murphy, Alice; Head; 27; F

1596; ---; Murphy, Elizabeth; Head; 24; F

1597; ---; Murphy, Amy; Head; 48; F
1598; ---; Murphy, Nettie; Daut; 20; F

1599; ---; Musgrove, William; Head; 32; M
1600; ---; Musgrove, Carl R.; Son; 5; M
1601; ---; Musgrove, Willis E.; Daut; 4; F

1602; ---; Newman, George; Head; 28; M

1603; ---; Noble, Ida; Head; 28; F

1604; ---; Nolegs, Larry; Head; 55; M

1605; ---; Odell, Clyde; Son; 3; M

1606; ---; Owens, Catherine; Daut; 5; F

1607; ---; Pappan, Samuel T.; Son; 19; M
1608; ---; Pappan, Lee A.; Son; 17; M
1609; ---; Pappan, Oakley; Son; 15; M
1610; ---; Pappan, Lester; Son; 13; M

1611; ---; Pappin, Alex; Head; 51; M
1612; ---; Pappin, Herbert; Son; 13; M
1613; ---; Pappin, Franklin A.; Son; 8; M
1614; ---; Pappin, Roosevelt; Son; 5; M
1615; ---; Pappin, Nora I.; Daut; 3; F

1616; ---; Pappin, Jesse L.; Son; 20;M
1617; ---; Pappin, John L.; Son; 18; M
1618; ---; Pappin, Jeanette; Daut; 15; F
1619; ---; Pappin, Joseph L.; Son; 13; M
1620; ---; Pappin, Jules C.; Son; 11; M
1621; ---; Pappin, Joshua J.; Son; 7; M

1622; ---; Pappin, James; Head; 25; M

1623; ---; Palmer, John F.; Head; 49; M
1624; ---; Palmer, Martha; Wife; 37; F
1625; ---; Palmer, Mary E.; Daut; 16; F

254

Key: NUMBER; Indian Name; English Name; Sex; Relation; Age
* An Askerisk will be next to a number if repeated or out of sequence and inserted among a different family.

1626; ---; Palmer, Clementine; Daut; 14; F
1627; ---; Palmer, Martha M.; Daut; 3; F
1628; ---; Palmer, Mable; Daut; 20; F

1629; ---; Park, Estella; Head; 22; F

1630; ---; Pease, Minnie A.; Head; 36; F
1631; ---; Pease, Marion H.; Son; 5; M

1632; ---; Perrier, Joseph; Head; 33; M

1633; ---; Perrier, Samuel; Head; 42; M

1634; ---; Perrier, Leo; Head; 29; M
1635; ---; Perrier, Clifford R.; Son; 4; M

1636; ---; Perrier, James; Head; 34; M
1637; ---; Perrier, John T.; Son; 16; M
1638; ---; Perrier, James R.; Son; 10; M

1639; ---; Perrier, Napoleon; Head; 52; M
1640; ---; Perrier, Nina; Daut; 19; F
1641; ---; Perrier, Leo; Son; 16; M
1642; ---; Perrier, Peter; Son; 13; M
1643; ---; Perrier, Lola; Daut; 12; F
1644; ---; Perrier, Owen; Son; 8; M

1645; ---; Perrier, Louis F.; Head; 21; M

1646; ---; Perrier, Thomas; Head; 26; M
1647; ---; Perrier, Roy B.; Son; 4; M

1648; ---; Perrier, Eugene; Head; 27; M
1649; ---; Perrier, Ray L.D.; Son; 4; M
1650; ---; Perrier, Kenneth; Son; 2; M

1651; ---; Penn, Leo; Son; 13; M
1652; ---; Penn, Oscar; Son; 11; M
1653; ---; Penn, Wayne M.; Son; 5; M

1654; ---; Pettit, S.W.; Head; 65; M

1655; ---; Pettit, Charles; Head; 37; M
1656; ---; Pettit, Hattie B.; Daut; 13; F
1657; ---; Pettit, Lela M.; Daut; 9; F

Key: NUMBER; Indian Name; English Name; Sex; Relation; Age
* An Askerisk will be next to a number if repeated or out of sequence and inserted among a different family.

1658; ---; Pettit, George; Head; 35; M
1659; ---; Pettit, George R.; Son; 11; M
1660; ---; Pettit, Lula B.; Daut; 8; F
1661; ---; Pettit, William A.; Son; 3; M

1662; ---; Pettit, John; Head; 33; M

1663; ---; Perkins, Elizabeth; Head; 55; F

1664; ---; Peters, James M.; Son; 11; M

1665; ---; Pearson, Rosa; Head; 47; F
1666; ---; Kent, Cordelia C.; Daut; 19; F
1667; ---; Pearson, Lillian F; Daut; 18; F
1668; ---; Pearson, Bertha L.; Daut; 16; F
1669; ---; Pearson, Kate V.: Daut; 13; F
1670; ---; Pearson, Willie J.; Son; 10; M
1671; ---; Pearson, Rose E.; Daut; 7; F

1672; ---; Pearson, October; Head; 27; M
1673; ---; Pearson, Mary C.; Wife; 23; F
1674; ---; Pearson, Bernice M.; Daut; 4; F

1675; ---; Phillips, William; Head; 40; M
1676; ---; Phillips, Angeline M.; Daut; 16; F
1677; ---; Phillips, Iva M.; Daut; 14; F
1678; ---; Phillips, James W.; Son; 12; M

1679; ---; Plomondon, Clemy; Head; 56; F
1680; ---; Plomondon, Daniel B.; Son; 18; M
1681; ---; Plomondon, Julia A.; Daut; 16; F
1682; ---; Plomondon, Louisa; Daut; 13; F

1683; ---; Plomondon, Louis; Head; 25; M

1684; ---; Plomondon, Barnard; Head; 40; M
1685; ---; Plomondon, Ella; Wife; 36; F
1686; ---; Plomondon, Grace; Daut; 18; F
1687; ---; Plomondon, Clementine; Daut; 16; F
1688; ---; Plomondon, Moses E.; Son; 14; M
1689; ---; Plomondon, George A.; Son; 11; M

1690; ---; Potter, Ethel; Head; 32; F
1691; ---; Potter, Francis A.; Son; 15; M
1692; ---; Potter, Oliver L.; Son; 10; M
1693; ---; Potter, James L.; Son; 7; M

Key: NUMBER; Indian Name; English Name; Sex; Relation; Age
* An Askerisk will be next to a number if repeated or out of sequence and inserted among a different family.

1694; ---; Potter, Zelma; Daut; 3; F

1695; ---; Prudom, Charles N.; Head; 55; M

1696; ---; Prudom, Nora; Head; 27; F

1697; ---; Prudom, Frank; Head; 44; M

1698; ---; Prue, Henry; Head; 35; M
1699; ---; Prue, Maude; Wife; 28; F
1700; ---; Prue, Hattie M.; Daut; 12; F
1701; ---; Prue, Charles F.; Son; 11; M
1702; ---; Prue, Henry E.; Son; 9; M
1703; ---; Prue, Floyd B.; Son; 6; M
1704; ---; Prue, Anna B. Daut; 4; F

1705; ---; Quinton, Franklin; Head; 23; M

1706; ---; Rairdon, Jane R.; Head; 51; F
1707; ---; Miller, Ida J.; Daut; 18; F
1708; ---; Rairdon, Wendall H.; Son; 10; M

1709; ---; Miller, Louis S.; Head; 21; M

1710; ---; Rapp, Barbara; Head; 24; F

1711; ---; Reece, Elizabeth; Head; 26; F
1712; ---; Reece, Hallie; Daut; 8; F
1713; ---; Reece, Ethel; Daut; 6; F

1714; ---; Revelette, James; Head; 33; M
1715; ---; Revelette, Teresa; Daut; 11; F
1716; ---; Revelette, William L.; Son; 9
1717; ---; Revelette, Mary E.; Daut; 4; F
1718; ---; Revelette, Minnie F.; Daut; 4; F

1719; ---; Revelette, Fred; Head; 31; M
1720; ---; Revelette, Pauline; Daut; 10; F
1721; ---; Revelette, Fred L.; Son; 8; M

1722; ---; Revelette, Frank; Head; 69; M

1723; ---; Revelette, Franklin; Head; 21; M

1724; ---; Revelette, Charles; Head; 37; M
1725; ---; Revelette, Joseph; Son; 4; M

Key: NUMBER; Indian Name; English Name; Sex; Relation; Age
* An Askerisk will be next to a number if repeated or out of sequence and inserted among a different family.

1726; ---; Revard, William; Head; 45; M
1727; ---; Revard, William E.; Son; 9; M
1728; ---; Revard, Della M.; Daut; 7: F
1729; ---; Revard, Gladis; Daut; 5; F

1730; ---; Revard, Solomon; Head; 51; M

1731; ---; Revard, Charles; Head; 51; M

1732; ---; Revard, Alex; Head; 50; M

1733; ---; Revard, Benjamin; Head; 29; M

1734; ---; Revard, Paul; Head; 35; M
1735; ---; Revard, Susie; Daut; 15; F

1736; ---; Revard, Mary E.; Head; 62; M[sic]

1737; ---; Revard, Elsie E.; Daut; 18; F
1738; ---; Revard, Maynard; Son; 15; M

1739; ---; Revard, Francis; Head; 42; M
1740; ---; Revard, Mack; Son; 16; M
1741; ---; Revard, Emanuel M.; Son; 11; M
1742; ---; Revard, Pearl I.; Daut; 8; F
1743; ---; Revard, Ethel E.; Daut; 4; F

1744; ---; Revard, John W.; Head; 31; M
1745; ---; Revard, Edward L.; Son; 12; M
1746; ---; Revard, Evart A.; Son; 11; M

1747; ---; Revard, Joseph; Head; 50; M
1748; ---; Revard, Ursula; Daut; 20; F
1749; ---; Revard, Clementine; Daut; 17; F
1750; ---; Revard, William J,; Son; 15; M
1751; ---; Revard, Ronald V.; Son; 13; M

1752; ---; Revard, Ralph: Head; 22; M

1753; ---; Revard, Franklin; Head; 46; M
1754; ---; Revard, Nicholas N.; Son; 16; M
1755; ---; Revard, Pearl; Daut; 15; F
1756; ---; Revard, Myrta; Daut; 7; F
1757; ---; Revard, Kathryn L.; Daut; 3; F

1758; ---; Revard, Mark S.; Head; 22; M

258

Key: NUMBER; Indian Name; English Name; Sex; Relation; Age
* An Askerisk will be next to a number if repeated or out of sequence and inserted among a different family.

1759; ---; Revard, Charles E.; Head; 50; M
1760; ---; Revard, Clarence; Son; 20; M
1761; ---; Revard, Ed Clifford; Son; 18; M
1762; ---; Revard, Clara; Daut; 16; F
1763; ---; Revard, Carrie; Daut; 12; F
1764; ---; Revard, Cora; Daut; 12; F
1765; ---; Revard, Nora T.; Daut; 11; F
1766; ---; Revard, McGuire N.; Son; 6; M
1767; ---; Revard, Lena; Daut; 4; F

1768; ---; Revard, Leonard; Head; 52; M
1769; ---; Revard, Lode; Daut; 16; F
1770; ---; Revard, Opal A.; Daut; 13; F
1771; ---; Revard, Hazel; Daut; 10; F
1772; ---; Revard, Minnie; Daut; 7; F
1773; ---; Revard, Cleo; Daut; 4; F
1774; ---; Revard, Victoria; Daut; 2; F

1775; ---; Revard, Joseph Jr.; Head; 53; M

1776; ---; Revard, Nellie; Daut; 9; F
1777; ---; Revard, Edgar T.; Son; 6; M
1778; ---; Revard, Mary C.; Daut; 4; F

1779; ---; Revard, Curtis; Head; 24; M

1780; ---; Revard, Aaron T.; Son; 18; M

1781; ---; Riddle, Sherman; Son; 18; M
1782; ---; Riddle, Joseph; Son; 16; M
1783; ---; Riddle, Frank; Son; 14; M

1784; ---; Ririe, Effie E.; Daut; 17; F
1785; ---; Ririe, Scott F.; Son; 14; M
1786; ---; Ririe, Otis E.; Son; 10; M
1787; ---; Ririe, Nellie I.; Daut; 8; F
1788; ---; Ririe, Arthur M.; Son; 4; M

1789; ---; Ririe, Oscar A.; Head; 23; M

1790; ---; Rodman, Antwine; Head; 37; M

1791; ---; Rogers, Stephen; Head; 29; M

1792; ---; Rogers, Louis; Head; 67; M

Census of the   **Osage**   Indians of   **Osage**   Agency   **Okla.**
on   **June 30, 1910.**   , taken by,   **Hugh Pitzer, Supt. & Sp'l. Disb'g. Agent**

Key: NUMBER; Indian Name; English Name; Sex; Relation; Age
* An Askerisk will be next to a number if repeated or out of sequence and inserted among a different family.

1793; ---; Rogers, Louis Jr.; Head; 25; M

1794; ---; Rogers, Nancy; Head; 62; F

1795; ---; Rogers, T.L.; Head; 24; M

1796; ---; Rogers, Arthur; Head; 50; M
1797; ---; Rogers, Joseph L.; Son; 11; M
1798; ---; Rogers, Ellen E.; Daut; 9; F
1799; ---; Rogers, John R.; Son; 7; M
1800; ---; Rogers, William C.; Son; 5; M
1801; ---; Rogers, Isabell; Daut; 3; F

1802; ---; Rogers, Mary E.; Head; 36; F
1803; ---; Rogers, Irene; Daut; 18; F
1804; ---; Rogers, Mary A.; Daut; 16; F
1805; ---; Rogers, Coaina; Daut; 12; F
1806; ---; Rogers, Eldred T.; 10; M

1807; ---; Rogers, Antwine; Head; 65; M

1808; ---; Rogers, Mae; Head; 24; F

1809; ---; Rogers, Kenneth; Head; 30
1810; ---; Rogers, Helen; Daut; 7
1811; ---; Rogers; Antwine; Son; 5

1812; ---; Rogers, Jasper; Head; 40
1813; ---; Rogers, Rosa; Wife; 31; F
1814; ---; Rogers, Emmet; Son; 8; M
1815; ---; Rogers, Cecelia; Daut; 9; F
1816; ---; Rogers, Maude; Daut; 5; F
1817; ---; Rogers, Flora; Daut; 3; F

1818; ---; Rogers, Bertha D.; Daut; 16; F
1819; ---; Rogers, Helen C.; Daut; 14; F

1820; ---; Rogers, Willie L.; Son; 3; M

1821; ---; Rogers, Thomas L. Jr.; Head; 25; M

1822; ---; Rogers, Granville; Head; 22; M

1823; ---; Rogers, Rosa L.; Daut; 17; F
1824; ---; Rogers, Josephine; Daut; 14; F
1825; ---; Rogers, John H.; Son; 12; M

Key: NUMBER; Indian Name; English Name; Sex; Relation; Age

* An Askerisk will be next to a number if repeated or out of sequence and inserted among a different family.

1826; ---; Rogers, Nora; Head; 26; F
1827; ---; Rogers, Richard L.; Son; 5; M

1828; ---; Rogers, Lewis A.; Head; 35; M

1829; ---; Rogers, Isadore; Wife; 32; F

1830; ---; Rogers, Fred R.; Son; 9; M
1831; ---; Rogers, Frank; Son; 5; M

1832; ---; Roberts, Ola; Head; 24; F

1833; ---; Ross, John; Head; 65; M
1834; ---; Ross, Floyd F.; Son; 13; M

1835; ---; Roach, Wilfred D.; Head; 30; M
1836; ---; Roach, Bridget A.; Daut; 7; F
1837; ---; Roach, Melvin C.; Son; 5; M
1838; ---; Roach, Wilfred D. Jr.; Son; 3; M

1839; ---; Roach, Samuel; Head; 28; M
1840; ---; Roach Mikle J.; Son; 7; M
1841; ---; Roach Herman B.; Son; 4; M

1842; ---; Roach, George W.; Head; 24; M

1843; ---; Rutter, Gertrude; Head; 30; F

1844; ---; Rivera, Grace; Head; 20; F
1845; ---; Rivera, Alex; Son; 2; M

1846; ---; Saxon, Cora; Head; 36; F
1847; ---; Saxon, Veva M.; Daut; 6; F
1848; ---; Saxon, Harry H.; Son; 4; M

1849; ---; Scott, George; Head; 33; M
1850; ---; Scott, Mary M.; Daut; 5; F

1851; ---; Scott, William J.; Son; 5; M
1852; ---; Scott, Violet; Daut; 3; F

1853; ---; Selby, Georgia; Head; 24; F

1854; ---; Sherrif, Coeanna; Head; 23; F

1855; ---; Shaw, Franklin; Head; 23

261

Census of the_____**Osage**_____Indians of _____**Osage**_____ Agency _____**Okla.**_____

on _____**June 30, 1910.**_____ , taken by, _____**Hugh Pitzer, Supt. & Sp'l. Disb'g. Agent**_____

Key: NUMBER; Indian Name; English Name; Sex; Relation; Age

* An Askerisk will be next to a number if repeated or out of sequence and inserted among a different family.

1856; ---; Shaw, Rose M.; Wife; 22; F
1857; ---; Shaw, Moses; Son; 6; M
1858; ---; Shaw, John; Son; 4; M

1859; ---; Shobe, Anna U.; Head; 26; F

1860; ---; Simpson, Susan; Head; 68; F

1861; ---; Simpkins, Mary L.; Head; 38; F
1862; ---; Simpkins, Warren D.; Son; 17; M
1863; ---; Simpkins, Mary E.; Daut; 16; F
1864; ---; Simpkins, Vivian P.; Daut; 13; F
1865; ---; Simpkins, Oren F.; Son; 12; M
1866; ---; Simpkins, Edward; Son; 10; M
1867; ---; Simpkins, Virgil; Son; 4; M
1868; ---; Simpkins, Helen V.; Daut; 3; F

1869; ---; Slaughter, A.B.; Head; 26; M
1870; ---; Slaughter, Minnie; Wife; 24; F

1871; ---; Slaughter, Amanda; Head; 23; F

1872; ---; Slaughter, Harry E.; Son; 20; M

1873; ---; Smith, George B.; Son; 8; M
1874; ---; Smith, Genevieve; Daut; 11; F

1875; ---; Soderstrom, Gertrude; Head; 31; F
1876; ---; Dickey, Alta A.; Daut; 12; F
1877; ---; Soderstrom, Hanna N.; Daut; 9; F

1878; ---; Soldani, Sylvester J.; Head; 50; M
1879; ---; Soldani, Josephine; Wife; 41; F
1880; ---; Soldani, Myrtle; Daut; 19; F
1881; ---; Soldani, Emmert A.; Son; 18; M

1882; ---; Soldani, Louis E.; Head; 21; M

1883; ---; Soldani, Kate P.; Head; 22; F

1884; ---; Soldani, Ida M.; Head; 23; F

1885; ---; Soldani, Agnes; Head; 24; F

1886; ---; Soldani, Anthony; Head; 48; M
1887; ---; Soldani, Amelia K.; Wife; 42; F

Key: NUMBER; Indian Name; English Name; Sex; Relation; Age
* An Askerisk will be next to a number if repeated or out of sequence and inserted among a different family.

1888; ---; Soldani, Frank E.; Son; 19; M
1889; ---; Soldani, Charles L.; Son; 17; M
1890; ---; Soldani, Clarence; Son; 14; M
1891; ---; Soldani, Grace M.; Daut; 11; F
1892; ---; Soldani, Rose M.; Daut; 11; F
1893; ---; Soldani, George H.; Son; 9; M

1894; ---; Souligny, Laura; Head; 25; F
1895; ---; Souligny, Mildred V.; Daut; 6; F

1896; ---; Stevens, John H.; Head; 44; M
1897; ---; Stevens, Mildred V.; Daut; 6; F

1898; ---; Stephens, Madeline; Head; 58; M

1899; ---; Stotts, Emma; Head; 35; F
1900; ---; Stotts, Joseph L.; Son; 19; M
1901; ---; Stotts, William W.; 15; M
1902; ---; Stotts, James E.; Son; 6; M

1903; ---; Stobaugh, Alice; Head; 39; F
1904; ---; Riddle, John L.; Son; 20; M
1905; ---; Riddle, Arthur; Son; 8; M

1906; ---; Stewart, Lenora; Head; 48; F
1907; ---; Wilkie, George L.; Son; 20; M
1908; ---; Wilkie, Rose E.; Daut; 16; F

1909; ---; Swanson, Celestine; Head; 28; F
1910; ---; Swanson, Addison L.; Son; 6; M
1911; ---; Swanson, Joseph N.; Son; 5; M

1912; ---; Sweeney, Oscar E.; Son; 17; M

1913; ---; Slamans, Mary E.; Head; 27; F

1914; ---; Tall Chief, Enoch; Son; 4; M

1915; ---; Tapp, Belle; Head; 46; F
1916; ---; Chambers, James W.; Son; 14; M
1917; ---; Chambers, Minnie A.; Daut; 11; F
1918; ---; Tapp, Ruby; Daut; 3; F

1919; ---; Taylor, James E.; Orphan; 17; M
1920; ---; Taylor, John F.; Orphan; 15; M
1921; ---; Taylor, Hiran; Orphan; 13; M

Key: NUMBER; Indian Name; English Name; Sex; Relation; Age
* An Askerisk will be next to a number if repeated or out of sequence and inserted among a different family.

1922; ---; Taylor, Fanny; Orphan; 12 F
1923; ---; Taylor, Agnes; Orphan; 10; F
1924; ---; Taylor, Anna; Orphan; 6; F

1925; ---; Tayrien, John; Head; 28; M
1926; ---; Tayrien, Mary L.; Daut; 6; F
1927; ---; Tayrien, Agnes; Daut; 5; F
1928; ---; Tayrien, Gladys; Daut; 3; F

1929; ---; Tayrien, Charles; Head; 35; M
1930; ---; Tayrien, Edna; Daut; 12; F

1931; ---; Tayrien, Thomas; Head; 49; M
1932; ---; Tayrien, George A.; Son; 18; M
1933; ---; Tayrien, Andrew J.; Son; 16; M
1934; ---; Tayrien, Paul; Son; 14; M
1935; ---; Tayrien, Maud J.; Daut; 6; F
1936; ---; Tayrien, John C.; Son; 5; M

1937; ---; Tayrien, David W.; Head; 22; M

1938; ---; Tayrien, James; Head; 25; M
1939; ---; Tayrien, Alberty; Daut; 6; F
1940; ---; Tayrien, Elmer C.; Son; 4; M

1941; ---; Tayrien, Andrew; Head; 36; M
1942; ---; Tayrien, Jennie; Daut; 14; F
1943; ---; Tayrien, Viola; Daut; 13; F
1944; ---; Tayrien, Alfred J.; Son; 11; M
1945; ---; Tayrien, Violet M.; Daut; 10; F
1946; ---; Tayrien, William J.; Son; 7; M
1947; ---; Tayrien, Rose Anna; Daut; 7; F

1948; ---; Tayrien, Cyprian; Head; 72; M
1949; ---; Tayrien, William; Son; 20; M

1950; ---; Toothaker, Rena L.; Head; 20; F

1951; ---; Thompson, Leroy; Son; 16; M
1952; ---; Roe, Emery E.; Son; 9; M

1953; ---; Thomas, Nicholas; Head; 52; M

1954; ---; Thomas, Agnes; Head; 28; F
1955; ---; Thomas, Maggie C.; Daut; 8; F
1956; ---; Thomas, Julia H.; Daut; 5; F

Key: NUMBER; Indian Name; English Name; Sex; Relation; Age

* An Askerisk will be next to a number if repeated or out of sequence and inserted among a different family.

1957; ---; Thurman, Lola; Head; 24; F
1958; ---; Thurman, Geneva; Daut; 4; F

1959; ---; Tinker, Louis; Head; 43; M
1960; ---; Tinker, William; Son; 19; M
1961; ---; Tinker, Bessie; Daut; 16; F
1962; ---; Tinker, Nora; Daut; 12; F
1963; ---; Tinker, Ora; Daut; 12; F
1964; ---; Tinker, Eva; Daut; 10; F
1965; ---; Tinker, Isabella; Daut; 7; F
1966; ---; Tinker, Rose; Daut; 5; F
1967; ---; Tinker, Cora; Daut; 3; F

1968; ---; Tinker, Geo. E.; Head; 41; M
1969; ---; Tinker, Mary G.; Daut; 16; F
1970; ---; Tinker, Sarah Anna; Daut; 16; F
1971; ---; Tinker, Nicholas A.T.; Son; 14; M
1972; ---; Tinker, George E. Jr.; Son; 11; M
1973; ---; Tinker, Villa; Daut; 7; F

1974; ---; Tinker, Clarence; Head; 22; M

1975; ---; Tinker, Charley; Head; 38; M
1976; ---; Tinker, Mary J.; Daut; 19; F
1977; ---; Tinker, Roy B.; Son; 16; M
1978; ---; Tinker, Maude; Daut; 13; F
1979; ---; Tinker, Lucille; Daut; 12; F
1980; ---; Tinker, David; Son; 9; M
1981; ---; Tinker, Louis N.; Son; 5; M

1982; ---; Tinker, Frank; Head; 49; M
1983; ---; Tinker, Mary L.; Wife; 49; F
1984; ---; Tinker, Tom; Son; 16; M
1985; ---; Tinker, Mary E.; Daut; 14; F
1986; ---; Tinker, Eliza; Daut; 10; F
1987; ---; Tinker, Sylvester J.; Son; 7; M

1988; ---; Tinker, Norris J.; Head; 21; M

1989; ---; Todd, Maud; Head; 31; F
1990; ---; Todd, Harold; Son; 5; M
1991; ---; Todd, Gerald J.; Son; 9; M

1992; ---; Trumbly, Julian; Head; 59; M
1993; ---; Trumbly, Eliza; Wife; 54; F
1994; ---; Trumbly, Henry; Son; 20; M

265

Key: NUMBER; Indian Name; English Name; Sex; Relation; Age
* An Askerisk will be next to a number if repeated or out of sequence and inserted among a different family.

1995; ---; Trumbly, Tina O.; Daut; 18; F
1996; ---; Trumbly, Charles; Son; 17; M
1997; ---; Trumbly, Theresa; Daut; 12; F

1998; ---; Trumbly, Oliver; Head; 28; M

1999; ---; Trumbly, Clarence; Head; 29; M
2000; ---; Trumbly, Gladys; Daut; 7; F
2001; ---; Trumbly, Clarence E.; Son; 4; M

2002; ---; Trumbly, George; Head; 36; M

2003; ---; Trumbly, Andrew; Head; 35; M
2004; ---; Trumbly, Mary; Wife; 24; F
2005; ---; Trumbly, Oscar; Son; 4; M

2006; ---; Trumbly, J.B.; Head; 56; M
2007; ---; Trumbly, John F; Son; 19; M
2008; ---; Trumbly, Elizabeth; Daut; 16; F
2009; ---; Trumbly, Paul P.; Son; 10; M

2010; ---; Tucker, Anna; Head; 26; F
2011; ---; Tucker, Bulah G.; Daut; 5; F
2012; ---; Tucker, Stephen J. Jr.; Son; 3; M

2013; ---; Tucker, Angeline; Head; 75; F

2014; ---; Turner, Frederick D.; Son; 15; M

2015; ---; Turner, Mary B.; Head; 28; F

2016; ---; Tyner, Benjamin F; Head; 35; M
2017; ---; Tyner, Ethel M.; Daut; 11; F
2018; ---; Tyner, Roy F.; Son; 9; M
2019; ---; Tyner, William L.; Son; 5; M

2020; ---; Vesser, Ruth; Daut; 17; F

2021; ---; Voils, Kathleen; Daut; 8; F
2022; ---; Voils, Elsie L.; Daut; 4; F

2023; ---; Watkins, Rosalie; Head; 35; F
2024; ---; Watkins, Francis M.; Son; 16; M
2025; ---; Watkins, James; Son; 16; M
2026; ---; Watkins, John F.; Son; 8; M

Key: NUMBER; Indian Name; English Name; Sex; Relation; Age
* An Askerisk will be next to a number if repeated or out of sequence and inserted among a different family.

2027; ---; Watson, Viola; Head; 18; F

2028; ---; Ware, Victoria; Head; 59; F
2029; ---; Del Orier, Lillie; Daut; 20; F
2030; ---; Del Orier, Edna; Daut; 19; F

2031; ---; Ware, Aggie; Head; 40; F
2032; ---; Ware, Julia; Daut; 16; F
2033; ---; Ware, Nancy; Daut; 14; F
2034; ---; Ware, Bulah; Daut; 12; F
2035; ---; Ware, Rosa L.; Daut; 10; F
2036; ---; Ware, Henry H.; Son; 8; M
2037; ---; Ware, David; Son; 7; M

2038; ---; Wade, Effie; Head; 24; F
2039; ---; Wade, Merle C.; Son; 5; M

2040; ---; Walker, Letetia; Head; 18; F

2041; ---; Waters, Telina; Head; 27; F
2042; ---; Waters, Anna M.; Daut; 3; F

2043; ---; Whiles, Elmer; Head; 28; M

2044; ---; Whiles, Delilah; Head; 25; F

2045; ---; Whiles, Francis M.; Head; 21; M

2046; ---; Wheeler, Paul; Head; 38; M
2047; ---; Wheeler, Merrit J.; Son; 7; M
2048; ---; Wheeler, Geneva; Daut; 6; F
2049; ---; Wheeler, Louisa; Daut; 3; F

2050; ---; Wheeler, Elmer; Head; 31; F
2051; ---; Wheeler, Eva R.; Wife; 32; F
2052; ---; Wheeler, Virginia; Daut; 6; F

2053; ---; Wheeler, Alma; Head; 24; F

2054; ---; Weinrich, Anna; Head; 27; F
2055; ---; Weinrich, Alma; Daut; 1; F

2056; ---; Wheeler, Susan; Head; 33; F
2057; ---; Wheeler, Morris E.; Son; 9; M

2058; ---; Wilkie, Louis F.; Head; 24; M

267

Key: NUMBER; Indian Name; English Name; Sex; Relation; Age
* An Askerisk will be next to a number if repeated or out of sequence and inserted among a different family.

2059; ---; Wilkie, Andrew E.; Son; 4; M

2060; ---; Willis, Lillie; Head; 18; F

2061; ---; Wilson, Mary; Head; 32; F
2062; ---; Wilson, William E.; Son; 13; M
2063; ---; Wilson, Julia K.; Daut; 11; F
2064; ---; Wilson, Banie; Son; 9; M
2065; ---; Wilson, Audry; Daut; 6; F
2066; ---; Wilson, Howard; Son; 3; M

2067; ---; Woodring, Tena; Head; 35; F
2068; ---; Woodring, Carlton W.; Son; 15; M
2069; ---; Woodring, Orville W.; Son; 13; M
2070; ---; Woodring, Anna; Daut; 9; F

2071; ---; Woodham, Lucy; Head; 60; F

2072; ---; Woodward, Kate; Head; 33; F
2073; ---; Beekman, Sybil F.; Daut; 5; F
2074; ---; Gorman, Mary A.; Daut; 11; F

2075; ---; Wyrick, Mary; Head; 37; F
2076; ---; Wyrick, Jessie W.; Daut; 14; F
2077; ---; Wyrick, John H.; Son; 13; M
2078; ---; Wyrick, Elnora J.; Daut; 9; F
2079; ---; Wyrick, Elmer F.; Son; 6; M

2080; ---; Wynn, Madeline; Head; 21; F

2081; ---; Yeargain, Early I.; Son; 19; M
2082; ---; Yeargain, Verona C.; Daut; 17; F
2083; ---; Yeargain, Leona; Daut; 16; F

2084; ---; York, Adah M.; Head; 24; F

2085; ---; Hooper, Sallie; Head; 39; F
2086; ---; Hooper, Mary; Daut; 16; F

2087; ---; Siggins, Clara; Head; 47; F
2088; ---; Siggins, Andrew W.; Son; 19; M
2089; ---; Stephens, Mary; Daut; 16; F

NOTE: Total of this roll is 2100, Numbers. 159 1/2, 254 1/2, 424 1/2, 535 ½, 672 ½, 693 ½, 435 ½, 437 ½, 933 ½, 1142 ½, and 1532 ½, are interlined hereon.

Census of the _____**Osage**_____Indians of ____**Osage**____Agency ___**Okla.**___
on ____**June 30, 1910.**____ , taken by, ___**Hugh Pitzer, Supt. & Sp'l. Disb'g. Agent**___

Key: NUMBER; Indian Name; English Name; Sex; Relation; Age

* An Askerisk will be next to a number if repeated or out of sequence and inserted among a different family.

RECAPITULATION:

All ages (Males, 1063; Females, 1037)	2100
Full-bloods:	
All ages (Males, 418; Females 407)	825
18 years and over (males)	251
Between 6 and 16 (males)	96
14 years and over (female)	272
Between 6 and 16 (females)	109
Mixed-Bloods:	
All ages (Males, 645; Females 630)	1279
18 years and over (males)	281
Between 6 and 16 (males)	244
15 years and over (female)	344
Between 6 and 16 (females)	272

Census of the Osage Indians

of

Osage Indian Agency, Oklahoma,

As of June 30, 1911

Hugh Pitzer, Supt. & Spl. Disb. Agent

Census of Osage Indians
Taken in the 4th quar. 1911
By Hugh Pitzer, Supt.

DEPARTMENT OF THE INTERIOR
UNITED STATES INDIAN SERVICE

Osage Indian Agency,

Pawhuska, Oklahoma, Sept. 26, 1911.

Transmits Osage
census roll for 1911.

The Honorable Commissioner of Indian Affairs,

Washington, D. C.

Sir:

There is transmitted herewith under separate
cover census of the Osage Indians for the year ending June
30, 1911.

Very respectfully,

Superintendent.

TSG

*CENSUS of the*___ **Osage**___ *Indians of*___ **Osage**___ *Agency,* __Okla.__
on ___**June 30, 1911**___ *, 19__, taken by* __Hugh Pitzer, Supt. & Spl. Disb. Agent__

Key: Number - Last/Present; Indian Name (if given); English Name (if given); Relationship; Age; Sex.

BIG CHIEF BAND.

1;	1;	Pah-hu-scah; Tom Bighchief[sic]; Head; 51; M
2;	2;	Me-to-op-pe; ---; Wife; 37; F
3;	3;	He-ah-to-me; May White; Daut; 19; F
4;	4;	Heh-kah-mon-kah; ---; daut; 11; F
5;	5;	Gra-to-me; ---; Daut; 7; F
6;	6;	Mo-she-to-moie; ---; Head; 66; M
7;	7;	Mo-se-che-he; ---; Wife; 66; F
8;	8;	---; Richard Rusk; Head; Head[sic]
9;	9;	Wah-tsa-ah-tah; James McKinley; S. Son; 15; M
10;	10;	Mah-sah; Walter McKinley; S. Son; 12; M
11;	11;	---; May Rusk; Daut; 7; F
12;	12;	Hla-me-tsa-he; ---; Daut; 4; F
14;	13;	Moie-wah-kon-tah; Phillip Carson; Orphan; 16; M
15;	14;	Num-pah-wah-kon-tah; Tom Carson; Head; 21; M
16;	16;	Hun-kah-me; ---; Head; 53; F
17;	16 ½;	To-sho-ho; Charles Whitehorn; Son; 14; M
18;	17;	E-nah-min-tsa; ---; Son; 6; M
19;	18;	---; Fidelis Cheshowahkepah; Head; 29
20;	19;	Hum-pah-to-kah; ---; Wife; 56; F
21;	20;	He-ah-to-me; Agnes Ferhuson[sic]; S. Daut; 10; F
22;	21;	Gra-tah-wah-kah; ---; S. Son; 7; M
23;	22;	---; Howard Russell; Head; 23; M
24;	23;	---; Otis Russell; Head; 24; M
25;	24;	---; Angella Russell; Wife; 24; F
26;	25;	He-ah-to-me; ---; Daut; 4; F
27;	26;	---; Howard Buffalo; Head; 51; M
28;	27;	---; Pearl Buffalo; Wife; 32; F
29;	28;	Wah-she-ke-pah; Willie Russell; Son; 15; M
30;	29;	Min-kah-she; ---; Daut; 5; F
31;	30;	---; Herman McCarthy; Head; 32; M
32;	31;	---; Martha Neal; Wife; 20; F
33;	32;	Son-sah-kah-hah; Head; Head; 63; M
34;	33;	Hlu-ah-to-me; ---; Wife; 64; F

Key: Number - Last/Present; Indian Name (if given); English Name (if given); Relationship; Age; Sex.

35;   [Skipped #35.]
36;   34;   Wah-sho-shah; ---; Head; 49; M
37;   35;   Mo-se-che-he; ---; Wife; 42; F
38;   36;   Hlu-ah-me-tsa-he; ---; Daut; 5; F

39;   37;   Mon-kah-so-py; ---; Head; 62; M
40;   38;   He-ah-to-me; ---; Wife; 41; F
41;   39;   Wah-tsa-ah-tah; Joe Osage; S. Son; 17; M
42;   40;   E-ne-op-pe; Nellie Osage; S. Daut; 15; F
43;   41;   Hun-kah-me; ---; Daut; 6; F
44;   42;   Heh-sah-hah; ---; Son; 4; M

45;   43;   Wah-hre-she; Charles; Head; 47; M
46;   44;   Hlu-ah-me; ---; Wife; 41; F
47;   45;   Mo-se-che-he; Josephine Wahhreshe; Daut; 15; F
48;   46;   Mon-kah-hah; ---; Son; 10; M
49;   47;   Nah-me-tsa-he; ---; Daut; 6; F

50;   48;   ---; Luther Harvey; Head; 41; M
51;   49;   Ke-ah-som-pah; Mary Harvey; Wife; 38; F
52;   50;   He-ah-to-me; Minnie Harvey; Daut; 16; F
53;   41;   Hlu-ah-wah-kon-tah; Walter Harvey; Son; 13; M
54;   52;   Num-pah-q-ah; Theodore R. Harvey; Son; 12; M
55;   53;   Wah-tsa-su-sah; ---; Son; 8; M
56;   54;   ---. Luther Harvey, Jr.; Son; 4; M

57;   55;   Me-ke-wah-ti-an-kah; ---; Head; 54; M
58;   56;   Wah-hrah-lum-pah; ---; Wife; 40; F
59;   57;   Kah-he-ah-gra; Louis James; Son; 14; M
60;   58;   Me-to-op-pe; ---; daut; 6; F

61;   59;   ---; Roy James; Head; 25; M
62;   60;   ---; Laura James; Wife; 24; F

63;   61;   ---; Roscoe Conklin; Head; 48; M
64;   62;   ---; Edith White; Wife; 29; F
65;   63;   ---; Joseph White; S. Son; 7; M
66;   64;   ---; Abraham White; S. Son; 5; M
57;   65;   Wah-shah-ke-pah; ---; Son; 4; M

68;   66;   He-ah-to-me; Nellie White; Orphan; 15; F

69;   67;   Sho-e-ne-lah; ---; Head; 39; M

70;   68;   Wah-shin-kah-sop-py; ---; Head; 64; M
71;   69;   To-op-pe; ---; Wife; 63; F
72;   70;   E-gro-tah; Joseph Bird; Son; 18; M

Key: Number - Last/Present; Indian Name (if given); English Name (if given); Relationship; Age; Sex.

73;   71;   E-gron-kah-shin-kah; ---; Head; 51; M
74;   72;   Hum-pah-to-kah; ---; Wife; 39; F
75;   73;   We-heh; Margaret Little; Daut; 17; F
76;   74;   Wah-sop-py-wah-kah; Mary Pappin; Daut; 10; F

77;   75;   Sin-tsa-hu; Ralph Hamilton; Head; 22; M

78;   76;   Shun-kah-mo-lah; ---; Head; 65; M
79;   77;   Wah-tsa-me; ---; Wife; 57; F
80;   78;   Wah-shin-kah-hu; Joseph Shunkahmolah; Son; 21; M

81;   79;   ---; Daniel West; Head; 37; M
82;   80;   Hlu-ah-to-me; ---; Wife; 40; F
83;   81;   Kah-shin-kah; ---; Son; 10; M

84;   82;   Wah-hah-sah-e; ---; Head; 74; F

86;   83;   Hlu-ah-to-me; Mary Blackbird; Head; 36; F
87;   84;   Mon-shou-tsa-e-tah; Maud Blackbird; Daut; 16; F
88;   85;   Che-sho-ki-he-kah; ---; Son; 4; M

89;   86;   Wah-hrah-lum-pah; Mollie Mantel; Orphan; 20; F

90;   87;   ---; Mollie Kyle; Head; 24; M

91;   88;   He-ah-to-me; ---; Head; 35; F
92;   89;   Kah-scah; Charles Antwine; Son; 11; M

93;   90;   Kah-wah-o; Yellow Horse; Head; 54; M
94;   91;   Ke-ah-som-pah; ---; Wife; 44; F
95;   92;   Pun-kah-me-tsa-he; Maggie Bates; Daut; 18; F
96;   93;   Ah-kah-hu; John Bates; Son; 14; M
97;   94;   Hun-kah-me-tsa-he; ---; Daut; 12; F

99;   95;   ---; Joseph Bates; Head; 25; M
100;   96;   ---; Lizzie June; Wife; 23; F
101;   97;   Hun-kah; ---; Son; 5;   M

102;   98;   Hun-kah-me-tsa-he; ---; Head; 28; F
103;   99;   ---; Michel Wah-tsamoie; Son; 4; M
104;   100;   ---; Frank Wahtsamoie; Son; 4; M

105;   101;   Ki-he-gra-in-kah; Harry Wahtsamoie; Son; 2; M

106;   102;   Pun-q-tah; ---; Head; 60; F

107;   103;   ---; Andrew Berry; Head; 24; M

Key: Number - Last/Present; Indian Name (if given); English Name (if given); Relationship; Age; Sex.

108;   104;   ---; Esther Smith; Head; 26; F

109;   105;   Nun-tsa-wah-hu; ---; Head; 58; M
110;   106;   Num-pah-se; Joseph Cannon; Head; 20; M
111;   107;   ---; John Cannon; Son; 9; M

112;   108;   ---; Frank Cannon; Head; 26; M

113;   109;   ---; Alex Cannon; Head; 28; M

114;   110;   O-pah-su-ah; ---; Head; 42; M
115;   111;   Wah-to-sah; ---; Wife; 42; F
116;   112;   Pah-pah-ah-hah; Francis Opahsuah; Son; 17; M

117;   113;   Tsa-po-in-kah; ---; Head; 62; M

118;   114;   ---; Lawrence Gray; Head; 25; M

119;   115;   ---; Amoa[sic] Osage; Head; 39; M
120;   116;   ---; Liza Osage; Wife; 30; F
121;   117;   He-ah-to-me; Rosa Osage; Daut; 12

MOH E KAH MOIE BAND

122;   118;   Moh-e-kah-moie; ---; Head; 77; M
123;   119;   Hlu-ah-to-me; ---; Wife; 57; F
134;   120;   Me-ah-hre; Mary Mohekahmoie; Daut; 17; F

125;   121;   ---; Dair[sic] Hickey; Head; 35; M

126;   122;   ---; William Fletcher; Head; 40; M
127;   123;   Me-sah-e; ---; Wife; 29; F
128;   124;   Gra-to-metsa-he; ---; S. Daut; 10; F
129;   125;   Gra-to-me; ---; S. Daut; 7; F
130;   126;   Sin-tsa-wah-kon-tah; Charles Fletcher; Son; 14; M
131;   127;   E-to-moie; Anna Fletcher; Daut; 11; F
132;   128;   ---; Frances T. Fletcher; Daut; 5; F

134;   129;   To-wah-gah-she; ---; Head; 52; M
135;   130;   He-ah-to-me; ---; Wife; 48; F
136;   131;   Gra-tah-su-ah; Thomas Butler; Son; 18; M

137;   132;   ---; Eugene Butler; Head; 23; M
138;   133;   ---; Grace Butler; Wife; 26; F

139;   134;   Me-gra-to-me; ---; Head; 45; F

CENSUS of the _____ **Osage** _____ Indians of _____ **Osage** _____ Agency, __Okla.__
on ___ **June 30, 1911**___, 19__, taken by __Hugh Pitzer, Supt. & Spl. Disb. Agent__

Key: Number - Last/Present; Indian Name (if given); English Name (if given); Relationship; Age; Sex.

140;   135;   U-sea-tah-wah-hah; ---; Head; 45; M

141;   136;   ---; Gilbert Cox; Head; 40; M

142;   137;   Me-ti-an-kah; ---; Head; 48; M
143;   138;   Mo-se-che-he; ---; Wife; 42; F
144;   139;   Ne-wal-la; Edward Elkins; Son; 15; M
145;   140;   E-he-ke-op-pe; ---; Daut; 10; F
146;   141;   Wah-ne-en-kah; ---; Daut; 5; F

148;   142;   ---; Charles West; Head; Head; 28; M
149;   143;   ---; Louisa West; Daut; 4; F

150;   144;   ---; Don Dickinson; Head; 33; M

151;   145;   ---; Herbert Spencer; Head; 35; M
152;   146;   ---; Jennie Spencer; Wife; 27; F

153;   147;   Gra-tah-su-ah; Donnie Cole; Orphan; 20; F

154;   148;   To-wah-Gah-he; ---; Head; 52; M
155;   149;   Son-se-grah; ---; Wife; 38; F
156;   150;   He-ah-to-me; Fanny Frye; Daut; 20; F

157;   151;   ---; Edward Cox; Head; 35; M
158;   152;   A-non-to-op-pe; ---; Wife; 24; F
159;   153;   ---; Mary Cox; Daut; 2; F
159 ½; 154;   Wah-tsa-ah-tah; Joseph Cox; Son; 6; M

160;   155;   ---; Clinton Bigheart; Head; 40; M
161;   156;   Mon-shon-tsa-e-tah; ---; Wife; 30; F
162;   157;   Hum-pah-to-kah; Rose Bigheart; Daut; 15; F

163;   158;   Ne-wal-la; Oscar Neal; Orphan; 12; M

164;   159;   ---; Rose Neal; Head; 24; F
165;   160;   ---; Clara May Neal; Daut; 3; F

166;   161;   ---; Wilson Kirk; Head; 54; M
167;   162;   ---; Dora Kirk; Daut; 10; F
168;   163;   ---; Rosa Kirk; Daut; 6; F
169;   164;   ---; Charles Kirk; Son; 4; M

170;   165;   Pah-she-he; Mary Cox; Orphan; 21; F

171;   166;   Hun-tsa-me; Mable Cole; Head; 23; F

279

Key: Number - Last/Present; Indian Name (if given); English Name (if given); Relationship; Age; Sex.

NE KAH WAH SHE TUN KAH BAND.

172;   167;   Ne-kah-wah-she-tun-kah; ---; Head; 71; M
173;   168;   Wah-hrahlum-pah; ---; Wife; 59; F

174;   169;   ---; Nicholas Webster; Head; 36; M

175;   170;   E-to-moie; Little Star; Head; 42; M
176;   171;   Wah-to-sah-e; ---; Wife; 42; F
177;   172;   Gra-tah-ah-kah; John Star; Son; 11; M
178;   173;   Tom-pah-pe; ---; Daut; 8; F
179;   174;   E-kah-pah-she; ---; Son; 5; M
180;   174;*[5]Me-tsa-ah-tah; ---; Daut; 3; F

181;   176;   Che-sho-wah-ke-pah; ---; Head; 41; M
182;   177;   Wah-hrah-lum-pah; ---; Wife; 44; F
183;   178;   Hum-pah-to-kah; ---; Daut; 14; F
184;   179;   Ke-ah-som-pah; ---; Daut; 11; F
185;   180;   ---; Mary Cheshowahkepah; Daut; 8; F

186;   181;   ---; Millie Kirk; Head; 27; F
187;   182;   Ke-ah-som-pah; ---; Daut; 3; F

188;   183;   Hun-wah-ko; ---; Head; 75; F

189;   184;   Pun-kah-wah-ti-an-kah; ---; Head; 49; M
190;   185;   Wah-hrah-lum-pah; ---; Wife; 26; F
191;   186;   Wah-tsa-ah-hah; James Bigheart; Son; 15; M
192;   187;   Wah-te-sah; ---; Daut; 9; F
193;   188;   Wah-sis-tah; ---; Son; 5; M
194;   189;   Min-kah-she; ---; Daut; 2; F

195;   190;   Pah-nee-wah-with-tah; ---; Head; 69; M
196;   191;   Gra-tah-me-tsa-he; ---; Wife; 50; F

197;   192;   Ne-kah-lum-pah; ---; Head; 55; M
198;   193;   Hah-moie; Bird Tuman; Son; 20; M

199;   194;   ---; Gurney Miller; Head; 44; M
200;   195;   ---; Grace Miller; Daut; 10; F
201;   196;   ---; Howard Miller; Son; 8; M
202;   197;   ---; Chester Miller; Son; 5; M
203;   198;   Joseph Miller; Joseph Miller; Son; 3; M

204;   199;   Ne-ah-tse-pe; ---; Head; 69; F

205;   200;   ---; Annie Daniels, Nee Turpie; Head; 24; F

280

Key: Number - Last/Present; Indian Name (if given); English Name (if given); Relationship; Age; Sex.

206; 201; Bro-ki-he-kah; ---; Head; 55; M
207; 202; Wah-tsa-e-o-she; ---; Wife; 62; F
208; 203; E-he-op-pe; Annie Brokey; Daut; 17; F

209; 204; Herbert Brokey; Head; 23; M

211; 205; Shon-kah-tsa-a; ---; Head; 43; M

212; 206; ---; Polly Jones, nee Earl; Head; 20; F
213; 207; ---; Jesse Earl Jones; Son; 1; M

214; 208; Ke-ah-som-pah; ---; Head; 60; F
215; 209; Me-hun-kah; Rosa Scott; Daut; 20; F
216; 210; Hlu-ah-wah-kon-tah; Daniel Scott; Son; 17; M
217; 211; Shah-kah-wah-pe; Walter Scott; Son; 14; M

218; 212; Wah-tsa-ah-hah; ---; Head; 57; M
219; 213; Wah-hrah-lum-pah; ---; Wife; 33; F
220; 214; Wah-tsa-moie; Joseph Watson; Son; 15; M

221; 215; Ethel Bryant; Ethel Bryant; Head; 27; F

222; 216; Shah-wah-pe; ---; Head; 43; M

223; 217; Hun-kah-hop-py; Edward G. Gibson; Orphan; 18; M

224; 218; Son-se-o-grah; Ropemaker; Head; 65; M
226; 219; Wah-ko-sah-moie; Mary Clay; Daut; 17; F

227; 220; ---; Dudley Haskell; Head; 35; M
228; 221; Son-se-grah; ---; Wife; 29; F
229; 222; Wah-hrah-lum-pah; ---; Daut; 10; F
230; 223; Me-gra-to-me; ---; Daut; 8; F
231; 224; Hlu-ah-wah-kon-tah; ---; Son; 5; M

232; 225; He-shah-ah-hle; ---; Head; 52; M
233; 226; He-ah-to-me; ---; Wife; 45; F
234; 227; Ah-kah-me; ---; Daut; 12; F
235; 228; Hlu-ah-gla-she; ---; Daut; 8
236; 229; Hun-kah-me-tsa-he; ---; Daut; 4; F

237; 230; Mo-hah-ah-gra; ---; Head; 52; M
238; 231; Wah-kon-tah-he-umpah; ---; Wife; 68; F
239; 232; He-kin-to-op-pe; Angella Hanna; Orphan; 16; F

240; 233; ---; Peter Clark; Head; 28; M
241; 234; ---; Madeline Clark; Wife; 22; F

Key: Number - Last/Present; Indian Name (if given); English Name (if given); Relationship; Age; Sex.

242; 235; Tom-pah-pe; ---; Head; 85; F

243; 236; ---; Richard Kenny; Head; 55; M
244; 237; Gra-tah-su-ah; ---; Wife; 44; F
245; 238; He-kin-to-op-pe; Mary Jane; Daut; 19; F
246; 239; A-non-to-op-pe; ---; Daut; 7; F
247; 240; Hlu-lah-tsa-keh; ---; Son; 4; M

248; 241; ---; John Kenny; Head; 28; M

249; 242; Wah-hrah-lum-pah; Annie Kenny; Head; 26; F

250; 243; ---; Orlando Kenworthy; Head; 35; M

251; 244; ---; Tony Townsend; Head; 31; M

252; 245; Hun-kah-hop-py; ---; Head; 42; M
253; 246; He-ah-to-me; Mary Hunkahhoppy; Daut; 16; F
254; 247; Wah-hrah-lum-pah; Rosa Hunkahhoppy; Daut; 14; F
254 ½; 248; ---; Lucy Hunkahhoppy; Daut; 3; F

255; 249; Hun-kah-hoppy; William Stepson; Orphan; 20; M

256; 250; ---; Jack Hartley; Head; 35; M

257; 251; Nah-hah-scah-she; ---; Head; 57; F

258; 252; Wah-tsa-ki-he-kah; Charles Drum; Head; 40; M
259; 253; We-heh; Agnes Drum; Daut; 16; F
260; 254; Wah-te-sah; Lucy Drum; Daut; 10; F

261; 255; ---; Julia Dunlap; Orphan; 13; F

BIG HILL BAND.

262; 256; to-Wah-e-he; ---; Head; 55; M
263; 257; Che-sah-me; ---; Wife; 63; F

264; 258; Hun-kah; Alfred Mckinley; Head; 23; M
265; 259; Eu-pah-shon-kah-me; ---; Daut; 4; F

266; 260; ---; Daniel McDougan; Head; 41; M

267; 261; ---; Ben Harrison; Head; 39; M
268; 262; ---; Edna M. Harvey; S. Daut; 16; F
269; 263; ---; Emily Harrison; Daut; 13; F
270; 264; ---; Ben H. Harrison; Son; 9; M

Key: Number - Last/Present; Indian Name (if given); English Name (if given); Relationship; Age; Sex.

271; 265; Wauneta E. Harrison; Daut; 6; F

272; 266; Ne-kah-e-se-y; Jimmy; Head; 65; M
273; 267; ---; Lizzie Q.; Wife; 62; F
274; 268; Wah-shah-she; Rita Kyle; Daut; 20; F

275; 269; ---; Minnie Smith; Head; 24; F

276; 270; A-non-to-op-pe; ---; Head; 62; F

277; 271; Pah-pah-ah-hah; Thomas Dorry; Orphan; 19; M

278; 272; Num-pah-se; Philip Brokey: Son; 10; M

279; 273; ---; Earnest Roe; Head; 39; M

280; 274; ---; Perry King; Head; 36; M
281; 275; E-ne-ke-op-pe; ---; Wife; 36; F
282; 276; Min-tsakah; Walter King; Son; 12; M
283; 277; Pun-q-tah; Mary King; Daut; 9; F
284; 278; Cha-hun-kah-me; ---; Daut; 4; F
285; 279; Moh-en-gra-tah; ---; Son; 7; M

287; 280; Wah-hrah-lum-pah; ---; Head; 55; F
288; 281; Hun-kah-she; Clementine P. Harris; Daut; 15; F

WHITEHAIR BAND.

289; 282; ---; John Claremore; Head; 28; M
290; 283; ---; Amanda Claremore; Wife; 27; F
291; 284; Mon-shonah-she; ---; Son; 4; M

292; 285; Ne-wal-la-tsa-he; George W. Allen; Orphan; 20; M

293; 286; ---; Dominic Daniels; Head; 28; M

294; 287; ---; Joseph Daniels; Head; 29; M

296; 288; Hlu-ah-tsa-ke; John Kenworthy; Son; 21; M
297; 289; Wan-ne-ah-tah; William Kenworthy; Son; 18; M
298; 290; Wah-shun-kah-hah; ---; Son; 12; M

299; 291; E-gro-op-pe; Hall Goode; Head; 22; M

300; 292; Wah-hrah-lum-pah (D&D); ---; Orphan; 16; F

301; 293; Mo-se-che-he; ---; Head; 50; F

Key: Number - Last/Present; Indian Name (if given); English Name (if given); Relationship; Age; Sex.

302;   294;   E-som-pah; May Cullum; Daut; 17; F

303;   295;   Wah-ko-sah-moie; ---; Head; 42; F
304;   296;   Lah-tah-sah; Clara Colum[sic]; Daut; 20; F
305;   297;   Ho-tah-me; Anna Collum; Daut; 14; F
306;   298;   Hun-tsa-moie; ---; Son; 13; M

307;   299;   ---; Joseph Mason; Head; 24; M
308;   300;   ---; Rose Mason; Wife; 26; F
309;   301;   ---; Frank Mason; Son; 3; M

310;   302;   ---; Francis Drexil; Head; 34; M
311;   303;   Wah-ko-sah-moie; ---; Wife; 35; F
312;   304;   Ne-kah-ah-se; ---; Daut; 13; F
313;   305;   Me-tsa-kah; ---; Son; 9; M

314;   306;   Pah-se-to-pah; ---; Head; 64; M
315;   307;   Wah-shah-she-me-tsa-he; ---; Wife; 61; F

316;   308;   ---; Paul Peace; Head; 25; M
317;   309;   ---; Clara Marshall; Wife; 25; F

318;   310;   ---; Henry Peace; Head; 28; M

TALL CHIEF BAND.

319;   311;   ---; Eliza Tall Chief; Head; 39; F

320;   312;   Hlu-ah-wah-kon-tah; Alex Tall Chief Jr.; Son; 21; M

321;   313;   ---; Rosa Tall Chief; Head; 30; F

322;   314;   He-ah-to-me; Emma; Head; 58; F

323;   315;   ---; Eves Tall Chief; Head; 33; M
324;   316;   Wah-shah-hah-me; ---; Wife; 31; F
325;   317;   ---; Helen Tall Chief; Daut; 6; F
326;   318;   ---; Henry Tall Chief; Son; 4; M

327;   319;   Me-hun-kah; ---; Head; 27; F

328;   320;   Ho-tah-moie; John Stink; Head; 46; M

329;   321;   Wah-shah-hah-me; ---; Head; 64; F

330;   322;   ---; Henry Tall Chief; Head; 28; M

Key: Number - Last/Present; Indian Name (if given); English Name (if given); Relationship; Age; Sex.

331; 323; Nah-she-wal-la; ---; Head; 52; M
332; 324; Wah-sha-she-me-tsa-he; Mattie Walsh; Daut; 21; F

333; 325; Pah-she-he; Grace Entoka; Head; 26; F
334; 326; He-ah-to-me; ---; Daut; 6; F
335; 327; ---; Louis Entokah; Son; 3; M

KOSHE WAH TSE BAND.

336; 328; He-lo-ki-he; Bare Legs; Head; 73; M

337; 329; He-se-moie; ---; Head; 62; M
338; 330; Tsa-me-tsa; Mary Buffalo; Daut; 12; F

339; 331; ---; Charles Grant; Head; 38; M

340; 332; ---; George Dunlap; Orphan; 16; M

342; 333; Shon-shin-kah; Bryan Wilson; Orphan; 18; M
343; 334; E-to-hun-kah; ---; Orphan; 11; M

344; 335; Kah-wah-ho-tsa (Sassamoie); ---; Head; 43; M
345; 336; Ah-kah; James Mckinley; Son; 17; M
346; 337; Wah-tsa-hu-hah; William Mckinley; Son; 15; M
347; 338; Wah-he-sah; ---; Daut; 11; F

348; 339; Wah-to-sah-grah; ---; Wife; 43; F
349; 340; Ah-kah-me-tsa-he; Eva Mckinley; Daut; 20; F
350; 341; Lah-su-sah-pah; Henry Mckinley; Son; 20; M

351; 342; ---; Josephine Mckinley; Head; 23; F

352; 343; Ne-wal-la (Tsa-ah-in-kah); ---; Head; 45; M
353; 344; Hlu-ah-to-me; ---; Daut; 8; F
354; 345; To-wah-e-he; ---; Son; 4; M

356; 346; Wah-ko-ki-he-kah; ---; Head; 57; F
357; 347; Wah-ko-sah-moie; John Hunter; Son; 19; M
358; 348; Wah-ko-sah-moie; Mary Hunter; Daut; 15; F

BLACK DOG BAND.

360; 349; Gra-to-me-tsa; Louisa Black Dog; Head; 31; F

361; 350; ---; Edgar McCarthy; Head; 38; M
362; 351; Me-tsa-he; Nettie McCarthy; Wife; 28; F

285

CENSUS of the____ **Osage**____ Indians of ____ **Osage**____ Agency, **Okla.**
on ____ **June 30, 1911**____, 19__, taken by ___**Hugh Pitzer, Supt. & Spl. Disb. Agent**

Key: Number - Last/Present; Indian Name (if given); English Name (if given); Relationship; Age; Sex.

363;   352;   Son-se-gra; ---; Head; 53; F

363[4];353;   ---; Amos Hamilton; Head; 39; M
365;   354;   ---; Noah Hamilton; Son; 9; M
366;   355;   ---; Ira Hamilton; Son; 7; M
367;   356;   ---; Otto Hamilton; Son; 4; M

368;   357;   Me-ho-e; ---; Head; 72; F

369;   358;   ---; Allison Webb; Head; 27; M
370;   359;   ---; Grace Webb; Wife; 37; F

371;   360;   He-lo-ki-he; Long Bow; Head; 24; M
372;   361;   E-gro-tah; Charles Pettus; Son; 21; M

373;   362;   Wah-sop-py; Lucy Hahmoie Bangs; Head; 27; F
374;   363;   ---; Myron Bangs Jr.; Son; 3; M

375;   364;   ---; Silas Sanford; Head; 34; M
376;   365;   ---; Anna Sanford; Wife; 29; F

378;   366;   Hum-pah-to-kah; ---; Wife; 23; F
379;   367;   ---; Bertha Webb; Daut; 5; F
380;   368;   ---; Charles E. Webb; Son; 5; M

381;   369;   ---; Willie McCarthy (Incompt); Head; 30; M

382;   370;   ---; Andrew Jackson; Head; 42; M

SAUCY CHIEF BAND.

383;   371;   ---; Lawrence; Head; 56; M

384;   372;   ---; Joseph Mills; Head; 22; M

385;   373;   ---; Alex Eagle Feather; Head; 37; M

386;   374;   Wah-te-sah; ---; Head; 70; F

387;   375;   Gra-to-me-tsa-he; Ida Gibson; Orphan; 16; F

388;   376;   ---; Prudie Martin; Head; 36; F
389;   377;   ---; Christine Martin; Daut; 8; F
390;   378;   ---; Cecil Martin; Son; 5; M

391;   379;   ---; James G. Blaine; Head; 38; M
392;   380;   ---; Hazel Blaine; Wife; 27; F

CENSUS of the_____Osage_____ Indians of ___Osage___ Agency, __Okla.__
on ___June 30, 1911__, 19__, taken by __Hugh Pitzer, Supt. & Spl. Disb. Agent__
Key: Number - Last/Present; Indian Name (if given); English Name (if given); Relationship; Age; Sex.

393;   381;   ---; Laura Gray; S. Daut; 9; F

395;   382;   E-ne-op-pe; ---; Head; 30; [F]
396;   383;   ---; Eugne[sic] Blaine; Son; 11; M
397;   384;   Me-shah-e; ---; Daut; 9; F
398;   385;   ---; James G. Blaine Jr.; Son; 7; M

399;   386;   ---; Hayes Little Bear; Head; M

400;   387;   Lo-hah-me; Dora Little Bear; 23; F

401;   388;   Ah-hu-shin-kah; ---; Head; 51; M
402;   389;   Wah-hah-sah-me; ---; Wife; 64; F

403;   390;   ---; Augustine Crowe; Head; 36; F
404;   391;   ---; Josephine Jump, nee Strike Axe; Daut; 17; F
405;   392;   ---; Augustus Chouteau; Son; 16; M
406;   393;   ---; Charles Chouteau; Son; 13; M

407;   394;   ---; Robert Panther; Head; 48; M
408;   395;   ---; Charles Panther; Son; 21; M
409;   396;   ---; Clark Panther; Son; 19; M
410;   397;   ---; Nettie Panther; Daut; 17; F
411;   398;   ---; Maud Panther; Daut; 14; F

412;   399;   ---; Mary Pryor; Head; 60; F

413;   400;   ---; Edna La Batte; Head; 39; F

414;   401;   Charles Me-she-tsa-he; ---; Head; 52; M
415;   402;   Wah-ko-sah-moie; ---; Wife; 57; F
416;   403;   Hlu-ah-me; Eva Bean; Daut; 19; F
417;   404;   Pah-she-he; Emma Hoover; Daut; 15; F

418;   405;   ---; Ben Mushunkashey; Head; 28; M
420;   406;   ---; Charley Mushunkashey; Son; 4; M

421;   407;   ---; William Pryor; Head; 36; M
422;   408;   Min-kah-she; Mary Pryor; Wife; 38; F
423;   409;   ---; Josephine Pryor; Daut; 11; F
424;   410;   Shon-kah; Charles Mushunkashey; S. Son; 15; M
424 ½; 411;   ---; John Pryor; Son; 8; M
425;   412;   ---; Susie L. Hutchinson; Head; 29; F
426;   413;   ---; Vernie L. Hutchinson; Daut; 10; F
427;   414;   ---; Charles V. Hutchinson; Son; 8; M
428;   415;   ---; Carllos H. Hutchinson; Son; 6; M
429;   416;   ---; Genvis Hutchinson; Daut; 4; F

287

Key: Number - Last/Present; Indian Name (if given); English Name (if given); Relationship; Age; Sex.

420;   417;   Ke-le-kom-pah; ---; Haed[sic]; 61; M
431;   418;   Mo-se-che-he; ---; Wife; 56; F

432;   419;   Wah-kon-tah-ah; Wakon Iron; Son; 20; M

433;   420;   ---; Paul Albert; Head; 42; M

434;   421;   Pah-she-he; ---; Head; 51; M

435;   422;   Hum-pah-to-kah; ---; Head; 57; F

435 ½; 423;   Wah-shah-she-me-tsa-he; Augustine Black; Head; 38; F
436;   424;   ---; John P. White Tail; Son; 14; M
437;   425;   Hom-me-tsa-he; May Black; Daut; 5; F

437 ½; 426;   Me-shah-e; ---; Head; 52; F

438;   427;   ---; Harry Kopay; Head; 39; M
439;   428;   ---; Elsie Kopay; Daut; 12; F
440;   429;   ---; Hugh Kopay; Son; 11; M
441;   430;   ---; Loretto Kopay; Son; 4; M

442;   431;   Wy-e-gla-in-kah; Red Corn; Head; 57; M
443;   432;   Wah-kon-tah-he-um-pah; ---; Wife; 60; F
444;   433;   Wah-tsa-kon-lah; Ralph Malone; S. Son; 19; M

445;   434;   ---; Raymond Red Corn; Head; 25; M

446;   435;   ---; Pearl Hartley; Head; 31; F

447;   436;   ---; Julia White Tail; Head; 65; F

448;   437;   Ne-kah-she-he; ---; Head; 37; F
449;   438;   Wah-pah-ah-hah; Edward Elkins; Son; 14; M
450;   439;   Gra-tome; Minnie Elkins; Daut; 6; F
451;   440;   Com-pox-she; Kate Albert; Daut; 4; F

452;   441;   ---; Charles Michelle; Head; 43; M
453;   442;   Me-sah-e; ---; Wife; 39; F
454;   443;   ---; Ida Michelle; Daut; 15; F

455;   444;   ---; Harry Big Eagle; Head; 25; M
456;   445;   Wah-shah-hah-me; Elsie Big Eagle; Wife; 21; F
457;   446;   Me-tsa-he; Metsa Big Eagle; Daut; 5; F

460;   447;   ---; Harry Pyahhunkah; Head; 24; M

288

Key: Number - Last/Present; Indian Name (if given); English Name (if given); Relationship; Age; Sex.

461;   448;   ---; Charles Brave; Head; 33; M
462;   449;   Mum-brum-pah; Mary Strike Axe Brave; Wife; 26; F
463;   450;   ---; Andrew Brave; Son; 10; M
464;   451;   ---; Louis Brave; Son; 5; M

465;   452;   ---; Laban Miles; Head; 51; M
466;   453;   Mo-se-che-he; Anna Miles; Daut; 21; F
467;   454;   Wah-shah-ah-pe; Mary Miles; Daut; 17; F
468;   455;   Pap-pah-ah-he; Leo Miles; Son; 17; F

469;   456;   Hlu-ah-shu-tsa; John Miles; Head; 21; M

470;   457;   Wah-shah-she-me-tsa-he; ---; Head; 42; F
471;   458;   ---; Walker Penn; son; 20; M
472;   459;   ---; Laban Miles Jr.; Son; 10; M

473;   460;   ---; Eddie Penn; Head; 22; M

474;   461;   ---; John Whitehorn; Head; 28; M
475;   462;   ---; Arthur Whitehorn; Son; 6; M

476;   463;   Hu-lah-tun-kah; Big Eagle; Head; 59; M
477;   464;   Pah-pu-son-tsa; ---; Wife; 61; F
469[7];465;   Pah-se-he; Mary Warrior; S. Daut; 16; F

480;   466;   Hun-kah-ah-gra; Robert Warrior; Head; 21; M
481;   467;   Tsa-me-hun-kah; Mamie Warrior; Wife; 21; F

482;   468;   ---; Russell Warrior; Head; 27; M

483;   469;   E-stah-o-gre-she; ---; Head; 47; M
484;   470;   Shon-blah-scah; ---; Wife; 43; F

485;   471;   ---; Frank Pyahhunkah; Orphan; 17; M

BEAVER BAND

486;   472;   ---; Rose L. Bigheart; Daut; 19; F
487;   473;   ---; Sarah L. Bigheart; Daut; 13; F
488;   474;   ---; Belle L. Bigheart; Daut; 8; F

489;   475;   Che-she-sin-kah; Henry Red Eagle; Head; 62; M
490;   476;   ---; Rosa Red Eagle; Wife; 60; F

491;   477;   ---; Paul Red Eagle; Head; 31; M
492;   478;   ---; Cecelia Red Eagle; Wife; 29; F
493;   479;   ---; Harry Red Eagle; Son; 9; M

CENSUS of the _____ **Osage** _____ *Indians of* _____ **Osage** _____ *Agency,* __Okla.__
on __June 30, 1911__ *, 19___, taken by* __Hugh Pitzer, Supt. & Spl. Disb. Agent__

Key: Number - Last/Present; Indian Name (if given); English Name (if given); Relationship; Age; Sex.

494;   480;   ---; Lucis Red Eagle; Son; 6; M
495;   481;   ---; Joseph Red Eagle; Son; 5; M
496;   482;   ---; May Louisa Red Eagle; Daut; 3; F
497;   483;   ---; Henry Red Eagle; son; 2; M

498;   484;   Hlu-ah-shu-tsa (D & D); Joseph Red Eagle; Head; 35; M

499;   485;   Beg-gah-hah-he; Brave; Head; 77; M
500;   486;   ---; Mary Brave; Wife; 80; F

501;   487;   ---; Andrew Bighorse; Head; 34; M
502;   488;   Hum-pah-to-kah; ---; Wife; 40; F
503;   489;   We-heh; Rose McDougan; S. Daut; 19; F
504;   490;   ---; Peter Bighorse; Son; 12; M
505;   491;   ---; Joseph Bighorse; Son; 10; M
506;   492;   ---; Mary Bighorse; Daut; 7; F
507;   493;   ---; Edward; Bighorse [?]; 4; M

508;   494;   ---; Charles McDougan; Head; 23; M

509;   495;   ---; John Wagoshe; Head; 33; M
510;   496;   Wah-shah-she-me-tsa-he; Agnes Bigheart; Wife; 33; F
511;   497;   ---; George Vest; S. Son; 15; M
512;   498;   ---; Charles Wahoshe[?]; Son; 7; M
513;   499;   A-non-to-op-pe; ---; Daut; 5; F
514;   500;   Wah-sah-po; ---; Daut; 4; F
----;   501;   ---; Louis Wagoshe; Son; 1; M

515;   502;   John Lookout; Head; 34; M

516;   503;   Heh-kah-mon-kah; ---; Wife; 25; F
517;   504;   ---; William Lookout; Son; 4; M

518;   505;   ---; Louis Bighorse; Head; 46; M
519;   506;   To-op-pe; Ida Bighorse; Wife; 31; F
520;   507;   ---; Rose Bighorse; Daut; 15; F
521;   508;   ---; Lillie Bighorse; Daut; 10; F
522;   509;   ---; Minnie Bighorse; Daut; 7; F
523;   510;   ---; Louisa Bighorse; Daut; 4; F

525;   511;   Pah-pu-son-tsa; ---; Wife; 53; F

526;   512;   Ah-tsa-shin-kah; Mary Wild Cat; Orphan; 13; F

527;   513;   Mo-ho-gla; ---; Head; 56; M
528;   514;   Me-tsa-hi-ke; ---; Wife; 67; F

Key: Number - Last/Present; Indian Name (if given); English Name (if given); Relationship; Age; Sex.

529; 515; ---; Antwine Pryor; Head; 31; M
530; 516; Julia; Julia Pryor; Daut; 6; F
531; 517; ---; Susie Pryor; Daut; 4; F

532; 518; ---; Henry Coshehe; Head; 38; M
533; 519; Wah-kon-tah-he-um-pah; ---; Wife; 35; F
534; 520; ---; Clem Coshehe; Son; 19; M
535; 521; ---; George Coshehe; Son; 5; M
535 ½; 522; ---; John Coshehe; Son; 11; M

536; 523; Wah-tsa-ah-tah; Ralph On Hand; Orphan; 20; M

537; 524; He-he-kin-to-op-pe; Minne[sic] On Hand; Orphan; 15; F

538; 525; ---; John McFall; Head; 44; M
539; 526; Gra-tah-shin-kah; Mary McFall; Wife; 32; F

540; 527; ---; Minnie Whitehorn; Orphan; 21; F

541; 528; ---; George Michelle; Head; 37; M
542; 529; ---; Wesley W. Michelle; Son; 6; M

543; 530; Mo-se-che-he; ---; Head; 71; F

STRIKE AXE BAND.

544; 531; ---; Fred Lookout; Head; 53; M
545; 532; Mo-se-che-he; Julia Lookout; Wife; 42; F
546; 532 ½; ---; Charles Lookout; son; 19; M
547; 533; ---; Frederick Lookout; Son; 16; M
548; 534; ---; Nora Lookout; Daut; 11; F
549; 535; ---; Henry Lookout; Son; 5; M

550; 536; ---; James Strike Axe; Orphan; 17; M

551; 537; Wy-e-nah-she; ---;Head; 63; M

552; 538; Tsa-shin-kah-wah-ti-an-kah; Saucy Chief; Head; 67; M
553; 539; ---; Sophia Chouteau; Wife; 69; F

554; 540; ---; Joseph Buffalohide; Head; 25; M
555; 541; ---; Agnes Buffalohide; Wife' 24; F

556; 542; Tom-pah-pah; ---; Head; 57; F

557; 543; ---; Pendleton Strike Axe; Head; 30; M
558; 544; Mo-se-che-he; ---; Wife; 23; F

CENSUS of the____Osage____ Indians of ____Osage____ Agency, _Okla._
on ___June 30, 1911__, 19__, taken by _Hugh Pitzer, Supt. & Spl. Disb. Agent_

Key: Number - Last/Present; Indian Name (if given); English Name (if given); Relationship; Age; Sex.

559; 545; ---; Emma Strike Axe; Daut; 7; F
560; 546; ---; Ida Strike Axe; Daut; 5; F

561; 547; ---; Foster Strike Axe; Head; 37; M
562; 548; ---; Jennie Strike Axe; Daut; 15; F
563; 549; ---; Emma Strike Axe; Daut; 13; F
564; 550; ---; Dora Strike Axe; Daut; 5; F

565; 551; ---; Louis Pryor; Head; 32; M
566; 552; ---; Andrew Pryor; Son; 5; M

567; 553; O-sah-ke-pah; Cap Strike Axe; Head; 53; M

568; 554; Pah-se-to-pah (D & D); ---; Head; 41; M
569; 555; Me-sah-e; Veva Pahsetopah; Wife; 31; F
570; 556; ---; Cora Pahsetopah; Daut; 10; F
571; 557; ---; Carrie Pahsetopah; Daut; 8; F
572; 558; ---; Louis Pahsetopah; Son; 6; M

573; 559; Me-hun-kah (He-ah-to-me); ---; Head; 61; F
574; 560; Ke-nun-tah; William Shahpahnahshe; Son; 21; M

575; 561; ---; Pierce St. John; Head; 35; M
576; 562; Ke-ah-som-pah; ---; Wife; 37; F
577; 563; Gra-tah-scah; Jocob[sic] Jump; S. Son; 19; M
578; 564; ---; Dora St. John; Daut; 9; F
579; 565; ---; Herbert St. John; Son; 7; M
580; 566; ---; William St. John; Son; 5; M
[5]481;567; ---; Anna St. John; Daut; 4; F

582; 568; ---; Frank Corndropper; Head; 63; M
583; 569; Gra-tah-me-tsa-he; ---; Wife; 65; F

584; 570; Peh-tsa-moie; ---; Head; 68; M
585; 571; Wah-tsa-u-sah; ---; Wife; 39; F

586; 572; ---; Richard Firewalk; Head; 27; M
587; 573; Son-se-grah; May Firewalk; Wife; 21; F

588; 574; Lah-blah-wal-la; Three Striker (Incompt); Head; 67; M

589; 575; Wy-u-hah-kah; ---; Head; 53; M
590; 576; Hlu-ah-me-tsa-he; ---; Wife; 61; F

591; 577; ---; John Oberly; Head; 31; M
592; 578; Me-tsa-he; ---; Wife; 29; F
593; 579; A-non-to-op-pe; ---; Daut; 4; F

CENSUS of the___Osage___Indians of___Osage___Agency, __Okla.__
on ___June 30, 1911_, 19__, taken by __Hugh Pitzer, Supt. & Spl. Disb. Agent__

Key: Number - Last/Present; Indian Name (if given); English Name (if given); Relationship; Age; Sex.

594;   580;   Pah-pah-ah-ho; ---; Son; 3; M

595;   581;   ---; John A. Logan; Head; 38; M
596;   582;   ---; Mary Logan; Wife; 33; F
597;   583;   ---; Joseph Logan; Son; 12; M
598;   584;   ---; Roas[sic] Logan; Daut; 6; F
599;   585;   ---; Oscar Logan; Son; 3; M
600;   586;   Tompah-pah; ---; Daut; 4; F

NE KAH KE PAH NEE BAND.

601;   587;   ---; Robert A-she-gah-hre; Head; 61; M
602;   588;   Gra-to-me-tsa-he; ---; Wife; 55; F
603;   589;   Me-tun-kah; Susan Killon; Daut; 21; F
604;   590;   Vah-sah-pah-shin; ---; Daut; 6; F
605;   591;   Sho-tsa; ---; Son; 4; M

606;   592;   Ke-mo-hah; ---; Head; 52; M
607;   593;   Loh-tah-sah; ---; Wife; 36; F
608;   594;   Me-tsa-he; Elda Townsend; S. Daut; 19; F
609;   595;   ---; John R. Townsend; S. Son; 14; M
610;   596;   Hun-kah-me (D & D); ---; Daut; 12; F
611;   597;   Heh-mo-sah; ---; Son; 11; M
612;   598;   Moh-e-kah-shah; ---; Son; 9; M
613;   599;   Mone[-]shon-kah-hah; ---; Son; 7; M

614;   600;   Tsa-e-kon-lah (Crazy); Mrs. Womack; Head; 67; F

615;   601;   ---; Clarence Gray; Head; 34; M
616;   602;   He-kin-to-op-pe; Jennie Gray; Wife; 24; F
617;   603;   ---; Mary Gray; Daut; 7; F

618;   604;   Tsa-pah-ah-in-kah; John; Head; 57; M
619;   605;   Wah-shah-pe-wah-ko; ---; Wife; 61; F
620;   606;   E-to-wah-hrah-lum-pah; Mary Brown; Head; 23; M

621;   607;   Shon-kah; Charles Brown; Head; 23; M

622;   608;   ---; David Copperfield; Head; 35; M
623;   609;   Hun-kah-me-tsa-he; Maggie Copperfield; Wife; 37; F
624;   610;   Me-tsa-he; ---; Daut; 11; F
625;   611;   Hun-kah-she; ---; Son; 9; M
626;   612;   Hun-kah-ah-gra; ---; Son; 6; M
627;   613;   Wah-she-pah; ---; Son; 4; M

628;   614;   ---; William Pitts; Head; 33; M
629;   615;   Me-tsa-he; Isabella Pitts; Wife; 33; F

293

Key: Number - Last/Present; Indian Name (if given); English Name (if given); Relationship; Age; Sex.

630; 616; George T. Pitts; Son; 4; M

631; 617; Hun-kah-tun-kah; Roman Logan; Head; 51; M
632; 618; Pah-she-he; Mary Logan; Wife; 30; F
633; 619; Me-tsa-he; Agnes Logan; Daut; 15; F
634; 620; Tom-pah-pe; ---; Daut; 9; F

635; 621; Che-sho-shin-kah; ---; Head; 72; M

637; 622; ---; Frank Lohowa; Head; 26; M
638; 623; ---; Mary Lohowa; Wife; 29; F

640; 624; Me-tsa-he; ---; Wife; 71; F

641; 625; Ah-hu-scah; Walla Fish; Head; 22; M
642; 626; E-ne-op-pe; Mary Fish; Wife; 20; F

643; 627; Hun-tsa-moie; ---; Head; 47; M
644; 628; Hlu-ah-to-me; ---; Wife; 67; F

645; 629; Mo-se-che-he; ---; Head; 93; F

CLAREMORE BAND.

646; 630; ---; Francis Claremore; Head; 46; M
647; 631; Wah-hrah-lum-pah; ---; Wife; 40; F
648; 632; Tsa-pah-ke-ah; Louis Claremore; Son; 18; M

649; 633; ---; John Abott[sic]; Head; 30; M
650; 634; Ne-kah-she-tsa; ---; Wife; 27; F
651; 635; Wah-shah-she-me-tsa-he; ---; Daut; 9; F
64[5]2; 636; ---; Margurite Abbott; Daut; 4; F

653; 637; ---; Henry Pratt; Head; 39; M
654; 638; Hun-kah-me; Josephine Pratt; Wife; 38; F
655; 639; ---; Helen Pratt; Daut; 16; F
656; 640; Gra-tah-scah; Geroge[sic] Pratt; Son; 10; M
657; 641; ---; Charles Pratt; Son; 6; M

658; 642; Me-gra-to-me; ---; Head; 55; F

659; 643; Pah-hu-gre-she; ---; Head; 23; F
660; 644; ---; Andrew Opah; Son; 5; M

661; 645; ---; Charles Big Elk; Head; 32; M
662; 646; Mose-che-he; Cora Big Elk; Wife; 29; F
663; 647; ---; Mary Big Elk; Daut; 11; F

CENSUS of the_____**Osage**_____ Indians of _____**Osage**_____ Agency, __**Okla.**__
on ___**June 30, 1911**___, 19__, taken by __**Hugh Pitzer, Supt. & Spl. Disb. Agent**__

Key: Number - Last/Present; Indian Name (if given); English Name (if given); Relationship; Age; Sex.

664;   648;   ---; Don S. Big Elk; Son; 5; M

665;   649;   E-ah-scah-wal-la; James Browning; Orphan; 18; M
666;   650;   Mon-kah-hah; John Browning; Orphan; 13; M

667;   651;   ---; Eugene Ware; Head; 35; M
668;   652;   Hum-pah-to-kah; ---; Wife; 34; F
669;   653;   ---; Joseph Ware; SON; L"[sic] [12]; m
670;   654;   ---; Mary Ware; Daut; 10; F
671;   655;   ---; Elijah N. Ware; Son; 8; M
672;   656;   ---; Daisy L. Ware; Daut; 6; F
672 ½; 657;   ---; Charles Ware; Son; 5; M

673;   658;   ---; Henry Roan; Head; 28; M
674;   659;   He-ah-to-me; ---; Wife; 22; F
675;   660;   ---; Grace Roan; Daut; 5; F

676;   661;   ---; Arthur Bonnicastle H; Head; 34; M
6̶3̶[7]7;662;   ---; Angie Bonnicastle; Wife; 24; F
678;   663;   ---; Kathleen Bonnicastle; Daut; 1; F

679;   664;   ---; Maud Supernaw; Head; 67; F
680;   665;   ---; Mary Thompson; Daut; 13; F

681;   666;   ---; Jack Wheeler; Head; 69; M
682;   667;   Nah-me-tsa-he; ---; Wife; 64; F

683;   668;   ---; Rhoda Wheeler; Head; 26; F

684;   669;   ---; Ben Wheeler; Head; 35; M
685;   670;   Tsa-me-tsa-he; Fanny Wheeler; Wife; 29; F
686;   671;   Hun-kah-hre; Fred Wheeler; Son; 10; M
687;   672;   Me-tsa-he; ---; Daut; 5; F
688;   673;   Shah-kah-pah-he; ---; Son; 3; M

689;   674;   ---; Nannie Naranjo; Head; 39; F
690;   675;   ---; Clara Naranjo; Daut; 12; F

691;   676;   Hlu-ah-shu-tsa; Joe Red Eagle; Head; 41; M
693;   677;   ---; Alice Red Eagle; Daut; 6; F
693 ½; 678;   ---; Frederick Red Eagle; Son; 10; M

694;   679;   Wah-shah-she-metsa-he; ---; Head; 62; F

695;   680;   ---; Sophia Greenback; Head; 37; F

Key: Number - Last/Present; Indian Name (if given); English Name (if given); Relationship; Age; Sex.

WAH TI AN KAH NABD[sic].

696;	681;	Wah-she-hah; Bacon Rind; Head; 51; M
697;	692;	Wah-ko-ki-he-kah; Rosa Bacon Rind; Wife; 47; F
698;	683;	In-gro-tah; George Bacon Rind; Son; 20; M
699;	684;	Ah-tsa-shin-kah; Louisa Bacon Rind; Daut; 14; F
700;	685;	Mah-hu-sah; [M]?oses[sic] Bacon Rind; Son; 10; M
701;	686;	---; Julia Bacon Rind; Daut; 8; F
702;	687;	Mo-sah-mum-pah; ---; Head; 34; M
703;	688;	Hun-kah-me; ---; Wife; 38; F
704;	689;	Ki-he-kah-tun-kah; ---; Son; 15; M
705;	690;	To-wah-e-he; ---; Head; 66; M
706;	691;	She-she; ---; Head; 52; M
708;	692;	---; Simon Henderson; Head; 29; M
709;	693;	---; Louisa Henderson; Wife; 25; F
710;	694;	He-ah-to-se; ---; Daut; 5; F
711;	695;	---; George Pitts; Head; 30; M
712;	696;	---; Mary Pitts; Wife; 25; F
713;	697;	---; Warren Pitts; Son; 8; M
714;	698;	---; David Pitts; Son; 6; M
715;	699;	---; Elizabeth Pitts; Daut; 4; F
716;	700;	Ho-ki-ah-se; ---; Head; 43; M
717;	701;	Me-tsa-he; Louisa Hokiahse; Wife; 33; F
718;	702;	To-ho-ah; ---; Son; 7; M
719;	703;	E-nah-min-tsa-tun; ---; Son; 3; M

wILLIAM pENN BAND? [WILLIAM PENN BAND.]

720;	704;	---; Peter C. Bigheart; Head; 72; M
721;	705;	Wah-ko-li-he-kah; ---; Wife; 68; F
722;	706;	Hlu-ah-to-me ([D] & D); ---; Orphan; 19; F
723;	707;	---; George Bigheart; Head; 35; M
724;	708;	Pah-me-she-wah; ---; Wife; 25; F
725;	709;	---; Charles Bigheart; Son; 6; M
726;	710;	Um-pah-to-kah; ---; Daut; 4; F
727;	711;	Wah-ko-sah-moie; ---; Daut; 3; F
728;	712;	---; Claude Smith; Head; 37; M
729;	713;	Hlu-ah-to-me; Mamie Smith; Wife; 28; F

CENSUS of the_____ **Osage**_____ Indians of _____ **Osage**_____ Agency, __Okla.__

on ___ **June 30, 1911** __, 19__, taken by __Hugh Pitzer, Supt. & Spl. Disb. Agent__

Key: Number - Last/Present; Indian Name (if given); English Name (if given); Relationship; Age; Sex.

730;   714;   Wah-tsa-me; ---; Son; 9; M
731;   715;   Hum-pah-to-kah; ---; Daut; 8; F
732;   716;   Ke-ah-som-pah; ---; Daut; 5
733;   717;   Wah-ko-sah-moie; ---; Daut; 4; F

734;   718;   Wah-she-wah-hah; John Bigheart; Head; 45; M
735;   719;   Hlu-ah-to-me; Grace Bigheart; Wife; 42; F
736;   720;   Ne-kah-sto-kah; John Bigheart; Son; 14; M
737;   721;   Wah-ko-sah-moie; ---; daut; 13; F
738;   722;   Ne-kah-sto-wah; ---; Son; 10; --
739;   723;   Kahhescah; ---; Son; 7; M
740;   724;   Grah-e-grah-in-kah; ---; son; 5; M

741;   725;   Wah-tsa-tun-kah; Joseph Bigheart; Head; 22; M

742;   726;   ---; Edward Bigheart; Head; 23; M
743;   727;   ---; Rose Bigheart; Wife; 20; F

744;   728;   Ha-ah-to-me; ---; Head; 50; F
745;   729;   Ne-wal-la; Henry Lohah; Son; 19; M
746;   730;   Ah-hu-shin-kah; Albert Lohah; Son; 17; M

747;   731;   A-non-to-op-pe; Ellen Lohah; Daut; F
748;   732;   Heh-kah-mon-kah; Mary Lohah; Daut; 12; F
749;   733;   Tom-pah-pe-she; ---; Son; 6; M

750;   734;   ---; Samuel Parker[sic]; Head; 32; M
751;   735;   ---; Frances Barker; Wife; 23; F
752;   736;   ---; James Barker; Son; 3; M

754;   737;   Mo-se-che-he; ---; Head; 43; F
755;   738;   Hlu-ah-wah-kon-tah; Robert Olohamoie; Son; 19; M
756;   739;   Wah-tsa-a-tah; George Olohahmoie; Son; 16; M
757;   740;   Wah-hrah-lum-pah; ---; Daut; 13; 13[M]
758;   741;   Num-pahq-ah; ---; Son; 11; M
759;   742;   Me-gra-tome; ---; Daut; 9; F
760;   743;   Moie-ke-kah-she; ---; Son; 7; M

761;   744;   Tah-hah-gah-hah; ---; Head; 46; M
762;   745;   Wah-hu-sah-e; ---; Wife; 42; F
763;   746;   Ah-nah-me-tsa-he; Roy Maker; Son; 14; M
764;   747;   Ho-ke-ah-se; George Maker; Son; 7; M

765;   748;   ---; Ross Maker; Head; 23; M

766;   749;   Ah-kah-me; ---; Wife; 32; F
767;   750;   Shon-kah; James Maker; Son; 14; M

297

Key: Number - Last/Present; Indian Name (if given); English Name (if given); Relationship; Age; Sex.

768;	751;	---; Edgar Maker; Head; 26; M
769;	752;	---; Helen Maker; Wife; 21; F
770;	753;	---; Theodore Maker; Son; 3; M

771;   754;   Mo-shah-ke-tah; ---; Head; 47; M

772;   755;   Tom-pah-pe; ---; Head; 65; F
773;   756;   O-hun-pe-ah; John Bruce; Son; 21; M

774;   757;   ---; Albert Penn; Head; 41; M
775;   758;   ---; Dora Penn; Wife; 24; F
776;   759;   Wah-ses-tah; Andrew Penn; Son; 17; M
777;   760;   Wah-te-sah; Grace Penn; Daut; 16; F
778;   761;   ---; Mary Penn; Daut; 5; F
        762;   Keo-som-pah; ---; Daut; 2; F
        763;   Wah-ko-suh-moie; ---; Daut; 1; F

779;   764;   ---; Fred Penn; Head; 38; M

780;   765;   O-ke-sah; Tom West; Head; 37; M
781;   766;   Me-tsa-he; Rosa West; Wife; 38; F
782;   767;   ---; John Wood; S. Son; 17; M
783;   768;   Mo-se-che-he; ---; Daut; 7; F

784;   769;   ---; Dan G. West; Head; 33; M
785;   770;   Pah-pu-son-tsa; Fanny West; Wife; 30; F
786;   771;   He-ah-to-me; Lucy West; Daut; 10; F
787;   772;   ---; Howard M. West; Son; 5; M

LITTLE CHIEF BAND.

788;   773;   ---; Charles Whitehorn; Orphan; 21; M
789;   774;   ---; John Whitehorn; Head; 23; M

790;   775;   Nah-kah-sah-me; Kate Whitehorn; Head; 23; F

791;   776;   Wah-shah-hahme; ---; Head; 59; F

792;   777;   Ki-he-kah-nah-she; ---; Head; 48; M
793;   778;   Hlu-ah-to-me; Frances Kihekahshe; Wife; 38; F
794;   779;   Wah-shah-she-me-tsa-he; Magella Whitehorn; Daut; 17; F
795;   780;   Hum-pah-to-kah; Tresa Whitehorn; Daut; 15; F
796;   781;   Monk-she-hah-pe; ---; Son; 4; M

797;   782;   Me-tsa-he; ---; Head; 45; F
798;   783;   Wah-shah-she-me-tsa-he; ---; Daut; 10; F
799;   784;   Ho-ho; Clarence Daniel; Son; 16; M

Key: Number - Last/Present; Indian Name (if given); English Name (if given); Relationship; Age; Sex.

800; 785; Wah-shah-she; Daut; 8; F

801; 786; He-ah-to-me; ---; Head; 59; F

802; 787; ---; Frank Little Soldier; Head; 26; M
803; 788; ---; Esther Little Soldier; Wife; 25; F

804; 789; Me-tsa-he; ---; Head; 21; F
80~~3~~[5];790; Wah-shah-e-no-pah; ---; Son; 3; M

806; 791; ---; Ellen Spurgeon; Head; 30; F

807; 792; Hlu-ah-wah-tah; ---; Head; 45; M
808; 793; He-to-op-pe; ---; Wife; 42; F
809; 794; Mah-grah-lum-pah; ---; Daut; 12; F
810; 795; Hlu-ah-wah-kon-tah; ---; Son; 7; M
811; 796; Wah-shah-me-tsa-he; Lillie Hlu-ah-wah-tah; Daut; 4; F

812; 797; Me-tsa-no; Mary Mudd; Head; 55; F

813; 798; ---; Alex Mudd; Head; 28; M

814; 799; ---; Lucy Lotson; Head; 34; F
815; 800; ---; Lucius Lotson; Son; 15; M
      801; ---; Maud Lee Mudd; Daut; 3; F

HALF BREED BAND.

818; 802; ---; Aiken, Elizabeth; Head; 29; F

819; 803; ---; Aiken, John H.; Head; 27; M
820; 804; ---; Alberty, Cynthia; Head; 55; F
821; 805; ---; Alberty. Lizzie; Daut; 20; F

822; 806; ---; Alberty. George; Head; 24; M
823; 807; ---; Alberty. Flora; Wife; 24; F

824; 808; ---; Alexander, Levi; Head; 30; F
825; 809; ---; Alexander, Martha I.; Daut; 9; F

826; 810; ---; Alexander, Ida A.; Head; 22; F

827; 811; ---; Allen, Emily; Head; 47; F

828; 812; ---; Whalen, Esther; Daut; 17; F
829; 813; ---; Whalen, Dorothea; Daut; 15; F
830; 814; ---; Whalen, Charlotte; Daut; 21; F

299

Key: Number - Last/Present; Indian Name (if given); English Name (if given); Relationship; Age; Sex.

831; 815; ---; Anderson, Mary; Head; 28; F

832; 816; ---; Anderson, John B.; Head; 25; M
833; 817; ---; Anderson, Henry P.; Son; 5; M
834; 818; ---; Anderson, Viretta; Daut; 4; F

835; 819; ---; Anderson, Edward R.; Head; 23; M

836; 820; ---; Anderson, Skinner T.; Son; 17; M
837; 821; ---; Anderson, Ora D.; Daut; 13; F
838; 822; ---; Anderson, Noble M.; Son; 12; M

839; 823; ---; Anderson, Florence; Head; 22; F

840; 824; ---; Appleby; Jane; Head; 80; F
841; 825; ---; Captain, Peter (Incompt); Son; 47; M

842; 826; ---; Atkin John D. Jr.; Head; 23; M

843; 827; ---; Avant, Rosalie; Head; 34; F
844; 828; ---; Avant, Theodore R.; Son; 13; M
845; 829; ---; Avant, Ethel; Daut; 10; F

846; 830; ---; Barber, Ida; Head; 29; F
847; 831; ---; Barber, Augustus; Son; 8; M
848; 832; ---; Barber, Morris G.; Son; 5; M

849; 833; ---; Barber, Bridget A.; Head; 50; F
850; 834; ---; Barber, Clara M.; Daut; 19; F
851; 835; ---; Barber, Edgar E.; Son; 16; M
852; 836; ---; Barber, Lawrence L.; Son; 14; M
853; 837; ---; Barber, Paul G.; Son; 11; M
854; 838; ---; Barber, Lee R.; Son; 7; M

855; 839; ---; Barker, Mary J.; Head; 56; F
856; 840; ---; Simms, Cora E.; Daut; 17; F

857; 841; ---; Baker, John Thomas; Head; 42; M
858; 842; ---; Baker, Monette; Wife; 36; F
859; 843; ---; Baker, Myrtle C.; Daut; 15; F
860; 844; ---; Baker, Morris A.; Son; 11; M
861; 845; ---; Baker, Frank T.; Son; 10; M
862; 846; ---; Baker, Martha B.; Daut; 7; F
863; 847; ---; Baker, John Thomas Jr.; Son; 3; M

864; 848; ---; Baker, Myrtle; Head; 22; F

300

CENSUS of the_____**Osage**_____ Indians of_____**Osage**_____ Agency, **Okla.**
on _____**June 30, 1911**_____, 19__, taken by **Hugh Pitzer, Supt. & Spl. Disb. Agent**

Key: Number - Last/Present; Indian Name (if given); English Name (if given); Relationship; Age; Sex.

865; 849; ---; Baylis, Elizabeth; Head; 67; F

866; 850; ---; Baylis, Harry; Head; 27; M

867; 851; ---; Bellieu, Thomas A.; Head; 29; M

868; 852; ---; Baylis, Walter S.; Head; 24; M

869; 853; ---; Baylis, Stella; Daut; 19; F
870; 854; ---; Baylis, Leo F.; Son; 15; M
871; 855; ---; Baylis, Anna H.; Daut; 13; F
872; 856; ---; Baylis, Stephen M.; Son; 11; M

873; 857; ---; Bellmard, Eliza; Head; 24; F
874; 858; ---; Bellmard, Clarence; Son; 4; M

875; 859; ---; Bennett, William; Head; 35; M
876; 860; ---; Bennett, Isabella; Wife; 30; F
877; 861; ---; Bennett, William E.; Son; 11; M
878; 862; ---; Bennett, Teresa; Daut; 7; F
879; 863; ---; Bennett, Irene; Daut; 4; F

880; 864; ---; Blackburn, Rachel; Head; 31; F
881; 865; ---; Blackburn, Oliver O.; Son; 11; M
882; 866; ---; Blackburn, Luther A.; Son; 6; M

883; 867; ---; Boulanger, Joseph; Head; 62; M
884; 868; ---; Boulanger, Benjamin H.; Son; 21; H
885; 869; ---; Boulanger, James V.; Son; 20; M
886; 870; ---; Boulanger, Eulalie C.; Daut; 17; F
887; 871; ---; Boulanger, Anna V.; Daut; 16; F
888; 872; ---; Boulanger, Charles F.; son; M

889; 873; ---; Boulanger, Grover; Head; 26; M

890; 874; ---; Boulanger, Stephen E.; Head; 26; M
891; 875; ---; Boulanger, Minnie L.; Daut; 10; F
892; 876; ---; Boulanger, Augustine C.; Daut; 8

893; 877; ---; Boulanger, Isaac; Head; 32; M
894; 878; ---; Boulanger, Charles M.; Son; 11; M
895; 879; ---; Boulanger, Alta; Daut; 9; F
896; 880; ---; Boulanger, Lenora; Daut; 8; F
897; 881; ---; Boulanger, Nellie; Daut; 6; F

898; 882; ---; Boulanger, W.J.; Head; 37; M
899; 883; ---; Boulanger, Edward Mc; Son; 16; M

301

*CENSUS of the*_____ **Osage**_____ *Indians of*_____ **Osage**_____ *Agency,* __Okla.__
on ___**June 30, 1911**__ *, 19__, taken by* __**Hugh Pitzer, Supt. & Spl. Disb. Agent**__

Key: Number - Last/Present; Indian Name (if given); English Name (if given); Relationship; Age; Sex.

900; 884; ---; Boulanger, May; Daut; 15; F
901; 885; ---; Boulanger, Evart; Son; 11; M

902; 886; ---; Bockius, Dora; Head; 28; F
903; 887; ---; Bockius, Cyril D.; Son; 13; M
904; 888; ---; Bockius, Earnest F.; Son; 10; M
905; 889; ---; Bockius, Mary B.; Daut; 8; F
906; 890; ---; Bockius, Milton J.; Son; 4; M

907; 891; ---; Boren, Blanche; Head; 25; F
908; 892; ---; Boren, Kathleen; Daut; 6; F
909; 893; ---; Boren, Evaleen; Daut; 6; F

910; 894; ---; Bowhan, Ida M.; Head; 30; F
911; 895; ---; Bowhan, Francis D.; Son; 10; M
912; 896; ---; Bowhan, Sewel C.; Son; 7; M
913; 897; ---; Bowhan, Erin S.; Son; 5; M

914; 898; ---; Bowhan, Marie B.; Head; 25; F
915; 899; ---; Bowhan, John C.; Son; 6; M
916; 900; ---; Bowhan, Harry; Son; 3; M

917; 901; ---; Bowhan, Rosetta; Head; 24; F
918; 902; ---; Bowhan, Mildred L.; Daut; 7; F
919; 903; ---; Bowhan, Ben; Son; 5; M

920; 904; ---; Brook, Lavaria; Head; 31; F
921; 905; ---; Brook, Winona V.; Daut; 4; F

922; 906; ---; Bray, Emma; Head; 32; F
923; 907; ---; McGath, John W.; Son; 14; M

924; 908; ---; Bradshaw, Rose E.; Head; 37; F
925; 909; ---; Bradshaw, Thomas S.; Son; 20; M
926; 910; ---; Bradshaw, Harry A.; Son; 17; M
927; 911; ---; Bradshaw, Alvin S.; Son; 15; M
928; 912; ---; Bradshaw, Sarah A.; Daut; 13; F
929; 913; ---; Bradshaw, Greta E.; Daut; 11; F
930; 914; ---; Bradshaw, Alva F.; Daut; 9; F
931; 915; ---; Bradshaw, Irene A.; Daut; 7; F

932; 916; ---; Bradshaw, George W.; Son; 5; M
933; 917; ---; Bradshaw, Courtland A.; Son; 3; M

933 ½; 918; ---; Brown, Mable; Head; 25; F

934; 919; ---; Brown, Charles; Head; 50; M

Key: Number - Last/Present; Indian Name (if given); English Name (if given); Relationship; Age; Sex.

935;   920;   ---; Brown, Bernice; Daut; 19; F
936;   921;   ---; Brown, Treva; Daut; 13; F

937;   922;   ---; Brown, Edward; Head; 44; M

938;   923;   ---; Brown, Earnest; Head; 39; M
939;   924;   ---; Brown, Maude; Daut; 16; F
940;   925;   ---; Brown, Laura J.; Daut; 13; F
941;   926;   ---; Brown, William P.; Son; 12; M
942;   927;   ---; Brown, Lula B.; Daut; 7; F
943;   928;   ---; Brown, Helen M.; Daut; 4; F

944;   929;   ---; Brown, A.H.; Head; 51; M
945;   930;   ---; Brown, William S.; Son; 9; m
946;   931;   ---; Brown, Frank R.; Son; 6; m

947;   932;   ---; Brown, Mary J.; Head; 44; F
948;   933;   ---; Brown, Edith; Daut; 18; F
949;   934;   ---; Brown, Louis M.; Son; 16; M

950;   935;   ---; Brown, Hatie[sic] B.; Head; 23; F

951;   936;   ---; Brunt, Edward; Head; 51; M
952;   937;   ---; Brunt, George E.; Son; 20; M
953;   938;   ---; Brunt, Joseph L.; Son; 12; M

954;   939;   ---; Brunt, Theodore; Head; 25; M

955;   940;   ---; Bruce, Elsie F; Head; 41; F
956;   941;   ---; Bruce, Louisa; Daut; 17; F
957;   942;   ---; Bruce, Lena; Daut; 15; F
958;   943;   ---; Bruce, Adelbert; Son; 19; M

959;   944;   ---; Nix, Josephine, nee Bratton; Head; 31; F
960;   945;   ---; Bratton, William E.; Son; 12; M
961;   946;   ---; Bratton, Edmund S.; Son; 9; M
962;   947;   ---; Bratton, John I.; Son; 6; M

963;   948;   ---; Breeding, Mary L.; Head; 46; F
964;   949;   ---; Breeding, Leta M.; Daut; 16; F
965;   950;   ---; Breeding, Francis; Son; 14; M
966;   951;   ---; Breeding, Elsie E.; Daut; 11; F

967;   952;   ---; Brooks, Philomena; Head; 31; F
968;   953;   ---; Brooks, Sylvester; Son; 13; M
969;   954;   ---; Brooks, Dolleretta; Daut; 12; F
970;   955;   ---; Brooks, Ruby A.; Daut; 10; F

303

*CENSUS of the*___**Osage**___*Indians of*___**Osage**___*Agency,*_**Okla.**_

*on*___**June 30, 1911**_, *19__, taken by*_**Hugh Pitzer, Supt. & Spl. Disb. Agent**_

Key: Number - Last/Present; Indian Name (if given); English Name (if given); Relationship; Age; Sex.

971;   956;   ---; Brooks, Del Orier; Son; 7; M

972;   957;   ---; Bryant, Joe; Head; 59; M
973;   958;   ---; Bryant, Frank; Son; 17; M
974;   959;   ---; Bryant, Della M.; Daut; 16; F
975;   960;   ---; Bryant, Carrie M.; Daut; 14; F
976;   961;   ---; Bryant, Cecil; Son; 12; M
977;   962;   ---; Bryant, Arthur; Son; 11; M
978;   963;   ---; Bryant, Anna B.; Daut; 8; F
979;   964;   ---; Bryant, Arena; Daut; 5; F

980;   965;   ---; Burton, Roy B.; Son; 15; M

981;   966;   ---; Carr, Nelson; Son; 15; M
982;   967;   ---; Carr, Cassie M.; Daut; 11; F

983;   968;   ---; Carpenter, Mary E.; Head; 41; F
984;   969;   ---; Carpenter, Floyd H.; Son; 20; M
985;   970;   ---; Carpenter, Charles E.; Son; 16; M
986;   971;   ---; Carpenter, Rose B.; Daut; 14; F
987;   972;   ---; Carpenter, Louis S.; Son; 12; M

988;   973;   ---; Carter, Alva E.; Son; 13; M
989;   974;   ---; Carter, Leota M.; Daut; 11; F
990;   975;   ---; Carter, Iarton[sic] D.; Son; 17; M
991;   976;   ---; Carter, Chrales[sic] A; Son; 15; M

992;   977;   ---; Callahan, Alfred; Head; 28; M

993;   978;   ---; Callahan, Cornelius; Head; 36; M

994;   979;   ---; Callahan, Julia; Head; 29; F
995;   980;   ---; Callahan, Rosemary; Daut; 5; F

996;   981;   ---; Callahan, William; Head; 33; M

997;   982;   ---; Callahan, Leo; Son; 13; M
998;   983;   ---; Callahan, Charles; Son; 11; M
999;   984;   ---; Callahan, Mary; Daut; 10; F
1000; 985;   ---; Callahan, Gertrude; Daut; 8; F

1001; 986;   ---; Canville, Clara; Daut; 13; F
1002; 987;   ---; Canville, John B.; Son; 10; M
1003; 988;   ---; Canville. Agnes L.; Daut; 8; F

1004; 989;   ---; Canville. Cecil; Son; 13; M
1005; 990;   ---; Canville. John; Son; 17; M

Key: Number - Last/Present; Indian Name (if given); English Name (if given); Relationship; Age; Sex.

1006;   991;   ---; Canville, Acuda; Daut; 7; F

1007;   992;   ---; Carlton, Anthony; Head; 39; M
1008;   993;   ---; Carlton, Mary E.; Wife; 30; F
1009;   994;   ---; Carlton, Eva M.; Daut; 13; F
1010;   995;   ---; Carlton, Ethel; Daut; 12; F
1011;   996;   ---; Carlton, Frances; Daut; 10; F

1012;   997;   ---; Carlton, George; Head; 34; M
1013;   998;   ---; Carlton, Augustine; Daut; 11; F
1014;   999;   ---; Carlton, Robert; Son; 9; M
1016;   1000;   ---; Carlton, George Jr.; Son; 6; M
1017;   1001;   ---; Carlton, Ella; Daut; 4; [F]

1018;   1002;   ---; Cedar, William; Son; 15; M

1019;   1003;   ---; Cedar, Paul; Orphan; 13; M

1020;   1004;   ---; Cheshewalla, Evart; Son; 14; M
1021;   1005;   ---; Cheshewalla, Floyd; Son; 12; M

1022;   1006;   ---; Childers, Nola; Orphan; 12; F

1023;   1007;   ---; Chouteau, Henry; Head; 26; M
1024;   1008;   ---; Chouteau, Robert; Son; 2; M

1025;   1009;   ---; Chouteau, Stewart; Head; 24; M

1026;   1010;   ---; Chouteau, Louis P.; Head; 23; M

1027;   1011;   ---; Clem, William; Head; 33; M
1028;   1012;   ---; Clem, William L.; Son; 11; M
1029;   1013;   ---; Clem, John E.; Son; 10; M
1030;   1014;   ---; Clem, James A.; Son; 6; M
1031;   1015;   ---; Clem, Frantz; Son; 5; M
1032;   1016;   ---; Clem, May M.; Daut; 2; F

1033;   1017;   ---; Clem, James J.; Head; 36; M
1034;   1018;   ---; Clem, Jessie M.; Daut; 15; F
1035;   1019;   ---; Clem, William H.; Son; 13; M
1036;   1020;   ---; Clem, James E.; Son; 10; m
1037;   1021;   ---; Clem, Sallie J.; Daut; 8; F

1038;   1022;   ---; Clewien, Anna; Head; 30; F
1039;   1023;   ---; Clewien, Clarabell; Daut; 6; F
1040;   1024;   ---; Clewien, Frances; Daut; 4; F

Key: Number - Last/Present; Indian Name (if given); English Name (if given); Relationship; Age; Sex.

1041; 1025; ---; Clawson, Josiah G.; Head; 23; M

1042; 1026'; ---; Clawson, Emma C.; Daut; 20; F
1043; 1027; ---; Clawson, Thomas A.; Son; 16; M

1044; 1028; ---; Clawson, George B.; Son; 14; M

1045; 1029; ---; Collins, Mary; Head; 75; F

1046; 1030; ---; Colby, Ora; Head; 31; F
1047; 1031; ---; Hardy, Orel; Son; 7; M
1048; 1032; ---; Hardy, Mary I.; Daut; 4; F

1049; 1033; ---; Cooper, Anna L.; Head; 29; F
1050; 1034; ---; Cooper, William O.; Son; 11; M
1051; 1035; ---; Cooper, Francis; Son; 8; M
1052; 1036; ---; Cooper, Edward E.; Son; 5; M

1053; 1037; ---; Conner, Woodie; Head; 28; M
1054; 1038; ---; Conner, Theil L.; Daut; 6; F

1055; 1039; ---; Conner, George; Head; 40; M
1056; 1040; ---; Conner, Adelia; Daut; 10; F
1057; 1041; ---; Conner, Victoria W.; 6; M
1058; 1042; ---; Conner, Daniel I.; Son; 4; M

1059; 1043; ---; Cottingham, Ida; Head; 25; F
1060; 1044; ---; Cottingham, Vera L.; Daut; 8; F
1061; 1045; ---; Cottingham, Logan; Son; 6; M

1062; 1046; ---; Collins, Lula; Head; 36; F
1063; 1047; ---; Collins, John W.; Son; 12; M
1064; 1048; ---; Collins, Roy W.; Son; 9; M

1065; 1049; ---; Conness, Veva; Head; 39; F
1066; 1050; ---; Conness, Geneva M.; Daut; 12; F
1067; 1051; ---; Conness, William S.; Son; 6; M

1068; 1052; ---; Conway, Jane; Head; 83; F

1069; 1053; ---; Crouse, Isabella Fuller; Head; 45; F
1070; 1054; ---; Crouse, Earl; Son; 19; M
1071; 1055; ---; Crouse, Laura I.; Daut; 15; F
1072; 1056; ---; Crouse, Stephen M.; Son; 12; M

1073; 1057; ---; Crouse, Dallas; Head; 25; M

306

Key: Number - Last/Present; Indian Name (if given); English Name (if given); Relationship; Age; Sex.

1074; 1058; ---; Crane, Marie; Head; 38; F
1075; 1059; ---; Crane, Frankie M.; Daut; 4; F

1076; 1060; ---; Cross, Ellen; Head; 30; F
1077; 1061; ---; Cross, Lou M.; Daut; 11; F
1078; 1062; ---; Cross, Charles L.; Son; 8; M
1079; 1063; ---; Cross, Candis J.; Daut; 4; F

1080; 1064; ---; Cunningham, Laura; Head; 37; F
1081; 1065; ---; Cunningham, Edward R.; Son; 12; M

1082; 1066; ---; Cunningham, Rose I.; Head; 41; F
1083; 1067; ---; Cunningham, Robert B.; Son; 12; M

1084; 1068; ---; Cunningham, John M.; Head; 23; M

1085; 1069; ---; Curtis, Mary; Head; 54; F
1086; 1070; ---; Farrell, Virgil L.; Son; 20; M
1087; 1071; ---; Curtis, Lethia B.; Daut; 16; F
1088; 1072; ---; Curtis, Ada; Daut; 13; F

1089; 1070[3]; ---; Daniel, Sophia; Head; 35; F
1090; 1074; ---; Daniel, Bessie; Daut; 17; F
1091; 1075; ---; Daniel, Vernie; Son; 15; M
1092; 1076; ---; Daniel, Pearl C.; Son; 13; M
1093; 1077; ---; Daniel, Ida I.; Daut; 10; F

1094; 1078; ---; Davis, Sophia; Head; 70; F

1095; 1079; ---; Davis, Mary J.; Head; 62; F
1096; 1080; ---; LaSarge, Minnie E.; Head; 22; F

1097; 1081; ---; Daily, Dora; Head; 29; F
1098; 1082; ---; Dial, Lawton M.; Son; 10; M
1099; 1083; ---; Dial, Elsie A,; Daut; 12; F

1100; 1084; ---; Darnell, Rebecca J.; Head; 48; F
1101; 1085; ---; Vadney, Amy V.; Daut; 20; F

1102; 1086; ---; Dennison, Eliza; Head; 42; F
1103; 1087; ---; Fugate, Frank B.; Son; 21; M
1104; 1088; ---; Fugate, John A.; Son; 20; M
1105; 1089; ---; Dennison, Nellie; Daut; 10; F
1106; 1090; ---; Dennison, George O.; Son; 5; M

1107; 1091; ---; Dennison, Bert; Head; 26
1108; 1092; ---; Dennison, Florence L.; Daut; 4; F

307

*CENSUS of the*___**Osage**___*Indians of*___**Osage**___*Agency,*__**Okla.**__
*on*___**June 30, 1911**__, *19*__, *taken by*__**Hugh Pitzer, Supt. & Spl. Disb. Agent**__

Key: Number - Last/Present; Indian Name (if given); English Name (if given); Relationship; Age; Sex.

1109; 1093; ---; Del Orier, Julia; Head; 61; F

1010; 1094; ---; Del Orier, Louis; Son; 5; M

1111; 1095; ---; De Noya, Louis; Head; 50; M
1112; 1096; ---; De Noya, Freferick[sic]; Son; 19; M
1113; 1097; ---; De Noya, Clement; Son; 17; M
1114; 1098; ---; De Noya, Josephine; Daut; 15; F
1115; 1099; ---; De Noya, Ruby P.; Daut; 13; F

1116; 1100; ---; De Noya, Frank; Head; 54; M
1118; 1101; ---; De Noya, Clara; Daut; 20; F
1119; 1102; ---; De Noya, Grace; Daut; 18; F
1120; 1103; ---; De Noya, Alfred R.; Son; 17; M
1121; 1104; ---; De Noya, Charlotte; Daut; 15; F
1122; 1105; ---; De Noya, Myrtle C.; Daut; 13; F
1123; 1106; ---; De Noya, Catherine I.; Daut; [8]; F
1124; 1107; ---; De Noya, Walter L.; Son; 5; M

1125; 1108; ---; De Noya, Jacob; Head; 32; M
1126; 1109; ---; De Noya, Belle; Wife; 31; F
1127; 1110; ---; De Noya, Virgil H.; Son; 10; M
1128; 1111; ---; De Noya, Maurice H.; Son; 8; M
1129; 1112; ---; De Noya, Lillian C.; Daut; 7; F
1130; 1113; ---; De Noya, Helen D; Daut; 5; F

1131; 1114; ---; De Noya, Joseph; Head; 34; M
1132; 1115; ---; De Noya, Charlotte E.; Daut; 7; F
1133; 1116; ---; De Noya, Margaret I.; Daut; 8; F
1134; 1117; ---; De Noya, Martha M.; Daut; 5; F

1135; 1118; ---; De Noya, Clement; Head; 44; M
1136; 1119; ---; De Noya, Emily; Wife; 40; F
1137; 1120; ---; De Noya, Clement Jr.; Son; 21; M
1138; 1121; ---; De Noya, Louis; Son; 17; M
1139; 1122; ---; De Noya, Sadie; Daut; 15; F
1140; 1123; ---; De Noya, Edna; Daut; 9; F
1141; 1124; ---; De Noya, Elizabeth; Daut; 7; F
1142; 1125; ---; De Noya, Millard; Son; 5; M
1142 ½; 1126; ---; De Noya, Elsie; Daut; 11; F

1143; 1127; ---; De Noya, Wesley; Head; 20; M
1144; 1128; ---; De Noya, Odell; Wife; 21; F

1145; 1129; ---; De Noya, Everette A.; Head; 24; M

1147; 1130; ---; Deal, Mary J.; Head; 22; F

CENSUS of the_____Osage_____ Indians of_____Osage_____ Agency, __Okla.__
on ___June 30, 1911__, 19__, taken by __Hugh Pitzer, Supt. & Spl. Disb. Agent__

Key: Number - Last/Present; Indian Name (if given); English Name (if given); Relationship; Age; Sex.

1148; 1131; ---; Deal, James C.; Son; 5; M
1149; 1132; ---; Deal, William M.; Son; 3; M

1150; 1133; ---; Deal, Julia A.; Head; 56; F
1151; 1134; ---; Deal, Sherman; Son; 20; M

1152; 1135; ---; Dickey, James A.; Head; 30; M

1153; 1136; ---; Dickey, John T.; Head; 27; M

1154; 1137; ---; Dial, Eliza; Head; 51; F
1155; 1138; ---; Penn, Augustus; Son; 21; M
1156; 1139; ---; Penn, Rose E.; Daut; 19; F
1157; 1140; ---; Dial, Cora E.; Daut; 14; F
1158; 1141; ---; Dial, Eva; Daut; 12; F
1159; 1142; ---; Dial, Chrales[sic] P.; Son; 6; M
1160; 1143; ---; Huston, John R.; Adpt. Son; 20; M

1161; 1144; ---; Donelson, Frances; Head; 28; F
1162; 1145; ---; Donelson, Robert L.; Son; 9; M
1163; 1146; ---; Donelson, James L.; Son; 12; M

1164; 1147; ---; Doolin, Martha; Head; 26; F
1165; 1148; ---; Doolin, Alta J.; Daut; 4; F

1166; 1149; ---; Donovan, Augustine; Head; 59; F
1167; 1150; ---; Donovan, Jesse C.; Son; 18; M

1168; 1151; ---; Donovan, Charles; Head; 22; M

1169; 1152; ---; Ducotey, Stanislaus; Head; 37; M
1170; 1153; ---; Ducotey, Versa; Daut; 13; F
1171; 1154; ---; Ducotey, Manza; Daut; 11; F
1172; 1155; ---; Ducotey, Bettie V.; Daut; 8; F
1173; 1156; ---; Ducotey, Frank S.; Son; 6; M

1174; 1157; ---; Dun[sic], Dora; Head; 33; F
1175; 1158; ---; Dun[sic], Ida M; Daut; 15; F
1176; 1159; ---; Dun[sic], Mary A.; Daut; 13; F
1177; 1160; ---; Dun[sic], Timothy J.; Son; 7; M

1178; 1161; ---; Durham, Martha; Head; 81; F

1179; 1162; ---; Dunn, Nettie M.; Head; 24; F

1180; 1163; ---; Easley, Margaret; Head; 39; F
1181; 1164; ---; Easley, Pearl; Daut; 19; F

Key: Number - Last/Present; Indian Name (if given); English Name (if given); Relationship; Age; Sex.

1182; 1165; ---; Easley, George E.; Son; 17; M
1183; 1166; ---; Easley, Leo B.; Son; 15; M
1184; 1167; ---; Easley, John W.; Son; 13; M
1185; 1168; ---; Easley, Mary E.; Daut; 10; F
1186; 1169; ---; Easley, Clarence A.; Son; 7; M
1187; 1170; ---; Easley, Robert J.; Son; 4; M

1188; 1171; ---; Edwards, Julia; Head; 45; F
1189; 1172; ---; Quinton, Agnes; Daut; 15; F
1190; 1173; ---; Quinton, Pearl C.; Daut; 13; F
1191; 1174; ---; Quinton, Elnora; Daut; 9; F
1192; 1175; ---; Edwards, Theodore; Son; 4; M

1193; 1176; ---; Quinton, Alex; Head; 22; M

1194; 1177; ---; Edmiston, Frances (Incompt); Head; 35; F
1195; 1178; ---; Edmiston, Bessie E.; Daut; 9; F

1196; 1179; ---; Evans, Mary E.; Head; 25; F

1197; 1180; ---; Easley, Irene; Head; 19; F

1198; 1181; ---; Farrell, Nathaniel; Head; 34; M
1199; 1182; ---; Farrell, Ruth; Daut; 11; F
1200; 1183; ---; Farrell, Andrew; Son; 8; M

1201; 1184; ---; Farrell, Mary; Head; 23; F

1202; 1185; ---; Farrell, Charles; Head; 29; M
1203; 1186; ---; Farrell, Mary; Daut; 8; F
1204; 1187; ---; Farrell, Pearl; Daut; 4; F

1205; 1188; ---; Farrell, Monica; Head; 56; F
1206; 1189; ---; Shaw, Moses R.; Son; 21; M

1207; 1190; ---; Shaw, Charles M.; Head; 22; M

1208; 1191; ---; Fenton, Margaret; Head; 28; F
1209; 1192; ---; Fenton, Sylvester R,; Son; 10; M
1210; 1193; ---; Fenton, Louis L.; Son; 9; M
1211; 1194; ---; Fenton, Curtis D.; Son; 6; M
1212; 1195; ---; Fenton, Lenora; Daut; 3; F

1213; 1196; ---; Fox, Susie; Head; 49; F
1214; 1197; ---; Lombard, Sylvester; Son; 21; M
1215; 1198; ---; Lombard, Augustine; Daut; 18; F
1216; 1199; ---; Lombard, Joseph; Son; 16; M

310

CENSUS of the_____**Osage**_____ Indians of _____**Osage**_____ Agency, __**Okla.**__
on ___**June 30, 1911**___, 19__, taken by __**Hugh Pitzer, Supt. & Spl. Disb. Agent**__

Key: Number - Last/Present; Indian Name (if given); English Name (if given); Relationship; Age; Sex.

1217; 1200; ---; Lombard, Paul; Son; 12; M
1218; 1201; ---; Fox, Alexander; Son; 9; M

1219; 1202; ---; Fronkier, Laban A.; Head; 21; M

1220; 1203; ---; Fronkier, William; Head; 40; M

1221; 1204; ---; Fronkier, Simon; Head; 39; M
1222; 1205; ---; Fronkier, Florence; Daut; 15; F
1223; 1206; ---; Fronkier, Blanche L.; Daut; 13; F
1224; 1207; ---; Fronkier, Benjamin; Son; 9; M

1225; 1208; ---; Fronkier, Philip; Head; 23; M

1226; 1209; ---; Fronkier, Augustus; Head; 33; M

1227; 1210; ---; Fronkier, James; Head; 32; M
1228; 1211; ---; Fronkier, Louis B.; Son; 5; M

1229; 1212; ---; Fuller, Thomas; Head; 30; M

1230; 1213; ---; Fuller, Louis; Head; 35; F
1231; 1214; ---; Fuller, Andrew B.; Son; 9; M
1232; 1215; ---; Fuller, Charles; Head; 27; M

1233; 1216; ---; Fish, Eliza; Head; 22; F

1234; 1217; ---; Gaylor, Victoria; Head; 46; F

1235; 1218; ---; George, James M.; Head; 58; M
1236; 1219; ---; George, James I.; Son; 5; M

1237; 1220; ---; George, Sylvester; Head; 27; M

1239; 1221; ---; Gilmore; S. J.; Orphan; 20; M

1240; 1222; ---; Gilmore, William H.; Son; 14; M

1241; 1223; ---; Girard, Amelia; Head; 37; F
1242; 1224; ---; Girard, Mary E. C.; Daut; 17; F
1243; 1225; ---; Girard, Corine A.; Daut; 16; F
1244; 1226; ---; Girard, Amelia V.; Daut; 15; F
1245; 1227; ---; Girard, Leona; Daut; 13; F

1246; 1228; ---; Grammer. Maggie; Head; 28; F

1247; 1229; ---; Goad, Clara; Head; 31; F

Key: Number - Last/Present; Indian Name (if given); English Name (if given); Relationship; Age; Sex.

1248; 1230;   ---; Goad, Cecil J.; Son; 9; M
1249; 1231;   ---; Goad, Ethel; Daut; 4; F

1250; 1232;   ---; Groves, Agnes; Head; 29; F
1251; 1233;   ---; Groves, Mural W.; Son; 9; M
1252; 1234;   ---; Groves, Mary L.; Daut; 7; F
1253; 1235;   ---; Groves, Harry L.; Son; 4; M

1254; 1236;   ---; Harrelson, Mary L. (Incpt); Head; 31; F
1255; 1237;   ---; Harrelson, Emerine; Daut; 13; F

1256; 1238;   ---; Hall, Ida; Head; 26; F
1257; 1239;   ---; Hall, Alfred; Son; 7; M

1258; 1240;   ---; Harruff, Margaret; Head; 47; M[sic] [F]
1259; 1241;   ---; Harruff, Julia; Daut; 15; F

1260; 1242;   ---; Hardy, Emily; Head; 38; M
1261; 1243;   ---; Hardy, Louisa V.; Daut; 17; F
1262; 1244;   ---; Hardy, Goldie; Daut; 14; F
1263; 1245;   ---; Hardy, Geneva; Daut; 11; F
1264; 1246;   ---; Hardy, William R.; Son; 7; M

1265; 1247;   ---; Hampton, Charles; Head; 31; M
1266; 1248;   ---; Hampton, Roland C.; Son; 5; M

1267; 1249;   ---; Hampton, Rosalie; Head; 50; F

1268; 1250;   ---; Hayes, Pearl; Head; 31; F
1269; 1251;   ---; Hayes, Olivia; Daut; 7; F
1270; 1252;   ---; Hayes, Elizabeth; Daut; 7; F
1271; 1253;   ---; Hayes, Margaret; Daut; 4; F

1272; 1254;   ---; Harlow, Josephine; Head; 32; F
1273; 1255;   ---; Harlow, John N.; Son; 14; M

1274; 1256;   ---; Hayes, Lawrence L.; Son; 6; M

1275; 1257;   ---; Harlow, Susan; Head; 49; F
1276; 1258;   ---; Akers, Grace; Daut; 20; F
1277; 1259;   ---; Gilcrease, Belle M; Daut; 17; F
1258[7]; 1260;   ---; Harlow, Charles C.; Son; 13; M

1279; 1261;   ---; Haynie, Mary; Head; 26; F
1280; 1262;   ---; Haynie, Willie; S. Son; 16; M
1281; 1263;   ---; Haynie, John C.; Son; 6; M
1282; 1264;   ---; Haynie, Emma; Daut; 5; F

CENSUS of the___**Osage**___ *Indians of*___**Osage**___ *Agency,* __Okla.__
on ___**June 30, 1911**___, *19__, taken by* __Hugh Pitzer, Supt. & Spl. Disb. Agent__

Key: Number - Last/Present; Indian Name (if given); English Name (if given); Relationship; Age; Sex.

1283; 1265; ---; Hackleman, Julia Ann; Head; 66; F

1284; 1266; ---; Harris, Mary E.; Head; 30; F

1285; 1267; ---; Harvey, Adeline; Head; 29; F

1286; 1268; ---; Heenan, Anna; Head; 29; F
1287; 1269; ---; Heeman, Beatrice M.; Daut; Daut[sic]--; --

1288; 1270; ---; Herard, Paul; Head; 43; M

1289; 1271; ---; Herard, Eugene; Head; 26; M

1290; 1272; ---; Herridge, Joseph; Son; 20; M
1291; 1273; ---; Herridge, Lula; Daut; 17; F
1292; 1274; ---; Hewitt, Rosa; Head; 25; F
1293; 1275; ---; Hewitt, Valaria; Daut; 5; F
1294; 1276; ---; Hewitt, Loretta M.; Daut; 4; F

1295; 1277; ---; Hildebrand, George; Head; 28; M

1296; 1278; ---; Hildebrand, Richard; Head; 32; M

1297; 1279; ---; Hildebrand, David; Head; 38; M
1298; 1280; ---; Hildebrand, Nancy; Daut; 10; F

1299; 1281; ---; Hildebrand, James; Head; 42; M
1300; 1282; ---; Hildebrand, Oragonia; Daut; 16; F
1301; 1283; ---; Hildebrand, Dica; Daut; 11; F
1302; 1284; ---; Hildebrand, Susan; Daut; 17; F

1303; 1285; ---; Hildebrand, Joseph; Head; 44; M
1304; 1286; ---; Hildebrand, Frank; Son; 13; M

1305; 1287; ---; Hickman, Clementine; Head; 34; F
1306; 1288; ---; Hickman, Homer; Son; 15; M
1307; 1289; ---; Hickman, Edna J.; Daut; 12; F
1308; 1290; ---; Hickman, Franklin; Son; 11; M
1309; 1291; ---; Hickman, Florence; Daut; 9; F
1310; 1292; ---; Hickman, Lillie V.; Daut; 7; F
1311; 1293; ---; Hickman, Bertha C.; Daut; 5; F
1312; 1294; ---; Hickman, Roy N.; Son; 4; M

1313; 1295; ---; Holloway, Jasper C.; Head; 59; M

1314; 1296; ---; Holloway, Milton; Head; 28; M
1315; 1297; ---; Holloway, Andrew L.; [Son]; 8; M

313

*CENSUS of the*___**Osage**___*Indians of*___**Osage**___*Agency,*__**Okla.**__
*on*___**June 30, 1911**___*, 19__, taken by*___**Hugh Pitzer, Supt. & Spl. Disb. Agent**

Key: Number - Last/Present; Indian Name (if given); English Name (if given); Relationship; Age; Sex.

1316;   1298;   ---; Holloway, Olita M.; Daut; 5; F

1317;   1299;   ---; Horn, Polly; Head; 29; F
1318;   1300;   ---; Buxbaum, Vernon E.; Son; 10; M

1319;   1301;   ---; Hoots, Rosa; Head; 42; F
1320;   1302;   ---; Hoots, Agnes; Daut; 16; F

1321;   1303;   ---; Hoots, Alfred; Head; 24; M

1322;   1304;   ---; Hunt, Mary A.; Head; 41; F
1323;   1305;   ---; Hunt, Lula B.; Daut; 14; F
1324;   1306;   ---; Hunt, Mary G.; Daut; 12; F
1325;   1307;   ---; Hunt, Andrew D.; Son; 9; M
1326;   1308;   ---; Hunt, Robert M. Jr; Son; 4; M

1327;   1309;   ---; Hunt, Antwine; Head; 23; M

1328;   1310;   ---; James, Jesse; Head; 23; M

1329;   1311;   ---; Javine, Peter; Head; 59; M
1330;   1312;   ---; Javine, Hasread; Son; 20; M
1331;   1313;   ---; Javine, Viola M.; Daut; --[16]; F
1332;   1314;   ---; Javine, Opal; Daut; 5; F
1333;   1315;   ---; Javine, Howard Taft; Son; 3; M

1334;   1316;   ---; Javine, Benjamin H.; Head; 22; M

1335;   1317;   ---; Javine, Roy V.; Son; 15; M

1336;   1318;   ---; Javine, John; Head; 56; M
1337;   1319;   ---; Javine, Ollie; Daut; 21; F
1338;   1320;   ---; Javine, Audra; Daut; 18; F
1339;   1321;   ---; Javine, Ora E.; Daut; 17; F
1340;   1322;   ---; Javine, Joseph; Son; 14; M

1341;   1323;   ---; Javine, Anthony; Head; 24; M

1342;   1324;   ---; Javine, John; Head; 29; M
1343;   1325;   ---; Javine, George M.; Son; 7; M
1344;   1326;   ---; Javine, Earl T.; Son; 5; M
1345;   1327;   ---; Javine, Ella C.; Daut; 3; F

1346;   1328;   ---; Johnson, Julia M.; Head; 56; F
1347;   1329;   ---; Johnson, John W.; Head; 22; M

1348;   1330;   ---; Jones, Laura; Head; 25; F

314

Key: Number - Last/Present; Indian Name (if given); English Name (if given); Relationship; Age; Sex.

1349; 1331;   ---; Jones, James F.; Son; 6; M

1350; 1332;   ---; Kennedy, Agnes; Head; 35; F
1351; 1333;   ---; Kennedy, James A.; Son; 13; M
1352; 1334;   ---; Kennedy, Forrest L.; Son; 10; M
1353; 1335;   ---; Kennedy, Thelma; Daut; 10; F
1354; 1336;   ---; Kennedy, Cordelia A.; Daut; 7; F
1355; 1337;   ---; Kennedy, Samuel G.; Son; 5; M

1356; 1338;   ---; Kennedy, Mable; Head; 31; F
1357; 1339;   ---; Kennedy, Albert A.; S. Son; 17; M

1358; 1340;   ---; Kennedy, Samuel; Head; 25; M
1359; 1341;   ---; Kennedy, Don C.; Son; 4; M

1360; 1342;   ---; Keeler, Blanche; Head; 29; F
1361; 1343;   ---; Keeler, Dixie; Son; 7; M
1362; 1344;   ---; Keeler Alberta M.; Daut; 5; F

1363; 1345;   ---; Kilbie, Benedict; Head; 25; M
1364; 1346;   ---; Kilbie, John A.; Son; 5; M

1365; 1347;   ---; Krebs, Henry; Son; 15; M

1366; 1348;   ---; Lawrence, Maggie; Head; 54; F

1367; 1349;   ---; Labadie, Charles; Head; 40; M
1368; 1350;   ---; Labadie, Hazel; Daut; 13; F
1369; 1351;   ---; Labadie, Frank; Son; 11; M
1370; 1352;   ---; Labadie, Alvin L.; Son; 9; M
1371; 1353;   ---; Labadie, Nita; Daut; 7; F
1372; 1354;   ---; Labadie, Ralph; Son; 3; M

1373; 1355;   ---; Labadie, William H,; Head; 26; M
1374; 1356;   ---; Labadie, Mary Ellen; Daut; 3; F

1375; 1357;   ---; Labadie, Ella; Head; 24; F

1376; 1358;   ---; Labadie, Frederick; Son; 21; M
1377; 1359;   ---; Labadie, Earnie; Son; 20; M
1378; 1360;   ---; Labadie, Joseph; Son; 18; M

1379; 1361;   ---; Labadie, Edwrad[sic]; Head; 45; M
1380; 1362;   ---; Labadie, Milton; Son; 13; M
1381; 1363;   ---; Labadie, Rose M.; Daut; 10; F
1382; 1364;   ---; Labadie, Robert E.; Son; 8; M
1383; 1365;   ---; Labadie, Charles W.; Son; 6; M

Key: Number - Last/Present; Indian Name (if given); English Name (if given); Relationship; Age; Sex.

1384; 1366; ---; Labadie, William H.; Son; 3; M

1385; 1367; ---; Labadie, Frank; Head; 50; M
1386; 1368; ---; Labadie, G.V.; Son; 19; M
1387; 1369; ---; Labadie, Paul F; Son; 16; M

1388; 1370; ---; Labadie, John; Head; 24; M

1389; 1371; ---; Lasarge, Marie; Daut; 17; F
1390; 1372; ---; Lasarge, Louis; Son; 15; M
1391; 1373; ---; Lasarge, Athur[sic]; Son; 14; M
1392; 1374; ---; Lasarge, Charles V.; Son; 12; M

1393; 1375; ---; Lasarge, Joseph; Head; 42; M
1394; [1376]; ---; Lasarge, Ellen; Daut; 11; F
1395; 1377; ---; Lasarge, Harold L.; Son; 4; M

1396; 1378; ---; Lane, Joseph; Head; 42; M
1397; 1379; ---; Lane, Zella A.; Wife; 41; F
1398; 1380; ---; Lane, Mary; Daut; 17; F
1399; 1381; ---; Lane, Bessie; Daut; 13; F
1400; 1382; ---; Lane, Joseph C.; Son; 8; M
1401; 1383; ---; Lane, Roy B.; Son; 6; M

1402; 1384; ---; Leahy, Mary L.; Head; 36; F
1403; 1385; ---; Leahy, Bertha; Head; 36; F
1404; 1386; ---; Leahy, Thomas R.; Son; 14; M
1405; 1387; ---; Leahy, Cora W.; Daut; 12; F
1406; 1388; ---; Leahy, Mable A.; Son[sic]; 8; F
1407; 1389; ---; Leahy, Edward A,; Son; 6; M

1408; 1390; ---; Leahy, W.T.; Head; 42; M
1409; 1391; ---; Leahy, Martha; Wife; 83; F [Age 32 in 1910.]
1410; 1392; ---; Leahy, William T. jr.; son; 13; M
1411; 1393; ---; Leahy, B. Thomas; Son; 12; M

1412; 1394; ---; Lewis, Mary; Head; 50; F

1413; 1395; ---; Lessert, Frank; Head; 69; M

1414; 1396; ---; Lessert, Walter; Head; 26; M

1415; 1397; ---; Lessert, Joseph; Head; 27; M

1416; 1398; ---; Lessert, David; Head; 33; M

1417; 1399; ---; Lessert, Guy; Son; 15; M

CENSUS of the **Osage** *Indians of* **Osage** *Agency,* **Okla.**
on **June 30, 1911**, 19__, *taken by* **Hugh Pitzer, Supt. & Spl. Disb. Agent**

Key: Number - Last/Present; Indian Name (if given); English Name (if given); Relationship; Age; Sex.

1418; 1400; ---; Lessert, Millie M.; Daut; 13; F
1419; 1401; ---; Lessert, Charles A.; Son; 11; F
1420; 1402; ---; Lessert, Hattie; Daut; 9; F

1421; 1403; ---; Lessert, Frank Jr.; Head; 47; M
1422; 1404; ---; Lessert, Mary J.; Daut; 16; F
1423; 1405; ---; Lessert, Robert A.; Son; 14; M
1424; 1406; ---; Lessert, Grace J.; Daut; 10; F
1425; 1407; ---; Lessert, Ray L.; Son; 8; M
1426; 1408; ---; Lessert, Dora L.; Daut; 5; F

1427; 1409; ---; Lessert, Benjamin; Head; 40; M
1428; 1410; ---; Lessert, Wade; Son; 20; M
1429; 1411; ---; Lessert, Susie; Daut; 15; F
1430; 1412; ---; Lessert, Benjamin L.; Son; 8; M
1431; 1413; ---; Lessert, Fay; Daut; 13; Daut; 13; F
1432; 1414; ---; Lessert, Fanny; Daut; 5; F

1433; 1415; ---; Lessert, William E.; Head; 22; M

1434; 1416; ---; Lessert, Charles; Head; 44; M

1435; 1417; ---; Liese; Coaina M; Head; 28; F
1436; 1418; ---; Liese; Washaki; Son; 6; M
1437; 1419; ---; Liese; Vivian; Daut; 1; F

1438; 1420; ---; Lohmann, Nettie; Head; 25; F

1439; 1421; ---; Lombard, Albert; Head; 65; M
1440; 1422; ---; Lombard, Bessie; Daut; 17; F
1441; 1423; ---; Lombard, Robert A.; Son; 10; M

1442; 1424; ---; Lombard, Nina; Head; 23; F

1443; 1425; ---; Lombard, Clara; Head; 25; F

1444; 1426; ---; Lombard, John; Head; 27; M

1445; 1427; ---; Lombard, George W.; Head; 32; M
1446; 1428; ---; Lombard, Frank H.; Son; 3; M

1447; 1429; ---; Lombard, John E.; Head; 25; M

1448; 1430; ---; Lombard, Walter; Head; 33; M
1449; 1431; ---; Lombard, Lucy; Daut; 10; F
1450; 1432; ---; Lombard, Lois; Daut; 8; F
1451; 1433; ---; Lombard, Samie; Daut; 7; F

317

CENSUS of the **Osage** *Indians of* **Osage** *Agency,* **Okla.**
on **June 30, 1911** *, 19__, taken by* **Hugh Pitzer, Supt. & Spl. Disb. Agent**

Key: Number - Last/Present; Indian Name (if given); English Name (if given); Relationship; Age; Sex.

1452; 1434; ---; Lyman, Paul S.; Head; 42; M
1453; 1435; ---; Lyman, Agnes; Daut; 8; F
1454; 1436; ---; Lyman, Capitola; Daut; 6; F
1455; 1437; ---; Lyman, Pauline; Daut; 3; F

1456; 1438; ---; Lyman, Arthur J.; Head; 41; M

1457; 1439; ---; Lynn, Mary A.; Head; 34; F
1458; 1440; ---; Lynn, John F.; Son; 16; M
1459; 1441; ---; Lynn, Theresa M.; Daut; 12; F
1460; 1442; ---; Lynn, Patrick; Son; 8; M
1461 1443; ---; Lynn, Joseph; Son; 10; M
1462; 1444; ---; Lynn, William R.; Son; 5; M

1463; 1445; ---; Logan, Ruby; Head; 22; F

1464; 1446; ---; Linley, Susanna; Head; 23; F

1465; 1447; ---; Lockwood, Adeline; Head; 63; F

1466; 1448; ---; Lavely, Anna; Head; 32; F

1467; 1449; ---; Mackey, Joseph; Head; 33; M
1468; 1450; ---; Mackey, Eva; Daut; 13; F
1469; 1451; ---; Mackey, Tenne; Daut; 8; F
1470; 1452; ---; Mackey, Agnes L.; Daut; 7; F
1471; 1453; ---; Mackey, Warren F.; Son; 5; M

1472; 1454; ---; Mackey, William B.; Head; 28; M
1473; 1455; ---; Mackey, Cecelia E.; Daut; 11; F
1474; 1456; ---; Mackey, Bertha M.; Daut; 6; F

1475; 1457; ---; Mackey, Grover; Head; 25; M

1476; 1458; ---; Mann, Stella; Head; 22; F

1477; 1459; ---; Mathews, W.S.; Head; 63; M
1478; 1460; ---; Mathews, John J.; Son; 17; M
1479; 1461; ---; Mathews, Mary I.; Daut; 14; F
1480; 1462; ---; Mathews, Lillian B.; Daut; 12; F
1481; 1463; ---; Mathews, Florence; Daut; 9; F

1482; 1464; ---; Mathews, Sarah J.; Head; 23; F

1483; 1465; ---; Mathews, W.W.; Head; 32; M
1484; 1466; ---; Mathews, Norman S.; Son; 6; M
1485; 1467; ---; Mathews, Anna M.; Daut; 4; F

318

Key: Number - Last/Present; Indian Name (if given); English Name (if given); Relationship; Age; Sex.

1486; 1468; ---; Mathews, John A.; Head; 35; M
1487; 1469; ---; Mathews, Lorenza; Wife; 28; F
1488; 1470; ---; Mathews, John A. Jr.; Son; 10; M
1489; 1471; ---; Mathews, Victoria; Daut; 9; F

1490; 1472; ---; Mathews, Edward O.; Head; 32; M
1491; 1473; ---; Mathews, Alfred E.; Son; 7; M

1492; 1474; ---; Mathes, Thomas S.; Head; 22; M

1493; 1475; ---; Marshall, Sarah; Head; 23; F

[Skipped #'s 1476 and 1477.]

1494; 1478; ---; Martin, Alex; Head; 65; M
1495; 1479; ---; Martin, Bertha; Daut; 16; F

1496; 1480; ---; Martin, Lombard; Head; 23; M

1497; 1481; ---; Martin, Lee; Head; 34; M
1498; 1482; ---; Martin, Dane L.; Daut; 13; F
1499; 1483; ---; Martin, Edgar E.; Son; 10; M
1500; 1484; ---; Martin, Linnie N.; Daut; 7; F

1501; 1485; ---; Martin, Emery; Head; 30; M
1502; 1486; ---; Martin, John D.; Son; 5; M
1503; 1487; ---; Martin, Delmas E.; Son; $[sic] [4]; M

1504; 1488; ---; Martin, Richard; Head; 37; M
1505; 1489; ---; Martin, Nannie V.; Daut; 4; F
1506; 1490; ---; Martin, Claude; Son; 14; M

1507; 1491; ---; Martin, James; Son; 18; M

1508; 1492; ---; Martin, Wilson; Son; 18; M

1509; 1493; ---; Martin, Joeanna; Head; 31; F
1510; 1494; ---; Flippin, Nettie B.; Daut; 13; F

1511; 1495; ---; McCarthy, Lenora; Head; 30; F
1512; 1496; ---; McCarthy, William H.; Son; 10; M
1513; 1497; ---; McCarthy, Solomon; Son; 9; M
1514; 1498; ---; McCarthy, Edna V.; Daut; 6; F
1515; 1499; ---; McCarthy, Charles V.; Son; 6; M

1516; 1500; ---; McCoy, Lillie; Head; 24; F
1517; 1501; ---; McCoy, Richard M.; Son; 4; M

CENSUS of the_____**Osage**_____ Indians of _____**Osage**_____ Agency, **Okla.**
on _____**June 30, 1911**___, 19__, taken by **Hugh Pitzer, Supt. & Spl. Disb. Agent**

Key: Number - Last/Present; Indian Name (if given); English Name (if given); Relationship; Age; Sex.

1518; 1502;   ---; McDaniel, Ellen; Head; 35; F
1519; 1503;   ---; McDaniel, Frederick W.; Son; 15; M

1520; 1504;   ---; McGuire, Mary E.; Head; 38; M
1521; 1505;   ---; McGuire, Ethel; Daut; 20; F
1522; 1506;   ---; McGuire, Leo; Son; 16; M
1523; 1507;   ---; McGuire, Bird A.; Son; 13; M
1524; 1508;   ---; McGuire, William T.; Son; 11; M
1525; 1509;   ---; McGuire, Charles A.; Son; 9; M

1526; 1510;   ---; McComb, Ellen; Head; 33; F
1527; 1511;   ---; McComb, Jessie; Daut; 16; F
1528; 1512;   ---; McComb, Willizam[sic] N.; 13; M
1529; 1513;   ---; McComb, Gladys I.; Daut; 10; F
1530; 1514;   ---; McComb, Rachel B.; Daut; 8; F
1531; 1515;   ---; McComb, Naioma; Daut; 5; F

1531 ½; 1516;   ---; McLaughlin, Nancy; Head; 47; F

1532; 1517;   ---; McLintic, Mary; Head; 34; F
1533; 1518;   ---; McLintic, Aloysia; Daut; 12; F

1534; 1519;   ---; McLain, Minnie; Head; 24; F
1535; 1520;   ---; McLain, Ray S.; Son; 6; M

1536; 1521;   ---; McCowan, Bessie; Head; 21; F

1537; 1522;   ---; Michelle, Estella; Daut; 13; F
1538; 1523;   ---; Michelle, Della; Daut; 10; F

1539; 1524;   ---; Mickels, Arania; Head; 34; F
1540; 1525;   ---; Carr, Delilah; Daut; 9; F
1541; 1526;   ---; Mickels, Clarence D.; Son; 6; M
1542; 1527;   ---; Mickels, Blanche O.; Daut; 3; F

1543; 1528;   ---; Miller, Gurney; Orphan; 13; M

1544; 1529;   ---; Mongrain, Rosa; Daut; 21; F

1545; 1530;   ---; Mongrain, Stewart; Head; 63; M
1546; 1531;   ---; Mongrain, Stewart Jr.; Son; 18; M

1547; 1532;   ---; Mongrain, Ernest; Head; 22; M

1548; 1533;   ---; Mongrain, Hattie; Head; 24; F

1549; 1534;   ---; Mosier; Thomas; Head; 68; M

320

CENSUS of the___**Osage**___Indians of___**Osage**___Agency, **Okla.**
on ___**June 30, 1911**__, 19__, taken by __**Hugh Pitzer, Supt. & Spl. Disb. Agent**__

Key: Number - Last/Present; Indian Name (if given); English Name (if given); Relationship; Age; Sex.

1550; 1535; ---; Mosier; Adeline; Head; 70; F

1551; 1536; ---; Mosier; W.T.; Head; 43; M
1552; 1537; ---; Mosier; Louisa; wife; 36; F
1553; 1538; ---; Mosier; Charles P.; Son; 15; M
1554; 1540; ---; Mosier; John T.; Son; 12; M [Skipped #1539.]
1555; 1541; ---; Mosier; Edwin P.; Son; 9; M
1556; 1542; ---; Mosier; Luther P.; Son; 6; M
1557; 1543; ---; Mosier; Agnes P.; Daut; 6; F
1558; 1544; ---; Mosier; James R.; Son; 4; M

1559; 1545; ---; Mosier; Jacob; Head; 49; M
1560; 1546; ---; Mosier; Stella; Daut; 19; F
1561; 1547; ---; Mosier; Claude; Son; 16; M
1562; 1548; ---; Mosier; Lione[?]; Daut; 13; F

1563; 1549; ---; Mosier; Kate; Head; 23; F

1564; 1550; ---; Mosier; Eugene; Head; 36; M
1565; 1551; ---; Mosier; Mary M.; Daut; 15; F
1566; 1552; ---; Mosier; John J.; Son; 9; M
1567; 1553; ---; Mosier; Ida M.; Daut; 7; F
1568; 1554; ---; Mosier; Walter L.; [Son]; 5; M

1569; 1555; ---; Mosier; Bismark; Head; 28; M
1570; 1556; ---; Mosier; Clara O.; Daut; 7; F
1571; 1557; ---; Mosier; Thelma V.; [Daut]; 5; F

1572; 1558; ---; Moore, James W.; Head; 25; M

1573; 1559; ---; Moore, Alice; Daut; 20; F

1574; 1560; ---; Moncravie, Charles; Head; 42; M
1575; 1561; ---; Moncravie, Rosa; Wife; 32; F
1576; 1562; ---; Moncravie, Augustine; Daut; 12; F
1577; 1563; ---; Moncravie, Virginia M; Daut; 9; F

1578; 1564; ---; Moncravie, Fred; Head; 36; M

1579; 1565; ---; Moncravie, Henry; Head; 38; M
1580; 1566; ---; Moncravie, Henri E.; Daut; 7; F

1581; 1567; ---; Moncravie, John; Head; 41; M
1582; 1568; ---; Moncravie, Sylvester A.; Son; 18; M
1583; 1569; ---; Moncravie, Jon N.; Son; 14; M
1584; 1570; ---; Moncravie, Alexander C.; Son; 12; M
1585; 1571; ---; Moncravie, Barada J.; Son; 10; M

Key: Number - Last/Present; Indian Name (if given); English Name (if given); Relationship; Age; Sex.

1586;	1572;	---; Moncravie, Vivian L.; Daut; 7; F
1587;	1573;	---; Moncravie, Anna A.; Daut; 5; F
1588;	1574;	---; Murray, Jennie; Head; 35; F
1589;	1575;	---; Murray, Morton J.; Son; 13; M
1590;	1576;	---; Murray, Ruby M.; Daut; 12; F
1591;	1577;	---; Murray, Arthur R.; Son; 9; M
1592;	1578;	---; Murray, Alfred G.; Son; 7; M
1593;	1579;	---; Murray, Maurice C.; Son; $[sic] [4]; M
1594;	1580;	---; Murphy, Gertrude; Head; 29; F
1595;	1581;	---; Murphy, Alice; Head; 28; F
1596;	1582;	---; Murphy, Elizabeth; Head; 25; F
1597;	1583;	---; Murphy, Amy; Head; 49; F
1598;	1584;	---; Murphy, Nettie; Daut; 21; F
1599;	1585;	---; Mudgrove, William; Head; 33; M,
1600;	1586;	---; Mudgrove, Carl R.; Son; 6; M
1601;	1586 ½;	---; Mudgrove, Willis E.; Daut; 5; F
1602;	1587;	---; Newman, George; Head; 29; M
1603;	1588;	---; Noble; Ida; Head; 29; F
1604;	1589;	---; Nolegs, Larry; Head; 56; M
1605;	1590;	---; Odell, Clyde; Son; 4; M
1606;	1591;	---; Owens, Cathrine; Daut; 4; F
1607;	1592;	---; Pappan, [S]Aamuel T.; Son; 20; M
1608;	1593;	---; Pappan, Lee A.; Son; 18; M
1609;	1594;	---; Pappan, Oakley; Son; 16; M
1610;	1595;	---; Pappan, Lester; Son; 14; M
1611;	1596;	---; Pappin, Alex; Head; 52; M
1612;	1597;	---; Pappin, Herbert; Son; 14; M
1613;	1598;	---; Pappin, Franklin A; Son; 9; M
1614;	1599;	---; Pappin, Roosevelt; Son; 6; M
1615;	1600;	---; Pappin, Nora I.; Daut; 4; F
1616;	1601;	---; Pappin, Jesse L.; Son; 21; M
1617;	1602;	---; Pappin, John L.; Son; 19; M
1618;	1603;	---; Pappin, Jeanette; Daut; 16; F

CENSUS of the_____ **Osage**_____ Indians of ____ **Osage** ____ Agency, **Okla.**
on ____ **June 30, 1911**__, 19__, taken by __**Hugh Pitzer, Supt. & Spl. Disb. Agent**__

Key: Number - Last/Present; Indian Name (if given); English Name (if given); Relationship; Age; Sex.

1619; 1604; ---; Pappin, Joseph L; Son; 14; M
1620; 1605; ---; Pappin, Jules C.; Son; 12; m
1621; 1606; ---; Pappin, Joshua J.; Son; 8; M

1622; 1607; ---; Pappin, James; Head; 27; M

1623; 1608; ---; Palmer, John F.; Head; 50; M
1624; 1609; ---; Palmer, Martha; Wife; 38; F
1625; 1610; ---; Palmer, Mary E.; Daut; 17; F
1626; 1611; ---; Palmer, Clementine; Daut; 15; F
1627; 1612; ---; Palmer, Martha M.; Daut; 4; F
1628; 1613; ---; Palmer, Mable; Daut; 21; F

1629; 1614; ---; Park, Estella; Head; 23; F

1630; 1615; ---; Pease, Minnie A.; Head; 23; F
1631; 1616; ---; Pease, Marion H.; Son; 6; M

1632; 1617; ---; Perrier, Joseph; Head; 34; M

1633; 1618; ---; Perrier, Samuel; Head; 43; M

1634; 1619; ---; Perrier, Leo; Head; 30; M
1635; 1620; ---; Perrier, Clifford R.; Son; 5; M

1636; 1621; ---; Perrier, James; Head; 35; M
1637; 1622; ---; Perrier, John T.; Son; 17; M
1638; 1623; ---; Perrier, James R.; Son; 11; M

1639; 1624; ---; Perrier, Napoleon; Head; 53; M
165[4]0;1625; ---; Perrier, Nin[sic]; Daut; 20; F
1641; 1626; ---; Perrier, Leo; Son; 17; M
1642; 1627; ---; Perrier, Peter; Son; 14; M
1643; 1628; ---; Perrier, Lola; Daut; 13; F
1644; 1629; ---; Perrier, Owen; Son; 9; M

1645; 1630; ---; Perrier, Louis F.; Head; 22; M

1646; 1631; ---; Perrier, Thomas; Head; 27; M
1647; 1632; ---; Perrier, Roy B.; Son; 5; M

1648; 1633; ---; Perrier, Eugene; Head; 28; M
1649; 1634; ---; Perrier, Ray L.D.; Son; 5; M
1650; 1635; ---; Perrier, Kenneth; Son; 3; M

1651; 1636; ---; Penn, Leo; Son; 14; M
1652; 1637; ---; Penn, Oscar; Son; 12; M

CENSUS of the _____ **Osage** _____ Indians of _____ **Osage** _____ Agency, **Okla.**
on _____ **June 30, 1911** _, 19__, taken by **Hugh Pitzer, Supt. & Spl. Disb. Agent**
Key: Number - Last/Present; Indian Name (if given); English Name (if given); Relationship; Age; Sex.

1653; 1638;   ---; Penn, Wayne M.; Son; 6; M

1654; 1639;   ---; Pettit, S.W.; Head; 66; M

1655; 1640;   ---; Pettit, Charles; Head; 38; M
1656; 1641;   ---; Pettit, Hattie B.; Daut; 14; F
1657; 1642;   ---; Pettit, Lela M.; Daut; 10; F

1658; 1642;   ---; Pettit, George; Head; 36; M [#1642, twice.]
1659; 1643;   ---; Pettit, George R.; Son; 12; M
1660; 1644;   ---; Pettit, Lula B.; Daut; 9; F
1661; 1645;   ---; Pettit, William A.; Son; 4; M

1662; 1646;   ---; Pettit, John; Head; 33; M

1663; 1647;   ---; Perkins, Elizabeth; Head; 56; F

1664; 1648;   ---; Peters, James M.; Son; 12; M

1665; 1649;   ---; Pearson, Rosa; Head; 48; F
1666; 1650;   ---; Kent, Cordelia C.; Daut; 20; F
1667; 1651;   ---; Pearson, Lillian F.; Daut; 19; F
1668; 1652;   ---; Pearson, Bettha[sic] L.; Daut; 17; F
1669; 1653;   ---; Pearson, Kate V.; Daut; 14; F
1670; 1654;   ---; Pearson, Willie J.; Son; 11; M
1671; 1655;   ---; Pearson, Rose E.; Daut; 8; F

1672; 1656;   ---; Pearson, October; Head;   28; M
1673; 1657;   ---; Pearson, Mary C.; Wife; 24; F
1674; 1658;   ---; Pearson, Bernice M.; Daut; 5; F

1675; 1659;   ---; Phillips, William; Head; 41; M
1676; 1660;   ---; Phillips, Angeline M.; Daut; 17; F
1677; 1661;   ---; Phillips, Iva M.; Daut; 15; F
1678; 1662;   ---; Phillips, James W.; Son; 13; M

1679; 1663;   ---; Plomondon, Clemy; Head; 57; M
1680; 1664;   ---; Plomondon, Daniel B.; Son; 19; M
1681; 1665;   ---; Plomondon, Julia A.; Daut; 17; F
1682; 1666;   ---; Plomondon, Louisa; Daut; 14; F

1683; 1667;   ---; Plomondon, Louis; Head; 26; M

1684; 1668;   ---; Plomondon, Barnard; Head; 41; M
1685; 1669;   ---; Plomondon, Ella; Wife; 37; F
1686; 1670;   ---; Plomondon, Grace; Daut; 19; F
1687; 1671;   ---; Plomondon, Clementine; Daut; 17; F

Key: Number - Last/Present; Indian Name (if given); English Name (if given); Relationship; Age; Sex.

1688; 1672; ---; Plomondon, Moses E.; Son; 15; M
1689; 1673; ---; Plomondon, George A.; Son; 12; M

1690; 1674; ---; Potter, Ethel; Head; 23; F
1691; 1675; ---; Potter, Frances A.; Son; 16; M
1692; 1676; ---; Potter, Oliver L.; Son; 11; M
1693; 1677; ---; Potter, James L.; Son; 8; M
1694; 1678; ---; Potter, Zelma; Daut; 4; F

1695; 1679; ---; Prudom, Charles N.; Head; 56; M

1696; 1680; ---; Prudom, Nora; Head; 28; F

1697; 1681; ---; Prudom, Frank; Head; 45; M

1698; 1682; ---; Prue, Henry; Head; 36; M
1699; 1683; ---; Prue, Maude; Wife; 27; F
1700; 1684; ---; Prue, Hattie M.; Daut; 13; F
1701; 1685; ---; Prue, Charles F.; Son; 12; M
1702; 1686; ---; Prue, Henry E.; Son; 10; M
1703; 1687; ---; Prue, Floyd B.; Daut; 5; F
1704; 1688; ---; Prue, Anna B.; Daut; 5; F
1705; 1689; ---; Quinton, Franklin; Head; 24; F

1706; 1690; ---; Rairdon, Jane R.; Head; 52; F
1707; 1691; ---; Miller, Ida J.; Daut; 19; F
1708; 1692; ---; Rairdon, Wendall H.; Son; 11; M

1709; 1693; ---; Miller, Louis S.; Head; 22; M

1710; 1694; ---; Rapp, Barbara; Head; 25; F

1711; 1695; ---; Reece, Elizabeth; Head; 27; F
1712; 1696; ---; Reece, Hallie; Daut; 9; F
1713; 1697; ---; Reece, Ethel; Daut; 7; F

1714; 1698; ---; Revelette, James; Head; 3[4]; M
1715; 1699; ---; Revelette, Teresa; Daut; 12; F
1716; 1700; ---; Revelette, William L.; Son; 10; M
1717; 1701; ---; Revelette, Mary E.; Daut; 5; F
1718; 1702; ---; Revelette, Minnie F.; Daut; 5; F

1719; 1703; ---; Revelette, Fred; Head; 32; M
1720; 1704; ---; Revelette, Pauline; Daut; 11; F
1721; 1705; ---; Revelette, Fred L.; Son; 9

1722; 1706; ---; Revelette, Frank; Head; 70; M

Key: Number - Last/Present; Indian Name (if given); English Name (if given); Relationship; Age; Sex.

1723; 1707; ---; Revelette, Franklin; Head; 22; M

1724; 1708; ---; Revelette, Charles; Head; 38; M
1725; 1709; ---; Revelette, Joseph; Son; 5; M

1726; 1710; ---; Revard, William; Head; 46; M
1727; 1711; ---; Revard, William E.; Son; 10; M
1728; 1712; ---; Revard, Della M; Daut; 8; F
1729; 1713; ---; Revard, Gladis; Daut; 6; F

1730; 1714; ---; Revard, Solomon; Head; 52; M

1731; 1715; ---; Revard, Charles; Head; 52; M

1732; 1716; ---; Revard, Alex; Head; 51; M

1733; 1717; ---; Revard, Benjamin; Head; 30; M

1734; 1718; ---; Revard, Paul; Head; 36; M
1735; 1719; ---; Revard, Susie; Daut; 16; F

1736; 1720; ---; Revard, Mary E.; Head; 63; M

1737; 1721; ---; Revard, Elsie E.; Daut; 19; F
1738; 1722; ---; Revard, Maynard; Son; 16; M

1739; 1723; ---; Revard, Francis; Head; 43; M
1740; 1724; ---; Revard, Mack; Son; 17; M
1741; 1725; ---; Revard, Emanuel M.; Son; 12; M
1742; 1726; ---; Revard, Pearl I.; Daut; 9; F
1743; 1727; ---; Revard, Ethel E.; Daut; 5; F

1744; 1728; ---; Revard, John W.; Head; 32; M
1745; 1729; ---; Revard, Edwrad[sic] L.; Son; 13; M
1746; 1730; ---; Revard, Evart A.; Son; 12; M

1747; 1731; ---; Revard, Joseph; Head; 81[?]; M [Age 50 in 1910.]
1748; 1732; ---; Revard, Ursula; Daut; 21; F
1749; 1733; ---; Revard, Clementine; Daut; 18; F
1750; 1734; ---; Revard, William J.; Son; 16; M
1751; 1735; ---; Revard, Ronald V.; Son; 14; M

1752; 1736; ---; Revard, Ralph; Head; 23; M

1753; 1737; ---; Revard, Franklin; Head; 47; M
1754; 1738; ---; Revard, Nicholas M.; Son; 17; M
1755; 1739; ---; Revard, Pearl; Daut; 16; F

326

CENSUS of the___ **Osage**___ Indians of ___ **Osage**___ Agency, __Okla.__
on ___ **June 30, 1911**___, 19__, taken by __Hugh Pitzer, Supt. & Spl. Disb. Agent__
Key: Number - Last/Present; Indian Name (if given); English Name (if given); Relationship; Age; Sex.

1756; 1740;   ---; Revard, Myrta; Daut; 8; F
1757; 1741;   ---; Revard, Kathryn L.; Daut; 4; F

1758; 1742;   ---; Revard, Mark S.; Head; 23; M

1759; 1743;   ---; Revard, Charles E.; Head; 51; M
1760; 1744;   ---; Revard, Clarence; Son; 21; M
1761; 1745;   ---; Revard, Ed Clifford; Son; 19; M
1762; 1746;   ---; Revard, Clara; Daut; 17; F
1763; 1747;   ---; Revard, Carrie; Daut; 13; F
1764; 1748;   ---; Revard, Cora; Daut; 13; F
1765; 1749;   ---; Revard, Nora T.; Daut; 12; F
1766; 1750;   ---; Revard, Mcguire N.; Son; 7; M
1767; 1751;   ---; Revard, Lena; Daut; 5; F

1768; 1752;   ---; Revard, Leonard; Head; 53; M
1769; 1753;   ---; Revard, Lode; Daut; 17; F
1770; 1754;   ---; Revard, Opal A.; Daut; 14; F
1771; 1755;   ---; Revard, Hazel; Daut; 11; F
1772; 1756;   ---; Revard, Minnie; Daut; 8; f
1773; 1757;   ---; Revard, Cleo; Daut; 5; F
1774; 1758;   ---; Revard, Victoria; Daut; 3; F

1775; 1759;   ---; Revard, Joseph Jr.; Head; 54; M

1776; 1760;   ---; Revard, Nellie; Daut; 10; F
1777; 1761;   ---; Revard, Edgar T.; Son; 7; M
1778; 1762;   ---; Revard, Mary C.; Daut; 5; F

1779; 1763;   ---; Revard, Curtis; Head; 25; M

1780; 1764;   ---; Revard, Aaron T.; Son; 19; M

1781; 1765;   ---; Riddle, Sherman; Son; 19; M
1782; 1766;   ---; Riddle, Joseph; Son; 17; M
1783; 1767;   ---; Riddle, Frank; Son; 15; M

1784; 1768;   ---; Ririe, Effie E.; Daut; 18; F
1785; 1769;   ---; Ririe, Scott F.; Son; 15; M
1786; 1770;   ---; Ririe, Otis E.; Son; 11; M
1787; 1771;   ---; Ririe, Nellie I.; Daut; 9; F
1788; 1772;   ---; Ririe, Arthur M.; Son; 5; M

1789; 1773;   ---; Ririe, Oscar A.; Head; 24; M

1790; 1774;   ---; Rodman, Antwine; Head; 38; M

327

Key: Number - Last/Present; Indian Name (if given); English Name (if given); Relationship; Age; Sex.

1791; 1775; ---; Rogersm[sic], Stephen; Head; 30; M

1792; 1776; ---; Rogers, Louis; Head; 68; M

1793; 1777; ---; Rogers, Louis Jr.; Head; 26; M

1794; 1778; ---; Rogers, Nancy; Head; 63; F

1795; 1779; ---; Rogers, TL.; Head; 25; M

1796; 1780; ---; Rogers, Arthur; Head; 51; M
1797; 1781; ---; Rogers, Joseph L.; Son; 12; M
1798; 1782; ---; Rogers, Ellen E.; Daut; 10; F
1799; 1783; ---; Rogers, John R.; Son; 8; M
1800; 1784; ---; Rogers, William C.; Son; 6; M
1801; 1785; ---; Rogers, Isabell; Daut; 4; F

1802; 1786; ---; Rogers, Mary E.; Head; 37; F
1803; 1787; ---; Rogers, Irene; Daut; 19; F
1804; 1788; ---; Rogers, Mary A.; Daut; 17; F
1806; 1789; ---; Rogers, Eldred T.; Son; 11; M

1807; 1790; ---; Rogers, Antwine; Head; 66; M

1808; 1791; ---; Rogers, Mae; Head; 25; M

1809; 1792; ---; Rogers, Kenneth; Head; 31; M
1810; 1793; ---; Rogers, Helen; Daut; 8; F
1811; 1794; ---; Rogers, Antwine; Son; 6; M

1812; 1795; ---; Rogers, Jasper; Head; 41; M
1813; 1796; ---; Rogers, Rosa; Wife; 32; F
1814; 1797; ---; Rogers, Emmet; Son; 9; M
1815; 1798; ---; Rogers, Cecelia; Daut; 10; F
1816; 1799; ---; Rogers, Maude; Daut; 6; F
1817; 1800; ---; Rogers, Flora; Daut; 4; F

1818; 1801; ---; Rogers, Bertha D.; Daut; 17; F
1819; 1802; ---; Rogers, Helen C.; Daut; 15; F

1820; 1803; ---; Rogers, Willie L.; Son; 4; M

1821; 1804; ---; Rogers, Thomas L. Jr.; Head; 26; M

1822; 1805; ---; Rogers, Granville; Head; 23; M

1823; 1806; ---; Rogers, Rosa L.; Daut; 18; F

Key: Number - Last/Present; Indian Name (if given); English Name (if given); Relationship; Age; Sex.

1824; 1807;   ---; Rogers, Josephine; Daut; 15; F
1825; 1808;   ---; Rogers, John H.; Son; 13; M

1826; 1809;   ---; Rogers, Nora; Head; 27; F
1827; 1810;   ---; Rogers, Richard L.; Son; 6; M

1828; 1811;   ---; Rogers, Lewis A.; Head; 36; M

1829; 1812;   ---; Rogers, Isadore; Wife; 33; F

1830; 1813;   ---; Rogers, Fred R.; Son; 10; M
1831; 1814;   ---; Rogers, Frank; Son; 6; M

1832[3];1816;   ---; Ross, John; Head; 66; M [Skipped #1815.]
1834; 1817;   ---; Ross, Floyd F.; Son; 14; M

1835; 1818;   ---; Roach, Wilfred D.; Head; 31; M
1836; 1819;   ---; Roach, Bridget A.; Daut; 8; F
1837; 1820;   ---; Roach, Melvin C.; Son; 6; M
1838; 1821;   ---; Roach, Wilfred D. Jr.; Son; 4; M

1839; 1822;   ---; Roach, Samuel; Head; 29; M
1840; 1823;   ---; Roach, Mikle J.; Son; 8; M
1841; 1824;   ---; Roach, Herman B.; Son; 5; M

1842; 1825;   ---; Roach, George W.; Head; 25; M

1843; 1826;   ---; Rutter, Gertrude; Head; 31; F

1844; 1827;   ---; Rivera, Grace; Head; 21; F
1845; 1828;   ---; Rivera, Alex; Son; 3; M

1846; 1829;   ---; Saxon, Cora; Head; 37; F
1847; 1830;   ---; Saxon, Veva M.; Daut; 7; F
1848; 1831;   ---; Saxon, Harry H.; Son; 5; M

1849; 1832;   ---; Scott, George; Head; 34; M
1850; 1833;   ---; Scott, Mary M.; Daut; 6; F

1851; 1834;   ---; Scott, William J.; Son; 6; M
1852; 1835;   ---; Scott, Violet; Daut; 4; F

1853; 1836;   ---; Selby, Georgia; Head; 25; F

1854; 1837;   ---; Sherrif, Coeanna; Head; 24; F

1855; 1838;   ---; Shaw, Franklin; Head; 24; F[sic] [M]

*CENSUS of the*___**Osage**___*Indians of*___**Osage**___*Agency,*__**Okla.**
*on*___**June 30, 1911**__*, 19__, taken by*__**Hugh Pitzer, Supt. & Spl. Disb. Agent**

Key: Number - Last/Present; Indian Name (if given); English Name (if given); Relationship; Age; Sex.

1856; 1839; ---; Shaw, Rose M.; Wife; 23; F
1857; 1840; ---; Shaw, Moses; Son; 7; M
1858; 1841; ---; Shaw, John; Son; 5; M

1859; 1842; ---; Shobe, Anna U.; Head; 27; F

1860; 1843; ---; Simpson, Susan; Head; 69; F

1861; 1844; ---; Simpkins, Mary L.; Head; 39; F
1862; 1845; ---; Simpkins, Warren D.; Son; 18; M
1863; 1846; ---; Simpkins, Mary E.; Daut; 17; F
1864; 1847; ---; Simpkins, Vivian P.; Daut; 14; F
1865; 1848; ---; Simpkins, Oren F.; Son; 13; M
1866; 1849; ---; Simpkins, Edward; Son; 11; M
1867; 1850; ---; Simpkins, Virgil; Son; 5; M
1868; 1851; ---; Simpkins, Helen V.; Daut; 4; F

1869; 1852; ---; Slaughter, A.B.; Head; 27; M
1870; 1853; ---; Slaughter, Minnie; Wife; 25; F

1871; 1854; ---; Slaughter, Amanda; Head; 24; F

1872; 1855; ---; Slaughter, Harry E.; Son; 21; M

1873; 1856; ---; Smith, George D.; Son; 9; M
1874; 1857; ---; Smith, Genevieve; Daut; 12; F

1875; 1858; ---; Soderstrom, Gertrude; Head; 32; F
1876; 1859; ---; Dickey, Alta A.; Daut; 13; F
1877; 1860; ---; Soderstrom, Hanna N.; Daut; 10; F

1878; 1861; ---; Soldani, Sylvester J.; Head; 51; M
1879; 1862; ---; Soldani, Josephine; Wife; 42; F
1880; 1863; ---; Soldani, Myrtle; Daut; 20; F
1881; 1864; ---; Soldani, Emmert A.; Son; 19; M

1882; 1865; ---; Soldani, Louis E.; Head; 22; M

1883; 1866; ---; Soldani, Kate P.; Head; 23; F

1884; 1867; ---; Soldani, Idam[sic] M.; Head; 24; F

1885; 1868; ---; Soldani, Agnes; Head; 25; F

1886; 1869; ---; Soldani, Anthony; Head; 49; M
1887; 1870; ---; Soldani, Amelia K.; Wife; 43; F

Key: Number - Last/Present; Indian Name (if given); English Name (if given); Relationship; Age; Sex.

1888; 1871; ---; Soldani, Frank E.; Son; 20; M
1889; 1872; ---; Soldani, Charles L.; Son; 18; M
1890; 1873; ---; Soldani, Clarence; Son; 15; M
1891; 1874; ---; Soldani, Grace M.; Daut; 12; F
1892; 1875; ---; Soldani, Rose M.; Daut; 12; F
1893; 1876; ---; Soldani, George H.; Son; 10; M

1894; 1877; ---; Souligny, Laura; 26; M[sic] [F]
1895; 1878; ---; Souligny, Mildred V.; Daut; 7; F

1896; 1879; ---; Stevens, John H.; Head; 45; M
1897; 1880; ---; Stevens, Mildred V.; Daut; 7; F

1898; 1881; ---; Stephens, Madeline; Head; 69; F [58 in 1910.]

1899; 1882; ---; Stotts, Emma; Head; 36; F
1900; 1883; ---; Stotts, Joseph L.; Son; 20; M
1901; 1884; ---; Stotts, William W.; Son; 16; M
1902; 1885; ---; Stotts, James E.; Son; 7; M

1903; 1886; ---; Stobaugh, Alice; Head; 40; F
1904; 1887; ---; Riddle, John L.; Son; 21; M
1905; 1888; ---; Riddle, Arthur; Son; 9; M

1906; 1889; ---; Stewart, Lenora; Head; 49; F
1907; 1890; ---; Wilkie, George L.; Son; 21; M
1908; 1891; ---; Wilkie, Rose E.; Daut; 17; F

1909; 1892; ---; Swanson, Celestine; Head; 29; F
1910; 1893; ---; Swanson, Addison L.; Son; 7; M
1911; 1894; ---; Swanson, Joseph N.; Son; 6; M

1912; 1895; ---; Sweeney, Oscar E.; Son; 18; M

1913; 1896; ---; Slamans, Mary E.; Head; 28; F

1914; 1897; ---; Tall Chief, Enoch; Son; 5; M

1915; 1898; ---; Tapp, Belle; Head; 47; F
1916; 1899; ---; Chambers, James W.; Son; 15; M
1917; 1900; ---; Chambers, Minnie A.; Daut; 12; F
1918; 1901; ---; Tapp, Ruby; Daut; 4; F

1919; 1902; ---; Taylor, James E.; Orphan; 17; M
1920; 1903; ---; Taylor, John G.; Orphan; 16; M
1921; 1904; ---; Taylor, Hiram; Orphan; 14; M
1922; 1905; ---; Taylor, Fanny; Orphan; 13; F

*CENSUS of the*___**Osage**___*Indians of*___**Osage**___*Agency,* **Okla.**
*on*___**June 30, 1911**___, *19*___, *taken by*___**Hugh Pitzer, Supt. & Spl. Disb. Agent**
Key: Number - Last/Present; Indian Name (if given); English Name (if given); Relationship; Age; Sex.

1923; 1906; ---; Taylor, Agnes; Orphan; 11; F
1924; 1907; ---; Taylor, Anna; Orphan; 7; F

1925; 1908; ---; Tayrien, John; Head; 28; M
1926; 1909; ---; Tayrien, Mary L.; Daut; 7; F
1927; 1910; ---; Tayrien, Agnes; Daut; 6; F
1928; 1911; ---; Tayrien, Gladys; Daut; 4; F

1929; 1912; ---; Tayrien, Charles; Head; 36; M
1930; 1913; ---; Tayrien, Edna; Daut; 13; F

1931; 1914; ---; Tayrien, Thomas; Head; 50; M
1932; 1915; ---; Tayrien, George A.; Son; 19; M
1933; 1916; ---; Tayrien, Andrew J.; Son; 17; M
1934; 1917; ---; Tayrien, Paul; Son; 15; M
1935; 1918; ---; Tayrien, Maud J.; Daut; 7; F
1936; 1919; ---; Tayrien, John C.; Son; 6; M

1937; 1920; ---; Tayrien, David W.; Head; 23; M

1938; 1921; ---; Tayrien, James; Head; 26; M
1939; 1922; ---; Tayrien, Alberty; Daut; 7; F
1940; 1923; ---; Tayrien, Elmer C.; Son; 5; M

1941; 1924; ---; Tayrien, Andrew; Head; 37; M
1942; 1925; ---; Tayrien, Jennie; Daut; 15; F
1943; 1926; ---; Tayrien, Viola; Daut; 14; F
1944; 1927; ---; Tayrien, Alfred J.; Son; 12; M
1945; 1928; ---; Tayrien, Violet M.; Daut; 11; F
1946; 1929; ---; Tayrien, William J.; Son; 8; M
1947; 1930; ---; Tayrien, Rose Anna; Daut; 8; F

1948; 1931; ---; Tayrien, Cyprien; Head; 73; M
1949; 1932; ---; Tayrien, William; Son; 21; M

1950; 1933; ---; Toothaker, Rean[sic] L.; Head; 21; F

1951; 1934; ---; Thompson, Leroy; Son; 17; M
1952; 1935; ---; Roe, Emery E.; Son; 10; M

1953; 1936; ---; Thompson, Nicholas; Head; 53; M

1954; 1937; ---; Thomas, Agnes; Head; 29; F
1955; 1938; ---; Thomas, Maggie C.; Daut; 9; F
1956; 1939; ---; Thomas, Julia H.; Daut; 6; F

1957; 1940; ---; Thurman, Lola; Head; 25; F

CENSUS of the __Osage__ *Indians of* __Osage__ *Agency,* __Okla.__
on __June 30, 1911__ *, 19__, taken by* __Hugh Pitzer, Supt. & Spl. Disb. Agent__

Key: Number - Last/Present; Indian Name (if given); English Name (if given); Relationship; Age; Sex.

1958; 1941; ---; Thurman, Geneva; Daut; 5; F

1959; 1942; ---; Tinker, Louis; Head; 44; M
1960; 1943; ---; Tinker, William; Son; 20; M
1961; 1944; ---; Tinker, Bessie; Daut; 17; F
1962; 1945; ---; Tinker, Nora; Daut; 13; F
1963; 1946; ---; Tinker, Ora; Daut; 13; F
1964; 1947; ---; Tinker, Eva; Daut; 11; F
1965; 1948; ---; Tinker, Isabella; Daut; 8; F
1966; 1949; ---; Tinker, Rose; Daut; 6; F
1967; 1950; ---; Tinker, Cora; Daut; 4; F

1968; 1951; ---; Tinker, Geo. E.; Head; 42; M
1969; 1952; ---; Tinker, Mary G.; Daut; 19; F
1970; 1953; ---; Tinker, Sarah Anna; Daut; 17; F
1971; 1954; ---; Tinker, Nicholas A.T.; Son; 15; M
1972; 1955; ---; Tinker, George E. Jr.; Son; 12; M
1973; 1956; ---; Tinker, Villa; Daut; 8; F

1974; 1957; ---; Tinker, Clarence; Head; 23; M

1975; 1958; ---; Tinker, Charley; Head; 39; M
1976; 1959; ---; Tinker, Mary J.; Daut; 20; F
1977; 1960; ---; Tinker, Roy B.; Son; 17; M
1978; 1961; ---; Tinker, Maude; Daut; 14; F
1979; 1962; ---; Tinker, Lucille; Daut; 13; F
1980; 1963; ---; Tinker, David; Son; 10; M
1981; 1964; ---; Tinker, Louis N.; Son; 6; M

1982; 1965; ---; Tinker, Frank; Head; 50; M
1983; 1966; ---; Tinker, Mary L.; Wife; 50; F
1984; 1967; ---; Tinker, Tom; Son; 17; M
1985; 1968; ---; Tinker, Mary E.; Daut; 15; F
1986; 1969; ---; Tinker, Eliza; Daut; 11; F
1987; 1970; ---; Tinker, Sylvester J.; Son; 8; M
1988; 1971; ---; Tinker, Norris J.; Head; 22; M

1989; 1972; ---; Todd, Maud; Head; 32; F
1990; 1973; ---; Todd, Harold; Son; 6; M
1991; 1974; ---; Todd, Gerald J,; Son; 10; M

1992; 1975; ---; Trumbly, Julian; Head; 60; M
1993; 1976; ---; Trumbly, Eliza; Wife; 55; F
1994; 1977; ---; Trumbly, Henry; Son; 21; M
1995; 1978; ---; Trumbly, Tina O.; Daut; 19; F
1996; 1979; ---; Trumbly, Charles; Son; 18; M
1997; 1980; ---; Trumbly, Theresa; Daut; 13; F

Key: Number - Last/Present; Indian Name (if given); English Name (if given); Relationship; Age; Sex.

1998; 1981;   ---; Trumbly, Oliver; Head; 29; M

1999; 1982;   ---; Trumbly, Clarence; Head; 30; M
2000; 1983;   ---; Trumbly, Gladys' Daut; 8; F
2001; 1984;   ---; Trumbly, Clarence E.; Son; 5; M

2002; 1985;   ---; Trumbly, George; Head; 37; M

2003; 1986;   ---; Trumbly, Andrew; Head; 36; M
2004; 1987;   ---; Trumbly, Mary; Wife; 25; F
2005; 1988;   ---; Trumbly, Oscar; Son; 5; M

2006; 1989;   ---; Trumbly, J.B.; Head; 57; M
2007; 1990;   ---; Trumbly, John F.; Son; 20; M
2008; 1991;   ---; Trumbly, Elizabeth; Daut; 17; F
2009; 1992;   ---; Trumbly, Paul P.; Son; 11; M

2010; 1993;   ---; Tucker, Anna; Head; 27; F
2111; 1994;   ---; Tucker, Bulah G.; Daut; 6; F
2112; 1995;   ---; Tucker, Stephen J. Jr.; Son; 4; M

2113; 1996;   ---; Tucker, Angeline; Head; 76; F

2114; 1997;   ---; Turner, Frederick D.; Son; 16; M

2115; 1998;   ---; Turner, Mary B.; Head; 29; F

2116; 1999;   ---; Tyner, Benjamin F.; Head; 36; M
2117; 2000;   ---; Tyner, Ethel M.; Daut; 12; F
2118; 2001;   ---; Tyner, Roy F.; Son; 10; M
2119; 2002;   ---; Tyner, William L.; Son; 5; M

2020; 2003;   ---; Vesser, Ruth; Daut; 18; F

2021; 2004;   ---; Voils, Kathleen; Daut; 9; F
2022; 2005;   ---; Voils, Elsie E.; Daut; 5; F

2023; 2006;   ---; Watkins, Rosalie; Head; 36; F
2024; 2007;   ---; Watkins, Francis M.; Son; 17; M
2025; 2008;   ---; Watkins, James; Son; 17; M
2026; 2009;   ---; Watkins, John F; [Son]; 9; M

2027; 2010;   ---; Watson, Viola; Head; 19; F

2029; 2011;   ---; Del Orier, Lillie; Daut; 21; F
2030; 2012;   ---; Del Orier, Edna; Daut; 20; F

Key: Number - Last/Present; Indian Name (if given); English Name (if given); Relationship; Age; Sex.

2031;	2013;	---; Ware, Aggie; Head; 41; F
2032;	2014;	---; Ware, Julia; Daut; 17; F
2033;	2015;	---; Ware, Nancy; Daut; 15; F
2034;	2016;	---; Ware, Bulah; Daut; 13; F
2035;	2017;	---; Ware, Rosa L.; Daut; 11; F
2036;	2018;	---; Ware, Henry H.; Son; 9; M
2037;	2019;	---; Ware, David; Son; 8; M
2038;	2020;	---; Wadw[sic][e], Effie; Head; 25; F
2039;	2021;	---; Wade, Merle C.; Son; 6; M
2040;	2022;	---; Wal[k]er[sic], Letetia; Head; 19; F
2041;	2023;	---; Waters, Telina; Head; 28; F
2042;	2024;	---; Waters, Anna M.; Daut; 4; F
2043;	2025;	---; Whiles, Elmer; Head; 29; M
2044;	2026;	---; Whiles, Delilah; Head; 26; F
2045;	2027;	---; Whiles, Francis M.; Head; 22; M
2046;	2028;	---; Wheeler, Paul; Head; 39; M
2047;	2029;	---; Wheeler, Merrit J.; Son; 8; M
2048;	2030;	---; Wheeler, Geneva; Daut; 7; F
2049;	2031;	---; Wheeler, Louise; Daut; 4; F
2050;	2032;	---; Wheeler, Elmer; Head; 32; M
2051;	2033;	---; Wheeler, Eva R.; Wife; 33; F
2052;	2034;	---; Wheeler, Virginia; Daut; 7; F
2053;	2035;	---; Wheeler, Alma; Head; 25; F
2054;	2036;	---; Weinrich, Anna; Head; 28; F
2055;	2037;	---; Weinrich, Alma; Daut; 2; F
	2038;	---; Weinrich, Elmer; Son; 6m; M
2056;	2039;	---; Wheeler, Susan; Head; 33; F
2057;	2040;	---; Wheeler, Morris E.; Son; 9; M
2058;	2041;	---; Wilkie, Louis F; Head; 25; M
2059;	2042;	---; Wilkie, Andrew E.; Son; 5; M
2060;	2043;	---; Willis, Lillie; Head; 19; F
2061;	2044;	---; Wilson, Mary; Head; 33; F
2062;	2045;	---; Wilson, William E.; Son; 14; M
2063;	2046;	---; Wilson, Julia K.; Daut; 12; F

*CENSUS of the*_____**Osage**_____*Indians of*_____**Osage**_____*Agency,*__**Okla.**
*on*___**June 30, 1911**__*, 19__, taken by*__**Hugh Pitzer, Supt. & Spl. Disb. Agent**

Key: Number - Last/Present; Indian Name (if given); English Name (if given); Relationship; Age; Sex.

2064; [2047;]   ---; Wilson, Banie; Son; 10; M
2065; 2048;   ---; Wilson, Audry; Daut; 7; F
2066; 2049;   ---; Wilson, Howard; Son; 4; M

2067; 2050;   ---; Woodring, Tena; Head; 36; F
2068; 2051;   ---; Woodring, Carlton W.; Son; 16; M
2069; 2052;   ---; Woodring, Orville W.; Son; 14; M
2070; 2053;   ---; Woodring, Anna; Daut; 10; F

2071; 2054;   ---; Woodham, Lucy; Head; 61; F

2072; 2055;   ---; Woodard, Kate; Head; 34; F
2073; 2056;   ---; Beekman, Sybil F; Daut; 6; F
2074; 2057;   ---; Gorman, Mary A.; Daut; 12; F

2075; 2058;   ---; Wyrick, Mary; Head; 38; F
2076; 2059;   ---; Wyrick, Jessie W.; Daut; 15; F
2077; 2060;   ---; Wyrick, John H.; Son; 14; M
2078; 2061;   ---; Wyrick, Elnora J.; Daut; 10; F
2079; 2062;   ---; Wyrick, Elmer F.; Son; 7; M

2080; 2063;   ---; Wynn, Madeline; Head; 22; F

2081; 2064;   ---; Yeargain, Early I; Son; 20; M
2082; 2065;   ---; Yeargain, Verona C.; Daut; 18; F
2083; 2066;   ---; Yeargain, Leona; Daut; 17; F

2084; 2067;   ---; York, Adah M.; Head; 25; F

2085; 2068;   ---; Hooper, Sallie; Head; 40; F
2086; 2069;   ---; Hooper, Mary; Daut; 17; F

2087; 2070;   ---; Siggins, Clara; Head; 48; F
2088; 2071;   ---; Siggins, Andrew W.; Son; 20; M

2089; 2072;   ---; Stephens, Mary; Daut; 17; F

Note: Total of this roll is 2072. Numbers 16 ½ and 332 ½ inserted.
Numbers 1476 and 1477 omitted.

Key: Number - Last/Present; Indian Name (if given); English Name (if given); Relationship; Age; Sex.

RECAPITULATION:

All ages (Males, 1079; Females, 993)	2072
Full-Bloods:	
All ages (males, 407; females 394)	801
18 years and over (males)	240
Between 6 and 16 (males)	96
14 years and over (females)	259
Between 6 and 16 (females)	107
Mixed-Bloods:	
All ages (Males, 646; Females 625)	1271
18 years and over (males)	277
Between 6 and 16 (males)	243
15 years and over (females)	344
Between 6 and 16 (females)	272

Research Books

Catlin, George, *Letters and Notes on the Matters, Customs, and Conditions of North American Indians, Volume I,* Dover Publications, New York,   (Note: The Dover Edition first published in 1973 is an unabridged republication of the work first published in London in 1844.)

Dickerson, Philip, *History of the Osage Nation,* Oklahoma City, 1906, Library of Congress

Drinnon, Richard, *White Savage, The Case of John Dunn Hunter,* Schocken Books/New York, 1972

Grann, David, *Killers of the Flower Moon*, Doubleday, New York, London, Toronto, Sydney and Auckland, 2017

Hassrick, Royal B., *The George Catlin Book of American Indians*, Folio Society, London, 1994 also Watson-Guptill, New York, 1977

Roehm, Marjorie Catlin, *The Letters of George Catlin and His Family, A Chronicle of the American West*, University of California Press, Berkeley, Los Angeles, 1966

Thirty-sixth Annual Report of the Bureau of Ethnology, 1914-1915, accompanying paper Osage Tribe: Rite of the Chiefs; Sayings of the Ancient Men, by Francis La Flesche

Index

Index

....205,275
WAH-SHE-PAH...........18,79,84,150,
.................................155,220,224,293
WAH-SHE-SHAH.................76,136
WAH-SHE-WAH-HAH...........25,87,
.....................................158,228,297
WAH-SHIN-KAH-HU................5,65,
.................................137,207,277
WAH-SHIN-KAH-SOP-PY.......4,64,
.................................137,207,276
WAH-SHO-SHAH........4,64,206,276
WAH-SHUN-KAH-HAH........12,72,
.....................................144,283
WAH-SHUN-KAH-KAH-HAH..214
WAH-SIS-TAH.........69,141,210,280
WAH-SOP-PY......14,75,147,216,286
WAH-SOP-PY-WAH-KAH.......5,65,
.................................137,207,277
WAH-TAIN-DU-SAH................22,84
WAH-TE-SAH.......8,15,26,69,76,89,
141,147,160,210,213,217,229,280,282,
286,298
WAH-TI-AN-KAH....................24,86
WAH-TI-AN-KAH BAND........24,86
WAH-TO-AH-NAH-SHE..............22
WAH-TO-SAH.................6,10,15,66,
.........................71,138,143,208,278
WAH-TO-SAH-E...8,68,140,210,280
WAH-TO-SAH-GRAH...........13,74,
.................................146,216,285
WAH-TSA-A-HAH......................9
WAH-TSA-AH-HAH......69,141,210,
.....................................211,280,281
WAH-TSA-AH-TAH...7,25,64,68,75,
81,88,135,136,139,152,205,206,209,
.................222,275,276,279,291
WAH-TSA-A-TAH.............4,8,14,19,
.................................159,228,297
WAH-TSA-E-C-SHE....................74
WAH-TSA-E-O-SHE.......13,211,281
WAH-TSA-EO-SHE...................141
WAH-TSA-HU-HAH...........216,285
WAH-TSA-KI-HE-KAH........10,71,
....143,213,282
WAH-TSA-KON-LAH...........16,78,
.................................149,219,288
WAH-TSA-ME.........5,25,65,87,137,
.....................158,207,228,277,297

WAH-TSA-MOIE.....5,9,13,65,69,75,
.................138,141,146,211,216,281
Frank 138
Michel.....................................138
WAH-TSAMOIE, Michel...........277
WAHTSAMOIE
Frank 208,277
Harry 208,277
Michel................................208
WAH-TSA-SU-SAH 4,64,136,
.....................................206,276
WAH-TSA-TUN-KAH............25,88,
.....................................228,297
WAH-TSA-U-SAH 21,83,154,
.....................................223,292
WALKER
Letetia....................267,335
Letitia 198
WALSH, Mattie..........74,145,215,285
WALTER 64
WALTER L..............................35
WAN-NE-AH-TAH 214,283
WARE
Aggie 58,127,198,267,335
Bulah 128,198,267,335
Charles......................161,226,295
Daisy L 156,226,295
David..............58,128,198,267,335
Edna.............................198
Effie.............................128
Elijah N 156,226,295
Eugene...............23,85,156,226,295
Henry H..........58,128,198,267,335
Joseph 156,226,295
Julia 58,127,198,267,335
Mary 156,226,295
Merle C.........................128
Nancy 58,128,198,267,335
Rosa L 58,128,198,267,335
Victoria.................58,127,198,267
WARREN..............................24,87
WARRIOR
Mamie........................150,220,289
Mary 79,150,220,289
Robert....................79,150,220,289
Russell..............18,79,151,220,289
Wash...........................79,150,220
WATERS

380

www.ingramcontent.com/pod-product-compliance
Lightning Source LLC
Chambersburg PA
CBHW031136020426
42333CB00013B/402